We're in DANGER!
Who Will HELP Us?

We're in DANGER!
Who Will HELP Us?

Refugees and Migrants: A Test of Civilization

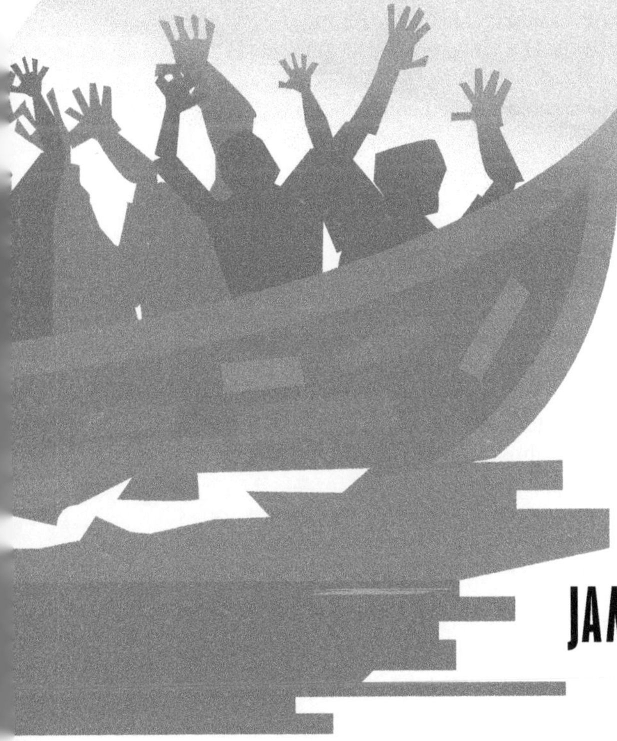

JAMES N. PURCELL JR.

Copyright © 2019 James N. Purcell Jr.

All rights reserved. No part of this book may be used or reproduced by any means, graphic, electronic, or mechanical, including photocopying, recording, taping or by any information storage retrieval system without the written permission of the author except in the case of brief quotations embodied in critical articles and reviews.

This book is a work of non-fiction. Unless otherwise noted, the author and the publisher make no explicit guarantees as to the accuracy of the information contained in this book and in some cases, names of people and places have been altered to protect their privacy.

The opinions and characterizations in this piece are those of the author, and do not necessarily represent official positions of the United States Government.

Author Photo – Author, UN Palais des Nations, Geneva
Photo Credit: Purcell library

Back Cover –Author at missile site Chechnya 1995
Photo Credit: International Organization for Migration

Archway Publishing books may be ordered through booksellers or by contacting:

Archway Publishing
1663 Liberty Drive
Bloomington, IN 47403
www.archwaypublishing.com
1 (888) 242-5904

Because of the dynamic nature of the Internet, any web addresses or links contained in this book may have changed since publication and may no longer be valid. The views expressed in this work are solely those of the author and do not necessarily reflect the views of the publisher, and the publisher hereby disclaims any responsibility for them.

Any people depicted in stock imagery provided by Getty Images are models, and such images are being used for illustrative purposes only. Certain stock imagery © Getty Images.

ISBN: 978-1-4808-6880-9 (sc)
ISBN: 978-1-4808-6881-6 (hc)
ISBN: 978-1-4808-6879-3 (e)

Library of Congress Control Number: 2018914887

Print information available on the last page.

Archway Publishing rev. date: 3/15/2019

DEDICATION

THIS BOOK IS DEDICATED TO TWO COURAGEOUS GROUPS OF people throughout the world, past and present: one, the millions who escaped persecution and torture and those who would no longer accept marginalization by their governments—all made life-changing decisions to change their circumstances; and two, the partners who stepped up to help in their quests.

ACKNOWLEDGEMENTS

My special thanks and appreciation to former Secretary of State George P. Shultz for his Foreword to this book, for meeting with me first to discuss the book's theme and progress, and for encouraging my efforts to write the history of the accomplishments of the Bureau for Refugee Programs in the US State Department. I value his views and will always consider him one of the most influential mentors of my life and career.

Special thanks and appreciation also go to Arthur E. (Gene) Dewey, my RP deputy and friend for continued close collaboration. I also acknowledge the valuable contributions of deputies Bob Funseth (deceased) and Richard English. I thank Robert (Bob) Gersony, Andy Michaels, Irena Omalaniuk, and Robert (Bob) Paiva for their encouragements and editorial comments on the manuscript.

Special thanks and appreciation for being available for personal interviews and through email and/or work papers, as cited in the text of the book: Elliott Abrams, John Bouche, James (Jim) Bullington, Margaret Carpenter, Priscilla Clapp, Patty Culpepper, Ralie Deffenbaugh, Bruce Flatin, Charles Freeman, Tex Harris, Carol Hecklinger, Doug Hunter, Mary Kavaliunas, Bill Krug, Don Krumm, Jim Lawrence, Paula Lynch, Tom Miller, Doris Meissner, Ann Morgan, Ken Quinn, Anne Richards, Lionel Rosenblatt, Terry Rusch, Phil Sargisson, Frank Wisner, and Lacy Wright. I appreciate the contributions of each of these outstanding professionals and former colleagues and all members of the global refugee team, past and present, who worked on behalf of the world's persecuted and disenfranchised people.

Treasured colleagues (deceased) that are part of the story and held in memory: John Baker, James Carlin, Judy Chavchavadze, Leo Cherne, Warren Christopher, James Cline, Wells Cline, Hank Cushing, Patricia Darien, Hamilton Fish, Robert (Bob) Funseth, John Glenn, Philip Habib, Poul Hartling, Mark Hatfield, Richard Holbrooke, Daniel Inouye, Bill Jordan, Ted Kennedy, Jeanne Kirkpatrick, Shep Lowman, Princeton Lyman, John McCarthy, Clay McManaway, Joe Meresman, Jonathan Moore, David Newsom, Robert Oakley, Ben Read, Peter Rodino, Bruce Sasser, Frank Sieverts, Steve Solarz, Carel Sternberg, Julia Taft, Jerry Tinker, Cyrus Vance, Dick Vine, Ingrid Walters, Jerry Weaver, and Warren Zimmerman. In special memory are my early professor and mentor Ernest Harrill, PhD, political science, Furman University, and professors of The Maxwell Graduate School of Citizenship and Public Affairs, Syracuse University.

Special thanks to Dr. Latayne Scott for her expertise and encouragement for the book's proposal; to Tim Beal for his comments and encouragements; and to Carrie Hesson and Lindsay Swisher for splendid technical support. Special thanks and appreciation to the Washington support teams at the State Department, including the research team at the Office of the Historian; the Bureau for Refugee Programs, now called the bureau of Population, Refugees, and Migration (PRM); the International Organization for Migration (IOM); and to Doug Hunter for helping me gain access to the papers of the late George Warren.

I acknowledge and express my eternal love and gratitude to my partner and wife, Jean Purcell, who has been with me every step of this amazing journey of life together and without whom this book would not exist. Also, salutes to daughters Deirdre Reilly and Carole Purcell, son-in-law Fred, and grandsons Fred, Matt, and James for their continuous love and encouragement.

Former Directors of Forty Years of RP/PRM

James Purcell (acting), June to August 1979
John Baker, August 1979 to November 1979
Frank Loy, January 1980 to January 1981
Richard Smyser, January 1981 to July 1981
Richard Vine, October 1981 to July 1982
James Purcell, August 1982 to September 1986
Jonathan Moore, September 1986 to December 1988
Princeton Lyman, September 1989 to June 1992
Warren Zimmerman, June 1992 to March 1994
Phyllis Oakley, August 1994 to November 1997
Julia Taft, November 1997 to January 2001
Arthur E. Dewey, January 2002 to July 2005
Ellen Sauerbrey, January 2006 to December 2007
Eric P. Schwartz, July 2009 to April 2012
Anne C. Richard, April 2012 to January 2017

CONTENTS

FOREWORD..xv
AUTHOR'S NOTE..xxi

BOOK ONE
AWAKE AND RISE
Desperation Engulfs Warring Indochina

1	Into the Storm	1
2	Vietnam and Five US Presidents	7
3	Rescue the Perishing	17
4	Tragic Triangle	21
5	Urgent Early Warnings	30
6	Wreckage Repair	38
7	From These Ashes, Will I Rise?	43
8	Weak Foundation	53
9	Durable Solutions Quest	66
10	Presidential Decision	73
11	Signs of Life	80
12	Existential Threats	88
13	Recalibrate for Global Response	95
14	Sharpening whilst Salvaging	100
15	Survive and Prosper	109

16	Refugee Act of 1980	118
17	Dark Clouds	122
18	Pivotal Startup	132
19	From the Management Hub	136
20	The Carter Refugee Record	148
21	The Significance of Public Service	152

BOOK TWO
CREATE LIFT
America's Refugee Exceptionalism

22	Transitional Leadership	157
23	Struggling to Stay on Course	173
24	Refugees in the Reagan Years	182
25	Phase 1. Stabilization	183
26	Phase 2. Protection	195
27	Protection—Political Prisoners and Amerasians	213
28	Phase 3. Reform	225
29	Phase 4. Solutions	235
30	The Meaning of Vietnam	242

BOOK THREE
"WE ARE HERE"
The World in Danger

31	Eastern Europe and the Soviet Union	247
32	Soviet Religious Minorities	254
33	Africa	272
34	The Middle East 1979 and Forward	306
35	Afghanistan and South Asia	325
36	Central America and the Caribbean	336
37	Summing Up the Refugee Decade	351
38	Changes in Direction	361

BOOK FOUR
AND NOW ...
A Test of Civilization

39	Above All, Do No Harm	367
40	Mystifying Breakdown	388
41	Is America Still Reliable?	395
42	Searching a Way Forward	410
43	Ending War and Moving Ahead	419
44	A Test of Civilization	424

NOTES	429
APPENDIXES	455
TABLES	461
INDEX	473

FOREWORD

ANOTHER HUMAN DISASTER WAS IN THE OFFING IN 1984. Governments and multilateral agencies were failing to sense the gravity of the spreading famine in Africa, which the UN called "the most massive catastrophe that has been visited upon the planet." Upwards of 150 million people in the Horn of Africa were trapped in the twentieth century's worst famine, and as many as thirty million were at risk of starving to death. Turning such a big ship around, even if it could be done, would take too long under normal circumstances. Anyway, if the UN and other multilateral agencies were failing, who else had the capability to step in?

Our answer then was that no new actors were either available or needed. We and other governments just had to muster the gumption to step up and force the multilateral system to work. Out of time and surrounded by government and international bureaucrats who would thwart immediate action, Jim Purcell and his deputy Gene Dewey took the unorthodox action—on my behalf—of going directly to the UN Secretary General to leverage the United States' vast financial and political contributions to the UN for immediate action on this crisis. With the help of UNICEF's Jim Grant, who saw the problem as we did, Secretary General Perez de Cuellar established the UN Office of Emergency Operations in Africa (OEOA) in one afternoon. It worked far better than even we expected, and the ensuing international response spared over six million lives. OEOA became one of the most successful UN operations of its kind and set the standard for multilateral crisis response in that era. Seeing the results, we in the State Department soon hailed the United Nations for clearly demonstrating its capability to make important and unique contributions to international efforts to relieve dire human suffering.

I met Jim Purcell in 1970 on my first day as the new director of the Nixon administration's Office of Management and Budget. The president had requested a review of the federal budget, and Jim was part of the team briefing me. These discussions factored into the full-employment budget concept that guided the administration's fiscal policy. A few years later we parted ways, as I was appointed Secretary of the Treasury and Jim ended up in the State Department.

When President Reagan appointed me secretary of state in 1982, I was not surprised to find that my friends Cy Vance and Warren Christopher had turned to Jim to create a new organization in the State Department, the Bureau for Refugee Programs (RP) to rescue the hundreds of thousands of Vietnamese allies and colleagues we had left behind after the Vietnam War. For the next three years, as RP's senior deputy and usually as acting director, he guided America's humanitarian operations not only in Southeast Asia but also in erupting crises throughout the world.

Knowing of the president's desire for a victims-first, nonpartisan approach to international humanitarian affairs, I designated Jim as one of my earliest appointees to be the permanent director of RP, and I gave him wide latitude for independent, quick-response maneuvering.

President Reagan had made known his passionate commitment to refugees from the outset. He spoke of it at the end of his July 17, 1980, speech accepting the Republican nomination:

> I have thought of something that is not part of my speech and I'm worried over whether I should do it. Can we doubt that only a Divine Providence placed this land, this island of freedom, here as a refuge for all those people in the world who yearn to breathe freely: Jews and Christians enduring persecution behind the Iron

Curtain, the boat people of Southeast Asia, of Cuba and Haiti, the victims of drought and famine in Africa, the freedom fighters of Afghanistan and our own countrymen held in savage captivity. I'll confess that I've been a little afraid to suggest what I'm going to suggest—I'm more afraid not to. Can we begin our crusade joined together in a moment of silent prayer. [Minute of Silence] God bless America.

He reiterated his conviction later when he said, "A hungry child knows no politics." I could sense from our many private discussions about world humanitarian crises over the years that his passion to help refugees never diminished.

We're in Danger! Who Will Help Us? traces the remarkable history of those years and recounts seemingly intractable human crises around the world that were plucked from the ashes of defeat and misery and moved toward humane and durable solutions by the State Department's refugee team. By motivating the United Nations to lead and by holding its feet to the fire to assure high performance, the State Department enabled remarkable results that all could see.

Indochina was the first refugee crisis the global humanitarian community addressed after World War II. It started with the hasty withdrawal of American forces from Vietnam in 1975 and the scramble to save as many Vietnamese colleagues as possible in those last few hours and days. It continued through the surge of dramatic boat and land departures from Vietnam a few years later and through the devastating spillover impacts that the war had on neighboring Cambodia and Laos. Over the next twenty years, the international community, with the United States in the lead, would devise new and creative approaches to complex humanitarian responses as it worked toward lasting durable solutions. No one could have expected that so many more humanitarian crises in other regions would cry out for similar efforts and that the knowledge gained in Indochina would become so valuable.

A major contributor to the eventual solution was the Indochina review panel that I set up in 1985 under the leadership of former governor Robert Ray of Iowa. His report charted the path forward, and the office of the UN High Commissioner for Refugees used its recommendations to bring the affected governments, including Vietnam, to agreement on a humane solution.

The clearest illustration of putting victims first was President Reagan's work to rescue Soviet Jews, even as he and President Gorbachev were working their way toward groundbreaking understandings on arms control, trade, and human rights. As we talked about Soviet–American relations, I sensed that the president wanted to move forward but, as he had never met with a Soviet official, he was unsure about the best tactics to use. As a start, I arranged his first-ever meeting with a Soviet official by inviting Soviet Ambassador Anatoly Dobrynin for a White House chat with Reagan in 1983. With a wide range of problems confronting the world's two superpowers, Reagan dominated the meeting with his concern over human rights, refuseniks, and religious freedom.

With the Soviet economy tanking, Gorbachev needed arms control relief and trade. These issues were hotly debated in four Reagan–Gorbachev summits between 1985 and 1988 in Moscow, Reykjavik, Washington, and Geneva. But Reagan refused to budge while Soviet Jews were still denied the right to emigrate. I used every possible occasion to make clear the president's policy during those hectic negotiations, including a speech I delivered just prior to a critical meeting of the Organization for Security and Co-operation in Europe: "Until there is substantial progress in the vital area of human rights, advances in other areas of the relationship are bound to be constrained. Token gestures for short-term lowering of barriers will not suffice."

By holding firm, both sides won as summit agreements led to a major de-escalation of the arms race, free emigration for Jews who wanted to leave the Soviet Union, and full cultural, religious, and educational rights for those who remained in Russia. Eventually, almost a million Jews left the Soviet Union for Israel, America, or other countries.

As the world witnessed, the United States put victims at the center of foreign policy decision-making, and many lives were spared and enriched. Even though emigration from the Soviet Union was at first quite limited, Jim and his organization kept the US welcome mat out and let it be known that we supported "Freedom of Choice" for Soviet Jews and were ready to receive all who could get to the United States.

These principles were applied with equal caring and firmness in refugee crises in other regions as well, in Africa and the Middle East (where the refugee program worked hard to avoid tilting), in South Asia, and in Central America and the Caribbean. The US approach did not necessarily result in more refugees reaching America. Far from it. Our response in most crises was to stabilize and protect refugees in their home regions until more permanent durable solutions were available right there. Resettlement in the US was reserved for those for whom no other safe solution was available. This approach reflected the skyrocketing growth of the world refugee population from six million to almost fifteen million during what we came to call the refugee decade, all during a period of federal budget reductions to deal with growing deficits.

As much as anything, the value of this book is its demonstration that programs that solve critical problems and save lives can be conducted by governments in professional and caring ways. Jim's book reveals intrigues and dynamics behind the scenes. From Ford to Carter to Reagan, the refugee program kept victims at the center of foreign policy decision-making and achieved consistency and spectacular results in a nonpartisan spirit. I regard this as one of my major achievements as secretary of state during the Reagan administration.

Why write or read a book like *We're in Danger! Who Will Help Us?* so far removed from contemporary life? I will answer the same way I responded to the American Jewish Historical Society in 2007 discussing Soviet Jews:

> The reason to record and remember how Soviet Jews were saved is to be prepared to act again when the need arises. If we are ever to live in a civilized world, what was accomplished for the Soviet Jews must become the rule

rather than the exception. We must not only preach the doctrine of human rights, we must learn how actually to be our brother's keeper.

As we scan today's headlines—with literally millions of at-risk refugees dispersed throughout the Middle East, hundreds of North African migrants and refugees drowning in the Mediterranean, and tens of thousands more contemplating the same journey—we should not fail to recall that the same kinds of problems were faced and resolved in the 1980s. We should keep lessons learned in that decade uppermost in mind as life-saving responses are developed for today's crises.

Secretary of State 1982–88
Hoover Institution, Stanford University

AUTHOR'S NOTE

THE HISTORIC PERIOD COVERED IN *WE'RE IN DANGER! WHO Will Help Us?* has been called the *refugee decade*, 1979–89. The book also treats what I will call the *Syrian refugee era* that began in 2011.

Major humanitarian crises erupted simultaneously in every region of the world during the refugee decade, needing new domestic and international response machinery. The US effort was led by the State Department's Bureau for Refugee Programs, known as RP, a humanitarian organization I played a leading role in creating and directing for most of that decade.

The contributions of RP in domestic and international refugee matters during the refugee decade are the principal subject of this book and are used to discuss implications for the Syrian crisis that began in 2011.

The book deals with the key events and people behind the building of a new organization from the ground up after the "Fall of Saigon" and the speedy withdrawal of American forces from Vietnam. The spreading upheavals around the world led US policymakers to confront human threats like the ones that nations face today. In *We're in Danger! Who Will Help Us?* I show how those existential threats were ably defeated, primarily because of political leadership. That leadership valued crisis victims and assured they had a central place in foreign policy decision-making. Our leaders recognized that governments, like individuals, are charged by civilization to "rescue the perishing," especially victims of war, famine, disease, and government corruption. They insisted that we keep victims central in programs and initiatives undertaken on their behalf. Collectively, we were to be our brothers' and sisters' keepers.

The American presidents at the front of the global refugee responses of that era were Gerald Ford, Jimmy Carter, and Ronald Reagan. Their leadership helped motivate public- and private-sector leaders around the world eager to join a "coalition of the willing." Rather than simply managing problems and responses, those global leaders insisted that diplomacy forge cooperative responses and burden-sharing solutions. Results of joint actions could be seen throughout the world, in Southeast Asia with the Comprehensive Plan of Action for Indochinese Refugees, in the USSR through gaining the freedom and emigration of almost a million Jews, in Africa in the saving of millions from famine, wars and corruption, in the Middle East by assuring the survival of the UN Relief and Works Agency for Palestinian Refugees, and in potentially destabilizing humanitarian crises in South Asia (Afghanistan) and Central America. The results those joint efforts produced would not have been possible had the US State Department been denied the necessary diplomatic tools to do the job.

We're in Danger! Who Will Help Us? is divided into four books covering the refugee decade and offers comment on lessons learned for the future.

Book One, "Awake and Rise," highlights the groundbreaking work of Presidents Ford and Carter to rescue trapped American allies following the Vietnam War and the corresponding impacts on the nations of Southeast Asia and other helping partners. This book also covers simultaneous crises arising in the Middle East, Afghanistan, the Horn of Africa, Central America, Eastern Europe, and the Soviet Union.

Book Two, "Create Lift," reveals the work of the Reagan team to cope with destabilizing Indochina refugee problems and to set in place protection, reform and solution mechanisms that eventually led to *comprehensive durable solutions.*

Book Three, "We Are Here," covers RP's problem-solving work in Eastern Europe and the Soviet Union, Africa, the Middle East, South Asia, Central America, and the Caribbean.

Book Four, "And Now…," brings my work as founder and director of the Department of State's Bureau for Refugee Programs to a conclusion with observations about contributors to the successes our team enjoyed. In Book Four, I also posit the solutions compact strategy of the refugee decade as a sustainable and flexible approach for current and future humanitarian crises.

We're in Danger! Who Will Help Us? is my story, written in my own voice, entirely by myself, from the perspective of where I sat. It is based largely on recollections of closest colleagues and my own and on documentation I saved, found, or others offered. I believe I have recalled events and stories accurately. I alone am responsible for the book's contents.

If I left out the contributions of any, it was inadvertent. I hope that did not happen. Writing this history took far longer than I had imagined, as life kept intervening. For that, I do not apologize, and trust colleagues will understand.

My narrative shows the bureau I helped create at the center of events in which others played critical and central roles. My goal has been to include the actions of many. I have not tried to rewrite history or to use knowledge gained later to go back and settle scores. Rather, this roller-coaster journey covers key historic events of a heartfelt era and warns of human risks we face once again—our test of civilization. I hope you will glean a new appreciation of that era defined by the suffering of innocents on a grand scale and the exceptional efforts to rescue them. Survivors rebuilt their lives with much courage, as you will see.

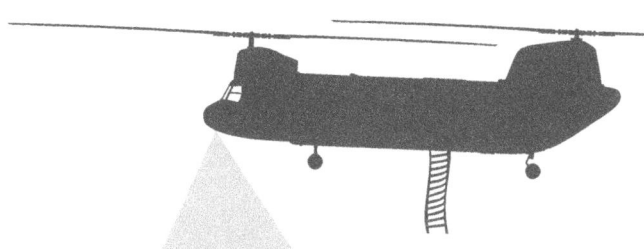

BOOK ONE

AWAKE AND RISE

Desperation Engulfs Warring Indochina

1

INTO THE STORM

VIETNAM. THAT EMBATTLED AND WAR-WEARY COUNTRY first showed up on my professional radar during the Nixon administration's first year. Hopes had risen and then stalled over Nixon's campaign promise to end the Vietnam War through a "secret plan."

Like many Americans, I saw the war as a painful chapter in America's history that just needed to end, and fast. I was thirty-one years old, a husband and father with a fast-rising career in fiscal management and budget analysis. For a year, I had worked on Vietnam and other budget items in the president's budget office, the Bureau of the Budget, or BOB. We were in a grand old building next door to the White House West Wing, on the opposite end from the Treasury Building. Our outfit was an energized, elite group. Our work was demanding, and I loved it.

White House Press Briefing, 1969

Joe Laitin, Budget Bureau counterpart to the White House press secretary, called to ask a question: "Jim, do you want to go to a White House press conference today?"[1] Nixon's first supplemental appropriation request to Congress would come up, Joe said, knowing I had coordinated the supplemental proposal; I jumped at the chance to go over to the White House. The last thing on my mind was the Vietnam War, although I knew war problems had ended President Johnson's run for a second term.

Joe stopped by, and when I jumped up to grab my coat, he commented, "It'll be a good experience for you to witness this press conference. I don't think they will have major questions about the supplemental; it's straightforward."

We reached the press room early, and I could sense the big import of that small space. There was the BOB deputy director Sam Hughes and White House Press Secretary Ron Ziegler, who sat in the front of the room at a small U-shaped desk, a phone in each hand. Ziegler spotted Sam and Joe and motioned them forward. I heard Joe tell him we were there as back-up on budget matters. "I'm glad you're here," Ron said. "Take a seat and I'll call on you if I need help."

When Ziegler got off the phones, he moved to a lectern and signaled an aide to open the door. The press corps flooded in, and I recognized faces from television and names from newspaper bylines. Ziegler read a list of administration announcements and initiatives and then played verbal ping pong with the press over different issues. He explained a budget item in Sam's bailiwick, but he did not call on him. Sam left, and Joe and I stayed, engrossed in the back and forth between Ziegler and the press.

As the briefing wound down, Joe leaned over and said: "Things seem to be going well. I'm going back to the office. Jim, I'm sure nothing will come up about the supplemental."

I said nothing but took note that Sam had left and now Joe was leaving. About thirty minutes later, Ziegler announced that the president had signed his first budget supplemental appropriation request that day, and it was on its way to Congress.

"There's nothing controversial here, just routine business. Copies are on the back table."

I thought Zeigler looked pleased as he called the conference to a close, before a voice from the back called out, "I've just scanned the supplemental appropriation document and there's a proposed reduction of $140.7 million for Southeast Asia operations in DoD. What's that for?"

Ziegler looked down at briefing documents I had prepared. "It's just routine housekeeping. DoD has found miscellaneous savings in its Southeast Asia operations. They can be used to help reduce pending appropriations requests in other parts of the defense budget. That's it."

To the press, Southeast Asia operations meant Vietnam, with immediate suspicions. For months, news organizations had waited for information about the new president's campaign claim—a secret plan to end the Vietnam War.

"What specifically is being cut? Which line items?" another reporter asked.

Other questions flew fast, and the orderly meeting devolved into pandemonium. A nearby journalist whispered, "I hear the national security advisor has scheduled a press conference soon."

Keen ears missed nothing, and a spontaneous chorus arose: "This is probably the budgetary impact of the secret plan they'll be revealing!"

Ziegler looked uncharacteristically befuddled. Things had been going well and now were unraveling. And then he pulled a straw out of thin air: "We have a representative from the BOB here, who put this package together. He can come up and explain this item." Ron Ziegler's straw had my name on it.

My bosses had already left, right? I held my breath and somehow made it to the lectern. I read the words in the supplemental, but the hungry press was not satisfied. I tried to explain that all federal operations are reviewed monthly, and those of DoD's size inevitably develop miscellaneous savings. They are bundled together and, where possible, offered as reductions to pending multibillion-dollar appropriations requests. And so on.

My reasonable answer fueled more suspicion. A powerful groupthink seemed to take over, a conviction that Nixon's secret plan was about to be revealed. *This supplemental appropriations request represents the secret plan's first budgetary implications.* I could almost hear them thinking. The national security advisor Henry Kissinger's notional press conference in coming days reinforced the idea.

Ziegler turned to me again and directed, "Call DoD for clarification."

Instead I called my boss, Ray Clark, who was amazed to learn about the ruckus. He kept me on hold and called Ellis Veatch, chief of the national security division of the president's budget office. Back with me, Ray said Ellis had grumbled, "It's just routine business. Tell them I'm not going to bother the secretary of defense with such trivia."

When I returned to Ziegler empty-handed, the uproar had not died down, and Ron seemed eager to welcome me back. I reminded the press corps of the normalcy of this situation, but they stood firm in disbelief.

"A list of specific line-items proposed for reduction will be available for you soon," I said, while knowing they probably saw me as the career stooge put out there to keep them in the dark. Addressing the front press row, I said, "Believe me, folks, if the president and national security advisor have a secret plan, they wouldn't use me to unveil it. I just work here."

Ziegler called a close to the meeting and motioned for me to come to his lectern. "Sorry," he said, "but that's the press corps. They believe little and question everything."

Back to Base

When I returned to my office, I was summoned to see the director, Bob Mayo. I wondered whether he was concerned that John Ehrlichman and Bob Haldeman, tough Nixon aides, might come after him because of the press briefing. However, with a serious look, he said, "Good job, Jim."

Ray Clark said, "I think you had better take a few days off, Jim, and let this cool down." Phone calls from the press were flooding the White House, the National Security Council (NSC), and the Department of Defense (DoD). Incoming calls to the bureau included requests to interview me.

My thoughts rambled that evening on my one-hour drive home to the rented townhouse in Rockville, Maryland. I walked through the front door in a state of dismay and concern. Jean and I had company for dinner, and later I confided to her, "I believe I may have just lost the Vietnam War." *And I might have ruined my career.*

I stayed at home a few days to wait for an all clear. Eventually, speculation about a secret plan in the budget lost steam. When I returned to work, the situation was hectic, and President Nixon revealed no special plan, secret or otherwise, to end the Vietnam War, which would grind on for six more cruel years.

After that White House press briefing, my boss promoted me to deputy director of the budget preparation staff.[2] One late question about a Southeast Asia budget item had shone a light directly on me, and I naturally paid more attention to the tumult that Southeast Asia and Vietnam topics could generate.

Forward to 1975—Delayed Evacuation Planning

Five years after the notable White House press conference, President Nixon resigned in disgrace, and the vice president Gerald Ford succeeded him, inheriting the ongoing war in Vietnam.

By early 1975, many diplomatic, defense, and intelligence officers accepted that a disastrous military defeat could be in the offing; most informed analysts regarded continuation of the war to be useless. Yet, the ambassador to South Vietnam Graham Martin and the secretary of state Henry Kissinger kept up the drumbeat.

An unofficial group of young Foreign Service Officers (FSO) could not tolerate failure to make evacuation plans for Vietnamese allies and colleagues. They dissented through the only channel then available, clandestine meetings—most often as a lunch group in the cafeteria or a conference room—to discuss evacuation planning. At their first meeting, January 1975, were Frank Wisner, director of plans and management in the bureau of Public Affairs; Paul Hare, deputy director of Press Relations; Kenneth Quinn, NSC; Lionel Rosenblatt, deputy secretary's staff; Craig Johnstone, director of the secretariat staff; Jim Bullington, Vietnam desk officer; and Parker Borg, of Secretary Kissinger's staff. Evacuation planning, in their view, was imperative.[3]

As the Vietcong kept Saigon and victory in their sights, the young rebels led the American government to pursue, unofficially, dual but contradictory plans regarding future intentions in South Vietnam. A two-track policy, never publicly articulated, guided the last months of the war.[4]

In one direction, official policy continually reaffirmed American steadfastness with its South Vietnam allies. Officially, there could be no talk of planned evacuation. South Vietnam, struggling to stay afoot, would likely collapse if the resolve of their American partners was brought into the slightest question. Kissinger detected the dissatisfaction within his ranks and ordered that no officer was to travel to Saigon to assist evacuation. State's public affairs official, Frank Wisner, later told me that "to plan evacuations would be to admit defeat and would amount to pulling the tent pole out, leading to the collapse of the whole tent."

Yet, dissenters at the State Department believed it imperative that evacuation planning proceed immediately, even as military losses piled up fast, to save lives.

On March 10, 1975, the South Vietnam highland city of Ban Me Thuot fell, soon followed by sister cities Hue and Da Nang. About seventy thousand people fled Da Nang, most to Cam Ranh Bay. Untold numbers perished. Nha Trang was in panic mode by early April, when senior South Vietnamese officers self-evacuated to Saigon by helicopter, leaving behind loyal and unprotected troops. Cam Ranh Bay, a mighty US Navy base about 200 miles north of Saigon, was abandoned.[5]

2

VIETNAM AND FIVE US PRESIDENTS

MILITARY RADAR HAD BEEN ON VIETNAM FOR AT LEAST fifteen years by 1969, my first year at the federal budget bureau. In 1954, the small country alongside the South China Sea had won independence from French colonization at the Battle of Dien Bien Phu. Afterward, as northern and southern factions bitterly slugged it out, a United States–Vietnam accord in Paris led to a cease-fire and a temporary partition between north and south; elections on reunification or continuing partition were to be held within two years. While both factions sought independence, their conflicting ideologies distinguished them. The Soviet Union backed North Vietnam, and America backed the South. Most observers accepted that the North Vietnamese later provoked the breakdown of the cease-fire, which led to full scale civil war. US leadership watched these events and commiserated with South Vietnamese allies. It was a time of US-USSR Cold War power struggles.

In a 2009 *Newsweek* article, Evan Thomas and John Barry traced key US actions covering the insertion of troops to Vietnam in 1959 and continuing through their withdrawal in 1975. For example, in 1959, President Dwight D. Eisenhower, a retired five-star general and World War II hero, remained concerned about Vietnam, yet he did not want US forces at war. He sent a few military advisors to Southeast Asia with the mission to help train the new South Vietnamese army. The first American casualties at the hands of North Vietnam from that mission were Major Dale Buis and Sergeant Chester Ovnand. Three years later, 1962, the new president John F. Kennedy kept military advisors in place in Vietnam. He also sent the vice president Lyndon Johnson to make an assessment. On return, Johnson recommended increased US assistance. After the Vietcong, the North's ally, won the battle of Ap Bac, a dispirited South Vietnam military (abetted by surprising US acquiescence) assassinated their president, Ngo Dinh Diem. The next year, President John F. Kennedy was assassinated in Texas, and Lyndon Johnson became the president.

The Evan Thomas and John Barry article in *Newsweek* included events that led to the Gulf of Tonkin Resolution.[1] I have summarized it.

Gulf of Tonkin Resolution

North Vietnamese torpedo boats reportedly attacked US destroyers in the Gulf of Tonkin in August 1964, leading President Johnson to ask Congress to enact necessary measures to defend Southeast Asia. Sen. J. William Fulbright (D-AK) was the floor manager for the Gulf of Tonkin resolution that became a declaration of war, authorizing direct military action (P.L. 88–408). (But the senator later had other words to say, in public, about that experience.)

As media coverage of military setbacks increased, and the nation divided over the war, President Johnson decided not to run again in 1968. In President Richard Nixon's first year in office, 1969, the press conference I attended had shown me the intense press sensitivities toward Vietnam.

President Nixon began early small troop withdrawals from the more than one-half million US troops in Vietnam. After the tragic anti-war protests at Kent State University in 1970, troop levels were dropped to about 215,000.[2]

In 1971, I was responsible for oversight of several international affairs agencies—including the US Information Agency (USIA)—at the Bureau of the Budget, which by then had been renamed the Office of Management and Budget (OMB). At a Senate Foreign Relations Committee hearing on USIA funding chaired by Sen. Fulbright, I heard the senator voice skepticism about the alleged Gulf of Tonkin attack that had spawned the resolution. A USIA witness responded there had been no choice but to accept President Johnson's view of the attack that led to the war resolution.

I watched in stunned amazement as Sen. Fulbright slammed his fist against his podium desk and bellowed: "I didn't know he (President Johnson) was lying either!"

President Nixon ordered more air campaigns in 1972. He approved the bombing of Vietnam's neighbor, Cambodia, as enemy attacks proliferated and American military and public resolve for the war weakened further. US troop levels were about thirty-five thousand by then. News of the bombings over Cambodia fell flat at home.

In January 1973, a cease-fire agreement signed in Paris by the US secretary of state Henry Kissinger and the North Vietnam negotiator Le Duc Tho meant more reductions of US forces. The North Vietnamese returned 591 American POWs, welcomed home in Operation Homecoming. President Nixon and Henry Kissinger regrouped, and then a domestic scandal called Watergate intervened. President Nixon resigned on August 9 the following year, and the vice president Gerald Ford was sworn in.

In 1974, Congress threatened to halve the administration's $722 million request for Vietnam operations. Appropriations Committee Chairman John Stennis (D-MS) told Secretary Kissinger to "… send someone out there to appraise it." Kissinger sent Jim Bullington, Vietnam desk officer, on December 20, 1974, for a three–week assessment. Commenting on Bullington's trip report, Henry Kissinger said, "He pointed out that even a supplemental of $300 million would only just barely cover expenditures for consumables and would leave no funds for replacements. A minimum of $1.3 billion would be needed for the same purpose in 1976. By then, the replacement of damaged and destroyed equipment could no longer be delayed." Kissinger added, "Bullington concluded that, without the supplemental, South Vietnam's position was hopeless. We had reached the point where, if the supplemental failed to materialize, only one option would be left to mitigate our country's dishonor: to save as many Vietnamese as possible."[3]

As Bullington told me, his earlier assessment had found that as many as one million people might need to be evacuated if American forces withdrew, including Americans and Vietnamese allies at risk. He also concluded that without replenishment, at the rate resources were being consumed, the war effort could not continue beyond the middle of 1975.

Key members of the Senate Foreign Relations Committee went to the White House for a face-to-face with President Ford on April 14, 1975. They talked about his budget request for $722 million to "stabilize the military situation" in Vietnam. The senators—including Jacob Javits (R-NY), Frank Church (D-ID), and Joe Biden (D-DE)—clarified to the president that no additional funds would be provided to continue the war, only funds for evacuation.[4]

In early 1975, Phuoc Binh, formerly a safe area of cassava and sweet potato farming, fell to the Vietcong, who bombed it in violation of the Paris agreement. President Ford met the breach with silence, and US troops did not reengage the enemy.

April 1975 Was a Cruel Month

As perceptions of a crumbling South Vietnam government mounted, concern heightened over the fate of over seventy thousand Vietnamese orphans. What would happen to them if the government collapses? Through the persistence of the deputy assistant secretary for human development Julia Taft of the Department of Health, Education and Welfare a rescue program was activated on April 3, 1975. President Ford announced that the United States would fly seventy thousand orphans out of Vietnam using two million dollars available from a special foreign aid children's fund. The evacuation would be named Operation Baby Lift.

Ann Blackman's biography of Julia Taft, *Off to Save the World*, described the harrowing departure of the first flight the following day as it left Tan Son Nhut airport at four in the afternoon with 328 children aboard. Twelve minutes into the flight a staggering disaster struck, an on-board explosion. The plane broke apart when the pilot landed in a rice paddy; over 150 passengers perished. This tragic accident brought anguish and tears throughout the world, but it did not halt evacuations. Over the next few weeks, Operation Baby Lift carried three thousand children safely out of Vietnam, before American troops left and the program came to a quick end.

The discreet pleadings of the young rebels emboldened the State Department's under secretary for management Larry Eagleburger to create the Interagency Task Force on Indochina Refugees (IATF) on April 14. Four days later, President Ford officially approved the task force, and evacuation planning for Vietnam became public. The IATF marked a significant move forward for official evacuation planning, with Ambassador L. Dean Brown in charge. Immediately joining were Frank Wisner, Julia Taft, Clay McManaway, and Gerald Rose. Eventually, over one hundred officials drawn from State, Defense, Labor, Central Intelligence, the Immigration and Naturalization Service, and the Department of Health, Education, and Welfare came on board. As Clay McManaway later related to me, evacuation planning and operations were in twenty-four seven mode.

On April 17, 1975, Secretary Kissinger gave the order to the ambassador Graham Martin in Saigon to expedite the withdrawal of nonessential American personnel and top Vietnamese officials. Five days later, immigration requirements were waived to allow *parole* of anticipated large numbers of Vietnamese. On April 23, 1975, shortly after the evacuation plan announcement, President Ford spoke at Tulane University. In reply to a question, he commented, "We, of course, are saddened by the events in Indochina. But these events, tragic as they are, portend neither the end of the world nor of America's leadership in the world ... the fate of responsible men and women everywhere, in the final decision, rests in their own hands, not in ours."[5]

President Ford's momentous words officially signaled the Vietnam War's approaching end. The historic, enormous streams of fleeing South Vietnamese people surged into rivers of desperate escape.

The State Department's amazing lore of that era reveals that Lionel Rosenblatt and Craig Johnstone hurriedly paid their way back to Saigon, contrary to Secretary Kissinger's orders. Lionel told me that Ambassador Graham Martin expressed outrage at their sudden arrival in Saigon on April 22. For four days, they ran an evacuation for over 200 Vietnamese by setting up special teams at a bowling alley near Tan Son Nhut Airport to identify and process South Vietnamese as refugees. Those approved got a document with an American consular seal, the ticket onto an evacuation flight. The US was preparing to evacuate Americans and any Vietnamese who could get past airport security and onto a plane.

Americans stationed in Vietnam bristled over inadequate evacuation preparations made by the American Embassy for Americans and South Vietnamese allies. For these obvious inadequacies, the American ambassador came under strong criticism then and later. Many thought the criticisms unjustified, but he was the responsible official, as many critics told me.

On April 29, North Vietnamese forces steadily drove toward Saigon and into a city in panic. Dramatic news film and photographs recorded the sight, as desperate citizens fled the city.

On that day, President Ford ordered evacuation of the embassy. Over the next fourteen hours, about one thousand Americans and six thousand South Vietnamese left by any way possible, many by risky helicopter rescues. As these events occurred, the South Vietnamese government ordered all American military forces and diplomats to leave within twenty-four hours. The last American troops and Ambassador Martin and most embassy staff evacuated. On the morning of April 30, 1975, North Vietnam tanks crashed through the gates of Independence Palace, and Vietcong troops swarmed the city. Saigon fell, the government of South Vietnam—the Republic of Vietnam (RVN)—collapsed. The war was lost and over. That day would be etched into American history as a culmination of dashed hopes, errors, and gross miscalculations.

Heroes of Saigon—Diplomats and Military Officers

Any understanding of the import of Vietnam and America's humanitarian response resides in awareness of events that led to the "Fall of Saigon" on the fateful day of April 30, 1975, and the brave life-saving actions that followed.

Of that awful day, President Ford said,

> One thing, however, is beyond question—the heroism of the marines who guarded the embassy during its darkest hours, and of those brave helicopter pilots who flew non-stop missions for eighteen hours, dodging relentless sniper fire to land on an embassy roof illuminated by nothing more than a thirty-five-millimeter slide projector.[6]

Obscured within the lagging, bungled, and tragic American-led evacuation from South Vietnam was the extraordinary and self-sacrificing bravery of many American diplomats, military officers, and intelligence personnel. Several staffers tried to fill the void by quietly launching evacuation schemes on their own.

Shep Lowman, then assigned to the embassy in Saigon, spoke on this subject and of his colleague and deputy, Lacy Wright:

> Political officer Lacy Wright, who had been working on evacuations with CIA's Frank Snepp and FSO Ken Quinn, ferried as many Vietnamese as he could find from designated safe houses to a barge on the Saigon River. He did not return until late on the afternoon of April 29, after the evacuation had been underway for many hours.[7]

He also recalled that Joe Gettier, a US Agency for International Development officer, was on the barge and did not evacuate by air at all. He received the State Department's Medal of Valor for riding shotgun down the Saigon River to the South China Sea. Shep later told me about the consul general Terry McNamara, his deputy Hank Cushing, and the officers of the US Consulate General in Can Tho who rejected evacuation by air and rode two river boats down the Bassac and Mekong Rivers to the South China Sea with South Vietnamese employees of the consulate and close contacts. He said they were swamped with messages from Foreign Service Officers all over the world with special concerns for Vietnamese friends.

Lowman scoured Saigon streets the last day, rounding up Vietnamese colleagues, including the mayor of Saigon, Nguyen Hop Doan. Shep gave about a hundred people directions to a meet-up location, and over 600 showed up. When evacuation buses failed to arrive, and time ran out, Shep urged last-minute evacuees to try to reach transport barges on their own. Other embassy and military officials drove around Saigon to collect evacuees. Shep Lowman and Lacy Wright left on one of the last flights out of Saigon.

Flotilla to Subic Bay

Sensing the imminent collapse of South Vietnam, US Navy officials had unofficially prepared for evacuation of Vietnamese allies. Navy Captain Paul Jacobs later said (the Cosmos Club in Washington, DC, 2015) that contingency plans had included four options: commercial ships in the Saigon River, commercial airlines, fixed-wing military aircraft, and helicopters and ships. He said that Ambassador Martin's refusal to order evacuation earlier left the US Navy with only the fourth option in the days leading to the, now iconic, Fall of Saigon.

By late April 1975, the Navy's Seventh Fleet Task Force 76, under the command of Rear Admiral Donald Whitmire, assembled all the evacuation ships available at the South Vietnam port of Vung Tau, about twenty miles offshore. Included were seventeen amphibious ships, two aircraft carriers, fourteen escorts (mostly destroyers and destroyer escorts), and eleven replenishment ships. Supporting this force but further out at sea was a second force to provide protection. The entire evacuation fleet comprised seventy-three ships. The evacuation was called Operation Frequent Wind.

Suddenly on April 29, the Task Force 76 ships reported the air filled with US Marine and Air Force helicopters loaded with evacuees from Saigon. They discharged their evacuees and headed back for another run. They had been followed out to sea by hundreds of Vietnamese Air Force Huey helicopters filled with escapees, hoping to land on the same ships.

In the often-told stories about the last days of the Vietnam War, and as relayed in Rory Kennedy's award-winning documentary, one ship in the force—the USS *Kirk* (a destroyer escort named for Admiral Alan Goodrich Kirk) under the command of Captain Paul Jacobs—was patrolling its assigned area.[8] At two in the afternoon on April 29, a South Vietnamese Huey helicopter turned toward the USS *Kirk* and commenced successful landing procedures. This was the first of twelve such landings over the next ten hours, rescuing 152 Vietnamese. Each Huey that landed and off-loaded was immediately pushed into the sea to make room for the next.

One rescue involved a twin-rotor CH-47 Chinook transport helicopter, a ninety-nine-foot aircraft—too large to land on the ship. Its rotating blades produced a continual swell in the sea. The Chinook dipped so low the crew could see faces at the windows. While the USS *Kirk*'s deck crew desperately tried to wave the pilot off, he lowered his craft even closer to the ship.

The crew realized the pilot was intending to discharge people from a side door, as they waited patiently at the deck's edge. They positioned themselves to catch jumping passengers, including a baby tossed to them. No life was lost. His passengers safely off, the pilot quickly turned his craft away, nosed it toward the sea, locked its controls, and plunged. The ship's crew feared the pilot had been trapped underwater. But he soon popped up and swam toward the ship, and the crew realized the red color in the water was fuel, not blood. Several crew members immediately jumped in to help the struggling pilot. He was Ba Van Nguyen of the Vietnamese Air Force, and his family had been on board the Chinook and were saved by the USS *Kirk*.

Captain Jacobs told the Cosmos Club audience about an unusual order he received on April 30 from Task Force 76 Commander Whitmire. That order placed his command in a leading and historic role in the next phases of the evacuation. He was instructed to pick up a civilian passenger, Richard Armitage, and follow his next-step instructions. The former Navy officer was working as a special agent for the US secretary of defense James Schlesinger. Earlier, he had negotiated the clandestine escape of the Vietnamese Navy with the chief of Vietnamese naval operations Vice Admiral Chung Tan Cang. Jacobs and Armitage were to rendezvous immediately with the remaining ships of Vietnam's Navy on Con Son Island, about a hundred miles southwest of Vung Tau.

Thirty Vietnamese ships and boats and two civilian fishing trawlers met the US Navy ship several days later at the designated island. They carried over thirty thousand escaping Vietnamese. The USS *Kirk* led the Vietnamese flotilla to Subic Bay; they arrived on May 5, 1975, and were refused permission to dock.

By that time, the Philippine Government had formally recognized the new communist party government of Vietnam, and the Philippine president Ferdinand Marcos feared allowing ships flying the flag of the former South Vietnam to harbor in his country. The American ambassador to the Philippines William Sullivan proposed a unique solution using provisions of the Military Assistance Program, under which American ships had been provided to the South Vietnam Navy. The ships could be returned and reflagged as American. The ambassador negotiated this arrangement with President Marcos, with the understanding the Vietnamese would quickly depart. The flotilla docked at Subic Bay. The Vietnamese were transferred to Military Sealift Command ships and moved to Guam.[9]

This was one of the most heroic rescues of the Operation Frequent Wind period, and the record justifiably overflows with numerous acts of bravery and kindness to thankful survivors.

3

RESCUE THE PERISHING

OPERATION NEW LIFE, THE RELOCATION ARM OF THE EMERgency evacuation program was underway as the last American military helicopter flew away from Saigon. Airlifted survivors went from ships to US bases in the Philippines, and later to other bases on Wake Island and Guam. Over 65,000 Vietnamese left under the auspices of the Interagency Task Force (IATF). About the same number arranged their own evacuations to designated transit points in the region, to be documented, processed, and moved to US military bases pending resettlement. In the planning stage, the ambassador L. Dean Brown of IATF contacted all stakeholders through the creation of two working groups. One was responsible for internal coordination within the State Department and the other for interagency relations with partners in the departments of Justice, HEW, Defense, and American private voluntary organizations (PVOs).

Operation New Life set up American transit camps to house Indochina refugees until the PVOs could arrange permanent resettlement locations. The transit camps were set up at Fort Chafee, Arkansas; Fort Indiantown Gap, Pennsylvania; Eglin Air Force Base, Florida; and Camp Pendleton, California. To pay for sizeable evacuation expenses, the Migration and Refugee Assistance Act of 1975 authorized $405 million, signed into law by President Ford in the evacuation month, April 1975.[1] By December 1975, all evacuees were resettled in America. Operation New Life, first led by Ambassador Brown and later by Julia Taft, gave many Americans their first experience with refugees in that remarkable resettlement program.

Significantly, informed observers thought (or hoped) the Vietnamese resettled from April to December 1975 would constitute the bulk of those needing help. Reality would soon hit hard, again.

Among the first State Department officers to anticipate Vietnam refugee disasters with a coming Vietcong victory, Lionel Rosenblatt and Craig Johnstone returned to Washington in July 1975 following their Saigon evacuation efforts and were summoned to Secretary Kissinger's office. They expected a tongue-lashing. But, after some initial criticisms, they received commendations.

When Secretary Kissinger asked Rosenblatt where he wanted to work next, Lionel later told me, he said he wanted to continue in refugee work. He thought the secretary seemed mystified by this career choice, since refugee work was then considered a dead end in the Washington bureaucracy. However, Kissinger sent Lionel to IATF to see the director Julia Taft.

By early 1976, the State Department hoped to wind down all refugee operations in Southeast Asia, and Taft sent Rosenblatt on a final observation and reporting mission to Thailand. Rosenblatt found many desperate people with no place to go, and he took special note of the pitiable conditions facing the Hmong refugees from Laos. The IATF was, thereafter, convinced that Southeast Asia refugee problems were not over.

Expanded Parole

To move specific refugees to the United States, the Interagency Task Force (IATF) launched a program that came to be the Expanded Parole Program (EPP). An additional 11,000 refugees would come to the United States under the admission numbers and funds leftover from the Saigon airlifts. The EPP would include three vulnerable groups of Indochina refugees: (1) close blood relatives of American citizens or permanent residents, (2) former US Government employees, and (3) persons unable to return home due to fear of persecution.

At the last possible moment—June 30, 1976, the end of the fiscal year—the House Judiciary Committee chairman Peter Rodino overrode the subcommittee chairman's reluctance to give congressional acquiescence for the EPP. Lionel Rosenblatt assembled his team in Bangkok, including Mac Thompson, Jerry Daniels, John Tucker, and Peace Corps volunteers Patty Culpepper, Sally Maxwell, Judy Kocher, Rich Kocher, Dick

Scott, Berta Romero, Pat Christman, Paul Christman, Lelia Webster, Steve Fick, and Chris Wharton. A major refugee processing partner, the Intergovernmental Committee for European Migration (ICEM), was headed by the legendary Albert Corcos in Bangkok.

Refugee processing included the participation of different professional specialists, beginning with pre-screening in refugee camps to determine US eligibility, then an interview by the Joint Voluntary Agency (JVA) and/or the embassy officer, followed by presentation to the US Immigration and Naturalization Service (INS) for decision, then US sponsor identification, medical screening and transportation arrangements by ICEM, and finally travel to the United States for permanent resettlement by the private partner organizations.

EPP concluded its work. Lionel went into the Foreign Service language training in Washington and others returned to their posts or began new assignments. Even the devoted refugee advocates concluded that the Southeast Asia refugee program was over, the end of a chilling drama. Memories of the Saigon evacuations and EPP faded. Refugee concerns slipped off Washington's radar.

Life only got worse for allies and friends left behind. America's swift, unplanned withdrawal from Saigon in April 1975 set in motion the systematic persecution and inevitable flight of multitudes of Indochinese. Strategic military and diplomatic withdrawal also affected Cambodia and Laos. Almost overnight, new communist regimes dominated fifty million Indochinese citizens. Abandoned, many tried to survive under harsh totalitarian regimes. Those able to cross borders into friendly neighboring countries throughout Southeast Asia exacted enormous costs on countries that, sometimes grudgingly, provided temporary haven. Pressure would build, with threats of expulsion for refugees and forced pushback of new escapees to vengeful communist systems.

Weakened Nation

The war's outcome and scathing impact changed our country. But the impact would take years to recognize. Decisions of five US presidents, influenced by advisors, policies, and growing public outrage over the war, set the stage for a historic US and Southeast Asia showdown. Many compatriots had put their faith in US advisors and fighters, assuming they would protect them if the worst came. America left Indochina with no exit plan and multitudes of loyal allies facing retribution at the hands of conquering forces.

After the US withdrawal from Southeast Asia, political, policy, and ideological divisions also sprang up throughout the American homeland, with significant reverberations. There was near condemnation of our national defense apparatus, for the war had consumed significant and precious resources in lives, materiel, and finances. Assaults on defense spending cost America vital defense investments, just when its Cold War adversary, the Soviet Union, continued the steady military buildup launched after the Cuban missile crisis.

The Vietnam War, its aftermath, and the Watergate scandal (directly related to President Nixon and his party's impropriety), brought significant congressional restrictions on presidential flexibility. The War Powers Resolution and a host of constraints on foreign aid, arms exports, and intelligence activities sought to constrain presidential ability to act independently in foreign policy. Many believed these constraints weakened America, signaling a pullback from its traditional global leadership.

After America's withdrawal from Vietnam, the Soviet Union used the interregnum to intervene in Angola, Ethiopia, South Yemen, and, yes, in Afghanistan, and to launch effective anti-US propaganda campaigns throughout the world. (The later Iranian hostage crisis gave another example of adversaries taking advantage of perceived American weakness.) After the war, several thoughtful analysts labeled this weakness as the most destabilizing factor on the global scene during that era. America was in retreat, rushing toward isolationism, whose destructive folly again was about to be revealed and show the dependence of world peace on American strength and resolve.[2]

Note: The acronym PVO (private voluntary organization) evolved into NGO (nongovernmental organization) over the next few years, especially following the establishment in 1984 of the umbrella organization, Interaction, (previously known as the American Council of Voluntary Agencies (ACVA). It was recognized that many affected organizations were state or corporate funded, with managed projects and professional staff. Hereafter, this book uses the acronym NGO.

4

TRAGIC TRIANGLE

Washington, DC

BY 1976, SAIGON EVACUEES AND THE EXPANDED PAROLE PROgram, known as "the first Indochinese refugee surge," had been resettled, mainly in the United States. The Interagency Task Force (IATF) on Indochinese Refugees, begun April 19, 1975, completed its work by mid-1977. State Department monthly resettlement reports show Indochina refugee admissions to the United States between April 1975 and June 1977 were 157,000, most of which were from Saigon or through the expanded parole program for evacuees, known as EPP (*see* Table 2).

Most US officials thought the Indochina refugee problems were over. Temporary organizational structures set up in Washington and Southeast Asia to deal with the first refugee surge were phased out. The small refugee office in the State Department returned to backwater status in Humanitarian Affairs (HA).

Meanwhile, refugee conditions in Indochina continued to deteriorate, as the victors applied brutal control over their defeated rivals. From mid-1977 to 1978, the refugee situation in Southeast Asia lurched toward another pressure point but received scant attention from Washington; the responsible bureau was preoccupied with human rights reporting and with an investigation of managerial short comings.

Vietnam

Life in the new Vietnam degenerated rapidly after Saigon fell on April 30, 1975. Darkness settled over the former Republic of South Vietnam like a cold moonless midnight. Many military, political, and diplomatic survivors were killed or imprisoned. Families, homes, and jobs were no more; education and medical care disappeared for many and reeducation camps or new economic zones were set up. Necessities were scarce, and survivors tried to avoid standing out in the communist restructuring.

Initially, fleeing Vietnamese were those who had fought the Vietcong or had been associated with the former South Vietnamese Government or with the Americans. But, in 1978 the communist government initiated harsher policies as Hanoi restructured society. It shifted city dwellers to the countryside and eliminated the business and professional classes. In March 1978, nearly thirty-five thousand large and small enterprises were closed or confiscated. In one swift stroke, the economic elite of the country were decapitated.

These new policies were aimed primarily at 1.5 million ethnic Chinese, South Vietnam's former commercial entrepreneurs, now viewed as security threats at a time of worsening Vietnam–China relations. Having lived peacefully in Vietnam for generations, the ethnic Chinese faced job dismissals, conscription, or transfer to the remote new economic zones.[1]

In the summer and fall of 1978, escapes from Vietnam increased markedly, including more ethnic Chinese. The North Vietnamese authorities were often complicit in organizing their flight, as in October 1978, when the *Hai Hong*, a 1,600-ton coastal cargo ship, arrived in Malaysia after being denied port in Indonesia.[2] It sought to offload over 2,500 Vietnamese refugees allegedly rescued at sea. The furious Malaysian government forced the Vietnamese to remain on the *Hai Hong* for eight weeks until agreement was reached for their authentication. Eventually, onboard processing allowed their immediate resettlement abroad.

The Malaysian and Indonesian authorities had discovered they had been duped a month earlier into assisting 1,200 Vietnamese brought to their shores by the *Southern Cross*, a 900-ton commercial freighter with a similar story. The *Southern Cross*, and later the *Hai Hong*, had been acquired by a Hong Kong syndicate to collect refugees for profit from the southern port of Vung Tau. The passengers paid $2,500 in gold and dollars to secure one-way passage. Three more vessels with 8,100 persons aboard made the same trip shortly after the *Hai Hong* and received similar treatment. Use of large vessels ended thereafter, as they met resistance at receiving Southeast Asia ports.

Using smaller craft, however, about 50,000 refugees arrived in first-asylum countries in the final three months of 1978.

Those who escaped Vietnam told of thousands of former US allies and compatriots either escaped or planning their escape via secretly organized departure schemes. In expanding numbers, sea and overland escapes were attempted. As the forcibly united Vietnam plunged into darkness, so too did its neighbors.

Cambodia

Led by Pol Pot, the murderous Khmer Rouge gradually took over and changed the country's official name to Democratic Kampuchea. (The name "Cambodia" would be restored with the monarchy in 1993.)

As the country plunged into anarchy, the American ambassador to Cambodia John Gunther Dean ordered the evacuation of nonessential American personnel in March 1975. Those remaining left by early April and America could offer no help to its former Cambodian allies. FSO Ken Quinn had been the lone voice reporting to Washington about the unfathomable hell that enveloped Cambodia between 1973 and 1975, including the use of children and young people as forward spears. No one had wanted to hear Quinn, as the American and international audiences had gone deaf on Cambodia.

Coinciding with the drive against Saigon in 1975, the North Vietnamese-backed Khmer Rouge ramped up their offensive against the Lon Nol government in Cambodia, causing over two million Cambodian citizens to flood into Phnom Penh, a capital city of acute deprivations, hardships, and suffering as the regime collapsed. The Khmer Rouge encountered little resistance in its takeover and launched a campaign to swallow up any remnant of traditional Cambodian society and construct a new and "pure" socialist society. They wanted to return to what they called "year zero." The devastatingly brutal social engineering experiment deliberately sealed off the country, as it created a Cambodian holocaust. Immediately, the sadistic Khmer Rouge forced almost everyone out of the capital city, ostensibly to avoid retaliatory American bombing. Reliable sources estimated that the devastating marches alone led 150,000 to 200,000 people to their deaths.

The Khmer Rouge (also known as KR) allowed no returns home, preferring to impose austere new settlements based on subsistence farming. No sign of earlier life remained, including family life. Parents, children, and spouses were dispersed to different work camps around the country. Human interaction for most people disappeared. Outward religious life, a source of hope, vanished as the regime demolished temples and either killed the monks or forced them into work gangs. Devotion was owed only to the Angka Loeu, the new communist regime. Punishments were meted out for any sign of education, wealth, or sophistication; wearing glasses or showing any knowledge of a foreign language posed serious risks. Many enslaved Cambodians were killed for any appearance of past opportunity or success, individual identity, or accomplishment. Those were flagrant violations of the new, "better" state.[3]

By late summer of 1975, unimaginable conditions deteriorated further. Famine swept Cambodia. Hunger, squalid living conditions, KR abuse, and almost the near absence of medical care made the death rate soar. During a reign of terror, the Khmer Rouge executed many Lon Nol soldiers and civil servants. Genocide consumed an estimated one to two million citizens. To prevent flight from Cambodia, the KR sealed the Thai border with landmines, making the frontier a danger zone through which escape was almost impossible. Very few got out, and panic reigned.

In December 1978, a new tide of refugees formed as the Vietnamese communists invaded Cambodia and overthrew the Khmer Rouge. Vietnam's army applied scorched earth tactics in pursuit of the retreating Khmer Rouge, and sowed more disaster by preventing the planting of the 1979 rice crop. So, the next year more famine ravaged Cambodia, and hundreds of thousands died. Khmer Rouge and Vietnamese domination blocked the movement out of Cambodia except for a small number. Escapee reports, backed up by intelligence, predicted human disaster of unimaginable proportions throughout Cambodia.

Laos

Laos, the third point of the tragic Indochina triangle, became a focus of United States planning for containing the regional conflict. During the Vietnam War, the communist Vietcong (VC) had looked to the Pathet Lao for sanctuary and resources. To avoid further communist expansion as US military forces weakened in the region, a strategic decision was made to bring in the Central Intelligence Agency (CIA). It organized a secret army in Laos to tie up the Pathet Lao, preventing them from coming to the aid of the North Vietnamese and Vietcong forces. The CIA mobilized a fiercely independent hilltribe people called the Hmong, noncommunist nationalists. They convinced the Hmong to wage guerilla warfare against the ruling Pathet Lao, which they did brilliantly for a time. Ultimately, the overwhelming military superiority of the Pathet Lao took its toll. By May 1975, the Hmong army had been subdued.

Local communists loyal to Hanoi, the center of communist power in the region, by 1975 had taken over the weakened neutralist government in Laos. The prime minister Souvanna Phouma surrendered and ordered government forces to cooperate with the communists. This made the Hmong's already perilous situation even more dangerous. The new government made clear to the Hmong what failure to submit would mean: decimation.

The Lao People's Democratic Republic was established in December 1975. Hmong residual forces, led by General Vang Pao, pulled back to their Long Tieng headquarters in the Plain of Jars, ancient rolling terrain set off by stones carved into jars, in Northeast Laos. The lush, green landscape had become a deadly war place, including hidden military landmines. Surrounded by the Pathet Lao, they knew they could no longer depend on outside governments for help. To avoid almost certain death if captured, General Vang Pao was forced to leave his troops behind and seek exile in Thailand.

Through the American Embassy in Bangkok, an arrangement was made to move up to three thousand Hmong refugees to Thailand. Refugee officer Jerry Daniels (a former CIA officer) tenaciously cobbled together an arrangement with Bird Air, evacuating people from Long Tieng to the Udorn Air Base in Thailand. It worked. However, over forty thousand other Hmong were left behind to face the Pathet Lao. General Vang Pao had hoped to regroup Laotian freedom fighters in Thailand for return to the homeland to defeat the communists. However, this was never to be, and he was later resettled in Montana, where he continued to hope and plan for a return.

The Pathet Lao entered Long Tieng without opposition. Other Laotian cities fell quickly. The war in Laos was officially over. The remaining Hmong community, at risk of slaughter, began a long, dangerous trek to Thailand on their own. Stories of the dangers and brutality they endured are part of the Hmong and refugee history. While many suffered along the way and others died, over forty thousand Laotians crossed into Thailand by the end of 1975, and more came later.

Also endangered were large numbers of lowland Lao, mostly urbanized and educated; many were former employees of the US Government. In the two years following the Lao People's Democratic Republic's establishment, about 150,000 Laotian refugees crossed into Thailand.

All of Indochina was in turmoil.

Washington Prepares for the Next Storm

A refugee tsunami was rumbling beneath the surface, forecast by developments in Vietnam, Cambodia, and Laos. From late 1977 to summer 1978, a few State Department officials in the region tracked increasing numbers of Vietnamese, Cambodians, and Laotians fleeing into Thailand and other asylum countries. But an unresponsive State Department leadership deflected and ignored their concerns. For most of 1976–77, the State refugee team had no officials involved in the first Indochinese refugee surge. Charles Whitehouse was the American ambassador in Thailand, the region's key country of refuge. At State, Art Hummel was the assistant secretary for East Asia and the Pacific. The refugee job in HA was vacant (Shep Lowman was being considered) and Lionel Rosenblatt was in language training at the Foreign Service Institute. For one year, 1977–78, new refugee arrival numbers in the region spiked, far exceeding minimal third-country resettlement capacities. The refugee populations climbed principally in Thailand, Malaysia, and Indonesia, all overwhelmed and reluctant to accept additional arrivals. No organizational structures existed for escalating refugee developments, and State Department officials in the field were on their own.

Embattled Humanitarian Bureau

The Human Rights and Humanitarian Affairs bureau (HA) was responsible for State's actions in the Tragic Triangle crisis, but it was paralyzed by congressional criticism so severe as to threaten future budgets and programs. This crisis would engulf HA responses to the refugee flows building up in Asia, and its implications would hound anyone working on immediate refugee solutions.[4]

◆

In the early 1970s, a House Appropriations Committee report noted that the State Department's involvement in European and African refugee matters had decreased substantially, and the US Government suffered from unusual administrative divisions: DoD and USAID handled Southeast Asian refugee assistance, while HEW handled Cuban refugees. The committee's report called for consolidation to avoid duplication and excess administrative costs.

By 1975, the Committee repeated its strong warning and demanded that the secretary of state provide detailed justification for prolonged inaction on its earlier call for consolidation. The Committee recognized that refugee concerns had fallen off State's radar.

After the Fall of Saigon, April 30, 1975, the State Department reacted to this outside pressure and to the growing interagency efforts following the Indochina evacuation, by establishing a coordinator position for refugees in Humanitarian Affairs. With forty staff positions, this office managed human rights, POWs, MIAs, and the people in danger crossing borders.

Congressional opposition was further intensified in mid-1978 when the secretary of state reported that HA had exceeded its annual refugee appropriation, violating the Antideficiency Act, a major violation of law.

On December 15, 1978, the House Appropriations Committee directed its investigative staff to review the programmatic management and administrative procedures of HA as they pertained to refugees. The result was a highly critical report released in April 1979, hinting at transferring the refugee portfolio from the State Department to USAID. State's inspector general launched a parallel investigation.

First Asylum at Risk

As the Bureau of Humanitarian Affairs (HA) was besieged with investigations, the number of Indochinese seeking asylum in noncommunist countries in Southeast Asia exploded, from fewer than three thousand per month in the 1976–77 period, to about six thousand people per month by August 1978, and fifteen thousand per month in the final quarter. In the first six months of 1979 about 200,000 Indochinese joined the 245,000-plus already in the first-asylum camps awaiting resettlement. Almost sixty thousand arrivals were recorded in June 1979 alone. During this period, only about seventy-five thousand survivors had been relocated from the camps to permanent resettlement in other countries.[5]

Therefore, by the end of June 1979, the Indochina refugee population in the noncommunist countries of Southeast Asia stood at approximately 370,000, including slightly over 200,000 boat refugees (principally in Thailand, Malaysia, Hong Kong, and Indonesia, plus smaller numbers in the Philippines, Macao, Singapore, Japan, and South Korea) and approximately 170,000 land refugees from all three Indochina states in Thailand.

Of concern was the large and growing proportion of Vietnamese boat refugees. Even the brutal pirate attacks against flimsy refugee boats could not deter desperate escapes.

Mushrooming boat people arrivals put the right of safe first asylum at risk for hundreds of thousands of Indochinese refugees. (In refugee parlance, *first asylum* refers to the legal obligation of the *first country of entry* to grant access to a person fleeing their home country for refuge and protection. (From here, I will italicize at least once the terms used regularly in refugee and immigration work.)

As the first-asylum populations multiplied, the Association of Southeast Asian Nations (ASEAN) announced a policy that Indochinese refugees could remain in their *first-asylum* countries only temporarily, in transit status; they could not settle there. As a condition of permitting even *temporary first asylum*, ASEAN insisted on international *third-country resettlement* (mainly the United States). Absent help from the major resettlement countries, an ASEAN refugee asylum moratorium would start after June 1979.

The CIA estimated that substantially larger numbers of Vietnamese could plan boat departure from June 1979 onward. In addition, new flows from Cambodia and Laos were making their way to the first-asylum nations. Malaysia indicated that in the second half of the year it would push off boats unless international help arrived.[6]

Those who sensed the brewing storm saw a bleak forecast. There were no rescue mechanisms in place in Southeast Asia in mid-1976 to mid-1978 era. The massive response needed did not appear to be on the drawing board, and little money was available. Other than a few single-minded State Department and NGO advocates, official Washington just wanted this problem to go away. A deeper look, however, revealed slight stirrings.

◇

The under secretary for political affairs Phil Habib—and the State Department's third-ranking official—understood and appreciated the dangers bubbling beneath the surface in Indochina in 1977. Tom Miller, one of Habib's special assistants, said Habib raised the Indochina and worldwide refugee problems with the secretary of state Cyrus Vance, who agreed that State should be better prepared for this looming global problem. When Habib suffered a heart attack in December 1977, his responsibilities, including the overview of refugees, was turned over to his successor, David Newsom. Miller was assigned to participate in drafting a memorandum to the secretary of state in 1978 recommending a new organizational configuration for refugee matters.

There should be, first, an interagency official to harmonize the work of external players, and second, an officer to manage the State Department's statutory refugee responsibilities. With Secretary Vance's approval, work on reform began. However, lacking significant organizational pronouncements from seventh floor top brass, breakthrough hopes languished, while a second wave of Indochinese refugees gained enormous strength at lightning speed. In HA, refugee concerns continued to take a backseat to the bureau's unquestioned priority: human rights analysis and reporting.

5

URGENT EARLY WARNINGS

ANOTHER POSTWAR REFUGEE SURGE WAS COMING. THE new refugee office director in HA, Shep Lowman had detected it in 1977. Yet, he had little success getting through to top leadership in HA or the department. Apprehensive about the massive challenge that lay ahead, Lowman went outside the government for help. In November that year, he went to New York to meet with an influential humanitarian, Leo Cherne.

A charismatic leader with the rare combination of knowledge, influence, and empathy, Leo Cherne was chairman of the board of directors of the International Rescue Committee (IRC), whose predecessor organization had been founded by Albert Einstein fifty years earlier.[1] Leo was respected as a humanitarian, a presidential advisor, an activist in many momentous events in modern history, a sculptor, a lawyer, a songwriter, a journalist, and an economist. (In 1984, he was awarded the Presidential Medal of Freedom by President Reagan.) As a knowledgeable man of action, Cherne did not require persuasion to help on the Indochina crisis.

Following his meeting with Shep Lowman in late 1977, Leo Cherne established the Citizens Commission on Indochinese Refugees (CCIR) to raise public awareness of the Indochina refugee dilemma and to press for urgent action by the United States. Cherne served as its chairman and recruited established figures from government, the private sector, business, and entertainment. CCIR members included, as vice chairman, Bill Casey (later to head the CIA), Bayard Rustin (president of the A. Philip Randolph Institute), Warren Meeker (chairman of the boards of the

Research Institute of America and the Lawyers Cooperative Publishing Company), author James Michener, Louis A. Wiesner (IRC staff executive), and other distinguished American humanitarians.

A New Refugee Team

The Department of State's deputy executive director Frank Wisner later recalled that work quietly moved forward to implement the secretary's 1978 decision on refugee organizational reform. Frank said that working groups like those set up in 1975 were established and featured a two-tiered structure, one for external stakeholders and a second dealing with internal operations within the State Department.

The actions coincided with the emergence of a new State Department team devoted to Indochinese refugees and a growing commitment to action.

In March 1977, Richard Holbrooke was named the assistant secretary of state for East Asia and the Pacific (EAP), and Indochina refugees fell under his bureau's purview. Dick Holbrooke was a life force like most had never known before. The son of Jewish immigrants from Germany and Poland, when his father died he was taken in at age sixteen by the future secretary of state Dean Rusk. He attended Brown University and edited the school newspaper.

He was hired by the US Agency for International Development (USAID) in 1963 and assigned to the lower Mekong Delta working on reconstruction and stabilization. He later served as the staff assistant to ambassadors Maxwell Taylor and Henry Cabot Lodge. In 1966, he joined the Johnson administration and advised on Vietnam matters, among other issues. He knew Vietnam issues like few others, and when appointed to head EAP in 1977, he was the youngest assistant secretary in State Department history to that time, and he became a driving force for Indochina refugees.[2] Holbrooke's deputy in EAP was the much-admired Bob Oakley.

The second man on the new refugee team was Morton Abramowitz. He would become the ambassador to Thailand in June 1978 and play a leading role in later developments. At that time, Shep Lowman was in

HA and Lionel Rosenblatt was back in Thailand as head of the American Embassy refugee operation there. Lionel assembled his team, including Mac Thompson and Dennis Grace, International Rescue Committee (IRC) and head of the joint voluntary agency (JVA).

Another key State official kept this issue alive in the face of leadership inattention during this period: Frank Wisner had been an original young dissenter in early 1975 while serving in the department's Bureau of Public Affairs. He had joined IATF, the Interagency Task Force on Indochina Refugees, at its formation in 1975, serving as its deputy director until selected as the special assistant to under secretary of state for political affairs Joseph Sisco. He served there until July 1976. In April 1977, he was named State's deputy executive secretary, where he engaged on Indochina.

Humanitarian Parole

Humanitarian parole was the legal mechanism used by the attorney general to admit refugees to the United States (prior to passage of the Refugee Act of 1980). State's new team, with help from Leo Cherne's Citizens Commission, immediately secured additional Indochina refugee humanitarian parole numbers from the Carter administration. Beginning in mid-1978, humanitarian parole numbers rose in increments and reached eighty-four thousand annually (seven thousand persons per month). Actual refugee resettlement—which lagged the approval of resettlement numbers because of processing—reached twenty-one thousand in 1978 and would spike over the next few years. Through the urgings of these and other committed individuals and organizations, the Indochinese refugee issue rose on America's foreign policy agenda. This timing was fortuitous, as the second refugee surge surfaced in mid-1978. For the next year, organizational and staffing changes, budget-busting decisions, and leadership involvement marked State's refugee programs.

External and Internal Actions

American refugee programs featured many partners beyond the State Department, including nine most familiar:

- US Congress
- White House
- Health, Education, and Welfare (HEW)
- US Agency for International Development (USAID)
- Department of Defense (DoD)
- Department of Justice (DOJ)
- International organizations
- Private groups and organizations
- Hosts of dedicated individual citizens

A high-ranking and overarching entity would be needed to direct, coordinate, and harmonize these interconnected efforts. This entity eventually was called the Office of the US Coordinator for Refugee Affairs and was to be positioned at a high enough level in the executive branch to command attention and respect. Initial plans called for locating this entity in the executive office of the president, but it was ultimately situated high in the State Department structure, reporting to the secretary.[3]

Tom Miller recalled seeing a list including several prestigious names for the first US coordinator position in late 1978. The White House and the secretary of state finally settled on former Sen. Dick Clark (D-IA). Clark, a friend and collaborator of President Carter, had lost his reelection bid the last time out. Dick Clark came onboard after his Senate confirmation, February 1979.

The refugee crisis became America's top foreign policy priority in Asia. Internal management of the State Department's refugee responsibility could no longer be avoided. State management ordered a special review of the coherence and effectiveness of State's internal structures, staffing, financial, and management practices in early 1979, to be led by the new coordinator office. High on the list of issues was the proper organizational structure and location for refugee programs, including the continuing role of HA.

Clearly, a special person was needed to lead this review, as it involved national interest programs and powerful personalities with political clout. There were political landmines all around for State, and a wrong step could bring everything crashing down, even loss of refugee programs to another federal agency. And the need was urgent and sensitive, given the refugee storm encircling Southeast Asia and managerial concerns in the refugee programs. The latter were a key subject of the internal review, and it was left to the deputy in the executive secretariat of state Frank Wisner to inform other department leaders, including those in HA.

Urgent! New Global Strategy Needed

The State Department's new refugee team was hard at work on a dynamic refugee strategy for Southeast Asia. Beyond new institutional arrangements, this is also a story about the re-awakening of the United States to the inevitable leadership role it was called to play again, during those tumultuous times.

Having been "weighed in the balances and found wanting," America woke up, dusted off, and got back into the game.[4] American values, grit, and sense of justice—so often called on in desperate times—would not allow the nation to stay on the sidelines when millions from Indochina and elsewhere were facing death and deprivation. First a few, and then many concerned advocates called for and/or accepted the call for renewed American leadership and commitment.

Governor Bob Ray

One frosty night in January 1979, Iowa Governor Ray was watching a film on Ed Bradley's *CBS Reports* about a Malaysian island. Watching with the governor was his key refugee aide, Ken Quinn, who reported they "were horrified to see a boat filled with Vietnamese refugees being pushed back out to sea and suddenly breaking up in the pounding waves. Helpless bodies plunged into the roaring surf, drowning literally before their eyes."

Governor Ray was deeply moved by what he saw and drafted a letter on the spot to President Carter, offering to double Iowa's resettlement of refugees. The president, he urged, must reopen America's doors to accept more Indochinese refugees.

The next morning Governor Ray held a press conference to make his pledge public. Two weeks later at the winter meeting of the National Governors Association in Washington, he asked that a task force be formed to deal with the Vietnamese boat people. Bill Milliken of Michigan, Brendan Byrne of New Jersey, and Dan Evans of Washington state agreed to serve with Governor Ray on this taskforce. What followed were strenuous lobbying efforts with the White House, the State Department, and Congress. The governors urged a change in policy and the reopening of America's doors for refugee resettlement. This was music to the ears of the refugee team at State.

Leo Cherne's Challenge of Congress

With Governor Ray, Leo Cherne became a significant nonfederal official for future action on refugees. In May 1979, about a year and a half after he had set up his Citizens Commission on Indochinese Refugees (CCIR), Cherne was called to give testimony to Congress about the CCIR's work on behalf of the Indochinese refugee program. Leo had his platform and did not lose the opportunity to warn of ever-worsening disaster:

> Unless action ... is taken, and is taken quickly, the catastrophe we are witnessing will deepen and become irreversible. In the words of a French doctor who served in the refugee camps of Thailand, 'the picture of little children hobbling toward their fate along dusty roads—and little children going to the bottom of the South China Sea—will serve history as the parallel to the famous photograph of the little Jewish boy in the Warsaw Ghetto, raising his arm as if to fend off the rifle of an indifferent German soldier.'... And yet, these pictures [from Southeast Asia] appear daily in the world press.[5]

That chilling imagery came from "The US Government Must Act Now," a Citizens Commission (CCIR) report submitted to a congressional hearing in May 1979. The CCIR had just completed factfinding trips to Southeast Asia. Its members were testifying before the Subcommittee on Immigration, Refugees, and International Law of the House Judiciary Committee, with Representative Elizabeth Holtzman (D-NY) presiding.

The witnesses were also saying that if the United States leads, others will follow. Testifying with Cherne were Commission members Bayard Rustin, Warren Meeker, and Louis Wiesner. During his testimony, Cherne highlighted discussions he had with government officials throughout Southeast Asia, particularly with the prime minister of Thailand. Cherne said the prime minister made his strongest point:

> ... the US response to the refugee problems ... could not be counted on, that it was ad hoc, that it came in fits and starts, that there was the constant sudden and unhappy inadequacy of parole numbers—that the entire parole process was beyond their understanding, that they found themselves increasingly carrying the burden of flight from Indochinese countries. They found in some ways they could rely more on the response of the government of France than of the government of the United States.[6]

Beyond a handful of State Department refugee stalwarts, now Governor Ray, Leo Cherne, and a few others had also thrown down the gauntlet. To its credit, the Carter administration found itself out front of their message, as it was already pushing itself into high gear. A new sense of urgency and generosity characterized efforts over the next months of 1979. These efforts activated a solution linchpin. America's foreign policy establishment now understood that a *third-country resettlement* effort unlike anything since World War II would need to be the centerpiece of the solutions puzzle. After consulting with allies and multilateral partners, the State Department agreed to an international Indochinese resettlement initiative.

This was a time of extraordinary promise and peril for the United States and for an extraordinary team brought together in the last half of the twentieth century. They would build a special humanitarian apparatus in the lumbering US State Department and then join it with international partners. Currents that began with the Saigon evacuations in April 1975 continued to accelerate, leading to this renewed American rescue mechanism that would reach millions upon millions of refugees and other victims in coming years. Most critical observers of that era, including myself, regard these events as foundational for modern American refugee policies and strategies. What followed sprang from these dynamic changes.

6

WRECKAGE REPAIR

AS THE SITUATION IN SOUTHEAST ASIA DETERIORATED, A crisis of equal proportions was taking place in Washington. The president and the secretary of state had big plans for refugee relief overseas, but the headquarters organization for planning these expanded programs was at the point of collapse. Congress had been so disappointed with the State Department's humanitarian performance in recent years that it threatened to move refugee programs to other organizations, in whole or in part. To accentuate its concerns, Congress delayed the funding needed for State's refugee programs just when the human disaster was growing in Asia. The under secretary for management Ben Read discussed the grave situation with the deputy secretary Warren Christopher. Building confidence required urgent reforms.

Legal Violation in the State Department

The unusually cold January of 1979 was a time of hard facts in a new calendar year. The seventh floor is the top authority level logistically and figuratively in the State Department. The seventh-floor fix-it manager Ben Read told me he had warned top officials that refugee programs were in trouble. Read said the mushrooming problems in Asia plus HA's violation of the Antideficiency Act brought into question State's ability. "If we don't fix this soon, we'll probably lose the programs." He reminded Warren Christopher of the administration's decision for an interagency refugee coordinator in the State Department; Sen. Dick Clark should arrive soon for that position, once confirmed by the Senate. However, nothing had changed regarding the management and oversight of State's statutory responsibilities.[1]

When HA violated the feared Antideficiency Act, Ben Read grappled with the blowback. The spending violation had come when the refugee crisis was heating up in Southeast Asia, and he saw a firestorm brewing. Congressional foreign operations appropriations committees already had HA in their sights. Ben sensed the full magnitude of this problem was not on the secretary Cyrus Vance's nor the deputy secretary Christopher's radar. Ben had to energize them: "Our challenge is whether State can move on from here … and build refugee programs that work." He noted HA's high visibility after President Carter highlighted the human rights performance of other countries. Naturally, the HA assistant secretary had focused attention on that specific area, and refugee issues had not received the same priority.

Vance and Christopher were shocked by the severe assessment and were soon in the game. The deputy secretary called a next-day meeting where he told the participants he had met with the secretary the previous evening. He wanted quick remedial action.

Foreign Service Officer Freeman

To conduct an internal assessment of the refugee function, including HA's management, Ben Read approached Asia expert and Foreign Service Officer Chas Freeman. Working in another bureau in State, I had heard that my boss, the highly respected assistant secretary for administration John Thomas had endorsed Chas for this task as one showing brilliant intellectual and analytical capabilities throughout his foreign affairs career as a problem solver and straight shooter.

Chas Freeman knew that an assessment would challenge powerful officials and interests at the State Department and beyond, so he wanted assurances that Secretary Vance would cover his back if he took this on. He got those assurances, with one instruction for this mission impossible, *Carry out the assessment in a discreet and sensitive way*. When Chas came on board in February 1979, he had about five months to complete the work before his next assignment. By prior agreement with Secretary Vance, he would function as deputy refugee coordinator while his assessment of the refugee function was underway. Concurrently, Sen. Dick Clark was confirmed and assumed his new position as refugee coordinator.

Ben Read wanted the problem fixed and gave Chas Freeman leeway for a decision about either keeping the refugee function in HA or moving it elsewhere. There was no predetermined conclusion. Freeman conducted extensive interviews with the staff and stakeholders and completed his assessment in record time. He later said that his most difficult job was to convince the HA assistant secretary Pat Derian that reorganization would be good for HA. She had been heard to remark that her bureau's primary function was human rights analysis and reporting. She came to see the reorganization for refugee programs as being good for State and HA.

The Freeman Report

The Freeman Report went at once to the top, where Warren Christopher and Ben Read reviewed it, disheartened by revelations of extraordinary weakness. Without immediate corrective actions, State faced a management disaster with potential for more investigations and diminished reputation. Already, the Carter administration had pulled the commercial, educational, and cultural affairs functions from State, sending them to other government departments. If State lost a program as mission-central as refugees, its reputation would take a big hit.

The report's major recommendation was the creation of a new standalone directorate—a bureau (originally designated as an "office") for refugee programs—to absorb the department's scattered refugee functions. It would remove the refugee portfolio from HA. The core staff and those from other State and USAID bureaus would be moved to the new bureau after a brief transit at the refugee coordinator's office.[2]

The president, through the secretary of state, would appoint a Bureau for Refugee Programs director to serve in a new senior position at the assistant secretary level, initially reporting to the refugee coordinator. The new bureau would be State's first standalone organization with refugees as its exclusive raison d'être. Instituting these reforms might allow State to hold off the congressional investigative wolves scratching at the door while reforms were underway.

Specific bold implementation actions included: recruit new leadership and staff; increase refugee resettlement levels; seek higher funding; improve relations within State and with other government entities; install modern management and financial systems; globalize refugee programs; reenergize resettlement capabilities, restore deteriorating congressional relationships (including enactment of the proposed Refugee Act); and develop stronger international partnerships.

◇

Approved in late April 1979, the Freeman Report came just in time for congressional hearings and set a record for speed. There had been no time for opposition backfires to ignite. Hopeful changes were in the air for refugees and US partners. Immediately, work began to set up the new bureau: Refugee Programs. His work complete, Chas Freeman began his next Foreign Service assignment. He left a transformative legacy as a modern refugee programs pioneer.

◇

The deputy secretary assigned Freeman Report implementation to Ben Read. A savvy manager and strategist, Ben had anticipated this assignment and was ready to move quickly. For starters, in May 1979, he requested the director general of the Foreign Service to identify senior FSOs from which to choose the new bureau's leader. The position would be named *director*, pending further negotiations with Congress on a statutory base for the assistant secretary-equivalent position.

Ben Read was in a hurry. He knew director recruitment and selection would take more than a month. He asked central personnel to identify a seasoned manager to function immediately as the senior deputy for reorganization oversight and direction. This official would lead until the permanent director came onboard, after which the interim incumbent would become senior deputy and chief management/operations officer.

From State's personnel database, three candidates were identified:

Roger Feldman (comptroller), Don Eller (executive director of IO), and me (executive director of State's Administration bureau). Ben Read passed his recommendation for my selection to Warren Christopher that day and suggested we meet soon.

7

FROM THESE ASHES, WILL I RISE?

JIM! I JUST HEARD YOU'VE BEEN TAGGED FOR THE REFUGEE job!"

Dayton (Day) Mount, my right hand in the Administration bureau, had more to say but stopped there. He had helped me set up the new executive office in John Thomas' bureau, known as "A." Day Mount was also one of Thomas's protégés and an ally I trusted.

When Ben's office called me to see him the next morning, I asked my trusted secretary Peggy Hite to cancel late afternoon appointments and to hold calls. I wanted uninterrupted time for soul-searching and reflection. I knew refugee problems in Southeast Asia absorbed department leadership in crisis management. Some in State opined, "Which donkey will get the tail of this disaster pinned to him or her?"

I met the next morning with Ben Read and Deputy Secretary Christopher in the deputy secretary's office. They wanted to pin down Ben's decision. I listened to their proposal and realized its strange twist: that I would oversee and lead this big reform in vital programs from a subordinate position. *If they need me so desperately, why don't they ask me to head this program?* I mused. Aloud I said, "Perhaps a Foreign Service Officer assigned to this function would be a better choice." I was thinking someone already in the refugee office in HA.

They said that would not be possible, because they wanted someone from outside the existing HA network—new blood, as Chas Freeman's report recommended. Christopher emphasized there were programs of special concern to the Foreign Service and others to the national interest. Refugee programs, he said, are the latter—in the national interest.

What a pitch, I thought. Is it persuasion, manipulation, or what?

I argued that my civil service status would be a disadvantage in a Foreign Service-dominated culture. They argued the opposite: my civil service status would provide needed continuity. My compromise, then, was to devote one week to making an assessment. They agreed. Warren Christopher offered a word of guidance: "Whatever you do, if you take this job, don't let these programs leave the State Department."

Later that afternoon I stood at the corners of Twenty-third and C Streets in Foggy Bottom, Washington, DC, Northwest. Armed guards stood duty in front of a massive gray structure with flags flying. The Federal Reserve building was next door, the Washington Monument in the far distance. I was in the shadows of the mighty US State Department. At age forty, I held an important foreign affairs management position there, and I had just been asked to gamble my career. This humanitarian challenge had meager chances of success. Reflecting on what I recently learned about the months of upheaval due to Southeast Asia/Indochina refugee concerns, I knew the year so far had been catastrophic for refugee first asylum in Southeast Asia. As the first point of refuge by land or sea, regional first asylum held together by a fraying thread, which the State Department was hoping to salvage with my help. That evening I sat in my office thinking. *There must be a reason this seemingly insurmountable 'opportunity' has come now.*

Assessment of the Environment for Refugee Programs

After my agreed one-week trial, Ben Read pressed me to stay permanently. I agreed to remain a few more weeks and give my observations about urgent program and financial matters that had arisen. One morning I received an informal note from Ben. The seventh floor was worried about the worsening situation in Asia and the congressional investigations underway. There were concerns about American participation in upcoming refugee conferences. Further organizing delays might jeopardize State's ability to get desperately needed funds from Congress or even keep refugee programs. Could we start up soon? Was I near a decision about staying?

It's too soon to know, I thought. *I have no idea where things stand in terms of readiness to launch.* Unknowns abounded. I needed to canvas preparations on the ground before a reliable assessment could be made. I informed Ben Read and set off to get answers.

Staffing, Funds, and Legislation

My first concern was staff quantity and quality. There were about fifty fulltime positions in the new bureau, and that number was projected to rise to eighty in next year's budget. Many were new, vacant, or temporary duty positions. A considerable number had been seconded from USAID. It would take time to sort them out and get fresh staff in place, and State had a reputation for being notoriously slow on personnel actions. We would rely on the bureau's new one-man personnel office Stuart Neilson to make things happen.

My second concern was funding: was there enough to meet rapidly expanding programs? In the patchwork congressional system, the Foreign Operations Appropriations Act (foreign aid) funded the former HA refugee program, whereas a different appropriations measure funded the State Department. Because Congress could not pass the FY 1979 foreign aid bill, State's new refugee bureau was to be funded through a restrictive continuing resolution geared to the previous year's spending.

No additional funding had been approved for FY 1979, although the Carter administration was planning more Indochina refugee initiatives and had requested urgent supplemental funding. Already, the United States had been forced to cut back admissions in April and May 1979 because of funding, and first-asylum governments had reacted in panic.

In May and June, refugee advocates, including Dick Clark and Leo Cherne, had implored Congress to act on urgent refugee funding requests, but to no avail. For FY 1979 (ending on September 30), a refugee supplemental appropriation request of $100 million (about half requested in January 1979 and the rest in April) languished in committee. For the coming fiscal year, FY 1980, beginning October 1, 1979, an appropriations amendment of $87 million awaited congressional action.[1] Funding to carry out the Indochina initiatives was, therefore, not in the bank. If Congress did not provide the funds soon, the State Department would have no choice but to slash resettlement at the very time it urgently needed to increase. Congressional hesitancy arose from concerns about State's competence to oversee and administer appropriated refugee funds. Also, refugee financial transactions were being reviewed at several levels, given the ongoing investigations. Future budgets might give relief, but for now money was a real concern.

Upcoming legislation needed attention. The proposed law to create a new statutory base for the US refugee program was making its way through Congress, and necessary changes in domestic refugee processing were under consideration, as well as an envisioned worldwide focus. What impact would derive from this important lawmaking, and how would the new RP deal with it?

Boat People Initiative

Finally, what about a rumored Indochinese boat people initiative that would require strong input from the new bureau? Unfortunately, time for such thinking was limited, as Southeast Asia operations consumed RP's attention, and refugee issues in other regions were percolating. Later that day I went to my office in the bureau of Administration, still my official post, to mull over what I had learned and to talk with Day Mount.

"You're going to have little to work with," Day counseled, knowing I was considering the move to RP. "And don't look to the department to make things better soon." He had heard that PER was already eyeing the new bureau as a dumping ground for problem staff.

Sandbagged

The next day during a briefing, RP's Office of Asian Refugees (OAR) asked me to accompany them to a meeting with State's Bureau for East Asia and the Pacific (EAP), Dick Holbrooke's domain. I told them I did not want to get pulled into day-to-day business yet. "Don't worry, you can just listen and get current on some of the management issues we're dealing with," they reassured me.

But the issue driving that meeting was lots of money owed for refugees; EAP had been advance-financing refugee field operations in embassies in Southeast Asia while new refugee funds languished in Congress. The amount owed was growing, and EAP wanted immediate repayment. During an active back and forth discussion, I noticed reluctance by former HA refugee staff to acknowledge possibilities for repaying this legitimate debt. In exasperation, the chairing deputy assistant secretary Bob Oakley finally turned to me and asked when they could expect to get paid. If we did not make reimbursement immediately, he stated, they would have no option but to terminate services and support in the field.

I had received no prior briefing or warning about this sensitive issue. I promised that someone in the refugee bureau would review the matter immediately and get back to them with a realistic reimbursement schedule. When I could not give more specific assurances, EAP attendees grumbled and made faces. The meeting adjourned. Back in the hallway, I pulled the refugee staff aside: "Don't ever set me up like that again. When I go into a meeting, I do not want to face these kinds of surprises."

Later that evening a cable from Hong Kong reported our lights had been turned off, phone service cut, in country staff travel forbidden, and administrative support shut down. EAP had carried out its threat. I reached EAP's senior deputy assistant secretary, only to hear that he had no maneuvering room: "Our assistant secretary is livid about the overdue reimbursements. He won't relent unless ordered."

As no congressional funding was on the immediate horizon, I knew shutdowns would soon happen in other Asian posts. The Refugee Programs bureau could not tolerate even one day's shutdown. I turned to Ben Read, who did not want to deal with this problem.

"Unless we get immediate help," I warned, "we will soon be out of business in Asia." Our staff in Hong Kong and other Asian posts were dealing with tens of thousands of refugees, either to provide relief assistance or processing for resettlement.

Continuing, I said, "I know EAP should be paid, and they will be, but don't they also have an interest in seeing that the refugees in EAP countries are cared for? Surely," I argued, "this is not just a concern for the small refugee office here in Washington."

Ben ordered the East Asia office to turn the lights back on. He promised to help cover expenses until proper refugee funding was arranged. We were back in business.

As sometimes happens, administrative help appeared unexpectedly. In May, without notice or fanfare, one of the State Department's most senior administrative officers, Kitty Kemp, strolled into my office as I was completing my discussion with Ben Read. I had visited with Kitty when she was administrative counselor at the American Embassy in Rome years earlier. She was a superstar, and I relaxed when she floated in.

"Jim, I've been assigned to help you get things shaped up. Where do we start?" (This development continues in Chapter 11.)

Unrealistic Pressures

The next day on a lunchtime walk, I had an unfortunate encounter where expectations of others and my stresses collided. A friend and key official in State's central management operations office crossed my path and suddenly laid into me: "Jim, we think you and your staff should quit stalling and complaining! Just finish the staff work to allow us to approve what you need to get up and running. The seventh floor wants this to happen immediately."

I presumed Ben Read had shared the gist of our earlier discussions. This friend, with whom I had worked closely before, knew me to be levelheaded, open to dialogue, and not easily provoked. But I just stood there speechless, red-faced, and stared at him for what seemed like an eternity. Then I uttered a few well-chosen words, turned, and walked away, certain my outburst would soon reach Ben.

Teambuilding Obstacles

Later that afternoon I met again with RP's new personnel officer Stu Neilson, for an update. I had laid out a notional agenda and schedule for Stu, including getting our positions authorized, writing the job descriptions, and getting them classified. As expected, he reported little progress, and let me know that the investigators from State's inspector general (IG) wanted to meet with me. Stuart also told me that central personnel had already begun to identify Foreign Service Officers that might fill some new positions, although the refugee bureau was not yet formally established. They wanted me to interview a candidate the next day to head our new Africa office.

This presumptive move on State's part at once reminded me of Day Mount's caution, and I ran the name by him. Day threw up his hands in disgust. His prediction that Refugee Programs would get all the hard-to-place FSOs was coming true. This recruit could work only half time, and personnel had been trying to place her for more than a year. At ten the next morning, I began the interview by explaining what the job would entail: a small office with big programs, big budgets, many complicated issues, only one other officer, and long hours. She explained her situation, and we agreed the two were incompatible. I suggested she let PER know this was the wrong job for her.

After that experience, I asked Stu to show me the other names central casting had in mind. When I saw the list, I knew these were not the people for building a strong bureau. I prepared a memorandum to tell central personnel that the present candidate list was unsuitable. The next day a young officer in Foreign Service assignments visited me. He brought me a personal and confidential message from his boss: "You are being difficult. We each have our jobs to do, and we need to work together in a more cooperative spirit."

I sent him back with my reply: "I am working at the direction of the deputy secretary and Ben Read to create a viable bureau to handle the State Department's most urgent foreign policy problem. I cannot and will not try that mission with unqualified staff. When we can get to a level of serious responsiveness, then, I think, we can better work together."

One more assessment was on my list.

◇

Where is Our Space, Literally?

I went to see the space allocated for the new bureau. Clearly, it met no outsider's imagination of work in the esteemed State Department. It showed we were expected to function in a maze of disconnected, disjointed, and puzzling parts that even now boggles the mind. The bureau's "elite" front office would sit within four cubicles reserved for us in another person's suite on Main State's seventh floor.

The guts of the new bureau would spill beyond there into *four separate* sites in Foggy Bottom (the nickname for the Main State building and its complex of buildings), including an annex known as SA-2, a decrepit building located a city block from Main State; SA-2 would house management staff and some program staff; on an early morning reconnaissance, I saw mice droppings on desks—altogether, refugee programs and their personnel faced a humbling and disappointing arrangement.

Start Up

When I was ready to respond to Ben's question about the start-up timing, I went back to my old office, told Day Mount and the others not to disturb me, closed the door, and went to work on a draft memorandum, drawing from recollections and notes, ending in a long missive.

> Ben,
>
> In the few weeks I've been here, I have come to the opinion that the proposed Bureau for Refugee Programs is nowhere near ready to start business. Even though the Freeman Report identified urgent reforms, little has been done to implement them. A few good staffers are coming over from HA, but the rest are problematic.
>
> Given the explosive nature of the refugee problem and the vast expansion of program services and support, funding is inadequate. With present funding, we can go on only for a few more weeks. Congress has not acted on the recent urgent supplemental appropriations requests, even in the face of a likely international refugee initiative. This no doubt reflects their low regard for State's previous oversight and management of refugee programs.
>
> There is no long-range planning capability or anticipation of funding for services sure to be needed soon. The bureau lurches from one crisis to the next, one episode to the next. The pending Refugee Act will add

even greater responsibilities on the bureau, and there has been almost no planning for this exponential explosion of service demands as the new bureau becomes a worldwide operation.

The reputation of the programs is bad and could get worse. Reorganization cannot solve this; it will take time and work. There are multiple investigations of previous management now underway. These are serious and will not go away short of sustained and provable reform. The problems the investigators identified can be corrected, but it will take time. These investigative groups can be convinced to hold off if they see a firm commitment from leadership that State is addressing these problems in serious and professional ways.

I have been disappointed by the lack of support this reorganization effort has received from the central offices instructed to assist it and me (the recent temporary assignment of Kitty Kemp is a notable exception). Personnel must be instructed that the best it can offer is the minimum that can be accepted. The central management offices must be made to understand that we need hands-on help. Until the new bureau can be competently staffed, it's not enough for central management to stand back and critique; they must roll up their sleeves and jump in to help. As the bureau gets its own competency, this will become less necessary, but for the time being it is essential.

As for a date, I just don't know. A lot of unfinished preparatory work must be done, and I will volunteer to oversee it. It could take three months, six months, who knows? I will try to bring the work to completion quickly. But it's more important that the preparatory work be done correctly than that we meet an unrealistic startup date. I believe our external stakeholders will be impressed with this commitment. You must convince the secretary.

You know better than I the pressures calling for a quick startup. If you decide on a more accelerated schedule, so be it. But it must be done without me. I've done several impossible missions in my time, and I do not wish to take on another.

Ben, if you accept my offer and conditions, I believe you know me well enough to know that I won't stop until we've brought State Department refugee programs where they should be, at the forefront of American diplomacy and outreach.

I carefully reread my long memorandum and realized it was like an ultimatum. (I hadn't absorbed how many frustrated emotions I was revealing!) This approach would put Ben in a difficult position, and a written response would have to be staffed out, coordinated, and dispatched through bureaucratic channels. What was needed was for Ben to absorb these points and formulate his own plan of action. I asked for a meeting, and the points became talk notes. The bureau must get off the ground soon.

Point of No Return

The foundation for modern American refugee programs was being laid. It needed new and dynamic organizational structures in the State Department, featuring the interagency coordinator's office and the new bureau, to manage State's burgeoning refugee responsibilities. A significant proposal to address the vexing Indochinese refugee problems was gathering momentum, with the funding pending in Congress. What remained was someone named to bring the strands together and make them work. Ben was a respected and trusted friend who deserved to know where I stood now. He also needed maneuvering room.

We had a private meeting that day, and I put the whole story before him, left it there, and awaited his decision. Then I realized I had stumbled across a very personal Rubicon.

8

WEAK FOUNDATION

IN 1979, I KNEW ONLY A LITTLE ABOUT AMERICA'S POSITIVE role in refugee relief during World War II, but what I knew raised questions about the present situation: *Why do the government and the State Department seem so unprepared to address the Indochinese problem four years after the Fall of Saigon?* There was a contradiction of America's past record of high achievement and its current unpreparedness. Further research showed a consensus that American attitudes about foreigners had been guided by three evolving approaches up to the present.

The First American Approach

The first national approach to foreigners was our founders' nation-building preoccupation with independent thinking, demanding work, overcoming obstacles, defending allies and friends, and securing hard-won liberties. This attitude included guarded good neighborliness, where "community" was valued, and strangers had to earn trust. Self-protecting attitudes were almost inevitable for pioneers carving out their places in a wild new land. From Europe came a heritage of industriousness and rugged individualism. America's founding fathers and mothers also welcomed the immigrants who wanted to help build a new nation. The appalling history of slavery in America, England, and other colonizing powers left blights that would take wars and years to put our countries and societies on the right side of morality and justice, with work ongoing to address lingering vestiges.

In *They Are Us,* co-authors Ralie Deffenbaugh and David Bouman noted that American colonies' view of immigration found formal expression in the Declaration of Independence. In 1776, seventh on the list of grievances against the British crown was "injuries or usurpations," and that "He (King George) has endeavored to prevent the population of these states; for that purpose, obstructing the laws of naturalization of foreigners; refusing to pass others to encourage their migration hither; and raising the conditions of new appropriations of lands."[1]

The 1787 US Constitution made immigration a concern of the federal government, stating in Article 1 that Congress would have the power to establish a uniform rule of naturalization. The first immigration law, the Naturalization Act of 1790, set a racial standard for citizenship, to any "free white person, who shall have resided within the limits and under the jurisdiction of the United States for the term of two years" provided he or she was "a person of good character."[2] So conflicted were the country's views on American citizenship that in 1886, the year the Statue of Liberty was dedicated in New York harbor to welcoming "your poor, your huddled masses yearning to be breathe free," mobs rioted in Seattle. More than half the city's Chinese residents were forced onto a ship to San Francisco.

Chinese workers had been recruited in America's West in the 1880s to help build the railroads and mines.[3] According to Deffenbaugh and Bouman, the Chinese presence was controversial because of others' perception of them as unfair competition and a general prejudice against foreigners. Legal opposition culminated in the Chinese Exclusion Act of 1882, not repealed until 1943 as part of America's World War II alliance with China.[4]

The nineteenth century saw large increases in US immigration. In the first half, the primary source countries were Germany, Britain, and Ireland, and later, eastern and southern Europe. During the Civil War, immigration patterns were a major difference between the North and the South. Most immigrants went to Northern Free States. The "great migration" to America occurred in the half century between the Civil War, ending 1865, and World War I, ending 1919. Over thirty-three million immigrants came to the United States in the century before 1920.[5]

Until restrictions imposed around World War I, immigration trends reflected America's guarded openness.

The Second American Approach

A mood of isolation and self-sufficiency emerged as the second approach to foreigners: disdain for outsiders who tried to involve themselves in US affairs or expected Americans to return to the overseas involvement of pre-World War I years. One measure of the changing American attitudes about immigration during those years was the vacillating percentage of foreign born in the American population. From 1860 to 1920, foreign born persons averaged 14 percent of the total American population; from 1920s to the 1960s, historical lows were just under 5 percent.[6]

◇

Until the restrictions imposed around World War I, America's immigration trends reflected guarded openness. Reacting to fears of a militarily aggressive Germany and concerns over uncontrollable immigration, America retrenched. The 1921 Quota Act gave preference to northern and western European immigrants. The 1924 Johnson-Reed Act shifted the legal dynamics of immigration so the law would no longer assume to allow more immigrants but would assume to disallow them. Overall limits on immigration numbers were set at levels far below those of the previous half century.[7] Even more restrictive immigration laws preceded the Great Depression in the 1930s, years of catastrophic economic decline. Before significant recovery took hold, American entry into World War II in 1941 led to a sharp immigration decline. America did not want Europe's violence and displacement at its shores, and there was net US out-migration.[8]

◇

President Franklin D. Roosevelt's Évian Conference initiative before US involvement in World War II tragically expressed the American hesitation to stop looking inward. The conference was convened at Évian les Bains, France, July 6–15, 1938, to respond to the plight of increasing numbers of Jewish refugees fleeing Nazi persecution in Europe.[9] Representatives from thirty-two countries, thirty-nine private organizations, and twenty-four voluntary organizations attended. Two hundred international journalists and other observers reported on the conclave. Dispossessed and displaced Jews of Austria and Germany hoped this conference would influence the acceptance of more refugees in what was termed *safe haven*, especially because the Americans had called for it. This presidential initiative was the first US undertaking in intergovernmental refugee efforts. Honorary chairman, Ambassador Henry Berenger of France, noted in his opening address to the assembled: "We should all desire to emphasize the novelty and originality of what has taken place here. This is the first time the United States has agreed to take part in intergovernmental action going beyond the limits of the United States itself."[10] The two main objectives of the Évian initiative were to secure *orderly emigration* from Germany and to develop settlement opportunities and financing for large numbers of refugees. President Roosevelt hoped to obtain commitments from governments to accept more refugees, although he took pains to avoid saying it plainly.

The United States sent American businessman Myron C. Taylor, rather than a government official. Before the Évian conference, the United States and Great Britain made a critical agreement: the British promised not to bring up the fact that the United States was not filling its immigration quotas, and any mention of Palestine as a possible destination for Jewish refugees was excluded from the agenda (Palestine was then a British mandate territory).[11] Golda Meir, the attendee from Palestine, was the only representative of a landed Jewish constituency, but she was permitted only to observe, not to speak or participate in the proceedings.

Despite the expectations of the president and Myron Taylor, the two main objectives, to secure orderly emigration from Germany and to develop settlement opportunities and financing for many refugees, were not achieved. To state the outcome boldly, the conference was a failure. The United States and Britain refused to accept substantially more refugees, and most countries at the conference followed their lead. Only the Dominican Republic agreed to take many Jews (one hundred thousand).

Forty years later, Vice President Walter Mondale would remind international leaders: "If each nation at Évian had agreed on that day to take in 17,000 Jews at once, every Jew in the Reich could have been saved."[12]

Another clear sign of America's isolation and its self-sufficient national mood had been its self-imposed hesitancy to engage in World War II, until Pearl Harbor, December 7, 1941.

The Third Dominant National Approach

America's third dominant approach evolved as its role in World War II progressed: *global engagement in humanitarian solutions.* That view would characterize America's evolving multilateral leadership style and carry over to its emerging consciousness about refugees.

As America was forced to recognize World War II's tragic results for many innocents in battleground countries, a long-restrained but countervailing attitude finally and gradually prevailed in our national psyche. No longer able to deny inbred impulses, America drew upon a national sense of generosity and heartfelt concerns that went out to the world's war victims and its displaced populations. But, it was difficult to overcome our national predisposition to look inward. As the American humanitarian attitudes evolved, we were more comfortable initially offering help to the war's victims over there, painfully not here.

These changing attitudes explain in part the words of State Department advisor George Warren, who participated in the conference and in the Washington meeting of the Intergovernmental Committee on Refugees, ICR, a year later:

> It must also be admitted that the Department of State was fully conscious that there was some reluctance in the United States to receive refugees. The predominant mood in Congress at the time was restrictive in immigration policy. There was concern that there could be no assurance that refugees once admitted to the United States during the war period would not present security risks. For the US president to assume leadership among governments in finding havens of asylum for refugees appeared to some to promise more in hospitality for refugees than United States law and practice could offer at the time.[13]

Dennis R. Laffer's *The Jewish Trail of Tears: The Évian Conference of July 1938* concludes that President Roosevelt recognized the looming threat of Nazi Germany and Imperial Japan but was unwilling to expend political capital on an issue that faced domestic and political opposition. Laffer cynically maintained that the conference was set up to fail while providing propaganda value for the participating democracies.[14]

Many agree that the "Kristallnacht" ("night of broken glass") of November 9-10, 1938, the first pogrom and only four months after the conference, was no coincidence. The achievement of either or both initial conference's objectives were to be brought to a halt by the invasion of Poland by the German armed forces in September and by the German occupation of the Sudeten areas of Czechoslovakia in October 1939.

George Warren maintained that the League of Nations was conspicuously unhelpful in this fluid situation, because it was unable to intervene with Germany to mitigate pressures on the refugees or burdens on neighboring governments. The presence of Germany, Italy, and Russia on its council impeded the League's influence.

Beyond Évian, noteworthy examples of the Roosevelt administration's ambivalence about accepting Jewish refugees on American shores included denial of landing for 734 Jews aboard the USS *St. Louis* in 1939.[15] A painful reception met a thousand Jews attempting to land in 1944 and facing internment and deportation.[16] America was stymied by predispositions.

Commerce shrank, and trade protectionism grew, hardening attitudes throughout the world. Many nations, particularly in Europe, fell under the influence of ethnic nationalism and totalitarian ideologies, leading to the twentieth century's most horrendous massacres, exclusions, and forced migrations. Authoritarian governments rose in number.

But, America's destiny would not be denied. As the world turned to the United States for World War II military leadership, it also came to see it as the essential linchpin for an international mechanism to rescue war victims. America welcomed that role with renewed confidence and resolve.

Post-World War II Refugee Institutions

The organizations created to save lives and settle refugees during and after World War II deserve special mention. Considerable growth and evolution had occurred in international humanitarian mechanisms by 1939 (*see* Appendix A). Even though America was sidelined during much of this time, three intergovernmental entities formed to address global refugee problems: the Nansen International Office for Refugees, the International Labor Organization, and the League of Nations. Protecting refugee civil rights was the function of the League, and relief was provided by voluntary agencies with encouragement and coordination by the League's high commissioner for refugees. Especially poignant was that America was not involved with the League of Nations.

The 1938 conference at Évian les Bains, France, resulted in the significant establishment of the Intergovernmental Committee on Refugees (ICR) with an office in London. As the war expanded, the British and American governments met later in Bermuda to explore ways of taking more effective rescue action. Over the ensuing years, the ICR expanded its mandate, membership, resource base, and activity on behalf of refugees. Until disbanded in 1947, it worked in close collaboration with the many intervening institutions.

Especially noteworthy was the UN Relief and Rehabilitation Administration (UNRRA) created by forty-four governments in 1943. UNRRA provided essential food, housing, and medical assistance to war victims, but was best known for its repatriation of displaced persons. Working with General Dwight D. Eisenhower and the Supreme Headquarters Allied Expeditionary Force (SHAEF), UNRRA repatriated millions of displaced persons in 1945.[17]

Nevertheless, over a million displaced persons could not repatriate, including 400,000 Poles, up to 200,000 displaced persons from the Baltic Republics (Wehrmacht and SS soldiers, slave laborers, and civilians fleeing Soviet forces), 150,000 ethnic Ukrainians, and about 250,000 Jewish death camp and death march survivors. To help those who could not repatriate, the United Nations created the International Refugee Organization (IRO) in 1946. The remaining populations consisted of (a) the victims of Nazi, Fascist, or collaborationist regimes; (b) the Spanish Republicans, and (c) those denied as refugees before the war. IRO pursued three *durable solutions: repatriation, emigration* (or *third-country resettlement*), and local *integration*. Few wanted to remain in Germany, and Cold War tensions made return to the Soviet Union undesirable for most. Therefore, third-country resettlement became the solution of preference.[18]

Knowledgeable international officials James Carlin and George Warren reported that over the twenty years following the 1939 creation of the Intergovernmental Committee on Refugees (ICR), the involved organizations—with help of private voluntary agencies—moved over 2.5 million migrants and refugees out of danger in Europe and the Far East. From 1947 to 1951, IRO spent almost $430 million on the care, protection, and resettlement of refugees and resettled more than one million persons under its auspices in forty-eight receiving countries—the largest institutionally organized migration in history. Under the Displaced Persons Act enacted by Congress in 1948, the United States received over 325,000, the largest number received by one country.[19]

Beyond UNRRA and IRO, the international community created and financed a succession of intergovernmental humanitarian organizations under the auspices of the United Nations from 1945 to 1951. This new international structure was further strengthened by the later establishment of other key global organizations devoted to human needs, such as the World Food Program (WFP) (*see* Appendix A). The strengthened international structure was significant because it showed a new commitment to multilateralism. This change was especially important to the isolationist United States (that had stayed out of the League of Nations) because it revealed its new "outward looking approach" toward global engagement.

The United States was a prime mover behind the creation of each organization that rallied to meet evolving humanitarian needs. The nations employed conceptual approaches and incorporated experiences gained from predecessor organizations. Often, the governments' failure to provide adequate budget support had been a precipitating cause for successor organizations to develop different methods of financing.

Other significant actors during the post-World War II period included the Red Cross movement. The International Committee of the Red Cross (ICRC) was founded in 1863 by Swiss citizens under the leadership of Henri Dunant to help people affected by conflict and armed violence and to promote the protection of war victims. Ultimately, it authored and sponsored the Geneva Convention of 1949, which enshrined many protections in an international covenant for conflict victims. The International Federation of the Red Cross and Red Crescent Societies (IFRC) dates to 1919, when the American Red Cross president Henry Davison gave impetus to forming a federation of national societies in the aftermath of World War I.

The International Refugee Organization (IRO) ceased in December 1951, and the US Displaced Persons Act was sunset that year. The Iron Curtain name, which described the Soviet-West divisions after World War II, explained the need for immediate assistance to people fleeing communist countries. Giving help to those trapped and beleaguered behind the Iron Curtain became crucial to US political and humanitarian interests. To address these needs, according to former RP official John Buche, President Truman established the United States Escapee Program, USEP, in March 1952 to serve escapees fleeing communism. Working primarily with NGOs, the escapee program helped over 350,000 escapees resettle in free countries.

By 1962, the responsibility for the escapee program was consolidated at the US Mission in Geneva. Over the next few years, remaining resettlement programs, including the escapee program, were folded into established refugee mechanisms and renamed the US Refugee Program, known then as USRP. Participating countries favored this change, as they believed the word "escapee" reinforced notions of the punishing communist regime of the Cold War. They were ready to move on.

Other breakthroughs came in rapid succession. Doug Hunter, a Refugee Programs official, later recalled that extraordinary parole provisions were authorized for Hungarians in the early 1950s, followed later for Czechoslovakian, Romanian, and Polish refugees. Other noteworthy improvements brought changes to immigration law favoring the persons fleeing communist countries and the Middle East; landmark Immigration and Nationality Act reforms in 1965 (opening immigration to denied regions of the world and providing for immigrant visas in a seven-category system); and the welcome to hundreds of thousands of World War II victims, anti–communist Cubans, Soviet Jews and other religious minorities fleeing oppression.

US immigration had featured racially-based national origin quotas into the mid-1960s. Anchored in a 1924 law, that system had employed race, ancestry, and country of origin to set priorities. The goal had been to maintain ethnic balance in the United States. By design, the country-of-origin quotas favored northern and western Europeans over other nationalities. Reacting to the Civil Rights movement of the 1960s, President Johnson, through his Great Society initiative, collaborated with Sen. Phil Hart (D-MI) and Rep. Emanuel Celler (D-NY) to convince the conservative chairman of the House Judiciary subcommittee on Immigration Rep. Michael Feighan (D-OH) to abandon the national-origin quota system for a new system that preserved families and attracted skilled workers.

Immigrant qualifications, rather than national origin quotas, would thereafter guide US immigration, a merit-based system, according to President Johnson. He signed the Immigration and Nationality Act of 1965 on New York's Liberty Island, October 3, 1965. The law "changed the face of the United States as much as any measure enacted in the twentieth century."[20]

Beyond government, and perhaps even more significant, was the awakening of an energized and aggressive civil society in the United States. It engaged the passions and energy of tens of thousands of the private voluntary organizations and citizens dedicated to relieving human suffering, including war victims and the world's neediest people.

In decades after World War II, the refugees gained recognition as an important category of people requiring respect and action. Some developments of this critically important period deserve special mention, as they show a process of change internationally and domestically:

- American First Lady Eleanor Roosevelt led the fight for a global agreement on the Universal Declaration of Human Rights, recognizing the world's obligation to protect the defenseless, adopted by the UN General Assembly in December 1948.
- In 1951, the international community folded previous refugee organizations (other than the UN Relief and Works Agency, (UNRWA) into a new UN High Commission for Refugees (UNHCR), to address the dilemma of the war-created refugees

needing international protection and assistance. The 1951 Refugee Convention defined the refugees as persons forced to flee for reasons of race, religion, or ethnicity and unable to avail themselves of the protection of their home government. The American government did not sign the binding obligation at that time.
- An American initiative in 1951 led to a Brussels meeting to address the logistical arrangements for relocating Europe's remaining refugees, displaced persons, and other migrants at risk. The resulting organization was the Provisional Intergovernmental Committee for the Movement of Migrants in Europe, known as PICMME. This organization eventually became permanent as the Intergovernmental Committee for European Migration, known as ICEM, and evolved into today's International Organization for Migration, IOM, with a global mandate.
- In 1967, America formally accepted the 1951 UN Refugee Convention, due to amendments made to the implementing protocol.

America, a Global Leader Cautious at Home

America had distinguished itself as a global leader through its contribution to the establishment of many international organizations and its outstanding work with World War II evacuees. However, it was much more cautious in building or retaining permanent national capabilities for migration and refugee solutions. Paradoxically, America's post-World War II capabilities and structures, which worked well earlier, were in substantial disrepair or decline as the new challenges arose in the 1970s and beyond.

In Washington, no forward planning or strategic analysis existed for the future humanitarian engagement. For most of the World War II and post-war periods, there was no felt need to develop longer-term capacities or a permanent US Government organizational home, especially for refugee matters. Carol Becker of the State Department Office of the Historian, said the post-World War II national structures for addressing the refugee and migration issues reflected America's old ambivalence toward immigration. At the State Department, the refugee and migration programs bounced around, clearly regarded as backwater areas that only reacted when forced, short-term, to sudden events or episodes. They quickly faded from serious engagement.

Becker reported that from 1944 until 1962 (with passage of the 1962 US Migration and Refugee Assistance Act), refugee and migration affairs were a collateral responsibility of four State assistant secretaries before they fell to a small office in UN affairs, after which the refugee and migration responsibilities were vested in the Security and Consular Affairs (SCA) bureau. In 1961, the Immigration and Nationality Act of 1952 was amended, terminating assistance to the refugees from Eastern Europe (especially Hungary). The refugee and migration staff were cut to eight and its annual budget halved to $72,000.[21]

While the locus of responsibility for refugee issues in Washington was in flux, the Refugee and Migration Assistance (RMA) office was at the US Mission in Geneva. RMA provided significant operational stability and continuity. The office interacted with the international humanitarian institutions and the NGOs (volunteer, non-profit groups) to coordinate the processing of Eastern European refugees in Western Europe destined for resettlement in the United States. The original task of NGOs was this resettlement of the Eastern European refugees processed in Western Europe, under contractual agreements with the State Department. When the Southeast Asia refugees arrived in large numbers later, most NGOs expanded their operations exponentially to meet this new crisis.

But regardless of these involvements, the State Department's disengagement in domestic refugee affairs remained unchanged. Carol Becker noted that by 1965 State's Security and Consular Affairs administrator Abba Schwartz, a friend of Attorney General Robert Kennedy (and I also later counted Abba a friend), lost favor with the Johnson administration and left government service. The result for refugee affairs was a reorganization of State's management of refugee programs in 1966, when a special assistant to the secretary of state assumed responsibility for the department's refugee and migration programs. State's concern for refugee programs then diminished significantly, and its refugee budget dropped to less than $6 million by 1968.

The humanitarian international institutions of the post-World War II era, featuring America's emergence as a global leader, brought with them new structures, policies, and laws to help the people needing safety. Each organization had its own history, priorities, and requirements. But America's humanitarian foundation, formed by previous sufferings and struggles, was mothballed as the worsening global humanitarian challenges of the 1970s and beyond beckoned. It remained available, however, ready to be called on.

But in 1979, as I considered a role in the American refugee scene, I realized that State's post-World War II off-again, on-again focus had become, almost overnight, its highest priority. The new bureau was to be the primary action office in the State Department. However, it was struggling to get on its feet.

This brief retrospective gave me a clearer picture of the American hesitancy yet crucial involvement in the major refugee and humanitarian challenges of the past and why State found itself so unprepared to meet the Indochinese refugee problems of the late 1970s.

The international community continued to look to the United States for courageous leadership to confront the humanitarian challenges of the times, just as it had for other global imperatives. The new bureau revealed enormous potential. The question the American government had to face in 1979, after a humbling military setback in Vietnam, was whether we were up to the job.

The world was about to find out.

9

DURABLE SOLUTIONS QUEST

WHETHER I ANSWERED THE CALL TO STATE'S NEW REFUGEE bureau, one thing was clear: refugee crises facing us were not deferrable. Critical work had to be done at breakneck speed. Foremost was Southeast Asia (Indochina) and a possible international initiative. All hands were expected to help. The refugee problems in Indochina required, in UN terms, *durable solutions*. But, being new to the issues, I had to ask, "What are durable solutions and what do they look like?" The answers lay in the 1951 Refugee Convention.

The 1951 Refugee Convention is a United Nations multilateral treaty that defines which persons in dire need shall be helped under the *refugee status* definition. It sets out the rights of individuals granted asylum and specifies responsibilities of nations that provide it; also, it identifies the people who do not qualify as refugees, such as those still in their home country and war criminals.

The Refugee Convention was initially considered at the fifth session of the UN General Assembly in 1950 by its Third Committee. Mrs. Eleanor Roosevelt was the US representative, assisted by George Warren of the State Department. The Refugee Convention was approved (for three years) at a special UN conference in 1951 and went into force in 1954. It was limited initially to protecting the European refugees from before January 1951. To be binding, these provisions had to be formally ratified by subscribing UN member nations. The Truman administration did not ratify the Refugee Convention on behalf the United States at the time, asserting,

> ...virtually all of the rights and privileges to be provided by the Convention were already available to refugees under federal and state laws in the United States. No distinction is made between refugees and other aliens under United States legislation and all aliens are in most rights and privileges in the same position as nationals.[1]

President Truman faced extraordinary isolationist pressures and withheld formal American approval, even though he agreed with the Convention's underlying concepts and purposes. The American delegate to the UN Third Committee said the Truman administration thought this instrument "would contribute substantially to the achievement of progressive self-dependence on the part of refugees and thus to peace and order in European countries."[2]

The United States did, however, ratify the 1967 implementing protocol on the status of refugees; 148 countries had formally accepted one or both instruments by April 2015. The 1967 implementing Protocol removed the time limits and applied the Convention to all refugees "without any geographic limitation."

The Refugee Convention formally defined refugees.

> A person who, owing to a well-founded fear of being persecuted for reasons of race, religion, nationality, membership of a particular social group or political opinion, is outside the country of his nationality and is unable or, owing to such fear, is unwilling to avail himself of the protection of that country; or who, not having a nationality and being outside the country of his former habitual residence as a result of such events, is unable or, owing to such fear, is unwilling to return to it.[3]

Persons meeting all provisions of the definition but still in their home country could not qualify under this refugee definition, a consideration that would become important later.

Signatories to the 1951 Refugee Convention agreed (1) to refrain from *refoulement*, a French word for *forced return*, of refugees to their home countries while the threat of persecution persists; (2) to guarantee the right for fleeing refugees to request asylum and protection within the country of asylum; and (3) to work for solutions for refugees.

Three Main Durable Solutions for Refugees

Durable solutions are not defined specifically in the 1951 Refugee Convention or Protocol. However, by established practice, three durable solutions are accepted, in order of priority: *voluntary repatriation, regional settlement*, and *third country resettlement*.[4]

Voluntary repatriation to the home country with safety assured is the first and most desirable *durable solution*. If this solution is impossible in the reasonably foreseeable future, regional settlement within the home region, if safe, is the second most desirable durable solution—such as Asian refugees settle within Asia, African refugees within Africa, and so on. When the first two solutions are impossible, third-country resettlement comes into play. That involves transferring refugees from their country of first asylum to distant places to begin new lives.

Because of the obvious disruption of the refugees' lives with third-country resettlement and the burden on receiving countries, it is the least preferred, a last resort.

Regarding Indochinese, all Southeast Asian first-asylum countries maintained they could not consider permanent regional resettlement for the refugees from Vietnam, Cambodia, and Laos. And, I found they were not signatories to either the UN's 1951 Refugee Convention or the 1967 Refugee Protocol. However, they had agreed to follow the many provisions and practices of both if they got equitable burden-sharing from other governments. As expected, the Association of Southeast Asian Nations (ASEAN) agreed in 1979 *not* to allow refugees to remain in their territory permanently; they considered themselves only to be countries of transit.[5]

Special Durable Solutions for Southeast Asia

Because the Asian asylum countries rejected voluntary repatriation and regional settlement, favoring the almost exclusive reliance on third-country resettlement, the notion of three sequential durable solutions was stood on its head. The UN High Commissioner for Refugees, among others, believed the international community had been given an all or nothing/take it or leave it deal. However, because the major resettlement governments, led by the United States, accepted this solution for the time being, UNHCR had no choice but to close ranks behind it.

Going forward, the US plans for Southeast Asia had to anticipate continuous refugee flight, large *first-asylum* camps, limited *voluntary repatriation*, almost no regional settlement, and large *third-country resettlement* programs. We would stay alert to changing conditions that might make *repatriation* or *regional settlement* possible.

Our short to midterm policy course was set.

Beyond *durable solutions* for vulnerable Vietnamese, the international community must also establish durable solutions for the Cambodian and Laotian refugees, also on the move and at risk.

The hunt for Southeast Asia durable solutions was gathering speed, since only global action could avoid the looming human catastrophe. Already, when I arrived to form the refugee organization at State in May 1979, there was talk of a new international initiative, big enough to persuade resettlement governments to substantially increase their refugee offtake and quick enough to convince first-asylum governments to stay the course. How big and how fast would be up to the international community, but the United States would have a big say.

At a May 1979 congressional hearing on the US Refugee Act, Sen. Clark acknowledged that not enough had been done to ease the burden carried by first-asylum countries placed by geography in the refugees' flight path. He emphasized that the inadequacy of resettlement programs created a human crisis far beyond anything the international community anticipated.

Other Indochinese advocates for refugees in the State Department were equally adamant, led by Dick Holbrooke and including Morton (Mort) Abramowitz, Frank Wisner, Shep Lowman, and Lionel Rosenblatt. Southeast Asian first-asylum countries, they maintained, had shouldered the greatest burden caring for the Indochinese refugees and had reached their limits. Governments had already pushed the refugees back across borders and threatened even more forced returns unless they got greater help from the United States and the other resettlement countries.

In June 1979, the Thai pushed back forty thousand Cambodians at the Preah Vihear temple and three thousand perished. Simultaneously, Indonesia confirmed that its military had been ordered to turn back refugee groups; Malaysia had already pushed back or expelled over fifty thousand in the first half of 1979, including fifteen thousand in June alone, and in mid-June announced a shoot-on-sight policy and a decision to evict the seventy-six thousand "boat people in asylum camps.[6] These draconian measures were to be employed unless a major third-country resettlement effort reduced their burden. Otherwise, ASEAN asylum countries threatened to close borders to future refugees. The CIA reported that up to a quarter million more Vietnamese boat people would flee Vietnam in the second half of 1979. To clarify their position, the ASEAN governments announced they would accept no further arrivals after June 1979.[7] As none of these asylum countries was a signatory to the 1951 Refugee Convention or bound by its non-refoulment principles, they considered forced return a viable option.

To clarify options available to US policy makers, in Geneva the US ambassador William vanden Heuvel advised Secretary Vance in mid-June his view of the near impossibility of increasing resettlement levels in the numbers required for a decisive impact. He said the exodus had no visible limits and could approach a million by the end of the year as panic conditions spread. He suggested that the United States and the Soviet Union discuss the possibility of asking the Socialist Republic of Vietnam (SRV) to halt the exodus immediately and agree to establish refugee camps in Vietnam, under international jurisdiction. ASEAN boat refugees could be returned to Vietnam with the prospect of eventual and orderly resettlement. Absent SRV cooperation, he concluded that the only certain result "will be death of countless thousands of Vietnamese."[8]

The new refugee team did not agree with the viability of that approach and set about to forge an international resettlement solution to be led by the United States. Given these alarming realities, I got word that under secretary for political affairs David Newsom, coordinator Dick Clark, and East Asia and the Pacific's Dick Holbrooke were instructed to prepare immediate options for an Indochinese resettlement initiative for presidential decision. Helped by EAP, our small Asia staff prepared the resettlement options, while our management staff calculated the budget requirements. (RP was not officially established until July 1979, but staff had already been transferred from HA to the coordinator's office, in anticipation of its formal creation.)

There was a question in my mind whether it would even be possible to get funding from a reluctant Congress for such an initiative. I was also concerned about the reception and placement capacity in the United States. Could the private voluntary agencies and local and state governments cope with a domestic resettlement program that had increased vastly? Could they find more local sponsors?

Refugee arrivals had increased over the recent months, and in December 1978 President Carter had raised the US resettlement levels to 25,000; he increased them to 84,000 in April 1979. Most of the funding was tied up in a pending supplemental appropriation in Congress. Other governments were also gradually increasing their resettlement numbers. Given lengthy processing requirements, however, the number of refugees leaving the region was still small and new arrivals in first asylum were dwarfing the offtake.[9] Given the magnitude of the problem in Southeast Asia, the first-asylum countries remained dissatisfied with the help they were receiving.

Dick Holbrooke, chief among the protagonists, and his State allies wanted the president to go big, to do something guaranteed to get the attention of first-asylum countries. Such an initiative would require decisive US leadership. Every option was on the table.

The President Ponders

Word came down that President Carter planned to travel to Tokyo in late June 1979 to participate in the Asian Economic Summit, and he wanted to announce new American plans regarding the Indochinese resettlement. Working twenty-four seven over the next few days, our refugee team developed a range of resettlement options ranging from staying where we were to major expansions. My attention to program ramifications on budgets in earlier years at the Office of Management and Budget (OMB) had influenced me to highlight budget and programmatic implications of these proposals. No government had attempted resettlement of such magnitude since World War II, and Congress had not provided appropriations for even present operations, much less expansion. Their interests and reactions also had to be considered. (As it developed, the Congress did not enact the required supplemental appropriations until late July 1979.)

The State Department's work was completed in short order, and a decision memorandum from Secretary Vance and Coordinator Clark was sent to the president on June 21, increasing the monthly intake from seven thousand persons to ten thousand for the coming year. In my view, that was RP's outer limit. Clark had a follow-up telephone discussion with the president on June 22, but no decision was forthcoming as the presidential team left for Tokyo.[10]

10

PRESIDENTIAL DECISION

Air Force One, Late June 1979

PRESIDENT CARTER WAS EN ROUTE TO TOKYO FOR THE Asian Economic Summit scheduled for June 28, and his team noticed that throughout the flight Dick Holbrooke was relentlessly "banging away" at the president to make sure he got the full, bleak picture. *First asylum*, Holbrooke argued, was collapsing. As evidence, he said that *refugee arrivals* were expected to reach a new high that month, maybe 60,000. That month, the push-offs of boats and other *forced returns*, with countless deaths, had already occurred in Thailand and Malaysia. More were undoubtedly occurring at that very moment. The United States must take the lead to forge a new international consensus to solve this problem.

The formal record does not discuss the president's reaction to Holbrooke's impassioned pleas, but at the next day's summit gathering, President Carter announced that the United States was doubling its monthly intake of Indochinese refugees from 7,000 to 14,000. He challenged other governments to raise their contributions similarly.[1]

The British prime minister Margaret Thatcher further internationalized the response by suggesting that the UN secretary general Kurt Waldheim call for a conference on boat people under the auspices of the UN High Commission for Refugees (UNHCR).[2] The Asian governments' responses were quick and favorable; the helping governments then had to deliver.

The global search for an Indochina durable solution accelerated following President Carter's announcement. The UN secretary general announced a conference, later called the International Conference on Indochinese Refugees—or the Geneva Conference—to be held in Geneva the next month, July 1979. He left it up to the concerned governments (asylum, donor, and resettlement) and the international organizations to seize the moment. The conference was to answer a central question: could the *international community* move fast enough to keep first asylum open?

With a presidential decision in hand and a big international refugee conference coming in a few weeks, the US team had to develop plans for inserting these decisions into already strained refugee budgets. We had to develop proposals for the other programs affected by expanded asylum and resettlement, including increased funding for: (1) the vast array of refugee camps and services in Southeast Asia; (2) better preparation of the refugees for life in their new homes; (3) improving conditions in the overcrowded refugee camps; (4) combatting pirate attacks on the refugee boats; and (5) establishing a safe *orderly departure* program from Vietnam.

One economizing measure put forward during our deliberations was to fold ICEM into UNHCR. Ben Read sought my advice on this matter, as I was assuming the temporary leadership of RP. I had no basis for offering advice and suggested deferring this proposal for a few weeks, giving RP a chance to assess both organizations (later concluding that the United States was best served by keeping ICEM separate).

A Vance-to-Carter decision memorandum was sent to the White House on July 16, 1979, regarding initiatives the United States could announce at the Geneva Conference. The national security director Zbigniew Brzezinski forwarded the decision memorandum to the president on July 18.[3] We had an answer the following day in the heavily underlined returned memorandum. Its marginal notes seemed to jump out from all corners.[4]

President Carter had approved most of our recommendations. He had not hesitated to reconfirm doubling the resettlement program to fourteen thousand refugee admissions per month, or 168,000 persons annually. Funding requests to Congress and logistical assistance to augment the existing refugee camps in Southeast Asia were also approved. To reduce camp overcrowding, funding was set aside for new overflow and processing camps. Medical care, nutrition enhancements, and English language training were expanded. Refugee *protection* needs were highlighted, especially against the dangers to women, children, and other vulnerable refugees in risk at sea; he approved using US Military Sealift Command and Navy resources for transit and rescue of refugees. Special attention was paid to the planning of an orderly departure program.[5]

International Conference on Indochinese Refugees

The United States Government announced the American delegation to Geneva would be headed by Vice President Walter Mondale. That decision made his representation the highest ever for an international refugee meeting.

With the vice president would be: Dick Clark, Dick Holbrooke, William vanden Heuvel, Mort Abramowitz, Nick Platt (on detail to the National Security Council from State), Frank Wisner, congressional leaders, senior NSC officials, State Department seventh-floor staffers, Chris Russell and Shep Lowman from RP and Lionel Rosenblatt, who was flying to Geneva from Bangkok. Tom Miller was called out of Thai language training at the Foreign Service Institute by Ambassador Clark to assist him at the conference. Previously Tom had served as special assistant to undersecretaries Phil Habib and David Newsom and had played an active role in earlier refugee reforms. Also invited were the governor of Iowa Robert Ray and the New Jersey governor Brendan Byrne.

Geneva, Switzerland, July 20–21, 1979

At the International Conference on Indochinese Refugees, also known as the Geneva Conference, where sixty-two governments—including the Socialist Republic of Vietnam, speaking for all of Vietnam—gathered at the UN Palais des Nations in Geneva. While the Socialist Republic of Vietnam continued to deny responsibility for the refugee outflow, it attended as a first-asylum country, because it was hosting refugees from Kampuchea. In the runup to the conference, the US mission in Geneva was the key US interlocutor with UNHCR. Ambassador William vanden Heuvel and the mission staff worked closely with the UN high commissioner Hartling and his deputy Dale de Haan and other key actors to shape the desired outcomes. They maintained close working contact with the Southeast Asia representatives at their missions in Geneva.

The high commissioner's opening statement crystallized the daunting challenge. About two-thirds of the 600,000 people who had fled since 1975 were still languishing in the first-asylum *refugee camps.* Protection concerns had shot to the top of the priority list as pirate attacks on the boat people were shocking the world; and the refugees reaching Indonesia, Malaysia, and Thailand were no longer welcomed, often facing pushbacks and death.[6]

On July 20, 1979, forty-one years after the failed 1938 World War II Évian Conference, Vice President Walter Mondale anchored his address on what happened at the 1938 Évian Conference and what was at stake in Geneva, 1979:

> [At issue in Évian] were… human lives—and the decency and self-respect of the civilized world. It is heartbreaking to think of the … desperate human beings … waiting in suspense for what happens at Évian. But the question they underline is not simply humanitarian … it is a test of civilization.[7]

He urged governments "to avoid a similar outcome in Southeast Asia." He reminded them of Hitler's cruel sarcastic words after Évian:

> [I] hoped and expected that the world, which has such deep sympathy for these criminals (Jews), will at least be generous enough to convert this sympathy into practical aid. We, on our part, are ready to put all these criminals at the disposal of these countries, for all I care, even on luxury ships.

Mondale challenged the attendees:

> Let us not be like the others. Let us renounce that legacy of shame. Let us honor the moral principles we inherit. Let us do something meaningful—something profound—to stem the misery. We face a world problem. Let

us fashion a world solution. History will not forgive us if we fail. History will not forget us if we succeed.... As the delegates left Évian, Hitler again goaded 'the other world' for 'oozing sympathy for the poor, tormented people, but remaining hard and obdurate when it comes to helping them.'[8]

The vice president reminded the delegates that just days after Évian's failure "the final solution to the Jewish problem was conceived, and soon the night closed in."[9] He captivated hearers with the magnitude of the current US resettlement and financial pledges. The United States would double its resettlement, increase financial contributions, and urge others to do the same.

The vice president's emphasis had the desired effect. Attending nations responded with sizeable pledges, including offers to resettle over 260,000 refugees over the next year. Resettlement at those historic levels was considered enough to maintain *safe asylum* and to assure equitable burden-sharing. More than $190 million dollars were pledged for camp care and maintenance. Japan reaffirmed its pledge to underwrite 50 percent of UNHCR's budget for care and maintenance in first-asylum camps.

The vice president featured seven action areas drawn from the analysis State's refugee staff had presented.[10] To aid refugees in distress at sea, for example, Mondale reported the president had strengthened his orders to the Navy to help the drowning and the desperate:

> Today the president has ordered four additional ships from the Military Sealift Command to be dispatched to the South China Sea—where they will be available both to transport tens of thousands of refugees from camps to refugee processing centers and to assist refugees at sea. The president has also ordered long-range Navy planes to fly patrols to locate and seek help for refugee boats in distress. And the President is asking our private shipping industry and unions to persist with their time-honored efforts to help refugees at sea. We appeal

to other governments to do the same----and to accept for resettlement those who are picked up.[11]

◆

Ken Quinn, speaking for Governor Ray and himself, said the vice president's intervention was one of the most powerful moments either had ever experienced; America had been embraced for its humanitarian leadership. When Vice President Mondale announced that the United States would take 168,000 new refugees a year and would send the US Navy to rescue boat people, a spontaneous ovation for America brought everyone in the hall to their feet—except for the Soviet bloc, China, and the Socialist Republic of Vietnam attendees. As the vice president made his way back to rejoin the US delegation, Quinn recalled Governor Ray being one of the first to meet him, shaking his hand and saying it was one of his proudest moments as an American.

The international community left with a renewed commitment to a Southeast Asia *durable solution*. Vice President Mondale reported to President Carter that *solution parameters* to America's most vexing refugee problem were finally coming into view.

◆

When the US team returned to Washington, the implementation work began at once. Dick Clark reported ebulliently that the United States had succeeded beyond our wildest dreams. An international response had been formulated and US leadership had been acknowledged. And now, we had to deliver. We had to manage every dollar and every resettlement slot to assure that we were getting the maximum results and were seen to be succeeding. Clark said Secretary Vance had assigned this issue to State's refugee team, RP, and both he and the world would be watching.

Even though Vietnam was our primary focus then, we could not fail to recognize that, alas, Vietnam was not the only Southeast Asian country in turmoil. Kampuchea's Khmer Rouge atrocities, later to be reported by the journalists, had already presented the governments with an unfolding nightmare as the country closed itself off. As events in Vietnam and Kampuchea dangerously escalated, neighboring Laos was not far behind.

The parameters of the future refugee problems in Southeast Asia were clear: wherever one looked from Vietnam to Kampuchea to Laos, the unintended consequences of the tragic war were cascading down on the allies and friends who had thrown in their lot with the Americans. It was time to acknowledge our responsibility and do something about it. The Geneva Conference had provided critically important tools to confront these challenges. A comprehensive rescue effort of historic dimensions was underway.

11

SIGNS OF LIFE

EVEN AS THE SMALL REFUGEE TEAM PERFORMED BRILliantly organizing the Geneva Conference initiatives, it was struggling simultaneously on another track: to keep the RP bureau surviving as an official organization.

We had been grinding in this track as far back as my early talks with Ben Read in May 1979. Following that talk, Ben had sent word he and the deputy secretary agreed with my organizational assessment and next-step suggestions. That was when I was officially reassigned from the "A" bureau to State's Refugee Programs bureau, RP, and placed in charge of the reorganization as the acting director, pending a permanent appointee. The startup date was deferred. Seventh-floor leadership would help address the ongoing investigations, and the management organizations would assist materially in establishing the new refugee bureau.

Left unanswered was the proposed length of my stay, until the official establishment of the bureau, and I let that consideration ride for the moment. Putting aside strong reservations, I was officially a member of the new refugee team.

While planning and preparations for the Geneva Conference had been underway, I had devoted time and attention simultaneously to the most urgent priority: RP's formal startup and stabilization as soon as possible. Otherwise, a struggling enterprise with weak underpinnings would continue to drift or lurch from crisis to crisis, including the outside threats to move it to USAID.

Overhanging our reform plans were other existential threats posed by the multiple inspections and investigative reports of past mismanagement and the congressional plans to transfer refugee programs to USAID.[1] I felt caught between the deputy secretary's demand that the programs remain in State and the external reviewers' desires to move them elsewhere. Ben Read and I commiserated that these threats had to be overcome quickly, or State might lose the programs before we got off the ground. As we launched the new organization, that would be one of my highest and most time-sensitive priorities.

The urgent reform list included professional staffing competent to address bureaucratic and global challenges, adequate and predictable funding, and State Department acceptance of refugee programs as vital, ongoing, and accepted components of American foreign policy. Coming from State's well-structured, staffed, and supported Administration bureau, "A," I could see how far the new RP bureau had to go. And I had little to work with. Even with the department's promises of support. *Where to start, given so many needs?*

When administrative officer Kitty Kemp was assigned to help, I was dumbstruck at first. Good news was so rare. Her first question was, "Where do we start?"

"Kitty, we need a crackerjack staff. Mediocre won't do."

Within weeks, the comptroller and contracts officer left RP and returned to USAID. With Kitty's help in May and June, we quickly recruited Marvin Smith from State's inspector general's staff to become comptroller; Norman Runkles came in to head financial management; Addie Parker arrived as contracts officer. Norm and Addie had worked for me in State's educational exchange program earlier and I knew they were outstanding. My wife Jean recommended I talk with two colleagues at Peace Corps headquarters. We shared a cheer when I learned that Jim Lawrence and Louise Pope would soon come on board for information systems and funds management, respectively. Jim Lawrence recommended I talk with someone named Karl Beck, for Africa. We seemed finally to be on a good development curve.

More good news came that John Baker, assigned as liaison to the UN Food and Agriculture Organization (FAO) in Rome, had been approved as the RP director. He could not arrive immediately, however. I knew

John and considered him a suitable choice. While at the OMB, I had worked with him during the Nixon administration's battle to save Radio Free Europe and Radio Liberty. Unlike other FSOs under recruitment, Baker had not been scared off by the Refugee Programs' lack of a statutory assistant secretary designation.

Overall, it took three months, working overtime May through July, to get ready for the formal launch. Kitty Kemp helped get much of the required personnel and organizational work completed in record time. The problematic staff were encouraged to transfer elsewhere, and active replacement recruitment was ongoing.

The infamous reputation of the previous refugee program continued to cause problems, as Kitty and I discovered when we first provided Foreign Service job descriptions to PER for worldwide posting. Not a single FSO submitted a bid to work with us! Clearly, there was more work ahead to make RP an attractive place to work and to assure that humanitarian work became a high priority for the State Department. We felt we could and would change these attitudes and perceptions. The process begun in May brought most of the basic preparatory work to completion.

On July 30, 1979, much remained to be done, yet accomplishments thus far justified the official establishment of the Refugee Programs bureau.[2] We had built a sound foundation. The launch date was a remarkable nine days after the Geneva Conference on Indochinese Refugees. Ben Read's crucial decisions became the point from which we thereafter would measure progress.

With deep feelings of relief, I sat back in my chair and dictated a one-word note to Ben: "Thanks." I remembered what others had seen as a costly organizational misdirection waiting to happen; but Ben Read had stayed true. I trusted we had turned a significant corner. However, if this huge undertaking failed, it would be my misadventure to account for.

Underlying the Geneva Conference and the State Department's new bureau's formal establishment, milestones for State and for the refugees were the human tragedies that begged for renewed American commitment to respond. The bureau's startup months had heightened my awareness of similar tragedies beyond Asia:

- Eastern European and Soviet Jewry crises
- Middle East and Israel disputes about Palestinian and Jewish refugees
- African civil wars and developmental issues
- Afghanistan/Soviet crisis emerging
- Central America civil wars

At our first staff meeting, I felt wary. I knew about multiple refugee issues from what I had researched, heard about, and seen. I knew much less than I wanted to know about the *geopolitical environment* in which RP orbited and about the people I would direct. I feared imminent failure and my stomach stayed in knots, nervous energy propelling me. *With limited staff, how should these organizational crises be tackled over the next few months? And our ongoing programs are more prone to problems and growing faster than ever.*

When the meeting broke up, I was ushered into a similar meeting in the refugee coordinator's office. Present were Dick Clark, the US refugee coordinator, and his new deputy coordinator, George Garbis, along with their staff. Clark was especially concerned to have a successful follow-up to the recent Geneva Conference. The president was adamant, Clark insisted, that the United States seize this opportunity to focus the world's attention on solutions to the devastating refugee problems in Asia. Because of the conference, the United States would embark on one of the largest refugee resettlement programs ever undertaken by a single government. While other resettlement countries would make refugee resettlement commitments, only the resolute US leadership and a continuing strong example of US resettlement efforts would sustain and enlarge those commitments. Dick Clark looked at me: "Jim, I trust RP is geared up."

Driving home later that night, the congested Washington commuter traffic had already passed. I reflected on the day's issues. *They're insurmountable*, I thought. *There's too much here, even for an established organization. Given newness and weakness and our spiraling workload, we will self-destruct if we allow ourselves to get caught up in this accumulation.* To make headway, I must concentrate on key, unavoidable reforms for RP stabilization.

Given concurrent pressures on Geneva Conference follow-up and RP's launch requirements, I mused, You've got maybe five months, until the end of the year, to prove that RP can manage the programs and sidestep congressional transfer threats. What's most urgent and accomplishable for this time frame and RP's future reputation?

After a bite to eat at home, I began to put ideas on paper. I subdivided immediate challenges into three categories to guide RP's takeoff. *Foremost*, there was the steady and predictable leadership on my part as we waited for the political system to produce permanent RP leaders. I hoped John Baker would arrive soon. *Second*, RP would need to implement immediately the Freeman Report's organizational and management reforms. *Third*, and simultaneously, we had to begin work on the Geneva Conference reforms.

Before I closed my eyes that night, it hit me again that I was in way over my head. I rationalized that I would get going in the morning and start afresh, one day and one issue at a time. Maybe more angels like Kitty Kemp would show up soon. *Please, don't let it implode on me*, I prayed.

◇

The next morning, I awoke troubled, thinking, Might I be leading an already struggling organization into utter catastrophe? Who could I bounce ideas off and get an informed reaction? I remembered Ben Read's offer to be a sounding board. Ben must be brought back into the picture. This agenda was already far too complex for an inexperienced temporary leader and staff, still untrained in the global refugee programs' many moving parts. It was, unavoidably, the agenda I thought we needed to focus on, for at least the next five months and possibly for the remainder of the Carter administration.

I needed reinforcement about my ideas and intentions. I would look to the new director when he arrived. Presently, Chris Russell, deputy director for program management, and staff would carry a big share of this load while I was in the command seat.

Key Startup Parameters

Early the next morning I organized a quick meeting with Ben Read and again felt energized to share my solution ideas with someone else. He listened as I talked about my three priority categories. While action on the new and permanent leadership was proceeding, I reiterated the need for fast action. Ben affirmed the Baker appointment and tried to assuage my concerns.

Regarding the second category, Freeman Report reforms, Ben was quiet as I identified the immediate reforms needed:

- Repair damaged congressional relations
- Finish RP staffing
- Address multiple inspection reports to get inspectors off RP's back
- Prepare the first-ever global and comprehensive refugee budget.
- Anticipate the reforms of the pending Refugee Act
- Prepare for RP's worldwide focus, including simultaneous global crises, new in refugee response history

Significantly, repairing congressional relations was prerequisite for advancing other reforms.

Regarding the third category, I identified priorities:

- Protect refugees endangered at sea
- Reduce overcrowding in *first-asylum camps*
- Gain burden sharing support on Indochina durable solutions
- Expand and improve US domestic resettlement
- Establish a program for *orderly departure* as a safe alternative to clandestine boat departures (*see* chapter 15)

So many people approved for admission were arriving that the expansion and improvement of domestic resettlement required priority attention.

When I finished my comments, I felt disappointed and perplexed by Ben's silence and wondered if he was hesitant or skeptical about my plans.

When he spoke, Ben asked if I was taking on more than RP could realistically handle. He asked why we could not just concentrate on the Geneva Conference initiatives for the next few months and deal with the other management concerns as time and work pressures allowed.

"Ben, ignoring the management infrastructure requirements in favor of more compelling program matters is what brought the refugee programs almost to the point of collapse!"

It's so typical of the State Department to downplay the compelling need for practical support so program projects can actually work! I thought cynically, knowing that most bureaucracies tend to put off the compelling management needs.

Aloud I said, "These priorities are so interlinked that we can't move forward on the Geneva Conference initiatives without simultaneous progress in the management area."

Thoughts flew, and I elaborated. Implementing these initiatives would require congressional approval for quick and sizeable expansion of RP's budget, staffing, and domestic resettlement programs.

"You know better than most that both the House and Senate Appropriations Committees have great concerns about State's refugee stewardship, stemming from the Antideficiency Act violations and charges of mismanagement. They are not likely to approve additional funds unless we can change their perceptions and convince them of the new team's management competence."

Summarizing, I noted that the appropriations committees were still on record for moving the refugee programs to USAID. So, it was critical to address and resolve the violations and inspection reports quickly.

"We've got to get beyond these problems," I worried aloud, "so our discussions with Congress can concentrate on the conference initiatives, the new Refugee Act under congressional consideration, and our large worldwide budget and resettlement requests for next year. We must make progress simultaneously in each area if we're to have any chance of gaining congressional approval of the funding and support as we move forward."

When I finished, Ben was quiet for a minute, then responded: "I suggest we expand the time frame from the end of the year to the duration of the Carter administration's first term. We must assume that we *will* overcome congressional notions about moving the program to USAID."

Agreement on Priorities

Ben Read's suggested time frame was early August 1979 to January 20, 1981, nearly a year and a half. I took in the words. They meant I must stay longer than anticipated. But I wanted to see this done. Ben asked me to keep him informed regularly about progress.

With this framework set, our small RP team turned its attention to my second and third priority categories: implementing Freeman Report reforms and assuring that the elusive *durable solutions* agreed to in Geneva did not slip away.

All points raised with Ben Read would energize refugee programs. Over years ahead, they would be recalled as important contributors to the record about policies and human stories of the first and second years of the Indochina refugee programs at State.

12

EXISTENTIAL THREATS

A SIGNIFICANT PART OF THE HISTORY OF MODERN US REFUgee programs emanates from the groundbreaking work to resolve their potentially imperiling threats. Awaiting John Baker's arrival at the State Department as first official refugee programs director, I concentrated on implementing the Freeman Report's organizational and management reforms in keeping with my agreement with Ben Read. We were simultaneously taking on the startup reforms, especially shoring up congressional relations, and important Geneva Conference initiatives.

Even though many balls were in the air at launch time, our immediate priorities were to resolve: (1) the existential threats to RP's continued existence in the State Department, (2) the negative inspection and investigative reports, and (3) the poor relations with all-important congressional appropriations committees, a prerequisite for other reforms.

◇

High on the Freeman Report reform agenda were corrections of deficiencies in contracting, procurement, planning and budgeting, financial management, information technology, coordination among partners, questionable assignment of functions, and leadership and staffing. To correct those deficiencies, I assigned specific RP staff teams to propose the corrective actions.[1] (Key management reforms are further discussed in the next chapters.)

As our teams produced the reform recommendations, I spent considerable time with the external investigative teams to discuss their findings and recommendations. I wanted to convince them to hold off further criticism while the reforms were underway. Except for the appropriations committees, the external critics liked the changes we were putting in place and backed off to give us time.

The inspection reports were helpful in making needed reforms. Especially helpful was the internal inspection report by Jerry Goldman, a State management expert assigned by Ben Read. He identified several glaring weaknesses and provided remedial recommendations. Goldman's report also confirmed what we thought: "refugee assistance efforts of the US Government were no longer exclusively emergency programs to meet temporary needs…"[2]

Beyond issuing a critical and negative report, Jerry Goldman got to know me, explained his critique well, and invested time in helping bring about suggested reforms. I later told Ben Read that Jerry's help was exactly the kind we needed.

Within a brief time, the demanding work of RP teams paid off, as many critics began to understand our plans and ease the pressure. Without question, however, I needed to concentrate more on the congressional reforms.

◇

The structure for executive/legislative branch relationships in the United States is complicated, involving numerous federal agencies and congressional committees. It is necessary to understand these complicated relationships to grasp the significance of the problems we faced and the reforms we were trying.

Executive Branch

The primary locus for refugees within the executive branch was the State Department, a designation that recognized both the foreign policy implications and the overseas origins of refugees.[3]

Important parts of the government's refugee efforts were dispersed to other federal agencies, given the domestic impacts. For example, the Justice Department (DOJ) held authority for the admission of refugees for permanent resettlement, through the Immigration and Naturalization Service (INS). The Department of Health, Education, and Welfare (HEW), later called Health and Human Services (HHS), provided the longer-term cash and medical assistance to resettled refugees, supplementing the initial reception and placement grants provided by the State Department. The US Agency for International Development (USAID) and the Department of Defense (DoD) were also involved in the overseas refugee relief. Both State and HEW gave grants to non-profit groups—known as nongovernmental organizations, or NGOs—including those working as refugee resettlement agencies, for different purposes.

Integrating the work of these executive branch agencies was the responsibility of four entities: the new office at the State Department, the US coordinator for refugee affairs, the president's Office of Management and Budget (OMB), the National Security Council (NSC), and the White House.

Legislative Branch

Congress is required, as with all federal programs, to authorize the international and domestic components of the refugee programs and appropriate funds to carry them out. The authorizing committees—the Senate Foreign Relations Committee and the House International Relations Committee—focused on the foreign policy concerns. Each had regional subcommittees to deal with specific geographic issues. Like the State Department, these committees adopted a more expansive view of refugee programs than did the counterpart domestic and law enforcement committees.

Authorized programs for US refugee admissions fell under the jurisdiction of the Justice Department's Immigration and Naturalization Service (INS). Relevant committees of the House and Senate authorized the refugee-related programs of the department of health and human services (HHS). These committees displayed restrictive views on refugee admissions.

Appropriating Committees

The overall State Department budget fell under the annual departmental Appropriations Acts of State, Justice, and Commerce; the refugee programs fell under the jurisdiction of the Foreign Assistance (foreign aid) Appropriations Act. This split had historic roots.[4] The congressional committees overseeing foreign assistance appropriations had oversight and appropriation powers for RP's funding for both domestic resettlement and international refugee assistance programs.

Consultations Committees

The Refugee Act of 1980 required annual consultations between the House and Senate Judiciary committees and the executive branch representatives regarding the number and origins of refugees to be admitted to the United States in the coming year. The consultation hearings usually occurred in September, just before the start of the Federal Fiscal Year, October 1.

The Judiciary Committees did not want foreign policy concerns to overshadow the legitimate domestic considerations. They regarded the growing public-assistance costs for resettled refugees as unsustainable.

Major Existential Threats

The congressional appropriating committees, insistent about transferring the Refugee Programs bureau to the US Agency for International Development (USAID), were holding up action on the urgent supplemental appropriations for Indochina.[5] Lionel Rosenblatt told me the Judiciary committees had tried to kill the Expanded Parole Program several years earlier, and they were now considering transfer of domestic reception and placement, our largest funded program, to HEW.[6] Working with these key committees, I could not forget the words of Deputy Secretary Warren Christopher, "Jim, don't let the State Department lose the refugee programs."

Congressional Antagonisms

The powerful appropriating committees developed antagonistic attitudes toward the State Department's previous management of refugee programs. Their clear intention, spelled out in appropriations reports, was to transfer the refugee programs from State to USAID, in part because of the perceived management deficiencies, including the 1978 Antideficiency Act violation that hounded the new refugee bureau. They had vowed that would never happen again. The Senate's transfer effort was led by Sen. Richard Russell (D-GA), former long-term chairman of the Senate Appropriations Committee, who also served as chairman of the subcommittee on Foreign Operations (foreign aid). Bill Jordan, also from Georgia, had served as the subcommittee staff director for over thirty years and was known for his intimidation of executive branch officials. Often accused of not seeing the forest for the trees, Jordan happily regarded himself as the one who kept the foreign aid programs under control. (There was a story that former Sen. Hubert Humphrey once gave up on a Food for Peace initiative out of fear he couldn't get it pass Bill Jordan).

The House Appropriations subcommittee staff director, Terry Peel, was equally influential and concerned about State's past management of refugee programs. Less flamboyant than Jordan, he was another serious player who favored transfer of the refugee account to USAID.

Gaining Support

An old saying is that "the proof of the pudding is in the eating." As they observed the new bureau's reform measures, the appropriations committees evolved from critics of State's refugee programs to advocates.

An anecdote about the congressional hearings on the refugee program bureau's fiscal year 1981 budget bears out this claim. Frank Loy was, by then, RP director (*see* chapter 19). The administration's record budget request that year was juxtaposed with the aftermath of the unpopular Vietnam War. Before participating in the refugee budget consultations hearing with the Judiciary committees in September, we first had to defend our budget requests before the House Foreign Affairs, Senate Foreign Relations, and Foreign Operations subcommittees of the important appropriations committees of both houses of Congress. With three committees, we expected to get reasonable agreement for increased funding and admissions numbers for that year. We felt unsure about the Senate Appropriations Committee hearing, where we would face the chairman Sen. Daniel Inouye (D-HI) and his tough staff director Bill Jordan.

The day before the hearing, Jordan called me, to review final arrangements. As he was signing off, he offered his commentary: "I have several organizations and agencies that come before the Senate Appropriations Committee who know their stuff, will be honest with me and the committee, and will use the money we appropriate well. Once you get on that list and continue to deal honestly with me, I give your program the benefit of the doubt. I've tested you over many months, and I like how this organization is now run. I've briefed Sen. Inouye and he wants to be helpful to refugees in Southeast Asia. I believe we will be able to work well together."[7]

Jordan's comment signaled a significant breakthrough for us, and its timing was much needed and appreciated. Lengthy hearings in Fall 1980 with Frank Loy as the principal witness went smoothly; RP later received an excellent appropriation from the Senate, as from the House. Jim Bond replaced Bill Jordan when Republicans took over the majority, and we had many battles—some wins, some losses—with this Senate committee over the coming years. I came to consider them honest but aggressive adversaries. The same held true in our relations with the corresponding House committee.

RP and Congress—Significant Accomplishments

I attributed much of the bureau's later success to the strong congressional funding base established during the takeoff period. We were a funding agency, and the international refugee system depended heavily on predictable American support. Following the transfer of refugee programs from HA to RP in May 1979 and continuing through the remaining years of the Carter administration, the new team had the responsibility for proposing, defending, and executing State's refugee budgets for all or parts of Fiscal Years 1978 to 1982.

We felt exonerated when former critics acknowledged that our work to repair tattered congressional relations produced weighty record-breaking accomplishments for refugees.[8] (Multiple examples are also included in the regional chapters. *See* Book Three.)

A discussion of US refugee programs vis-à-vis Congress would be incomplete without mentioning the critical advocacy and support over many years of the late Sen. Ted Kennedy and Jerry Tinker, his Judiciary subcommittee staff director. Their persistent interest and prodding kept the United States at the forefront of refugee issues around the world. Their leadership was crucial to enactment of the visionary Refugee Act of 1980.

Seeing progress in confronting these existential threats, RP could turn attention to my second and third priority categories: implementing other Freeman Report reforms and assuring that the elusive durable solutions for Indochina, agreed to in Geneva, did not slip away.

13

RECALIBRATE FOR GLOBAL RESPONSE

AMERICAN LEADERSHIP WITHIN THE GLOBAL REFUGEE SYStem required the Bureau for Refugee Programs to field a strong professional team of committed officers, both in headquarters and overseas. Standing at the starting line in July 1979, I feared we had a long way to go. I thought, *If I'm to play even a temporary leadership role in this effort, I need to be better acquainted with the team members already here.*

I met or learned about most of the refugee staffers and accepted they would be the core of our team at headquarters and overseas. Though some staff were problematic, most seemed up to the job. I hoped for added qualified staff soon. I was introduced to other State Department bureaus and offices that would continue to interface regularly with RP, such as the geographic bureaus, particularly East Asia and the Pacific (EAP); International Organizations (IO), Consular Affairs (CA) and the central budget and management offices.

The more I learned, the more my paradigm widened. The State Department was only one component of a broader American commitment to refugees. Other critically important components included the partner federal agencies, Congress, nongovernmental organizations (NGOs), state and local governments, committed individuals and organizations, multilateral and intergovernmental organizations, and partner governments. This vast array contributed immensely to the work of the global effort. I knew I must understand more about them.

On behalf of the United States, the RP bureau would be the dynamo to help catalyze America's role in a broad, diverse global network. Interfacing with that network would be daunting, but I took hope that a strengthened network dedicated to mutually important purposes could be a potent global force. As it was, however, RP needed a lot of shoring up, too. Even though it was our job to bring such a strong interactive refugee team into being and keep it stimulated, I had strong doubts RP had or could quickly get the required tools and skills.

Rescue Needs a Plan, a Map, and Resources

Forming a global and comprehensive refugee budget for the first time was a necessary and critical building block. I remembered Ben Read talking in the spring of 1979 about refugee budgeting and financial management.

First, he had said they were in a chaotic mess. Congress was so upset with us they were threatening to take action. We were living off emergency supplemental appropriations, but humanitarian crises were anything but temporary. They were a permanent feature of the foreign affairs landscape and likely to stay that way for the foreseeable future. He said there was no anticipation or planning and there was limited global cooperation among our allies for cost sharing. We lurched from crisis to crisis and the United States was carrying too heavy a load.

Refugee programs were becoming the largest single item in the Department's budget and its greatest vulnerability. Most investigations underway sprang from financial improprieties. The former budgeting and financial shortcomings, Ben Read had warned, were prompting calls to move the programs to USAID and questioning State's management competence.

"Jim, we've got to do better."

The State Department was in a life and death battle with Congress over refugee funding. To deal with the threatening refugee surge in Southeast Asia, the department had been forced to send yet another urgent supplemental appropriations request to Congress in April 1979. With other department leaders—including Dick Holbrooke and Dick Clark—I spent considerable time and energy lobbying the appropriations committees for these needed funds. I had already decided that we would not risk a repeat of the Antideficiency Act debacle of the year before. So, I was prepared to recommend stopping resettlement operations at the end of August. unless Congress approved the requisite funding.

At a May 1979 hearing on the proposed Refugee Act, Dick Clark had made an urgent appeal:

> We face an imminent collapse of all our programs unless Congress enacts our pending supplemental requests for $104.9 million (for FY 1980) by the beginning of June. This means that not only will refugees have to spend more time in camps—often in inadequate conditions—but also that growing refugee populations in countries of first asylum of Southeast Asia will further strain aid resources and the willingness of asylum countries to admit new arrivals. I'm afraid we may see a tragic increase in deaths and drowning at sea because boats full of refugees are refused permission to land, and many more desperate land refugees may be forced back into the countries they are fleeing.[1]

Leo Cherne, chairman of both the International Rescue Committee (IRC) and the Citizens Commission on Indochinese Refugees, reinforced this warning in his testimony at the hearings:

> The paramount fact is this: the refugees will die unless legislation is quickly enacted that will enable voluntary and intergovernmental agencies to continue their work. We cannot continue beyond this month—some of us perhaps into June—until the supplemental funds requested by the executive branch are voted by the Congress.[2]

Thanks to last minute heroics by the State Department and many concerned advocates and supporters, we narrowly dodged another bullet. Congress approved the supplemental appropriation late in the fiscal year, after the Geneva Conference. But in approving the measure, they reiterated their continued unhappiness with the bureau's management. That narrow escape toughened my sense of urgency. Congressional imperatives required RP to undertake an immediate overhaul of its financial management, contracting, and budget systems. It took no genius to foresee that larger refugee funding demands were in the offing. Hefty amounts of money would be needed, and future refugee agency leaders must be able to attract them from both public and private coffers. We must assure potential funders that RP could anticipate, plan, and manage big programs and budgets.

By summer 1979, it was time to prepare RP's next fiscal year budget, FY 1981. Budget proposals must go through a succession of executive branch reviews, first within RP, then the State Department, and finally the OMB. Our budget proposals were due to the department's central budget office by mid-August.

I postponed a major overhaul of the bureau's budget formulation system until the next year. We had devoted much precious time to immediate needs, including the congressional funding crisis; the formation of at least a skeletal RP; a response to the Geneva Conference agreements; and the emerging world refugee crises. To our lean staff, I drew on an adage, "There's only so much blood we can get out of this turnip."

Mary Kavaliunas, Frank Moss, and I put our heads together and came up with the bureau's FY 1981 budget request, which was essentially a pricing-out of the Geneva Conference initiatives for Southeast Asia and an assumption of steady-state continuation for all the other global programs. We envisioned no other initiatives or programs beyond those already agreed. Our proposed budget was not long on narrative, but it was big in dollars because the scale of the initiatives (*see* Table 3). Because the Indochinese refugee crisis was at its peak, the FY 1981 budget made it through OMB and Congress with minimal changes. Each reviewing entity clarified, however, that FY 1981 was to be an exception. Later refugee budgets could not expect such extraordinary treatment. The real budget reform would come only the following year after we had time to conceptualize and plan for a revised program and budgeting system.

Reformed Accounting and Budgeting

In the remaining months of the Carter administration, the RP comptroller, Marvin Smith, and the financial management chief, Norman Runkles, reformed accounting, financial monitoring, and contracting systems to correct past flaws and to modernize RP's financial management. Controls were put in place to detect problems early, take fast corrective action, and inform the management regularly about the program's financial status. This progress was just the beginning, and reform and refinement would continue for years.

The budget formulation and execution systems designed for a less complicated era were inadequate for the expanding global needs. The focus henceforth would be global, while in the past, needs were confined to specific episodes or regions. We now had to relate the dollars with policies and programs with greater precision than ever.

Before even thinking about assigning dollar amounts to refugee programs and organizations, I created a conceptual, analytic process to review country, regional, and worldwide requirements. It was based on similar management review models I had seen used elsewhere and on my own design. RP's innovative Policy and Program Review Committee (PPRC) participants were the senior managers, program officers, and budget staff. (I would have been astounded if anyone had told me then that the PPRC process would endure and become a permanent fixture in refugee program management, even to the present.)

Following the record FY 1981 budget, we were concerned that the steep FY 1982 budget request would shock external groups that reviewed our budget. Because government protocol did not allow me to discuss the details or specific amounts before presidential approval, I began informally to apprise these groups of what lay ahead and why America's refugee budget required quantum leaps. Though I anticipated negative reactions, I was surprised that most organizations and groups were pleased to hear that the State Department finally had the backbone to propose annual refugee budgets commensurate with what, most agreed, were the ongoing and ballooning needs.

FY 1981 and 1982 budget requests were the largest ever proposed for refugees by a national government. We would have been shocked but pleased had we been able to comprehend that the framework Mary Kavaliunas proposed for RP's 1982 budget would endure over the years. As the executive branch FY 1982 cycle ended, global and comprehensive refugee budgeting were established as the new norm that would carry into the future.

14

SHARPENING WHILST SALVAGING

TO EXPLORE RESETTLEMENT ISSUES, DECISIONS, AND REforms, we go back to the July 1979 Geneva Conference. One of RP's most pressing concerns then was the US *domestic resettlement system*: Could it be expanded and improved quickly enough to meet the exponential growth targets set up at the Conference; and would it remain at State? House Immigration Subcommittee Chair Elizabeth Holtzman (D-NY) wanted to consider relocating this major function. As I perused our reform agenda, both concerns were up in the air. Any hope to salvage RP for the State Department would depend on sharpening the valuable tools we already possessed.

Domestic Resettlement Under Attack

At a May 1979 hearing before the House Judiciary Committee on the proposed Refugee Act, Holtzman questioned the HEW secretary Joseph Califano.

> Elizabeth Holtzman: Why shouldn't all the reception and placement [R & P] grant programs be consolidated in one place [HEW], once the refugee reaches this country? I am talking about the R & P grants from the State Department for the initial period.[1]
>
> Joseph Califano: There is no doubt in my mind that that is the best way to do it.[2]

In our view, however, a transfer of one of our biggest programs would harm RP and the State Department: It would remove our most valuable tool for integrating foreign and domestic aspects of refugee assistance; and it would sever our critical link to the private resettlement agencies. If the committee transferred the reception and placement functions to HEW, I envisioned RP as easy pickings for USAID to swoop in and grab the rest, thereby removing these vital diplomatic elements of international assistance to refugees.

We warned that congressional delay on our pending supplemental appropriations request was close to stopping these life-saving programs. The resolution of this problem would critically affect the next year.

Vulnerability

During the Geneva Conference, RP's coinciding startup, and its first two-and-a-half months, I'd had numerous talks with State Department leaders, inspection teams, and congressional staff about the domestic resettlement program. The Geneva Conference had notched up our domestic admissions program many levels. RP's Reception and Placement program had been a subject of intense scrutiny in recent House Judiciary Committee hearings that considered the pending Refugee Act. Under Reception and Placement, we provided per capita grants to *domestic voluntary resettlement agency partners* for each refugee sponsored and resettled in the United States through their networks. These initial ninety-day grants allowed us to assure that resettled refugees had a smooth landing and a good start in the United States.[3] HEW would provide cash and medical assistance, as needed.

I concluded that domestic resettlement represented RP's greatest vulnerability for a stealth takeover. If early on we lost the largest and most visible domestic program, the State Department would be in danger of losing all refugee programs; the international and foreign policy aspects would be separated. We, therefore, had many reasons to fight hard to keep domestic resettlement in the State Department and to avoid the disruption its loss would provoke.

Soon after the Geneva Conference, I called a meeting with the RP staff involved in domestic resettlement: "Tell me what *domestic resettlement* is and how it's done."

Nongovernmental Organization Agreements

Geneva, Switzerland, historically has been a center for humanitarian operations through networks focused on global needs. I was surprised to learn that the US domestic resettlement contract work with private refugee resettlement agencies, including daily interaction, was done by the refugee and migration section of the US Mission in Geneva. John Buche and Doug Hunter were the key resettlement officers at the mission, and I understood they were doing a remarkable job. This meant, however, that that RP had no official management or oversight capability in Washington for domestic resettlement.

Apparently, the State Department had contracts with twelve private voluntary organizations, NGOs, for resettlement. Most of the NGOs had been involved with refugee issues for years.[4] The contracts provided a per capita grant for each refugee resettled. The private agencies were expected to supplement the initial reception and placement grants with private resources raised from their organizational networks of congregations, parishes, synagogues, or other civic supporters. Each NGO also had a contractual relationship with HEW, Joe Califano's bailiwick, to provide each refugee, as needed, the access to longer-term federal cash and medical assistance. Initially, resettled refugees had been eligible for up to three years of federal support, but the duration was being reduced gradually.

Mary Kavaliunas showed me a copy of the existing NGO contracts. They included no federal guidance about expectations, suggested approaches, or outcomes. There was no provision for follow-up evaluation or performance assessment. The contracts had one brief paragraph describing resettlement, provisions regarding numbers to be resettled, the per capita amount, and the contract value.

The government's primarily anecdotal understanding of successful resettlement would not be acceptable going forward. Ingrid Walters and Jack Griswold of the Lutheran Immigration and Resettlement Service (LIRS) told me that the early agreements from the 1975 era basically said the government would admit refugees and LIRS would resettle them, providing a per capita grant to help defray the costs. As time went on, they said operations had become much more bureaucratic and complicated.

The RP team learned that we needed to provide guidance about service expectations and how resettlement was to be accomplished and tracked. As a first step, I established a contracting capability and transferred this work from Geneva to Washington. Mary Kavaliunas suggested I meet with some of the NGOs to get their take.

At a New York meeting, I saw several longstanding pros, including John McCarthy of the US Catholic Conference, Ingrid Walters of the Lutheran Immigrant Resettlement Services (LIRS), Carel Sternberg and Bob DeVecchi of the International Rescue Committee (IRC), and Wells Klein, reenergizer of the American Council for Nationality Service (ACNS).

These experienced resettlement pros knew about the substantial expansion in resettlement that President Carter had approved and were honestly worried that their networks would not be up to the task. The government, they maintained, did not understand resettlement fully and might not respond to the problems they were likely to face. I was disturbed, but inspired, by this meeting. I knew from experience that the formal agreement we needed was not a "contract" per se, but an arrangement called a "cooperative agreement." Under this collaborative arrangement, the government must be specific about the public/private cooperation expected, the activity planned, its modalities, funding, and the performance expectations. No such requirements were laid out in the existing agreements.

The more I learned about the domestic resettlement programs, the more my confidence plunged. How could a weak, newly-established RP possibly cope with what had become one of State's highest priority undertakings? And how could we do it quickly enough to satisfy the critics, meet the growing demand, and avoid losing the programs to another agency? I let the coordinator's staff know of my misgivings.

One morning after a meeting near the White House, at the New Executive Office Building, I asked friend and colleague Frank Moss to walk with me to a nearby McDonalds. Over coffee I told Frank, "I don't even have a knowledgeable person to write the expectations and modalities section of a decent cooperative agreement. We have no follow-up or monitoring capacity."

As we talked about this, a practical idea formed: Why don't we get the NGOs away with us for a few days and work out and agree on an acceptable cooperative agreement? They are the experts, so why don't we listen to them and invent a new cooperative agreement geared to the specific US resettlement needs? We would then develop national standards and expectations!

We developed these thoughts further over the next few days. I talked to NGO leaders and discovered they were in full agreement and amazed that anyone in the government cared or wanted their input. Clearly, we realized, there was need for better understanding on both sides. We invited the other federal departments to come onboard.

The Coolfont Conference Answer

In late 1979, after many conversations, RP met with the NGO leaders for three days at a conference center in wooded Coolfont, West Virginia. *Coolfont* would become a meaningful reference in RP lore of that time, marking where significant understandings took place among parties vital to refugee resettlement. We discussed the external help needed, the available options, and how to strengthen all parties.[5] Significant to the outcome was leadership from participants: the resettlement NGO community(including Iowa) and the affected federal agencies.

Frank Moss moderated the opening session, and I laid out RP's hopes and expectations. After that, the private agencies began to unburden, and it was a difficult session. NGOs spoke of feeling unappreciated or undervalued as well as resenting government's failure to talk to them as equal partners, not children.

My impression was that the agencies had been waiting for the new US refugee leaders to clarify precise expectations for domestic resettlement. I tried diplomatically to communicate our need for their help for a new cooperative agreement. However, the discussion did not move forward until a voluntary agency veteran, Wells Klein, spoke.

"They don't know what they want us to do. They've invited us here to do their job for them."

"I would put it differently, but yes, we need your help," I said.

After hours of critical NGO venting on the first day, I acknowledged their messages and tried to clear the air. "OK, let's move on."

The outcome was worth the time and the complexities of the discussions and emotions released. A new cooperative agreement was created to specify roles and responsibilities, goals and objectives, modalities, and funding arrangements. We debated and established performance evaluation and assessment mechanisms. Each NGO would constantly monitor their operations and take remedial steps where necessary. The government would undertake targeted audits and performance reviews and certify each agency's monitoring regime. Future agreements would incorporate the results. The government agreed to keep the per capita funding rates under review, and the agencies agreed to further supplement that amount with private resources.

We agreed to continue the existing practice whereby NGOs operating overseas selected one agency in each processing country to represent the interests of all NGOs vetting cases for presentation to the government, the Joint Voluntary Agency (JVA) system. In Thailand, for example, the International Rescue Committee (IRC) was the designated JVA.

The agencies to operate as JVAs in the field requested greater clarity on the *refugee resettlement priorities,* specifically categories identifying applicants and levels of persecution to be considered for US resettlement. I said we would undertake a review and soon assigned key RP staff. Shep Lowman, Victor Wolf, Jerry Hogenson, Judy Chavchavadze, with the Consular Affairs bureau, undertook an in-depth review that clarified and expanded the parameters of *six refugee processing priorities* (*see* Appendix C). They became the foundation for future *resettlement processing.* These resettlement priorities would continue as key elements, with situational refinements, to guide the American refugee selection efforts going forward.

We agreed to enhance the existing refugee transportation loan system, whereby approved refugees had to sign a promissory note guaranteeing to repay, eventually, funds advanced by the Intergovernmental Committee for European Migration, ICEM, to cover costs of their processing and transportation to the United States. The US Government, through our bureau, agreed to capitalize the ICEM Loan Fund, which refugee loan repayments would replenish. The NGOs agreed to collect the loan repayments, keeping 25 percent for processing costs. They also agreed to strengthen their refugee transportation loan repayment systems. The NGOs would have preferred grant-funded arrangements with no repayment requirement, but RP could not agree, due to sizeable funding involved and our belief that the loan repayment program gave refugees a personal stake in their own resettlement. HEW and Justice made specific contributions in their areas of competence at the conference, while acknowledging RP's lead role. They left it to us to carry the debate, and we left Coolfont as united as this disparate group could be.

Coolfont triggered significant breakthroughs in the process and advanced everyone toward improved government and private cooperation on domestic refugee resettlement. All of us had needed Coolfont.

Ralie Deffenbaugh, former head of Lutheran Immigration and Refugee Services (LIRS) told me that before the Coolfont Conference, most of the early allocations—which agency would handle which refugees, and where in the country they would be resettled—were organized by the private agencies (NGOs) among themselves. They were pragmatically filling the vacuum left by the government. Only later did the government gradually take over control of that important function.[6] I had promised to review, strengthen, and update the resettlement processing mechanisms. Most urgent was the antiquated way we allocated incoming refugees among the participating resettlement agencies. We needed to assure equitable and efficient geographic distribution throughout the country. If resettlement surged, this system had to sparkle with efficiency. Over the next few weeks, RP's Jim Lawrence was tasked to improve the existing process. With the installation of Wang computers, he modernized and improved the system.

During and after the Coolfont Conference, the surge in resettlement following the Geneva Conference was underway, and the revised cooperative agreements with NGOs went into effect. Real-time tests of the agreements' operational mechanisms showed that they worked as envisioned. The basic cooperative agreement carved out at Coolfont endured, with modifications and improvements.

Unlike several of our allies that implemented their domestic resettlement programs within their bureaucracies, the United States continued to rely on the private sector, including the faith-based agencies. We were interested in competence and capacity, including surge capacity, since large increases in US resettlement of Southeast Asia refugees were envisioned. In the coming weeks, the Presiding Bishop's Fund of the Episcopal Church (in discussions with Canon Samir Habibi and Marney Dawson) and the World Relief network representing evangelical churches (in discussions with Grady Mangrum) were added to our list of authorized refugee resettlement NGOs.

Dynamic Resettlement—"Constructive Ambiguity"

In the Refugee Programs bureau's early days, domestic refugee resettlement was one of the most contentious and hotly debated refugee issues between the executive and legislative branches. Domestic resettlement would remain controversial for years to come, yet we overcame the doubters. The unique contributions each partner brought to the program had to be harmonized for this valued venture to succeed. After the Geneva Conference, and due largely to Coolfont, a renewed and reinvigorated resettlement partnership developed.

As 1979 ended, a new, more dynamic legal arrangement had been negotiated and all partners agreed they had a better idea of the mutual expectations. Inevitable frictions and annoyances most often led to creative improvements in cooperation. I often referred to this arrangement as "constructive ambiguity." The endurance of this unique public-private cooperation in the contentious domestic resettlement world proved its greatest testimony.

In its consideration of the 1980 Refugee Act, Congress ultimately agreed to maintain the reception and placement (R and P) program in the State Department. We kept them apprised on reforms already in place and others about to come on line, and committees and inspectors became believers, especially when the NGOs testified that they thought the State Department programs would be more responsive to their needs than Health, Education, and Welfare (HEW).

The 1980 Refugee Act, soon to become law, recognized the State Department's primary role to set refugee policy and lead the executive branch in determining how many refugees would come into the country and from where. RP had come far on resettlement, the key initiative of the Geneva Conference, moving forward in more positive breakout ways than any of us had believed possible. The frankness and seriousness of Coolfont discussions precipitated changes that brought about state-of-the-art domestic resettlement programs for that era, including accountability at all levels.

15

SURVIVE AND PROSPER

THE EXISTENTIAL THREATS FACING RP IN ITS FIRST DAYS, plus the time-sensitive Geneva Conference imperatives, kept many balls constantly in the air—all demanding immediate attention. Delay was out of the question. Therefore, as RP overcame the congressional transfer threats in Washington, we simultaneously addressed the demands for better preparation of refugees for life in America, even as we sought safer protection and departure arrangements for the fleeing refugees in Southeast Asia. With the other reforms underway, RP's own short term survival agenda was set.

Plowshares of International Partnership

Surging refugee populations strained the reception and shelter capacities of Asian *first-asylum* countries, producing crowded and politically volatile refugee camps. Public health concerns were alarming. The UN High Commission for Refugees (UNHCR) identified this problem in its agenda for the Geneva Conference, and proposed two overflow camps to better handle the existing refugee populations and those still streaming in. UNHCR postulated that the overflow camps might have a calming effect on the nervous asylum countries, especially, Thailand, Indonesia and Malaysia.[1]

At the Geneva Conference, the United States had included $20 million in its budget for overflow or "refugee processing" camps. The Philippines, which could not make a financial or resettlement pledge at the conference, offered land to house a new camp. Shep Lowman told me that Indonesia offered similar facilities on Galang Island. UNHCR planned to establish overflow camps for fifty thousand refugees.

From Military Bataan to Refugee Bataan

Shep Lowman stopped in Manila on his way home from the Geneva Conference to tie down their offer. He met with President Ferdinand Marcos and Mrs. Imelda Marcos and through them with the key Philippine official responsible for this matter, General Gaudencio V. Tobias (Retd.), the head of the National Housing Authority (NHA). The general reviewed several proposed sites with Shep. They settled on a plot of land on historic Bataan Island, a key military post in World War II and a thirty-minute helicopter flight from Manila.

After waiting fruitless months for other governments to contribute, UNHCR moved ahead on the Philippine offer. A team of Philippine architects, engineers and construction specialists designed an overflow camp on Bataan Island and presented plans to UNHCR several months later. Unfortunately, available funding would accommodate only seventeen thousand refugees, fewer than originally expected. The UNHCR checked with the United States, still the only donor, for permission to proceed, to avoid breaking faith with first-asylum governments. They were watching all this closely. General Tobias informed us it would take about six months to complete camp construction.

Meanwhile, unexpected developments occurred throughout Southeast Asia: declines in camp populations and overcrowding. Several explanations were possible, including the impact of the expanded *third-country resettlement* programs; the weather constraints on new arrivals; possibly the Vietnamese government moratorium on mass boat exodus; and lack of follow-through on the SRV promise to promote orderly departures. Or, maybe, the SRV was buying time, now that world attention was spotlighting Vietnam. Whatever the reason, many workers breathed sighs of relief. This favorable trend was encouraging and raised a question: did we still need the overflow camps as earlier envisioned?

Expanded US resettlement had produced serious assimilation problems for the incoming refugees in language, employment (most refugees lacked basic skills for the US job market), and health, particularly tuberculosis. Congress was threatening to halt further resettlement unless these problems were addressed, especially the medical concerns. While we considered possible locations for a new training center to address the assimilation needs, a light went on regarding the overflow facility under construction on Bataan Island. We could add language training and other preparation skills there, alongside resettlement processing at the Philippine Refugee Processing Center (PRPC). The same could be done at a similar camp in Indonesia.

As these events unfolded in late 1979, a new refugee coordinator, Victor Palmieri, replaced Dick Clark. Before departing on an Asia orientation trip, Palmieri agreed to our plans for the Bataan training programs, including the recruitment of a qualified leader. On arrival in Thailand, he met with the country director for the Peace Corps Ann Morgan, whose record with the Peace Corps revealed extraordinary accomplishments. She was the person for implementing the language training and assimilation programs. Within weeks she was on the job in Washington, organizing the training programs in English language, vocational skills, and cultural orientation. Concurrently, the Intergovernmental Committee for European Migration (ICEM) (later named International Organization for Migration (IOM)) organized health screening, a principal concern of Congress.

Starting from nothing, Ann Morgan quickly decided on the goals, objectives, funding requirements, linkages with US partners, and her own staffing and logistical needs for an innovative Philippine Refugee Processing Center (PPRC).[2] Our first discussion persuaded me of her commitment and willingness to work with me and with Congress to obtain the funding required for this program.

I feared trouble getting State Department help for qualified PRPC staffing and logistical support and, thereby, losing our new team member. But Ann said, "If you'll stand with me all the way, I can pull the pieces together myself. I know many people who can help me do this. I'll need the money and lots of flexibility. I can make this happen."

Without questioning her optimism, I offered my hand and said, "Ann, we've got a deal." We were all amazed as we observed the program taking shape. Ann identified an assistant, Ed Geibel, a former

Peace Corps volunteer in Thailand then working at the headquarters in Washington. Ed became her only permanent RP support staff, an asset on the job.

Building English as a Second Language (ESL)

Ann Morgan recruited experienced agencies such as the Experiment in International Living (now World Learning) and the Center for Applied Linguistics to be the implementing partners. With them, she established the program's structure, curriculum, standards, practices, and operational guidelines. She hired the International Catholic Migration Commission (ICMC), in the Philippines, already working in Bataan, to recruit and train the Filipino nationals to teach English as a Second Language courses. A consortium of agencies headed by World Learning took on the same training role in Indonesia and Thailand. The locally-hired teachers did the day-to-day teaching, supervised by the American staff. The competence, performance, an affordability of these dedicated instructors were extraordinary.

The traditional grammar methods of teaching English were not likely to work. A curriculum was developed to teach the basic language and survival skills to cope with life in America, such as finding and keeping a job, describing medical problems, or dealing with other issues that would likely arise during their first few months in the United States. The training program evolved in various locations over the ensuing fifteen years. Keeping it relevant to the immediate resettlement needs remained a guiding principle. Refugee groups from other regions joined the mix over time and components were added to address their special needs. The success of this enterprise changed the perception of the processing centers as only holding or overflow camps. Whether in the Philippines, Thailand, or Indonesia, they served as lively educational centers. The money to support these centers had to come from very stingy congressional committees, and Ann Morgan simply overwhelmed them. In a low key, professional manner, she answered members' questions and addressed their concerns. They responded with the funds and promises to add more, if needed.

The United States was on a path to become the largest English language training and cultural orientation provider in the world, serving 500,000 refugees from Southeast Asia and almost a million worldwide. As the longest-serving RP official bridging the Carter and Reagan administrations, I could assure Ann Morgan the long-term support and continuity she needed to develop and expand these essential programs. Critical questions about the overflow camps in Southeast Asia never came up again, and the bureaucratic threats against the ESL (English as a Second Language) program were overcome.

Protection: Rescue at Sea and Anti-Piracy

It is irrefutable that Vietnamese escapees were aware from the start of the dangers inherent in clandestine boat departures. Motivations far outweighed the odds for survival. They stepped onto unseaworthy and overcrowded boats not because the grass was greener somewhere else but because draconian forces were driving them away. Pirates, an old scourge in the Southeast Asia region, took advantage of their desperation and intercepted rickety refugee boats to plunder and abuse. They knew refugees often had a little gold or money, usually representing their life savings, and they mercilessly ransacked, killed, or left scores of mothers, fathers, children, and grandparents to drown. Some took girls aged ten-to-fourteen years old, often with sisters or mothers, onto their ships, gang raped them for days or weeks, then threw them overboard, expecting them to drown.

To corroborate this horror, *Reader's Digest* reported on the case of a boat that slipped away from Can Tho, Vietnam, on March 24, 1985, with 117 passengers aboard, including thirty-six children under ten. Four days later, it drifted across the path of five pirate vessels. Only one man survived.[3]

"More than half the boats don't make it," was the message passed along by many refugees. No one knew if this was true, but the most informed observers thought the numbers were in the tens to hundreds of thousands. Regardless of the numbers, I thought, *It's incredible that so many people continued to try, another measure of their extreme fears.* Though unseaworthy vessels doomed many boat people from the outset, many reported deaths resulted from the pirate attacks. Those grew in frequency and brutality, searing the world's conscience.

Anti-piracy and the Geneva Conference

It was not until July 1979 that extensive press coverage focused world attention on the appalling tragedies of piracy, including the attacks by Thai and Malaysian fishermen in the South China Sea and the Gulf of Siam. The specter of brutal attacks on the already-threatened, defenseless men, women, and children provoked universal condemnation, with calls for action at the Geneva Conference. Vice President Mondale reiterated President Carter's commitment to help refugees at risk on the high seas, including with American military assets.[4] The UN high commissioner for refugees, Poul Hartling, reminded governments and shippers of their special protection responsibilities to rescue the refugees in distress at sea.[5]

Following the Geneva Conference, the UNHCR renewed calls for commercial shipping vessels in those dangerous waters to abide by the "best traditions of the sea" and come to the aid of boats in distress. Most commercial shippers were hesitant and ignored these pleas that, if answered, could disrupt schedules or force them to incur delays and expense.

To support these calls for help and to overcome the asylum countries' reluctance to land refugees rescued at sea, UNHCR protection director, Michel Moussali, led governments to extend specific resettlement offers to rescued refugees. In August 1979, UNHCR established RASRO (Rescue at Sea Resettlement Offers) and DISERO (Disembarkation Resettlement Offers), backed with resettlement assurances from the United States and seven other governments. These programs assured "commercial ships that people rescued by merchant ships flying flags of states that did not resettle refugees would be disembarked at a welcoming port, primarily Singapore, to be resettled quickly [within 90 days]."[6]

The early results of RASRO and DISERO were slow and sporadic. But over time the program showed progress, largely due to the increased awareness of commercial shippers. Bilaterally, several governments and humanitarian agencies dispatched ships to Southeast Asian waters to rescue victims spotted on the rough seas. However, governmental rescue efforts—like the French Navy frigate *Balny*, the French cargo ship *Le Goelo*, and the German freighter *Cap Anamur*—proved to be more distraction than help. First-asylum governments saw them as magnets that attracted even more refugees.[7] Nevertheless, these efforts continued.

Humanitarians were inspired by the stories of heroism on behalf of refugees in danger at sea. The most remarkable was undoubtedly a Gulf of Thailand rescue in 1979, involving Ted Schweitzer, a UNHCR field officer stationed in Songkhla, Thailand. He dared to confront the lawless pirates abusing refugees on tiny Ko Kra Island, about thirty miles off Thailand's eastern coast and made repeated rescue attempts. Over several months, his efforts saved over a thousand men, women and children. His was truly an inspiring story of compassion and determination.

International antipiracy efforts began early the next year, 1980, on a large scale. The Royal Thai Government launched sea and air patrols with US funding. When continuation funding could not be assured without more donors, other interested governments stepped in to avoid the shutdown of this essential program.

Assuring safe passage by sea remained a key refugee protection concern, and the United States raised the piracy troubles at the thirtieth- and thirty-first sessions of UNHCR's executive committee meetings in October 1980 and 1981. The United States played a significant role in addressing this issue in the remaining years of the Carter administration and beyond.

Concerns over refugee safety gave birth to an alternative protection concept: *orderly departures* from Vietnam. As envisioned, this program would operate with the acquiescence of the new communist government and be available for high priority refugee and immigration cases. If successful, it could dramatically lessen the need for clandestine boat departures.

Orderly Departure Program

To almost everyone's amazement, the Socialist Republic of Vietnam (SRV) agreed to discuss an *orderly departure mechanism*, resulting in a January 1979 SRV announcement initiating the formal discussions. To represent interests of resettlement countries, the UN High Commission for Refugees in Geneva was asked to take the lead. The deputy high commissioner, Dale de Haan, an American colleague of long-standing and a former senior staff aide to Sen. Ted Kennedy (D-MA), led the UNHCR delegation to Hanoi. He initiated the orderly departure negotiations with the SRV in early 1979 and the formal discussions took place in Hanoi in February and May 1979, culminating in a formal agreement to initiate the Orderly Departure Program (ODP).[8] Developments continued to move quickly. The SRV attended the Geneva Conference in July and made a surprising pledge to stop the mass exodus of boat refugees and promote orderly departure. The SRV pledged to allow ten thousand emigrants to leave each month through the ODP, but the initial results, as expected, were poor. Two months after the Vietnamese pledge, only 200 exit permits had been issued.[9]

Gaining agreement on the ODP procedures was complex and time-consuming, but arrangements were eventually agreed for adding applicants to the ODP rolls and organizing departures. Travelers destined for the United States spent an additional week in the Phanot Nikhon Transit Center near Bangkok for the final immigration clearance. Transportation, medical screening, and document processing were coordinated by ICEM.

Almost from the beginning, the Soviet Republic of Vietnam (SRV) wanted to fill the departure lists with people they considered undesirable and to deny the approval to many persons in whom the United States expressed strong interest. The SRV seemed especially eager to rid itself of the ethnic Chinese and those considered politically unreliable. An official SRV–UNHCR working group met in Hanoi twice each month to resolve the differences. Vietnamese lethargy in granting the exit permits continued, with large fees exacted from the applicants, many without the means.

Why did the SRV agree to orderly departures after having forced so many to flee in boats? My discussions with many knowledgeable colleagues in Washington and overseas on this question led to a pragmatic answer: from the SRV's perspective, it looks better to see people flying out of Ho Chi Minh City on organized flights than having thousands embarking on flimsy boats in a chaotic exodus. Plus, they could better control the pace of ODP departures, and exact fees.[10]

To start the ODP, the United States and other resettlement countries made many compromises in the early years. To demonstrate interest, the American side immediately came up with a list of almost ten thousand ODP candidates. But, as 1979 ended, we realized that the departures would be minimal for the immediate future because of continued Vietnamese intransigence. At least there was reason for hope, which was later vindicated; a safe alternative to dangerous clandestine departures by sea was in place.

The work to create viable *orderly departure* mechanisms continued through the remaining months of the Carter administration. The incoming Reagan team would need to build on that work. If the mechanisms worked, ODP could break the back of perilous boat escapes.

16

REFUGEE ACT OF 1980

IAN SIMINGTON, A SENIOR OFFICIAL IN THE AUSTRALIAN Department of Immigration and Ethnic Affairs, was one of the first foreign officials I met while the acting RP director. We became close collaborators, and through Ian I met Gervais Appave and Rodney Inder, highly valued colleagues among the Australian immigration officials. When we met, the refugee issues were rocketing to the top of Australia's foreign policy agenda due to the large number of Southeast Asia refugee arrivals.

Ian and I talked about the Australian worries that, as a US ally and an asylum country, Australia might be overwhelmed if new resettlement programs got underway in Asia. Australians were concerned that the rest of the international refugee community sometimes believed the Americans isolated themselves or took unexpected approaches. Ian believed that co-operation from the other countries depended on American engagement in the global humanitarian system as partners. Australians, he emphasized, attached hopeful significance to the refugee legislation in the US Congress. I assured him the Australian concerns would be taken seriously.

When I met with refugee and foreign policy officials from both the United States and other countries, they agreed we were on the cusp of a global refugee explosion, and all agreed we must prepare for it. A key US requirement was to set up a forward-looking statutory base for the refugee programs. The legislative base for American involvement to that point existed in the 1948 Displaced Persons Act, the 1953 Refugee Relief Act, the 1962 Migration and Refugee Assistance Act, and general authorities offered to the attorney general and the HEW secretary.[1] However, the 1951 Refugee Convention and the 1967 Protocol were the reference points for international refugee matters; also, earlier provisions primarily covered refugee relief overseas, with minimal guidance for resettlement. The existing legislation did not anticipate the new international collaborative relationships required at that time.

The Genesis of the New Refugee Act

The proposed refugee act had its genesis at a February 1977 congressional hearing chaired by Rep. Joshua Eilberg (D-PA), chairman of the House Judiciary subcommittee on immigration, citizenship, and international law. Included at the hearing were the State Department's human rights leaders from HA including, George Warren, Jr., the senior advisor; James Carlin, the deputy assistant secretary; and Shep Lowman, the director of HA's program and asylum division. The hearing's purpose was to "establish a legislative policy governing the admission of refugees into the United States." The ideas that flowed from the 1977 and later hearings were incorporated into the proposed legislation submitted to Congress in 1979 by Coordinator Dick Clark and introduced by the House Judiciary chairman Peter Rodino the next month. A companion bill was introduced in the Senate.[2]

Dick Clark informed me that his office had proposed this new legislation and David Martin in Humanitarian Affairs (HA) had been working on it with the relevant congressional committees for over two years. The legislation was close to passage. Margaret Carpenter, the responsible officer on the coordinator's staff, worked with the legal advisor and the relevant congressional committee staffers: Jerry Tinker with Sen. Kennedy, Dick Day with Sen. Alan Simpson, Jim Cline with Chairman Rodino, and Skip Endres and Pete Regis with Subcommittee Chairman Romano Mazzoli. These people were the most vital to opening legislative doors for refugee matters.

When I arrived on the refugee scene, the Judiciary Committees were conducting hearings. Already, the admission of large numbers of Indochina refugees was a major concern that affected the discussions about the proposed Refugee Act. Concerns in Congress about a large Indochina refugee influx included the potential impact on American labor and on the minority communities. To counter these concerns, the refugee coordinator worked with the American NGO community and arranged special expert testimonies. Appearing, among others, were Lane Kirkland, the president of the AFL/CIO, and Bayard Rustin, a revered civil rights leader. In their testimony, each urged US assistance for the Indochina war victims. They objected to the congressional committees' past use of constituent concerns to justify denying help.

New Refugee Bureau and New Act

The proposed Refugee Act presented many immediate challenges for State's planned Bureau for Refugee Programs. The bureau would have to develop the proficiency to assess and document refugee needs in all regions of the world and to determine the applicability of durable solutions. Mechanisms to acquire the necessary global funding had to be established. Working with HEW, INS, and the NGO community, the bureau must overhaul the domestic resettlement regimes and prepare for major expansions.

Congressional hearings on the proposed refugee law were lengthy, instructive, and contentious. Each stakeholder had opportunities to argue views. Passage was originally envisioned for 1979; events forced delay into the next year.

Improvements by the US Refugee Act of 1980

The Refugee Act of 1980, Public Law 96–212, was enacted by Congress on March 3, 1980, and signed into law by President Jimmy Carter on March 17, 1980. It became effective on April 1 that year.

The new law made several significant improvements.[3] First, it brought the United States in line with the formal international Refugee Convention by defining refugees as persons of special humanitarian concern. Second, it established the worldwide focus of US refugee programs henceforth and removed past geographic or ideological restrictions, formerly focused on the persons from the communist countries or the Middle East. Third, it created a new mechanism for the legal admission of refugees, specifying that each applicant had to prove individual persecution under the criteria enumerated in the Act. Previously, absent a more formal legal mechanism, the attorney general had exercised *parole authority* to admit the refugees to the United States. Indochinese parolees had *presumptive eligibility* for US refugee admission if they were assessed as members of the *persecuted* classes. Proof of individual persecution had not been required.

The attorney general's parole authority was limited to 17,400 refugees annually but could be increased for emergencies, as had been done for the Hungarians, Cubans, and Indochinese. The initial intention of *parole authority* to address individual cases of humanitarian hardship had, in recent years, been stretched to cover emergency admissions. The revision transferred emergency admissions authority from the attorney general to the president, since admission decisions had both foreign and domestic policy implications. It also reduced from two years to one year the period when refugees were *conditional entrants* in the United States before being granted the status of permanent resident alien .

The fourth improvement was provision for an annual consultation between the president and Congress on refugee admissions. It gave the president unilateral permission to admit up to fifty thousand refugees annually as a normal flow, while requiring consultation with Congress on admissions above that level. This flexibility met current and future requirements, a major step toward action-oriented refugee programs. These provisions anticipated comprehensive worldwide planning and allowed Congress a voice in annual refugee admissions.

Fifth, the 1980 Refugee Act provided a more equitable way to assist refugees once they arrived, thereby integrating domestic refugee assistance into the welfare system. In HEW, a new Office for Refugee Resettlement (ORR) was established. After an eighteen-month transition period, the Refugee Act authorized the federal government to reimburse state and local governments one hundred percent for the costs to assist refugees for three years.

The sixth and final improvement was the formal authorization of the position of the US coordinator for refugee affairs to harmonize US interagency and international efforts.

This landmark legislation, which would guide future American refugee efforts, benefitted greatly from the untiring work of the late Sen. Edward Kennedy (D-MA).

17

DARK CLOUDS

IN THE MONTHS LEADING TO THE JULY 1979 GENEVA Conference, conditions had worsened for all the refugees in Southeast Asia. Fearing the donor and resettlement countries were abandoning them, first-asylum governments vowed to deal with the refugee problem on their own by drastic measures. They promised forced repatriation, denial of entry (especially by boat) and the harsh treatment of all refugees remaining in their territories unless they got massive and immediate help from the major donor and resettlement countries. They were aiming for an ASEAN ban on new arrivals by June 30, 1979, close to the conference.

Kampuchea (Cambodia), July 1979–January 1981

"Democratic Kampuchea" had become Cambodia's official name after Pol Pot's Khmer Rouge took power in 1975. (Cambodia, the former name, would not be restored until 1993, with the monarchy.)

Although Kampuchea did not generate "boat people," it had been the elephant in the room in Geneva. While the conference raised hopes that the Vietnamese refugee situation might move in a more positive direction, reports of the Kampuchean holocaust were sending shock waves around the world. This was happening in the aftermath of a Vietnamese military victory over Kampuchea a few months earlier (December 1978), that resulted in the establishment of a pro-Vietnamese Kampuchean state, the People's Republic of Kampuchea (PRK), with Heng Samrin as the chief of state.

The Vietnamese victory interrupted the Khmer Rouge enslavement of the people and sent them scattering in all directions. Some looked for family members, some headed for their former homes; some hunted for food and medical care; others just wanted to go anywhere for a fresh start. Thinking that international help would be found in Thailand, multitudes moved in that direction.

However, the Thai Government, already hosting large Khmer populations and anticipating the massive numbers of new arrivals, closed their border. New arrivals were to be kept on the Thai-Kampuchea border and designated as "displaced persons" or "illegal migrants," not "refugees," just as the Thai had earlier refused to recognize the Vietnamese and Laotians as refugees. The government instituted a policy of "humane deterrence" for the Khmer who had arrived inside Thailand earlier. That policy resulted in spartan living arrangements and no access to the resettlement governments. To reinforce their hardline policy, the Thai military forced thousands of previously-admitted Khmer back across the border in June 1979 at the ancient Preah Vihear Temple, which dated to the sixth-century Khmer, or Angkor, Empire. It had been a disputed border site between Thailand and the Khmer. The Thai military pushed some displaced people back through mine fields. UNHCR estimated that at least three thousand people were killed.[1] Reports of this hostility put Kampuchea on the world's radar.

Following pleas from the international community, the Thai made one exception to their hardline policy. Following the Preah Vihear pushbacks, the secretary of state Cyrus Vance promised at a July 1979 ASEAN meeting that the United States would coordinate international assistance for the endangered Khmer most at risk. Based on these promises, the Thai temporarily moved large numbers to the holding centers deeper inside Thailand.[2] They later opened several refugee camps in Thailand, including at Khao-I-Dang and Sa Kaeo, to house many of the 160,000 Khmer people who were thought to be the most at risk. However, the Thai Government continued to deny access to the resettlement countries, as they were concerned that resettlement would act as a magnet drawing even more to try and reach Thailand.

Conditions inside Kampuchea remained precarious; the country was so close to economic collapse that the new Vietnamese–imposed government (with Heng Samrin as president and Hun Sen as foreign minister) was forced to appeal to the international community for help. The foreign minister Hun Sen's July 1979 appeal claimed that over two million lives were at risk.

Kampuchea Border Tragedy

About eight o'clock one August evening, 1979, the Washington refugee programs team was introduced to the unfolding Kampuchean border crisis in an urgent way. We were reviewing the day's work in my cramped seventh floor cubicle when Nora Day, one of RP's secretaries, rushed in.

"Ambassador Abramowitz is calling from Thailand. He wants to talk about Kampuchea." Nora's voice sounded urgent.

Shep Lowman left to take the call and returned about twenty minutes later.

"Jim, I think you'd better join me on this call."

This was my first official contact with Mort Abramowitz, known for zinging calls and cables to State for failure to respond aggressively to atrocities in Kampuchea. When Mort realized he was on the line with the new guy in RP, he unloaded.

"Washington has been dragging its feet for months! People have been dying, and now it's really hit the fan. The long-awaited flow of refugees out of Kampuchea has finally begun to arrive in Thailand. We think maybe upwards of forty thousand people are congregated at the Thai border and more are on the way!"

The worst was yet to come: "It's raining. There is no shelter. They are hungry and sick. If we don't get help soon, they're all going to die. We can't depend on the Thai Government for immediate help."

"Mort, what's the most urgently-needed now?"

"Shelter, food, medical care, attention."

"I need to talk to colleagues here who know a lot more about this than I do," I said. "I promise that someone will call you back soon with a plan. We will not leave here tonight until help is on the way."

Mort had our response in an hour, as soon as our Asia team—Shep Lowman, Hank Cushing, Jim Schill, Bill Krug, and John Lloyd—came up with a temporary solution. A quick contact revealed that the Office of

Foreign Disaster Assistance (OFDA) in USAID had hundreds of tents in nearby warehouses that could be airlifted within hours. USAID's Food for Peace and the World Food Program (WFP) would get food on the way soon.

After others left, I stayed around that night, thinking over Mort's warning... *and more are on the way.*

I drafted a memo about the evening's developments to the under secretary for political affairs, stressing the need to plan for a larger Kampuchean tragedy.

The under secretary sent a quick response, establishing a new State task force, the Kampuchea Relief Group, KRG, with Refugee Programs (RP) in charge. In Bangkok, Mort Abramowitz established the Kampuchea Emergency Group (KEG) to manage events on the ground, with Lionel Rosenblatt in charge and Mike Eiland as the deputy.

Within a few days, Asia expert Tom Barnes was assigned to head up the KRG. He arrived at my cubicle, saying he would need an office, secretarial support, staff, and a telephone. He wanted to be housed on the seventh floor to have quick access to State's leaders.

I stared at him and then let out a chuckle of disbelief: "None of those things is available, apart from the telephone. Certainly, you must know this is RP ... but we'll work something out."

That day we moved another desk into my cubicle and arranged for another telephone hookup. My secretary would help Tom as well. Ben Read authorized me to issue a notice to all of the State and USAID offices, calling for volunteers to assist in this crisis. I also negotiated permanent office space on the first floor to be available in a few weeks. The Kampuchea Relief Group was up and running.

Another Asia expert, Andy Antipas showed up the next day to be KRG deputy. Tom and I looked at each other and laughed. "We simply cannot fit a third desk into this office," I opined, but no other space was immediately available.

I was impressed that the KRG attracted volunteers of high quality. Margaret McKelvey from USAID's Office of Foreign Disaster Assistance (OFDA) impressed me so much I later offered her an appointment in our Africa office. She became one of America's top Africa refugee experts.

Practical Issue, a Floating Office

State was offering little help finding permanent RP digs. I gave my seventh-floor cubicle to the Kampuchea group and decided, simultaneously, to demonstrate State's lack of serious office support. I began to float. Daily, RP's five Foggy Bottom locations needed my attention, and I moved among them, file folders and call slips in hand. I returned to RP's seventh-floor headquarters in the evenings to regroup with the other RP leaders to complete the day's business. I made a point of letting State Department leaders know of this irony. The CEO of State's most consequential foreign policy operation had no office, cubicle, or telephone.

Hun Sen's Appeal

The international community, including the United States, reacted quickly to Kampuchean Foreign Minister Hun Sen's July 1979 appeal. International attention was targeted on the border Khmer and those in Thailand, and the acute needs inside Kampuchea. Donor governments and the United Nations considered each need urgent, especially along the Thai border, where tens of thousands continued to arrive. America was to be a major donor to the massive UN appeal for Kampuchea, and RP was responsible to secure the US funding. On November 5, 1979, the UN secretary general convened a pledging conference on "Emergency relief to the people of Kampuchea." Seventy-six states and the European Union (EU) attended, and they pledged $210 million.

The United Nations agreed to institutional arrangements for responding to Hun Sen's urgent appeal: food inside Kampuchea through the World Food Program, WFP; border distribution by UNICEF, and medical care through ICRC, the International Committee of the Red Cross. The United States and several other donors wanted a lead agency for the border populations, and they agreed to a UN proposal for ICRC and UNICEF to be the temporary coordinating presence on the border. The Thai Government worried that a permanent presence would be a magnet drawing more into Thailand. We agreed to their terms although we disagreed with the rationale.

UNHCR played a minor role in these relief arrangements and drew heavy criticism from the United States for its lackluster performance and timidity. One notable exception was UNHCR field officer Mark Malloch Brown of the UK, who helped establish badly needed Kampuchean refugee camps in Thailand in the fall of 1979 and courageously thwarted the forcible repatriation (*refoulement*) of thousands of refugees.[3]

By November 1979 the Royal Thai Government had opened several refugee camps to handle the 160,000 Khmer inside Thailand, including at Khao-I-Dang and Sa Kaeo. By the end of 1979, Khao-I-Dang was the largest settlement of the Khmer outside Phnom Penh. These refugees came under the care and protection of UNHCR. However, they were still subject to the Thai humane deterrence policy, which meant they could not be considered for resettlement in third countries.

Even as it issued appeals for international aid, the new Kampuchean government was still trying to defeat the remaining Khmer Rouge forces inside the country. It launched a military offensive in September 1979 to destroy the Khmer Rouge remnants, forcing many to flee. Both the KR and the non-KR opposition were at or moving toward the Thai border.

As the border populations grew, the Thai permitted separate border camps for the KR and non KR populations, respectively. The KR camps were at Nong Pru and Tap Prik, and the non-KR camps were at Ban Sangae, Nong Samet, Mak Mun, and Nong Chan.[4] At its peak, there were over 750,000 people at the border, and the Thai still refused permission to cross into Thailand. Two Khmer groups were of concern: (1) nearly half a million congregated at the Thai border but denied entrance to Thailand; and (2) the 160,000 at-risk inside Thailand under special arrangements.

In October 1979, the Thai foreign minister was shocked by conditions when he visited the precarious Khmer border camps. Shortly thereafter, Thailand announced a new "open door policy" to allow the temporary asylum for border Khmer barely surviving—up to ninety thousand. The "open door" lasted a few months, until early 1980, when the Thai Government complained that the meager international response to its requests for refugee aid had convinced them once again to close the door, although the international community was providing unprecedented support.

The Land Bridge Initiative

In December 1979, British relief worker Robert Ashe, with Kampuchea colleagues, started what worked as a land bridge. Using the Nong Chan refugee camp as their logistics base, they distributed food, seeds and tools to Khmer drawn to the border in search of food. This initiative succeeded beyond expectations, and within six months it was feeding over seventy thousand people. In 1981, the land bridge provided food and seeds to almost 700,000 Khmer in Western Kampuchea.[5] During these years, the famine in Kampuchea was still a grave concern.

The Air Bridge

The dilapidated transport system in Kampuchea made getting food and other assistance into and across the country especially complicated. RP became involved when a plan formed for daily flights, an air bridge, starting in October 1979. Given the security and logistical concerns, major donors were assigned specific months for flying in food and medical supplies. The annual international budget for this program was over $100 million. The goal was to fly thirty thousand tons of food per month through the port of Sihanoukville (formerly Kompong Som). Daily flights begun in mid-October were expected to reach one thousand tons per day.

Most other countries were already operational when the US rotation drew near. No RP staff had logistical experience for air delivery nor could anyone in the State Department remember ever organizing such an airlift.

Perplexed, I thought, *How do I organize this venture and make it work?* I mentioned this concern to RP's Jim Lawrence, who responded without hesitation. "I can do that. I'll find out how things like this are done and make the contacts to get it underway."[6]

I appreciated another can-do attitude, especially from a new member of the team. Jim Lawrence chartered an Alaska Air C–130 cargo plane, had a UN logo painted on it, got it to Bangkok loaded with food, arranged for privately donated medical supplies, and with refugee emergency fund money got that lifeline ferrying between Bangkok, Thailand, and Sihanoukville, Kampuchea, during the month. Our air bridge plan worked flawlessly. This proved again the life-threatening obstacles an enthusiastic, confident spirit can overcome.

The air delivery goal of thirty-thousand tons per month was only partially achieved, however. This was out of our hands, as we learned that much of the food did not reach the countryside due to the large amounts being siphoned off to the Khmer Rouge. And, some food probably made its way to Vietnam. Also, eventually raised were questions on the extent of the real famine.

These developments reminded me of a US congressional hearing on the Kampuchea Relief Act in Fall 1979:

"Why should we send so much food if most up it ends up feeding the Vietnamese and Khmer Rouge armies?" one congressman had asked the head of Catholic Relief Services.

"Sir, if only half gets through to the people in need, then we should double our contribution."

American Governors' Perspectives

Iowa Governor Robert Ray was monitoring these same issues from his office in Des Moines. In November 1979, a few months after the Geneva Conference, the National Governors Association invited Governor Ray to join their delegation to China.[7] On the return leg, he suggested a stop in Thailand to visit camps holding long-term refugees hoping for US resettlement, like the Tai Dam people. Many of these urban-educated civil servants and former French soldiers had worked for the Americans, and about 1,200 had resettled in Iowa. However, when the group landed in Bangkok, Ambassador Abramowitz suggested inspecting the desperate situation of Khmer on the Thai border. Recent visits by Rosalynn Carter, Dick Holbrooke, Lionel Rosenblatt, and Mort Abramowitz had helped heighten public awareness of the appalling tragedy.

The governors arrived at the Sa Kaeo border camp on day five of its existence. Thirty-thousand Khmer were there in the roughest, most forlorn circumstances, dispersed across empty fields and no shelter. The death count was fifty to one hundred daily, and corpses were bulldozed into a mass grave. There was little food, and the relief organizations bought what they could find at local markets to distribute to anyone able to stand and get in line. When the governors returned to Bangkok, they met again with Ambassador Abramowitz to discuss action. Mort focused on the desperate need for food, medicine, and money.

On the flight home from Thailand, the group talked of little else but the most horrifying disaster they had ever seen. Back home, Governor Ray gave the Des Moines Register his camp photos, which flashed all around the state the next day and galvanized support for renewed humanitarian action. The governor turned to Ken Quinn, who quickly proposed Iowa's Sending Help to Aid Refugees and End Starvation (SHARES). Between Thanksgiving and Christmas 1979, Iowa raised over $500,000, about $1.5 million in current dollars. On Christmas Day, their food and medicine reached Khmer people stuck on the border; more food donated by Iowans went into Kampuchea through the relief organizations over the coming months. For the next two years, volunteer Iowan doctors and nurses treated patients at Khao-I-Dang.

Several hundred Khmer died during attacks by Vietnamese military on the Mak Mun and Nong Chan *displaced persons* camps in mid-1980. The ostensible reason for the aggression was UNHCR's earlier *repatriation* of Khmer fighters, who the Vietnamese regarded as something akin to terrorists. The Vietnamese stopped the food deliveries at the border, and ICRC and UNICEF withdrew in protest. UNICEF later returned. ICRC did not.

Some Khmer Return Home

Despite food diversions, logistics crises, interagency skirmishes, and warring factions everywhere, the 1979–1980 international efforts resulted in significant survival successes for the war-stressed Khmer. Eventually, many returned home from the Thai border, carrying rice seed given by their humanitarian partners. They planted the rice, their basic crop, in time for the monsoon rains. Within a year, they were taking home enough seed to sow more than one acre and increase rice production substantially.

This was a momentous period of hope.[8] It became normal again to see the Khmer rice farmers standing in newly planted fields, gazing over a watery landscape, hoping and waiting for the harvest ahead. For those farmers, the monsoon downpours were not nuisance rains but were what made survival possible. Being back home, however difficult, spoke of a possible future. Helped by the UN, farmers in the best rice-growing areas of Kampuchea produced enough food to allow much of the country slowly to regain agricultural self-sufficiency as fears of imminent famine diminished.

Khmer at the End of the Carter Administration

In late 1980, as the Carter administration was ending, the UN High Commission for Refugees (UNHCR) announced that 200,000 Khmer people living on or near the Thai border had returned home. However, the other 230,000 would remain precariously on the border until peace prospects improved and they too could return safely. A new UN organization specifically to serve the border Khmer was under discussion.

For the border Khmer and the Khmer inside Thailand, no *durable solution* was available or under consideration as the Carter years ended. No international agency had a protection mandate for the border Khmer. Durable solutions would become possible only in the years ahead.

Back at State, our Kampuchea Relief Group, KRG, moved to Main State's first floor. Significant to the RP team was the space found a bit later in a nearby building. My "shoe-leather protest" had succeeded.

Within a few months, RP would need to establish new task forces to plan and manage the US responses to complex crises in Afghanistan, the Horn of Africa, Cuba, and Haiti. Kampuchea had been the first of many.

18

PIVOTAL STARTUP

July 1979 to the End of the Carter Administration

EXPLOSIVE HUMAN EMERGENCIES IN KEY WORLD REGIONS confronted the new team in the early months, a time unlike any other in my professional experience (other RP staff later expressed the same view). Suddenly, refugee crisis places in South Asia, Central America, and the Horn of Africa erupted in the Carter administration's last year. Added to our work in Southeast Asia and incorporating the initiatives of the Geneva Conference on Indochinese Refugees and the Kampuchean holocaust, our massive mission quickly expanded.

The carefully crafted and vetted Refugee Act, making its way through Congress in 1979, had anticipated a future worldwide refugee scope. The RP team witnessed the global onslaught, forming fast and furiously in real time even before the Act became law. Adding global planning to the priority list months earlier seemed prescient.

Somalia, Horn of Africa

Within days of RP's formal establishment, Karl Beck, our new Africa office director from the Peace Corps, alerted me to another destabilizing crisis. This time it was a failed Somali invasion of Ethiopia's Ogaden region. Defeated in battle, hundreds of thousands of ethnic Somalis fled toward the Somali desert. Quickly, a special Somalia Task Force was formed outside RP's regular bureaucratic structure to manage American involvement in this newest crisis. We estimated over 700,000 refugees in flight, the first of many Horn of Africa crises to come.

Afghanistan

Between Christmas 1979 and the New Year 1980, most people in RP, including our recently arrived director and the US refugee coordinator's office, were out for a holiday break. As acting director, I planned to use that time to clean out accumulated paper and better organize my work. One morning I noticed unusually heavy cable traffic, but not from Southeast Asia. That was when I learned the USSR, intending to bring Afghanistan solidly back into the communist fold, had invaded Afghanistan, which they called that "rebel" country. Afghan population flows in the millions were expected, moving toward Pakistan and Iran. The upshot for the Refugee Programs bureau would be to organize a US response on behalf of millions in flight from Afghanistan.

As staff filtered back from the holiday break, we set up the Afghan Refugee Task Force (ARTF). Its work also was to include keeping eyes on the impact the Soviet invasion might have on the movement of Jews and other minorities from the Soviet Union.

Cuba and Haiti Boat People

Within days of the Horn of Africa news, a boat exodus arose close to home, involving thousands of Cuban citizens fleeing from the Port of Mariel and headed for the US shores. There were simultaneous boat departures from Haiti. Immediately, we set up the Cuba-Haiti Task Force to help those distressed populations requiring urgent US assistance.

Startup Accomplishments

RP's four individual task forces—Kampuchea, Afghanistan, Somalia, and Cuba-Haiti —joined the list of large ongoing refugee programs throughout the world, all involving the United States.

Geneva Conference decisions drove Indochina actions forward, coinciding with the formal establishment of refugee programs in State.

From their shaky beginnings, when survival prospects were questionable, the new team faced down these awesome global challenges and threats, as described later. They survived and reached higher than could have been imagined a few months earlier. The dedication, systems and practices established during that pivotal period equipped RP to face growing refugee challenges with confidence.

Through RP, the State Department's accomplishments during this pivotal period of the Carter administration and into the early Reagan months influenced and enhanced American foreign policy in numerous ways:

- Correcting self-inflicted and near-fatal wounds and infusing a lethargic refugee program with a vital mission, renewed energy, commitment, and purpose
- Guiding American and global refugee programs and operations through near and long-term actionable goals and objectives
- Creating an enduring financial resource base for responses to America's refugee challenges and to reinvigorate the emerging global humanitarian system through the first comprehensive American refugee budget
- Repairing frayed and critical relationships with the US Congress and the NGOs
- Implementing the anticipated Refugee Act of 1980 and its legal framework for US refugee assistance (which remains in place)
- Launching and implementing the world's largest refugee rescue initiative since World War II, via the Geneva Conference of 1979, with piracy on the agenda and orderly departure from Vietnam a reality, although used little, yet
- Assisting the rescue of Kampuchea's genocide survivors and addressing survival risks caused by war, famine, poor health and nutrition, and a hostile government in complete breakdown
- Responding to layers of refugee crises in the former Soviet Union, Horn of Africa, South Asia, and Central America
- Demonstrating State Department capability to manage crisis programs successfully

As 1980 ended, our team's responses in the first year proved to have been visibly swift. Beyond Southeast Asia, the refugee global landscape—Africa, the Middle East, Eastern Europe and the Soviet Union, South Asia, and the Americas—was less certain. Yet RP's people and systems were operational and deeply engaged to address those needs.

19

FROM THE MANAGEMENT HUB

I WAS ACTING DIRECTOR OF THE REFUGEE PROGRAMS BUreau, waiting for an appointed director scheduled to arrive by fall, 1979. There were management decisions that could not be deferred:

- Correct the problems identified by investigative and inspection reports
- Establish new communication links with the stakeholders
- Convince Congress to approve critical funding
- Reform domestic resettlement

Misgivings lingered about the State Department's on-again/off-again support for its new, critical bureau during its reorganization phase, and the implications were troubling. RP was not the ubiquitous *Star Trek Enterprise*, but we seemed to be going to places unknown. Many real lives depended on our deliberate "below the radar" efforts to develop solutions for dangerous places far from home. When new refugee leaders came and went during RP's first months, I was acutely aware of constantly juggling to "take the conn," taking note of untraveled territories within our mandate.

Leadership Carousel July to December 1979

While the Freeman Report reforms and the Geneva Conference initiatives were underway in the bureau, my top priority was to provide seamless, steady, and predictable leadership. The team hung on while the political system delayed appointing, or kept changing, the top leadership positions. I planned to honor my pledge to stay the course during the rest of the Carter administration.

Reflections on Leadership

The two key refugee posts in the State Department needing permanent appointments were the coordinator for Refugee Affairs and the director of the Refugee Programs bureau. The White House named the first coordinator for refugee affairs (*refugee coordinator*, in shorthand) on February 28, 1979, former Iowa Sen. Dick Clark, who was trumpeted as a sign of President Carter's seriousness about refugee concerns.[1] Sen. Clark worked hard with Congress to get refugee admissions numbers raised and to guide new refugee legislation. He left in September 1979 to join Sen. Edward Kennedy's challenge to President Carter's second-term campaign. Had he stayed longer, I believe he could have been a significant catalyst for American advancement in refugee matters.

The first director of the Refugee Programs bureau was appointed in late August 1979, Foreign Service Officer John Baker.[2] Unfortunately, Dick Clark's sudden departure after seven months set in motion the forces, not discussed here, that made Baker a sitting duck. His appointment was terminated by November 1979, and he confided a sense of betrayal in State leadership's failure to come to his defense. On his way out the door, he bristled that no one, including me, had let him know he had been a target.

"John," I said, "I didn't know; I've been too busy."

I suspected there were elements of truth in John's claims, since his departure fit in with the emerging plans for State's two top refugee jobs. The disheartening result—five months after startup the director and coordinator positions were again vacant—put me back in charge by default. And I had no real political authority or mandate.

The resilient RP staff dismissed the absence of formally-appointed leadership as probably insignificant in the short term. We knew what had to be done. We did fear, however, for the programs' reputation, as the organization would take another hit. We needed leaders for the long term. But where would they come from? When would they arrive?

I mused, *I hope I can get out of here with my career intact. Promises of help still have not been met.* That failing affected the work and the people in the bureau. In a meeting with Ben Read in late December 1979 to review these developments, I expressed my utter disappointment.

"How could you and Warren Christopher allow these calamities, especially after the promises you made to us?"

"Jim, just stay steady," he said. "The program's going to need you now more than ever." That did not allay my concerns.

Yet, of note was the progress made by the staff in those first five months, when political leadership was in a state of flux. The disappointing leadership scramble had brought more opportunities for the career staff to step forward.

The Palmieri-Loy Team
December 1979 to January 1981

President Carter selected Victor Palmieri as the US coordinator for refugee affairs. He was confirmed by the Senate in December 1979 and assumed the position immediately with the rank of ambassador-at-large.[3] Palmieri had a formidable reputation as a crisis management expert/institutional reform specialist in the private sector. We also heard that his business colleague, Frank Loy, would accompany him and become RP's second director. Congressional opposition ruled out an additional assistant secretary position for the State Department, and Loy arrived with the rank of ambassador.

The Palmieri-Loy team gave off impressive signals and, by reputation, held out great promise. There were a few significant diplomatic flourishes, such as the attention generated by their foreign travel and the heightened visibility they brought to State's refugee work. Overall, however, their time in office was limited, and we sensed their attention and focus in the last few months diverted to the pressing Cuba concerns of that era.

Frank Loy changed RP's structure from two deputies to four. Chris Holmes from USAID became deputy for management and coordinator of other deputies, including: Shep Lowman for Asia, new hire Dick Smyser for the rest of the world, and me for financial management.

Each deputy was designated as deputy assistant secretary (DAS). I thought the arrangement too much for a small bureau like RP, but I withheld comment, not planning to stay much longer. My personal antennae were up for interesting opportunities elsewhere, but I assured Ben Read I would stay until the new team got their sea legs. I felt very much at ease orienting and guiding Chris Holmes in his new responsibilities.

Frank Loy's chief interest was on the programmatic side of RP's mission. He left deputies free to operate with minimal oversight. I took the liaison lead within the department and with the OMB and the congressional committees on budget and management matters. Frank did a superb job presenting RP's budget before the OMB and testifying before Congress in 1980, and our teamwork produced outstanding results.

I got along famously with Victor Palmieri. He was smart, energetic, and debonair. Our conversations were friendly, professional, and usually casual. I enjoyed his company and could see why he succeeded in the private sector.

Several key crises already mentioned had erupted during the year Victor Palmieri and Frank Loy were in office, leaving a heavy imprint on their tenure. The crises included (1) the Soviet Union's invasion of Afghanistan in December 1979; (2) the Horn of Africa wars, beginning in Somalia, that were to produce millions of refugees in coming years; (3) Castro's expulsion of Cuban dissenters through the Port of Mariel; and (4) the Haitian outflows to the United States.

The Cuba and Haiti crises had the most telling impact on the Palmieri-Loy regime. When they left in January 1981, Victor and Frank were each grappling with separate Cuban undertakings of extreme complexity.

Castro Strikes Back

Significantly for the United States and for the Refugee Programs' involvement in the early 1980s, Fidel Castro vented his anger at the ongoing US human rights criticisms, especially as they pertained to dissidents wishing to flee Cuba. Since the Kennedy administration's disastrous Bay of Pigs escapade in April 1961, US policy had, without question, accepted as refugees any Cuban who escaped to America.

The Cuban Adjustment Act approved in 1966 had offered *permanent residency* to Cubans one year after arrival in the United States. Those intercepted at sea would be returned to Cuba. This was unlike the treatment accorded people from any other region where numerical limits, prior screening, and other restrictions applied. The theory was that any Cuban who escaped was another testimony to the brutality and illegitimacy of the communist dictator.[4] (The continued confusion produced by this practice eventually gave rise to the Clinton administration's "wet foot, dry foot" policy years later that allowed Cubans to stay in the United States if they touched American soil.)

Fidel Castro's confrontational message in 1980 was "… if you want Cubans, I'll give you Cubans." He ordered his troops to empty out Cuban prisons, hospitals, asylums, leper colonies, and other institutions for the sick, the weak, the disabled, the insane, and blatant criminals. He forcibly deported them through the Port of Mariel. Many other Cubans wanting to escape took advantage of this opening.

Cuban Americans in South Florida, angered at Castro for so misusing defenseless pawns and hoping to use this window to rescue family and friends still in Cuba, responded by organizing boat flotillas (even though US officials objected) to assist escapes. The result was catastrophic in Cuba, South Florida, and Washington. Thousands of aliens, including some of the most dangerous imaginable, were headed toward the US coast, and many Americans were concerned about the problems they might bring with them. Most were coming in unsafe craft.

The Mariel Crisis occurred as Victor Palmieri and Frank Loy assumed office, and the Carter administration was unprepared for the coming catastrophe. Over 125,000 Cuban aliens arrived in South Florida over the first few weeks of 1980. And beyond the Cubans, thousands of Haitian immigrants, who assumed that US doors would likewise be open for them, decided this was also a propitious moment to slip through. So, they too sailed toward South Florida.

In Washington, there was chaos. Was this an immigration problem or a refugee crisis? Depending on the answer, the responding federal department would be Justice, State, or both. With little reaction time available, the administration turned to Palmieri to chart the way forward.

As this crisis was unfolding, President Carter added fuel to the debate fires when, in a Philadelphia radio broadcast, he restated America's previous welcoming policy toward Cuban exiles (800,000 had been welcomed since 1960). Apparently, he departed from a script prepared by his staff intended to discourage the irregular Cuban immigration.

To his credit, Victor Palmieri knew he needed expert help, and he turned to RP as the only State Department office with the structure, apparatus, and experience to handle the large influx anticipated. He agreed immediately to establish a Cuba and Haiti Task Force, and he asked for leadership recommendations. Shep Lowman and I recommended Nick Thorne, well known for his refugee and diplomatic work in Manila as the embassy's administrative counselor.

Nick Thorne reported in. We could see there were obvious problems ahead. Palmieri was well-groomed and sophisticated; Nick was old school, former US Army, rough and tumble, a hands-on operator. But we hoped the urgency of the problems would impel them to bridge their differences.

Meanwhile, given the immediacy and considerable number of Cuban arrivals, the task force housed them in hastily organized detention camps until alternative arrangements were available. We knew this solution could last only days, because of the sheer number of arrivals and because some of the Cubans exhibited dangerous tendencies.

Palmieri asked the Federal Emergency Management Agency, FEMA, to identify military bases in the United States to house the Cubans. Eglin Air Force base in Florida, Indiantown Gap in Pennsylvania, and Fort Chafee in Arkansas were immediately identified, as they had been for Operation New Life survivors in Southeast Asia (*see* chapter 3). There were also possibilities in other states, including Maryland.

Within hours of the mention of Maryland, as I recall, I was cautioned by the staff of RP's House appropriations subcommittee chairman Doc Morgan (D-MD). They said if I wanted to get another dollar for refugees out of his committee, I would make sure that no Cuban camp was set up in Maryland. I notified FEMA, adding they should ignore this threat.

Arriving Cubans were transferred eventually to designated camps, each one problematic, as no state or community wanted to bring in criminals and undesirables. The Carter administration agreed to confine and deport the criminal aliens in this population. As with the Indochinese, the American NGOs were contracted to manage the *resettlement* of Cubans approved to remain in the United States.[5]

Serious security issues existed from the beginning, particularly involving minors. The first camp established at Eglin Air Force Base at Fort Walton Beach, Florida, temporarily housed ten thousand *unvetted* Cuban entrants. Carol Hecklinger of the coordinator's staff was dispatched to oversee and manage the camp. Almost immediately, she reported that the federal agencies and NGO representatives had much anxiety about the vulnerability of the unaccompanied male minors. Even the Air Force officials believed this hastily-assembled camp had placed tents too closely together, allowing undetectable movements between the minors and the possible predators.

Carol left the camp early one day to call Victor Palmieri to alert him to possible problems, suggesting he alert the White House. This warning had little impact as President Carter gave his "open arms" speech that week. Carol and her colleagues at Eglin took matters into their own hands and contacted the Justice Department (DOJ) community relations service. They immediately moved the young boys to Miami and placed them under the care of a priest with proven experience helping children.

The Cuba Task Force had to address similar security concerns at other camps. Fort Chafee in Arkansas was probably the most welcoming. The new Arkansas governor, Bill Clinton, saw the bigger picture. He welcomed the new arrivals but assumed the federal government would sort out the criminal element. He took a lot of criticism from Arkansans about the Cubans. Over time, the Fort Chafee operation worked well, but at the next election Governor Clinton suffered the only defeat in his political career. Some claimed his loss was partly due to the Cuban issue.

After several weeks' trial with Nick Thorne, Victor Palmieri told me he would replace Nick as the task force head. Victor insisted that I sit in when he met with Nick, even though I did not agree with the decision. Nick took the separation with grace. He also knew this had not been a match made in heaven. Then, Victor asked me to suggest names of possible replacements. For over an hour, I went through the names of everyone I knew who might do the job. None was acceptable to Victor. Finally, in desperation, I mentioned that RP's senior deputy, Chris Holmes, was the only person not yet mentioned. I thought Frank Loy would be reluctant to lose Chris, so I told Victor I could not suggest him.

At the mention of Chris' name, Victor sprang up.

"That's what I thought you would say! He's perfect, and Frank will understand why we need him to handle this critical task force."

My shocked rejoinder was, "You'd better check this out."

Victor immediately called Chris to join us. Chris (reluctantly, I thought) agreed to this new assignment. When informed of this robbing of a talented deputy, Frank's reaction was cool.

Temporary Promotion

With the move of Chris Holmes to the Cuba–Haiti Task Force, Frank Loy sent a late-July 1980 memorandum to RP staff.[6] As we neared the end of RP's first year, the memo announced my temporary assignment as the senior deputy assistant secretary (DAS) for refugee programs. This was added to my normal financial management responsibilities; I would be accountable for the day-to-day operations once again.

Over time, the screening process for Cuban entrants worked and the criminal element was identified and sent to a secure prison facility in Atlanta while diplomatic efforts were underway to arrange their return to Cuba. But while things were sorting themselves out in the field, at home the White House was in tumult. The administration was ravaged. Many in Congress and the press believed the United States had failed to deal effectively with a serious threat to our safety and sovereignty. Victor Palmieri (along with the State Department) was taking a lot of heat. For example, Jack Watson, Carter's chief of staff, invited Victor and me to the White House one afternoon, where he read us the daily press clippings. Most reported on how the Carter administration had failed to deal adequately with the Cuban issue. Watson was not happy.

This problem took years to play out. Over time, almost three thousand criminal aliens were returned to Cuba. A success story! Unfortunately, much of the good part did not occur during Victor Palmieri's tenure.

Frank Loy faced a different Cuba issue in President Carter's final months that I will describe below. Eventually, Victor and Frank left slightly over one year after their arrivals. The clock ran out.

Personal and Staff Concerns

I look back to that summer and fall of 1980 with a sense of trepidation. Work and life felt increasingly burdensome. Hard, long hours, seven days a week, and troubled sleep led to a feeling of being used up—approaching burnout mentally, physically, emotionally and spiritually. Family problems were rising; I sensed that my commitment time to establish RP was ending.

And I saw our small team, including myself, as "helper workaholics," constantly barraged by human tragedies. I was overseeing the bureau's daily work; Shep Lowman was our right hand on Asia; and Dick Smyser was responsible for the rest of the refugee world. Our regular and emergency programs were in flux as most moved constantly through their crisis stages.

I wanted to update Frank Loy on my thinking on numerous crises. But, he was too busy, I was told, and so we never talked. Frank had become unavailable because he dealt only with Cuba matters.

As the Carter administration worked through its final months, the Cuban government agreed to negotiate a special immigration deal. Carter diplomacy would score a big win if this could work. Frank Loy was to be the lead US negotiator opposite Cuba's foreign minister. The Cubans would not agree to enter the State Department, so Washington meetings took place at Frank's Georgetown home. He put aside his other responsibilities and pulled in Phil Chicola, a key RP officer, for the talks.

To conserve Frank's time, Shep Lowman and Dick Smyser agreed to merge their issues with mine so that all could be raised at one sitting. As the senior deputy assistant secretary, I had authority to act in Frank's absence, which I did. But I felt a need to touch base with him occasionally to assure that we still had the same outlook regarding several sensitive and urgent matters. There were also personal concerns to discuss.

I requested meetings through Frank's assistant, June Ward. He had made known his desire to be involved in major issues, and we had several percolating. After several postponements, June was apologetic: "Jim, he's so busy with the Cuba talks that he can't take out time for other meetings."

About that time, I visited my old friend Don Eller, executive director of State's International Organizations (IO) bureau. He was set to leave soon to become the US deputy chief of mission in Geneva.

Don said, "Why don't you let me talk with Bill Maynes about having you take over for me here in IO?"

When Bill Maynes offered me the job on the spot, I gave tentative approval. I said I needed to let Frank know first. I went back to RP and requested an urgent meeting, but again received a deferral.

"That's o.k.," I told June, "just tell him I've accepted an offer to be executive director of IO and will be leaving shortly."

"Does Victor know?"

"No."

My relief over this decision was immediate. I was happy, excited. I felt leaving this problematic bureau was the best personal decision.

Late that evening Victor called. He seemed shocked. "Jim, what have we done? We'll be leaving soon, and you'll be needed to carry on to the new administration. You can't leave."

When I balked, he said, "Meet me for breakfast tomorrow morning at the Watergate, ten o'clock."

The next morning, Saturday, I went into the office early and on my desk was a note from Ben Read, which I was sure Chris Holmes had instigated. Ben apologized and promised me all the help the department could provide over the few remaining months of the Carter administration. He pleaded with me to reconsider my decision about IO, saying I, of all people, would be needed as the new administration formulated its approach to refugee issues. I had heard Ben's arguments before, landing me in RP for, I had thought, a short while. The mission of RP was not what had irritated me; the uncertainties about steady leadership and the lack of dependable seventh-floor support had!

The breakfast at the Watergate with Victor, while interesting, did not change my mind.

The reaction in RP the next week was overwhelmingly negative.

"Who can take over?" That question was asked repeatedly.

"I don't know, and it's not my concern anymore," I responded.

Shep Lowman, by then one of my closest RP associates, seemed distraught. "Jim, they'll probably be moving me out of RP soon (he was due for Foreign Service rotation) and if you leave, there's no one else. I plead with you to reconsider."

"Shep," I said, "this job is not good for me, personally or professionally. I can't depend on State. I must look out for myself and my family."

At some deep level, however, the urgings from Shep and Victor did reach me. I reconsidered and then surprised myself by reaching a very painful conclusion: I could not, in clear conscience, just up and leave RP. As I had listened to others' concerns, I had found I agreed that the refugee apparatus was finally taking shape and so much was at stake for RP. I then reached a point of view where I felt compelled not to disappear when the refugee programs again needed continuity. Perhaps more than ever. I might help bring greater clarity to RP's role in the State Department or at least keep it from losing ground in a new administration. My thinking took a U-turn, and I cringed while informing IO.

There remained nagging, intensely private questions. Have I fallen prey to a superman syndrome? Have I let encouragement to continue the heavy lifting to make me a fallback guy? To resolve those questions, I had to settle within myself that I needed no one's approval going forward. I would consider myself the de facto director of RP. Anyway, the present administration would end soon.

The painful crossroads led to a determination for a more normal life. Considering my workaholic tendencies, I knew I needed to exert much discipline to avoid backsliding. A big perk at State for the key leadership people was a parking permit, a coveted privilege. Mine gave me unlimited access to the underground parking at Main State. Driving easily through the garage entrance and down into the dark parking areas saved those with permits extensive time and expense.

I had put my privilege to good use. It allowed me to arrive early without hassles. However, it also allowed me to stay late. Working late, for many of us in RP, had become a habit. And that was part of the problem. It was too easy to stay in the office into the late-night hours.

The obvious decision then was to give up reserved parking, use public transportation, or make other commuting arrangements to enforce a more regular schedule. The effect turned out to be amazing. I was off in a new, unexpected, and potentially invigorating direction.

20

THE CARTER REFUGEE RECORD

NOVEMBER 4, 1980 IS A DATE NOTEWORTHY FOR THE PRESI-dential election between President Jimmy Carter and his challenger, Ronald Reagan. In the coming days at work, while the election result brought a fresh presidency, it also brought the departure of Victor Palmieri and Frank Loy, the Carter administration's political and management leaders for refugees for just over a year. We were in for another leadership transition.

Victor seemed to accept the election result with a sense of happy resignation, while Frank seemed a bit reluctant. Their final months had been difficult, consumed with the aftermath of the Mariel crisis. Most of the hardened criminals had been rounded up and awaited deportation to Cuba from a federal prison in Atlanta. Victor had wanted to tie up this loose end in the two months before President Carter left office, but that, unfortunately, would take several more years.

On President Carter's last day, Dick Kennedy, soon to be named as Ben Read's replacement, relayed a message that all outgoing political appointees were to submit their resignation letters. Victor complied, as did Frank after a brief hesitation.

Victor saw me as one of his last farewells. When I went into his office, he was at his desk, a look of concern on his face. My last words to him were, "Victor, let history decide."

The next day the Reagan administration began.

The *emergency phase* of the Indochinese refugee programs, which began with the 1975 Saigon evacuations and continued through the

Carter administration, was without question RP's top refugee priority. The diplomats and refugee officials of the Ford and Carter administrations deserve much credit for their accomplishments during the critical exodus and emergency stage of the Indochinese refugee programs. They created time and space for the new team to move into the next critical phases.

Underpinnings and Accomplishments

It was heartening to see how far we had spread our wings in the previous year-and-a-half of dealing with dangerous situations in many world regions (mentioned earlier and covered in detail in the Book Three section). The bottom line was that we had made great progress developing the capacity to respond to the refugee crises globally, thanks to committed and professional teamwork.

- We had satisfied the threatening concerns of inspection teams critically focused on State's management; inspection teams had given us clean bills of health; some outside RP now considered the bureau as an example of managerial excellence.
- The 1980 Refugee Act was law, and we were carefully adapting to it.
- Refugee consultations with Congress had gone well in 1980. The record refugee budgets RP submitted in those years received extraordinarily positive reactions from the State Department, the White House, and Congress. Underwritten by successful consultation hearings and budget results, refugee resettlement and funding were at record levels.
- The Coolfont Conference, a watershed, had brought many positive changes to domestic resettlement, and the NGO partners were progressing as a team.
- Overseas processing was going well, and superb ESL and cultural orientation programs were underway.
- Having seen record Soviet Jewish emigration in 1979, we hoped the current emigration dip (due to Soviet obstruction) was only temporary.

- The worst of the Marielito problems were behind us as we waited to expel the criminal elements to Cuba.
- RP's various emergency task forces were operating as smoothly as crisis programs could.

These amazing efforts to save as many lives as possible under so many harrowing conditions might well be Carter's refugee legacy, I thought. However, as Carter was leaving office, Southeast Asian refugee dynamics and exploding global refugee movements were changing rapidly and their impacts would be significant going forward.

Gil Loescher wrote about the changing Asian dynamics.

> Over time, the generous and preferential treatment for Indochinese refugees had a magnet effect, attracting large numbers of people out of the embattled and impoverished countries of Indochina. It became extremely difficult to stem the flow. By the early 1980s, the impetus for Western countries to sustain their large resettlement programs diminished ... From 1975 to 1980, the United States accepted as many refugees as did the entire rest of the world, and hundreds of thousands of new arrivals were pouring in. Such large admissions inevitably led to a backlash from local communities and eventually to reductions in the numbers of overall quotas. Australia, Canada, and other resettlement countries soon followed suit.[1]

The bureau confronted a palpable explosion of refugee populations around the world. The UN reported that global refugee populations remained steady at about 2.5 million per year from 1968 to 1975. They rose by almost 300 percent between 1975 and 1980, the end of the Carter administration. Experts correctly predicted global refugee populations would accelerate even faster in coming years. As the office of the presidency prepared to change hands, two-thirds of RP's refugee budget, around one-half-billion dollars a year, was devoted to domestic resettlement programs, mostly Indochinese.

The exponentially growing refugee relief problems elsewhere in the world required far more attention than the resource base permitted. RP analyzed these realities and concluded this programmatic and resource mismatch could not continue. That would challenge the new leadership team coming in with the Reagan administration.

Circling in Place

Driving home from work on President Carter's next to last day, I took a scenic route from Foggy Bottom into Maryland via the quieter, tree-laden Rock Creek Park route, a favorite. During the ride, and replaying parts of the day, my head was abuzz with questions, like *What will work be like tomorrow when the Republicans take over? Will my better work habits withstand the demands of the increasingly stressful refugee programs?* Jean and I had discussed these unknowns and agreed to stay flexible.

21

THE SIGNIFICANCE OF PUBLIC SERVICE

THE SIGNIFICANCE OF PUBLIC SERVICE WAS VIVIDLY CLEAR to me as I reflected on RP's evolution. This was especially the case regarding the initiatives undertaken to get in sync, piece by piece, with the global refugee solutions framework under construction. I realized more than ever that a public service career involves so much more than just moving up a predictable professional ladder. To be meaningful, it involves dedicating your career and yourself to noble public causes that save endangered lives and improve well-being.

As the Indochina refugee program commenced, the American electorate's presidential choice was Jimmy Carter, governor of Georgia. And his vigil, 1976 to 1980, placed Indochinese refugees at the center of his foreign policy, allowing an unprecedented humanitarian solutions to emerge.

Let me illustrate with an excerpt, "Administrator Reflects on US Refugee Policy in the 1970s," published by The Carter Center, from early drafts of this book:

> President Jimmy Carter increased Indochinese refugee resettlement levels to the US to fourteen thousand persons per month. This landmark decision, announced by Vice President Mondale in July 1979 at the Geneva Conference on Indochinese Refugees, brought the American public into the Indochina refugee program in a big and special way, resulting in quantum boosts to American learning and understanding of foreigners.

Soon, almost every community, congregation, and parish in America was hard at work helping refugees assimilate and integrate into US society. Remarkably, many citizens and communities were concerning themselves with the needs of other nationalities and cultures for the first time. Our horizons and our outlook expanded and have continued to do so. This was American learning at its best.[1]

President Carter's 1979 initiatives led to the saving of hundreds of thousands of lives over the ensuing years and the stabilization of an important region of the world. Even though these decisions were made for foreign policy and humanitarian reasons, the by product—expanding American learning and understanding of the world beyond—was equally beneficial. I recall the Carter years as a time when America broadened its leadership paradigm in global humanitarian matters. Even though the political leaders assigned to refugee programs sometimes left a lot to be desired, President Carter's personal example guided many people to stay and keep their shoulders to the wheel.

I was proud to be among them.

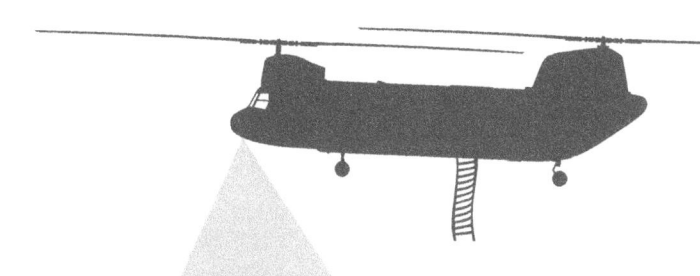

BOOK TWO

CREATE LIFT
America's Refugee Exceptionalism

"Let us fashion a world solution ..."
Walter F. Mondale

22

TRANSITIONAL LEADERSHIP

ON JANUARY 20, 1981, RONALD WILSON REAGAN BECAME THE fortieth US president. Former California governor, actor and television personality, avowed anticommunist and activist, Ronald Reagan exerted a calm, decisive presence like few before or since. The concluding statement from his July 17, 1980, nomination acceptance speech strongly hinted he would be good for refugee programs:

> I have thought of something that is not part of my speech and I'm worried over whether I should do it. Can we doubt that only a Divine Providence placed this land, this island of freedom, here as a refuge for all those people in the world who yearn to breathe freely: Jews and Christians enduring persecution behind the Iron Curtain, the boat people of Southeast Asia, of Cuba and Haiti, the victims of drought and famine in Africa, the freedom fighters of Afghanistan and our own countrymen held in savage captivity. I'll confess that I've been a little afraid to suggest what I'm going to suggest—I'm more afraid not to—that we begin our crusade joined together in a moment of silent prayer. [Minute of Silence] God bless America.[1]

President Reagan was a likeable person of warmth and clear views who would be an energetic, proactive American leader. He was a Cold War hawk with little sympathy for détente, and his foreign policy radiated with new American toughness. He was confrontational and did not tolerate idle chatter, he favored substance over form and believed that America could win the Cold War. When he assumed office as president, the American Refugee Programs bureau was in full speed mode.

Global Refugee Situation

In Southeast Asia, the *first-asylum* countries were eager to see whether this new administration would continue America's commitment to the 1979 Geneva Conference initiatives. The private resettlement agencies in the United States were working at full capacity under considerable stress to keep up with the rising Indochina refugee admissions. The need for self-sufficiency of those refugees already admitted was a huge concern for Health, Education, and Welfare, HEW). The overseas pre-departure English language training (ESL) and cultural orientation programs were underway and holding great promise. But the Immigration and Naturalization Service remained in flux as it struggled to implement the 1980 Refugee Act's processing and admissions requirements. The State Department's Refugee Programs bureau, RP, continued its recovery from the tumultuous launch in 1979, but still faced massive, although solvable, challenges.

Nine million of the world's people were classified as refugees according to the internationally agreed definition. The clear majority had been in that status for many years. An equal population called *displaced persons* remained in refugee-like situations in their own countries. As in Indochina, new refugee concerns were developing quickly in the other regions. In Athens, Rome, Paris, Vienna, and Madrid thousands of Eastern Europe refugees were being processed for admission to the United States. They were primarily from Hungary, Czechoslovakia, Bulgaria, Yugoslavia, and Albania.

Further east, the Soviet Union clamped down hard on Jews and other minorities following world outrage over its December 1979 invasion of Afghanistan. After achieving historically high Soviet Jewish emigration in 1979, the Soviet reaction to universal condemnation was to slam the emigration door shut.

In the Near East and South Asia, aggressive Soviet policies caused the continued massive exodus of Afghans fleeing the occupation of their homeland. Over three million Afghans were in regional refuge, most in Pakistan and Iran.

Meanwhile tens of thousands of Iranians had fled following the overthrow of Shah Pahlavi, a secular ruler, and the rise to power of the religious leader, Ayatollah Khomeini. They sought refuge in the region and beyond.

Elsewhere in the Middle East, the United States stayed the essential advocate and supporter for over two million Palestinian refugees under the care of the United Nations Relief and Works Agency for Palestinian Refugees (UNRWA).

In Central America, the flight of Salvadorans, Guatemalans, and Nicaraguans to Honduras and elsewhere in the region and to the United States challenged the administration for attention. They were fleeing repressive communist regimes or right-wing military dictatorships. Three thousand Cuban criminals were in US prisons, pending their return to Cuba.

Africa claimed the world's largest refugee populations and the largest share of the US global refugee relief assistance.

Victor Palmieri, the outgoing US refugee coordinator, had only recently completed consultations with Congress for admissions for 217,000 refugees in fiscal year 1981. For funding, RP was operating under a continuing resolution, and its record budget request for FY 1981 was still before Congress.

This was the daunting refugee situation a new president faced coming into office.

Transitioning—Sharp Right Turn

The presidential transition brought new leadership across the government, as well as uncertainties and surprises. President Reagan named Alexander Haig as the secretary of state, and he was confirmed quickly. I had dealt with Haig's National Security Council (NSC), during the Nixon administration, but had never met him. Richard Allen was named to head NSC. A California colleague of Reagan's, Judge William Clark, was named the NSC deputy but was shortly sent to State as the deputy secretary. Richard (Dick) Kennedy, a former Haig NSC colleague, was named to replace Ben Read as State's under secretary for management. He would be the department's primary contact with the White House transition team.

Until the appointment of a new director, I was again acting director in a drama carrying over from the previous administration. Word came down several weeks into the transition that Dick Smyser would be the acting director.[2] Dick had worked for several months on Europe, Africa, Central and South America, and the Soviet Union. He had earlier served at the NSC with Al Haig and Dick Kennedy.

Shep Lowman continued to oversee Asia, and when Smyser became acting director I concentrated on management and financial matters. Chris Holmes' position was not filled. Dick Smyser informed us he thought the new team planned to name a permanent RP director soon. My office was in the SA-2 satellite building again, and I was content to deal with regular assignments and keep my head down, happy to be free of the acting directorship.

Also, of interest was President Reagan's imminent naming of the appointees for key positions that affected our bureau, especially the State Department's geographic bureaus and central management offices. I vowed to get to know the new appointees soon; they would be instrumental in the decisions affecting refugees and funding.

We were interested in congressional changes, as well. The Judiciary Committees were reorganizing as Republicans took control of the Senate. New Democratic leadership was taking shape in the House.

"Why are you guys so happy?" I asked Frank Moss and Mary Kavaliunas, who seemed euphoric.

"We have great news!" they said, in unison. "We've just heard that Julia Taft is being appointed as the new refugee coordinator. She'll be terrific. This means the Reagan administration takes refugee issues seriously."

Julia Taft, a former White House fellow, had headed the Inter-Agency Task Force (IATF) on Indochinese Refugees (1975-76), when over 150,000 refugees moved from Saigon as American forces left. She also had been involved as a department consultant in the original planning for the refugee coordinator's office and the new refugee bureau. Regarded as both a quick study and a hard charger, she was universally well-liked, and the American refugee advocacy community was overjoyed that President Reagan had named her.

I knew Julia Taft by reputation and her husband, William (Will) Howard Taft, IV, for his work as staff assistant to deputy director Cap Weinberger in the Office of Management and Budget, when I was there.

In the State Department, presidential nominees were appointed as consultants, pending confirmation. Lying low allowed them to get up to speed on issues, prepare for confirmation hearings, and make the rounds on Capitol Hill, where they needed formal approval. The reasons for that protocol were about to become painfully clear.

Julia moved into the coordinator's office on the seventh floor, chaired staff meetings, and conducted other business. Assurances had her at ease about her confirmation. She held the confidence of all the key White House officials important to her nomination, including the president, vice president, and the NSC director. She seemed sure of the support of the secretary of state Alexander Haig, the HEW secretary Richard Schweiker, and the attorney general William French Smith. She had met with all the key congressional players, who seemed eager for her appointment.

She met with all key RP staff, many of whom knew her well. I heard she was eager for our first meeting, and she asked Frank Moss to introduce us. After a half hour's discussion, I mentioned her consultancy appointment and offered thoughts about the interim period. Julia disagreed with my view about the level of activity considered prudent for a nominee awaiting confirmation, so I backed off. As I left our first meeting, she said she would appoint a career deputy coordinator right away, likely Clay McManaway, a highly respected FSO. I knew Clay well and had worked closely with him earlier to establish the State Department classification/declassification center in the bureau of Administration. He had also helped establish IATF in 1975.

However, I hoped Julia would wait for confirmation before proceeding; she said Dick Kennedy had co-signed her consultancy papers to allow more freedom than usual. She made staffing decisions, participated in budget meetings, reorganized, and met with the NGOs and international organization officials who came through. She took an active interest in the management-by-objectives system set up for the new administration by David Stockman at OMB. She brought in McManaway as deputy. She put in long hours and seemed to thrive.

To prepare for Judiciary Committee consultation hearings in September 1981, Julia convinced Secretary Haig to appoint a special refugee advisory group to advise the administration on new Indochina refugee directions. The panel was headed by the former assistant secretary of state for East Asia and Pacific Affairs Marshall Green, who had also served as ambassador to Australia and Indonesia. From May–July 1981, the advisory group made the required rounds in Washington and traveled extensively— Southeast Asia and Geneva.[3] They completed work in July and reported to Julia, the coordinator nominee, and to the secretary.

Working from RP's satellite offices in SA-2, I was less involved than earlier in State's seventh-floor matters. I learned that the special refugee advisory group confirmed present directions and implored the administration to keep Indochinese admissions numbers high.

I became concerned when Julia made a key staffing change at the US Mission to the UN in Geneva, because such decisions were normally RP's responsibility. I did not want to start a precedent to involve the coordinator. However, as RP acting director Dick Smyser agreed with the change, the plan proceeded.

Julia brought Frank Sieverts back to Washington from Geneva and assigned Karl Beck, RP's Africa office director, as his replacement. I thought Karl would do an outstanding job in Geneva, but RP needed him at headquarters. Next thing I heard, Karl and Frank were on the move.

The next decision almost knocked me over. Before being officially approved for the job, Julia had arranged the nomination of Dick Smyser as the UNHCR deputy in Geneva to replace Dale DeHaan, a former staffer for Sen. Edward Kennedy. (A State Department nominee traditionally held the position.)

Congressional Hearings and a Shocking Blow

By August 1981, preparations were underway for September's congressional consultation hearings, the first for Reagan administration appointees.

Rather than battling with Congress over money, as executive branch witnesses usually did, these admissions hearings focused on the numbers and origins of refugees the United States planned to admit in the next year.

And that was when I discovered that Julia's nomination for the coordinator position was going off track. After months acting as coordinator, she still had no news or schedule for her confirmation. She talked to State Department, (NSC), and White House offices and learned the required paperwork had not been sent to the White House. She pressed Secretary Haig's office and learned her papers were still with the deputy secretary William Clark. She became concerned when she could not schedule a meeting with Clark.

In the middle of August, Clay McManaway called to bring me up to date on his concerns about upcoming consultation hearings. Dick Smyser was going to Geneva in a new capacity. Julia was having confirmation troubles, and Clay was temporary and not informed on current refugee matters.

Clay and I met with Julia, and neither of us understood what was behind the confirmation delay. She had already spoken with the HEW secretary Schweiker and learned he could do nothing further. By this time, we had developed a good working relationship. Clay and I advised her to abandon the normal office routine, at least until she was officially nominated. Why not await word of her nomination? Julia eventually agreed. Clay stayed for several more weeks. When no further word came about Julia's nomination, he returned to his previous job.

Dick Smyser's UNHCR appointment was approved, and he assured me that a new RP director would come in soon. Meanwhile, again, I would be acting director, per seventh-floor decision.

The formal appointment did not materialize for Julia. Her loss was an enormous loss for US refugee programs. It was rumored that State's new leaders had deemed too controversial one of her blue-ribbon commission choices.

"Don't worry," Smyser tried to reassure me, "you will be acting for a short while only, and don't worry about hearings, either."

Me worry? It was "déjà vu all over again," as popular Yankee Yogi Berra famously said about such situations.

After Dick Smyser left RP, I was the only official still in place, and the vital congressional consultations were around the corner. Everyone in RP worried about its fate.

The Judiciary Committees were up in arms because they could not learn who the key Reagan administration witnesses would be. They complained bitterly to the White House and the State Department. At the last minute, a message came that I alone would represent the State Department as Refugee Programs acting director, at a director no-show show.[4]

Hold on, I thought. Like I had felt when facing press corps questions in the White House with Ron Ziegler, I felt as if I'd been dropped from a high altitude with no parachute. I had sat beside congressional witnesses over the years and handed over budget data. But, I had never been in the witness chair, all eyes on me. No, I did not want to be there, feeling unprepared, unqualified, and more. I was the least traveled person in the bureau and had limited face-to-face experience with refugees. Yet I would have to become ready for high-stakes hearings in a few weeks. A poor showing could revive congressional threats to transfer substantial parts of Refugee Programs to USAID and/or HEW. My mind would not forget Warren Christopher's earlier command, "Don't lose this program, Jim!" RP's future was at stake.

The September 1981 hearings for FY 1982 refugee admissions were scheduled under the Refugee Act of 1980 (Public Law 96-212), which required the president's representatives to consult with the House and Senate Judiciary Committees about refugee programs, specifically admissions to the United States for the coming fiscal year. Julia Taft's summer negotiations had proposed admissions of 173,500, including 140,000 from Indochina. For FY 1981, the first year under the Refugee Act of 1980, President Carter had approved a level of 217,000 admissions after consultations with Congress. Actual refugee admissions, however, were much lower at 154,000, primarily due to processing delays in the field (*see* Table 2).

Customarily, under the terms of the Refugee Act of 1980, the US coordinator would serve as the administration's refugee spokesperson. Accompanying testimony would come from the secretary of state with the RP director present (regarding foreign policy implications), the attorney general (regarding processing and admission of refugees), and the secretary of HEW (regarding domestic assistance for resettled refugees).

Again, as had happened unexpectedly before, help arrived. Lionel Rosenblatt had been brought from Thailand to help Julia Taft prepare for her consultation hearings. Lionel was known to almost everyone I must deal with.

My closest RP advisors gathered every morning to go over the congressional schedule and discuss strategic approaches. Lionel Rosenblatt, Carol Hecklinger, Margaret Carpenter, Ada Adler, and Shep Lowman were part of this team. At one meeting, I commented about a new person sitting in our office complex. "That's Julia's and Bud McFarland's friend," someone explained. "He's coming to work with us." I invited our visitor, Arthur Eugene (Gene) Dewey, to join our early morning meetings. Gene Dewey and I would become trusting colleagues (and he a close advisor and colleague) through many future challenging years.

After my designation as the *sole* witness was announced, State's Office of Congressional Relations asked if I had arranged for other administration officials to provide accompanying testimony. I had not. Then, Secretary Haig passed word he would be unavailable (he had little interest in refugee matters) and the deputy secretary William P. (Bill) Clark, in Warren Christopher's old position, was incommunicado.

Therefore, State's third-tier official, the under secretary for political affairs Walter J. Stoessel would accompany me. Walt emphasized to me that he would make a statement but would not answer questions because he was uninformed on refugee issues.

My frazzled thoughts conjured up a Herblock cartoon-like image: higher ups are running off to Geneva and elsewhere as a high level State official unprepared and unwilling to take questions plays sidekick to a burdened civil servant and both men—question marks over their heads—are gawking speechlessly over the witness table at the powerful, literally elevated committee members. The cartoon image morphed grotesquely in my mind as the attorney general and his deputy became likewise unavailable and we learned that Justice responsibility for the hearing had passed to their number three, the associate attorney general Rudy Giuliani. Doris Meissner, the number two at INS, would back him up.

Worsening news arrived that Giuliani could not attend the hearing, nor could HEW Secretary Schweiker or his deputy. Doris Meisner would be Justice's lead witness and newly appointed director of the refugee resettlement office. Phil Hawkes would represent HEW.

Dangling Herblock question marks then tumbled over more cartoon heads in my imagination.

The Judiciary Committees were livid over this pared down panel. They had expected high-profile hearings garnering loads of media and public attention. Instead, they would be getting the "odd couple," Walt Stoessel and me, from the State Department. This truly capitol disaster caused the committees to be upset, primarily with State. I heard the congressional disapproval loudly and clearly from the Hill, as did other State, DOJ, INS, and HEW officials. The reactions were powerfully negative: "The Reagan administration is thumbing its nose at the Congress with such low-level witnesses!" They vowed revenge.

What would happen to RP's case in September 1981 as Stoessel and I were grilled by some of the most powerful politicians in Congress? Walt Stoessel, known in foreign policy circles, was an unknown quantity in this arena; I was viewed as only one of many civil servants working at the budget and management level. What did happen regarding the September hearings was unbelievably preposterous to me, testing credulity and my credibility to the core: I was scheduled for a marathon—every Monday through Friday of that month—of running through extensive in-house briefings or tough congressional hearings.

To prepare for that grueling month, I asked every Refugee Programs officer and the coordinator's staff to prepare answers for the questions they thought might be raised at the hearings. Their specific material to help me prepare produced three big Q and A notebooks, which I pored over every night.

Before being flung farther into this political briar patch, I met with the staff of the House subcommittee on Immigration, Refugees and International Law—familiarly known as the Mazzoli subcommittee. Present were Garner (Jim) Cline, staff director of the House Judiciary

Committee (he had called the roll at the 1973 Nixon impeachment hearings), Skip Endres of the Mazzoli subcommittee, and Pete Regis.

On my visit with Jim Cline, he greeted me with, "You poor sucker, they've sent you up here to get slaughtered. We will ravage your requests. I'll take bets now that you won't end up with more than 50,000 admissions."

Jokingly (or so I hoped), the three made bets on how low the final consultations numbers would go.

I could only respond, seriously, that "only fifty-thousand admissions would produce genocide." I hoped their mocking comments were only in jest, although they highlighted the difficulties we would likely face.

House Hearings

The first hearing was in the massive Rayburn House Office Building situated southwest of the capitol, with Chairman Romano Mazzoli (D-KY) presiding. Because refugee admission numbers were contentious and newsworthy, the spacious hearing room was packed tight. The noise and chatter of the mass of people waiting to find seats inside was unnerving. Members of the press were visible everywhere. Smoking in hallways was accepted practice then and—being a habitual smoker in those days—I put away nearly half a pack of cigarettes, I think. (And I had told my wife I would quit smoking—which I later did.)

Chairman Mazzoli gaveled the hearing to order. After his opening statement and those of the ranking minority members and my pal Walt Stoessel, he proceeded, as the congressional record showed.

> Chairman Romano Mazzoli: I would like to introduce our panel: Mr. James Purcell, the acting director of the Bureau for Refugee Programs in the Department of State; Ms. Doris Meissner, the acting commissioner of the Immigration and Naturalization Service; Mr. Phillip Hawkes, director of the Office for Refugee Resettlement, Department of Health and Human Services; and Mr. William Haratunian, deputy director of the Voice of America. I presume, Mr. Purcell, you will be the leader of the panel. We yield to you for your statement.[5]

Prepared opening statements took up the first hour before the merciless questions began. No camera could catch the taut-wire tensions in that room as this subcommittee looked eager to cut refugee admissions drastically. During a break for a vote on the House floor, Rep. Hamilton Fish (R-NY) came up to me at the witness table.

"Mr. Purcell, these hearings are not going well," he said sternly, and you're all we've got. I'm going to ask some leading questions and you need to make a strong case for what happens if admissions are cut. Give me everything you've got."

Rep. Fish's words helped. When the hearing resumed, facts and reasoning seemed to float automatically to the top of my memory as I made our case for high Indochinese and Soviet Jews admissions. After three hours of questioning, the hearing ended. From his chair on the raised platform, Ham Fish gave me a thumbs-up. Walt Stoessel, Doris Meissner, and Phil Hawkes offered me their warm congratulations. As we left, Doris and Phil, major collaborators in years to come, leaned over and said, in effect, "You did better than any political appointee they could have sent up here."

As I collected my papers to leave, I looked upward and thought, *Thanks! We did it.* My support team was overjoyed that we had beaten the odds. Except for one person, they were ecstatic. Margaret Carpenter had noticed my stumbling over an answer on English as a Second Language.

"You should have known the answer to that question!"

Maggie, give me a break, I thought, although I sensed she had been joking.

That hearing did not end the tensions. Yet it established that the Refugee Programs bureau had made a credible and aggressive case, and we would not be silenced by signs of opposition. Even my discussions the next day with the House Judiciary staffers convinced me they realized we had a serious game on our hands. We had not lost, yet.

Many other committees representing various geographical concerns requested briefings or hearings, and we willingly complied. During an important hearing before the full House Judiciary Committee, Rep. Sam Hall (D-TX) questioned whether the Indochinese refugees coming in were free of tuberculosis. I tried to explain the medical clearance checks we put each refugee through. The medical clearances were the responsibility of the Centers for Disease Control and Prevention (CDC); the US Public Health Service; and the Intergovernmental Committee for European Migration (ICEM).[6]

Rep. Hall was not satisfied and proposed a moratorium on further US admissions until this medical issue could be addressed. My reaction to this amendment was clear: it would lead to disaster and likely deaths in Southeast Asia. We needed to address the committee's concern.

The Judiciary Committee went ahead with a vote on the Hall resettlement moratorium amendment, which lost by one vote. We had avoided a disaster. The briefings and testimonies were over and, as usual, we expected to hear from the committees by the end of September. I thought we were in decent shape.

The US Public Health Service and the Centers for Disease Control spent many hours before the Senate Judiciary Committee providing explanations and data about two kinds of tuberculosis, TB: communicable and noncommunicable. They explained that no refugee with the communicable variety could depart for the United States. While a few refugees had been admitted with communicable TB, they were not a threat and could best be treated in the United States. I realized our explanations had not gotten through entirely when one of the national news headlines erroneously declared, "500,000 ticking time bombs in the US."

The Senate hearings were testy but less contentious. Staffers had attended the House hearings and knew that I could defend our programs. The more negative tendencies expressed by some members were overcome by the impassioned pleas from Sen. Ted Kennedy (D-MA) and a supportive statement by Sen. Mark Hatfield (R-OR). We left intact.

A September Surprise

Donna Alvarado of Sen. Simpson's staff had speculated that RP might plan a refugee admission surge in September to make up for lower arrivals in previous months. She had traveled to Hamilton Air Force base in California where many refugees landed and witnessed seemingly hasty preparations. I gave my word repeatedly that admissions in the current year would go no higher than fourteen thousand in any given month, the maximum the NGOs (nongovernmental organizations), said they could resettle in that period. Therefore, in formal testimony I had given assurances this limit would not be exceeded.

A litmus test of our credibility was measured by how the Judiciary Committees considered the fourteen-thousand-monthly limit. They believed the State Department would favor higher numbers for foreign policy reasons over quality domestic resettlement. Would we stick to my assurances?

Credibility on a Thin Line

For days before the hearings, I was so concerned about my promise being kept that I strongly pressed this issue at every morning's staff meeting like a foghorn blast. Therefore, I felt sure the team would honor my promise.

The reality soon became clear. On the last day of the fiscal year, September 30, 1982, I noted that Shep Lowman had added several Asia office colleagues to our early morning meeting. One, Hank Cushing, was ebullient, reporting: "We did it! We got record numbers in September. One lady being flown was about to give birth. She somehow was able to delay until the plane entered American airspace, so her offspring would count against September's numbers!"

The rest of us then learned that RP had admitted nineteen-thousand-plus refugees, in September. The room went quiet for about ten seconds before Margaret Carpenter, Carol Hecklinger, Ada Adler, and Gene Dewey exploded: "This will *kill* us with the Congress. They *warned*, and we *pledged* this would not happen! But now it has!"

I dreaded even the thought of passing this discrediting news to Rep. Mazzoli and Sen. Simpson. All arduous work by the RP team in the past month had officially and quickly been undone. Ruined.

I slumped in my chair and stared into a nothingness of disbelief. I couldn't understand or explain what we had just heard. Finally, looking to Shep, I said, "How could this happen?"

He explained that the processing system "had just caught up. No one expected anything like this was even possible."

It later became clear that my injunction to keep September admissions below fourteen thousand had not been passed to our colleagues in SA–2.

Compared to the reactions of the others, my hurt and anger were outwardly constrained. As the team accepted that our hard-won good reputation was now no more than scorched toast, they were inconsolable and uncontrollable.

After adjourning the meeting, I allowed depressing thoughts. Critics would say that if I had better control, this would not have happened. I had kept to myself personal hopes to stay with the refugee bureau. Now, hopes to become permanent head of RP someday, based on my record and the successful congressional testimony, were dashed. To close the loop, I told Shep, "We've got to inform the committees."

For the next hour we informed each committee and answered their questions. Reactions were fast and uniformly negative. From multiple congressional committees plus NSC, OMB, and State Department officials, I heard the same question: "How could you have let this happen?"

I learned that several of RP's Asia staff, not having been told of the importance of our admissions understanding with Congress, had manned the nightly phone lines to Asia to assure that overseas posts pushed as many admissions as possible for September, to make up ground lost in previous months. The entire episode came to be known in refugee circles as "the September surprise."

In 2010, a criticism of our handling of the September surprise claimed that I had blamed Hank Cushing.[7] That was false. Hank had not been present at my early morning meetings, and he would not have known of my instruction. I had looked to those in attendance to pass the word to their staffs. This criticism failed to note my pledge to the committees or Hank's subsequent position as head of one of RP's major field posts.

Given cynical reactions from congressional staffers before the September hearings and then the September surprise, I expected negative consultation letters. However, the Senate consultation letter signed by Strom Thurmond, Al Simpson, Joe Biden and Ted Kennedy proposed 125,000 annual admissions with no geographic restrictions. A House letter signed by Peter Rodino, Hamilton Fish, and Robert McClory proposed 140,000. A separate letter signed by Rep. Mazzoli proposed

120,000. When all letters were in, we were moving forward.[8] We advised the president to set the 1982 level at 160,000, slightly below the request. He agreed.

Other committees heard of RP's ultimate consultations victory, and I sensed their respect for the programs and for me, as a witness. The potentially punishing events had ended well. Personally, I remained wounded. In the middle of October, Lionel Rosenblatt came to see me in the office space usually used by the US coordinator, still unnamed.

"I see the State Department is replacing you," Lionel announced.

'What?! Not that I've been told.'

"I hear Dick Vine from State's EUR bureau (European Affairs) is coming in as director," Lionel shared.

It's all come to this, not an official word to me. Yet, by then was anything unbelievable? Again, I would leave the acting director duties.

13

STRUGGLING TO STAY ON COURSE

WHERE DID YOU HEAR THAT?" I ASKED LIONEL ROSENBLATT, who had just told me I had been replaced.

"It's all over the seventh floor," he said.

Well, not my part of it, I thought, then called deputy assistant secretary in PER Hank Cohen. I knew him as a straight shooter.

"Jim, I thought sure you had been informed by Dick Kennedy's office. Dick Vine has just been selected as director.[1] He's a good officer with a solid background in European matters. I'm so sorry if you're just hearing now. I believe Vine will want you to stay as the senior DAS (deputy assistant secretary)."

"How could this happen? Does Vine know anything about refugees? I guess this will become clear, but ... let me ask, is Dick Vine about sixty, thinning gray hair, about six feet tall?"

"Yes," said Hank.

"I'll bet that's who's sitting in our reception area. It's a good thing I called you, because he's here to see me!"

When Dick and I met for the first time, he seemed embarrassed that I had not been informed. He mentioned past assignments as ambassador to Switzerland, president of the Atlantic Council (a think tank) in Paris and, most recently, in the European Affairs (EUR) bureau at State. He had limited refugee experience but considered himself to be a quick study and looked forward to working with me to get oriented quickly. He wanted me to play an active role in RP management and hoped to take up this new assignment in a few weeks.

Dick Kennedy's office finally called to apologize for dropping the ball. I didn't know what to think. I talked with lots of people over the next days and learned that State's new management team had no real tie or commitment to the Refugee Programs bureau, unlike the Ben Read team. And the September surprise had not helped my case. I packed to return to SA-2, leaving the convenient seventh-floor office. Dick Vine would set up in the refugee coordinator's suite.

Vine selected Robert (Bob) Funseth, his EUR colleague, as deputy assistant secretary to replace Dick Smyser, already in Geneva. Bob Funseth was a well-traveled Foreign Service Officer with several key European posts behind him, and he had served a stint as the press spokesman for Secretary Kissinger. Bob brought a lot of Foreign Service credibility to RP.[2]

Dick Vine asked my advice and reorganized. He assigned Bob Funseth to domestic programs, including resettlement; Gene Dewey for *overseas refugee relief* programs except Asia, divided geographically; and me, for management. When Shep Lowman was reassigned overseas, Gene added Asia to his overseas relief portfolio. This reorganization made sense. *Dick Vine*, I thought, *is making good decisions.*

Continuity

Dick and I heatedly discussed other key staffing changes, such as his decision to terminate or not to renew the appointments of former Southeast Asia refugee officials in Washington and in the field. I disagreed with such a clean sweep. Some individuals were controversial, not always following rules precisely. Yet, as a team, they achieved superb programmatic results in Southeast Asia. Their experience and knowledge had brought continuity to RP in a critical part of the world, and I thought Dick was mistaken to lose them all at once.

I reminded Dick these decisions would leave me as the only RP continuity point for Indochina refugees, and we debated about this for many days. Dick argued, "This is a Foreign Service environment and officers don't stay around in one organization for as long as these people have been with refugees. They've been here too long for their good and ours. We need new blood." That view was popular with central personnel,

PER, which insisted that refugee jobs, filled by the same people for years, should be freed up for other rotating FSOs. Using my own reasoning, they claimed that a positive image for refugee work in the department could otherwise never emerge; we must provide opportunities for a wider universe of FSOs to serve in refugee work.

I discovered just how strongly central personnel and State management held this view when later I encountered strong opposition to my proposal to appoint Ken Quinn, a respected Asia expert, to a senior position. My insistence on Quinn ended in a hastily called meeting with the deputy secretary Ken Dam, the under secretary for management Ron Spiers, and the Foreign Service director general Joan Clark. I made a strong case for Quinn, the only senior FSO with relevant experience for the position under consideration. Joan Clark objected that he, like several other experienced refugee officers, had been outside the mainstream too long and needed to get back in if he wanted a Foreign Service career.[3] That was an argument I could not and did not win. Bob Funseth, the new DAS for domestic resettlement, went even further. In Thailand, Bob brought in a new processing team, including Bill Stubbs as Bangkok refugee coordinator (refcoord), replacing Mike Eiland (Lionel Rosenblatt's replacement), and Calvin Connors as deputy refugee coordinator.

After Dick Vine's first weeks, word came that H. Eugene Douglas from Texas had been named US coordinator for refugees.[4] Gene Douglas had been engaged with President Reagan's election campaign in Texas.

The Vine-Douglas team was incompatible from the get-go. Dick Vine believed Douglas was condescending; Douglas thought Dick too old-school. They clarified their mutual disrespect in words and actions. Both seemed to work better with me than each other. That led me into the unenviable position of bridging between them, which I hated.

Vine's leadership style was brusque intimidation of adversaries. He picked fights and lost many; staff had to glue things back together. I was biding my time until a good reassignment opportunity arose, and from Vine's first day I decided not to allow him to antagonize or force me into anger. Dick said he considered me indispensable to the program's operations; he trod softly around me.

Blowups between us occurred, however, on significant decisions that year, including Khmer resettlement and the evacuation of Palestine

Liberation Organization (PLO) combatants from Beirut. For the most part, we tamped down our emotions before the relationship was irreparably damaged.

Our last disagreement, however, was the final straw for me. It had to do with RP's indispensable planning for the next year's refugee consultations with the House and Senate Judiciary Committees. In early summer of 1982, we were making forward projections of refugee resettlement and related budget implications. In the past, RP had been the dominant actor in both. We knew the needs and the capabilities of the American resettlement community and the refugee bureau's funding constraints. Dick decided he would represent RP's interests in these discussions taking place under the auspices of his arch enemy, refugee coordinator Douglas.

Following one meeting, Dick called RP's budget officer Rosanne Oliver and me to his office. He was in a foul mood.

"Douglas wants to cut the numbers drastically and EAP is determined to raise them. Nobody listens to me," he said. "I'm fed up. I'm not going to another of these stupid meetings. Let them do whatever they want. We will live with whatever they decide. I don't care anymore."

Such an abdication would affect the bureau's future, and I recalled how we had managed similar disagreements in the past. I could not believe Dick was serious about ignoring the process. However, several times he repeated, "They can do whatever they want."

At one such time I could no longer contain myself and yelled, "You are the director. You represent all of us. We look to you for leadership, and you are dropping the ball. This is disgraceful. You owe us more!"

My anger was so hot I stopped myself there. Rosanne Oliver was quiet. Dick sat quietly, staring ahead; I had wounded him. The room felt explosively tense. I suggested we end the meeting, and Dick nodded agreement.

Outside, I talked briefly with Rosanne. "I was wrong to attack Dick in your presence. I am sorry you experienced my outburst."

This uncomfortable situation gave me the thought that it would be impossible to continue working with Dick. I returned to his office and found him still sitting there, staring ahead.

"Dick, I was wrong to get into this in front of staff. I'm sorry, please accept my apologies. I'll be leaving immediately."

The next moments, I would say, took a measure of the man. Dick looked up, smiled, and spoke: "I'm the one who was wrong. You're right, I'm the director, and I need to lead."

We sat in silence a little while, and I realized a peculiar bond had been forged. Although my mind did not change about this issue, it changed drastically about the character of the man.

Two events soon would profoundly affect RP and my life. Dick Vine left after fewer than nine months as director, and President Reagan appointed George P. Shultz as the secretary of state.

George P. Shultz had been the Office of Management and Budget (OMB) director when I worked there during the Nixon administration and the storms of the Vietnam War. I had high regard for him as a supervisor and mentor.

When he arrived to lead the State Department, RP was again without a permanent director following Dick Vine's departure. For the fourth time, I was designated acting director while the personnel office said they were identifying possible candidates, this time ostensibly to include me. However, I had lost confidence in the selection process and held no hope or expectation about my chances.

Many in the NGO community declared their intention to let Secretary Shultz know their support for me. I gave them no encouragement or support. Nor did I ever communicate with the secretary about this. I convinced myself that it would be foolish to pursue it. I was a career civil servant and had intentionally never sought political support for personal interests.

UNHCR, Geneva

Extensive global refugee issues were on the agenda that year, and UNHCR called for a mid-year review in Geneva. They planned to ask donors for more money. Representing US refugee programs bureau at such meetings, I usually invited a few key people from Congress to get a better sense of what we were facing. Most eagerly agreed, but one I could not convince was the chairman of the Senate Judiciary subcommittee on immigration and refugee policy Al Simpson. A fiscal conservative, Sen. Simpson maintained that his constituents in Wyoming would not understand his spending money on travel to Switzerland.

Although he had given us a rough time at the last consultation hearings, I put in a special, sugarcoated invitation for Simpson to attend this review. His Judiciary Committee staff director, Dick Day, convinced him to accept and agreed to accompany him.

On the first evening in Geneva, the US ambassador held a dinner for the American delegation. We went over the issues that would come up at the review and had time to socialize. When everyone kicked back, Sen. Simpson, noted for his dry humor, regaled the group with adventurous Wyoming stories. He and Dick Day rode back with me to the InterContinental Hotel. During the ride, Dick raised the question of who was slated to be the new RP director. I said I didn't know, but the nominee of the US ambassador to the UN Jeanne Kirkpatrick seemed to have the inside track. Sen. Simpson asked why I was not under consideration, since I had run the Bureau of the past few years. I explained that was an unlikely outcome for a civil service employee in the State Department, home of the Foreign Service.

Sen. Simpson commented, "That's stupid. They should go after the best person for the job. Jim, give me your CV and I'll talk with George."

I had no CV, as I had never actually applied for a job in the State Department. I stayed up late that night and prepared a simple version.

Back in Washington, things were quiet on the RP leadership front for a few weeks. Then I got word there had been developments regarding the appointment of a new director for RP. The reports said the White House had sent the RP nomination papers back to Secretary Shultz with a request he take another look. He was new in his job and had not been involved in the initial selection. The present candidate's involvement in a controversial policy decision years before had led to doubts at the White House.

Simultaneously, Shultz had been hearing from several people supporting my appointment as permanent director. These supporters included Sen. Simpson, several of the American NGOs, and others unnamed to me. Dick Day told me that Elliott Abrams had put in a good word. Otherwise, I lacked knowledge of any external support.

Secretary Shultz sent the nomination papers back to State's personnel office with a request for another list, instructing them to add my name this time. When I learned these details, I was not surprised to learn I had been excluded from previous lists.

Within a few days, word came in about the decision. I had been nominated, after all, and the Reagan White House team had agreed. As I took this in, my feelings matched comedian Jackie Gleason's line, "How sweet it is!"

Official Appointment

The official State Department announcement was issued on August 2, 1982. When the news of my appointment spread, people bounded into my office rejoicing that something special had happened. It was intoxicating. Gene Dewey, Bob Funseth, Jim Lawrence, Louise Pope, Ann Morgan, Mary Kavaliunas, and many others expressed excitement and amazement.

Bureaucratic wonders were still possible, according to calls and private comments in the State Department. A civil service professional in the State Department had slogged through the system to head a major programs bureau. I called Jean, my greatest supporter, to share the news, and she was silent for a moment before she said, "Thank God."

Former doubters then saw the struggling backwater refugee programs as the special efforts they were. Suddenly, refugee work was viewed differently in the department. Even FSOs were coming back for a second look.

The civil service community at State gained inspiration as one of their own sat at the head of a major programs bureau. The American NGO community and the bureaucracy in the executive branch and Congress were shocked to see merit triumph over politics. The international refugee community could sense a new determination by the Americans to play a leadership role in global humanitarian matters. It was not "business as usual."

I was to be an administratively-designated assistant secretary, pending resolution of disputes with the House International Relations Committee over the number of statutory assistant secretary slots available to the State Department. I would be the director, until then, "with the full privileges and benefits of an assistant secretary." I could even call myself assistant secretary, if I chose.

In Washington government circles, such details have always affected influence, or in milder terms, have opened doors. But title was not a critical issue to me. To be named director under George Shultz seemed incredible. The unthinkable would be to begin by focusing on titles. The extraordinary delegations of authority Secretary Shultz vested in me and the confidence they signaled made other bureaucratic concerns irrelevant. If I did right by RP's mission, I could count on the boss to watch my back.

The Secretary

I had worked with George Shultz at the White House Office of Management and Budget (OMB), in his early days as Nixon's budget director. Now, I was among his first appointees in his new role as Reagan's secretary of state. Significantly, early appointments, including Paul Wolfowitz for East Asia and the Pacific and the seventh-floor counselor Edward Derwinski sent strong positive messages throughout Shultz's foreign affairs empire.[5]

To appreciate the relationship we carved out to do the job, it is important to understand the ground rules we established. As much as anything, they set the tone of a future operating style. When the secretary asked for my views, I responded that the team would frequently deal with escalating human disasters needing timely, swift, and unbureaucratic responses.

"The team will sometimes need to act on the double in your stead and name," I said. I promised to keep him and his key staff informed of all significant developments and issues, but I would need his trust if occasions arose where I responded quickly.

"I'll not delay action," I said.

I hoped that Secretary Shultz knew and trusted me from our time together in the OMB during the Nixon administration and would give me a longer lead than usual. He said he would authorize me to act appropriately and immediately in his stead, as emergency refugee needs would arise.

"Keep me informed or seek my approval when policy is at issue," he told me. "If you do a good job, I'll pat you on the back and say, 'Atta boy,' but if you screw up, I'll fire you. Deal?"

A visit with the coordinator Gene Douglas was an effort to establish an early workable relationship. I had heard of his support for another candidate until he heard that Shultz was leaning toward me. A clear footing was what I wanted, and I reminded Douglas I worked for the person at the top, the secretary, and took my foreign policy guidance from him. Regarding interagency refugee matters, I considered RP to be one of the federal agencies Douglas was to harmonize and coordinate. I respected his job to represent the administration's program to American audiences and constituencies; I emphasized that State was the single voice on foreign policy matters.

Secretary Shultz had shown confidence in me, and I would do the same with RP's deputy assistant secretaries. To give them space to carry out RP goals with their teams, I redelegated most director's authorities to these trusted deputies.

I was ready to start work, again.

24

REFUGEES IN THE REAGAN YEARS

IN EARLY 1981, THE UNITED STATES AND THE INTERNAtional community were fully engaged in the dramatic concluding chapters of the exodus and emergency phase of the Indochinese refugee programs. Over the next two years, the new team under President Reagan completed the emergency period, involving protection.

Attention focused on the four major critical strategy phases next: stabilization, protection, reform, and solutions. They were not always mutually exclusive, because elements of one often overlapped with or led into others. For example, it would be incorrect to say that protection was not relevant to the exodus and emergency phases. Yet, protection later became a separate and distinct priority for especially vulnerable groups.

Despite their obvious imprecision, these phases give useful analytical and chronological segues. In the next chapters, one sees how they interconnect, how refugee solutions work to solve problems, and why an understanding of their rationales and contexts is so imperative.

25

PHASE 1. STABILIZATION

WHILE GOVERNMENTS AGREED TO HONOR THE COMMITments of the 1979 Geneva Conference on Indochinese Refugees, they worried about the magnet effect of the continued high levels of third-country resettlement.

Did the robust resettlement program for Vietnamese refugees provoke continuing outflows? To restore equilibrium and confidence, resettlement needed to rebalance with the other *durable solutions* options, such as safe voluntary repatriation, regional settlement, and orderly migration.

To do this, the RP team worked out a stabilization regime to anchor programs and operations while undertaking a concerted search for solutions. Under this regime, existing and new crises would be examined continually and monitored for operational effectiveness and durable solution potential.

There were agreed and basic understandings to guide the stabilization phase regime. Honoring the Geneva Conference resettlement commitments, as the situation required, was imperative. We would reserve future resettlement for persons with no other options. Under those conditions, repatriation and regional settlement would have high priority and constant assessment. Plans must aim to preserve safe regional asylum by assuring secure refugee camps and adequate funding. Alternatives to escape by boat must be realistic, aimed at safety. We would work transparently with governments in Asia and elsewhere as they studied their national measures to stabilize and manage refugee movements and security at home. Safe voluntary return programs would be set up wherever and whenever possible.

We would strengthen the US resettlement process to prepare incoming refugees for life in America.

For an RP deputy to oversee resettlement stabilization, the deputy secretary of state Ken Dam suggested Richard English, someone with solid analytical and political credentials. The secretary of state James Baker, President George H. W. Bush, and Barbara Bush highly recommended him. I was pleased to welcome Dick to the team.

The Ever-Changing Refugee Paradigm
Bangkok, Late Fall 1982

On a trip to Southeast Asia, the refugee coordinator Gene Douglas and I were dinner guests of the US ambassador to Thailand John Gunther Dean, once a refugee from Nazi Germany. Also present were about thirty officials from Thailand, other governments, NGOs, and international organizations.

During conversation, I mentioned that about eight thousand out of the twenty-one thousand Cambodians processed by US immigration services had been disapproved for resettlement. Ambassador Dean surmised that some of these declined refugees might be family reunification cases, and he passionately supported reuniting them in America with their families.

That's when conversation suddenly turned testy, when Gene Douglas muttered, "John, you might just turn out to be Abramowitz II."[1]

"Do not impugn the integrity of Mort Abramowitz in this house!" Ambassador Dean angrily pointed a finger at Gene Douglas. "Mort's a great ambassador," he continued, "a remarkable humanitarian, and a good friend."

Total silence fell over the room. Mort Abramowitz was held in highest esteem. Guests also knew that two months earlier Douglas had been gaveled "out of order" in Geneva by UNHCR's executive committee chairman, for inserting partisan American politics into the proceedings.

When he inserted the unwelcome dinner comment, Gene Douglas

had been highlighting coming changes in the US refugee scenario. These changes would inevitably occur with implementation of the 1980 Refugee Act, Douglas said, trying to explain that the previous free-flowing US resettlement channel was coming to an end. He'd implied that Abramowitz and the former refugee team had openly encouraged the free flow, and he opined that new refugee law would require more rigid discipline.

Unfortunately, the significance of the coming changes was likely lost on many guests that evening. By saying "Abramowitz II," Douglas had set the stage for Dean's outburst. I felt sure most guests would have identified with Dean; Douglas's remark had sidelined related issues. Eugene Douglas had awkwardly pointed to significant changes required by the 1980 Refugee Act. Previously, refugee admissions had been processed under the attorney general's parole authority; persecuted groups or classes (such as Vietnamese) could be considered to have *presumptive eligibility* for US admission if able to prove they belonged to a predetermined persecuted class. Few were denied.

The Refugee Act of 1980 replaced presumptive eligibility with a more stringent regime. The INS (Immigration and Naturalization Service) would make individual determinations based on criteria enumerated in the Act. Membership in a persecuted class, formerly the main criterion, had been replaced by individual persecution evidence. The Act made US admission far more difficult for refugee claimants. The role of the Justice Department was strengthened. Many accustomed to the processing prior to the 1980 Refugee Act, including some at the ambassador's dinner, had been caught unaware by these changes.

At the ambassador's table, though, one could sense the ending of the exodus and emergency phase of the Indochina refugee programs, an end that challenged the new RP team to harness and stabilize refugee processing and protection regimes for the complex future ahead.

As guests were leaving, Ambassador Dean motioned me over and confided, "Jim, I guess I went too far this time."

"No, you said what had to be said."

Within this unique environment, earlier comfortable and cozy relationships among the involved parties would evolve in new directions. This would affect Washington refugee officials, overseas refugee coordinators and embassies, INS, and the private resettlement agencies. State must give much more guidance and disciplined supervision to its headquarters and field staff and to the resettlement agencies, including the Joint Voluntary Agencies, JVAs. Life under the 1980 Refugee Act would be vastly different.

Washington, Fall 1982

Nowhere did institutional changes for resettlement call out more for adjustments than in RP's Washington headquarters. Prior to Dick Vine's 1981 reorganization, programmatic leadership for domestic resettlement was vested in each of RP's regional offices. Vietnamese resettlement had been the responsibility of Shep Lowman's Office for Asian Refugees (OAR). Now, we would have one central office exclusively responsible for directing and overseeing the global resettlement program. By that time there were 625,000 Indochinese refugees in the United States and more coming every year. They were dispersed to most US states. While we were confident in the overall merits and integrity of the resettlement program following the Coolfont Conference, our monitoring had revealed growing concerns about the quality of some placements, the impact on the local jurisdictions, and the sluggish pace of assimilation in some areas. Also, the Judiciary Committees in Congress were raising questions about the State Department's stewardship of the resettlement program, especially following the 1982 "September surprise" debacle and broken admissions promises.

For some time, Carol Hecklinger of the refugee coordinator's office and her colleague, Joe Coleman, had been exploring ideas about how to proceed toward a more systematic resettlement program. I called Carol to tell her I hoped she would consider moving to RP to head the new domestic resettlement office. She responded, "Are you kidding! I'm on my way!"

Carol immediately outlined a plan of action, and Richard English asked her to begin implementation. Key to her initial approach was onsite monitoring to assess resettlement performance in selected cities. Because we had no staff other than Carol Hecklinger and Carl Harris, we enlisted others in RP to join monitoring teams for short periods. Terry Rusch joined the team shortly after Carol, and the institution-building process was underway. Later to come were Anita Botti, Bruce Flatin, Peggy Barnhard, John Campbell, and others. The organizational capability they produced would bring major systemwide and nationwide improvements.

Managing Down

A year earlier, September 1981, as acting director I represented the State Department at the annual refugee consultation hearings before the Judiciary committees. It was the Reagan administration's first appearance before them. We proposed continued high Southeast Asia resettlement levels for FY 1982 (173,000) (*see* Table 2), and I vowed to Congress and the ASEAN governments that we would faithfully honor American commitments made at the 1979 Geneva Conference and intensify the search for comprehensive durable solutions. We announced plans to reduce resettlement programs gradually in the coming years as camp populations declined and other durable solutions became possible.

Shep Lowman, the deputy assistant secretary for Asia, named the gradual reduction approach "managing down." *First asylum* must not be endangered under this process. Rather than create a new monitoring and review mechanism, I incorporated *durable-solutions planning* into the Program and Policy Review Committee, PPRC, a review system established earlier for budget and program planning (*see* chapter 13). As we determined America's annual funding contributions to RP's domestic and international programs, we simultaneously agreed on appropriate durable solutions plans for each country and region.

Repatriation and *regional settlement* were difficult to organize because of the ingrained preference for the resettlement solution. But we wanted always to be ready when and if opportunities arose. In the FY 1983 budget for Southeast Asia, for example Asia, RP made a separate proposal for $10 million to be directed toward *nonresettlement durable solutions*. We tried to keep these frameworks alive so that, when the time came, they would to be readily available (*see* Table 3). As expected, nonresettlement initiatives proved decisive years later during the *solutions phase*. There were many difficulties over the years—many frightening and nearly calamitous—but eventually the *managing down* approach worked.

RP monitored available indicators of influence and/or progress. For example, US admission numbers rose when needed but slackened when needs decreased, 1979–87 (*see* Table 3).

Simultaneously, numbers of new refugee arrivals to first-asylum countries declined. The rate of new arrivals from Vietnam and Laos decreased from an average of twenty-four thousand per month in FY 1979 to ten thousand per month in FY 1981, and to fewer than seven thousand per month in FY 1983. They continued declining each year thereafter. Kampuchea was a special case.

Given continued resettlement by the United States and other countries, the decline in new arrivals, and small repatriation and regional settlement efforts, first-asylum numbers dropped progressively from 1979 to 1986.

12/79: 409,000	12/83: 191,000
12/80: 320,000	12/84: 150,000
12/81: 258,000	12/85: 120,000
12/82: 222,000	12/86: 110,000

First-asylum populations drop (1979–86)

In no year were first-asylum populations allowed to rise.

Significantly, managing down allowed the refugee program offices to free up resources devoted to resettlement and apply them to other durable solutions in Asia and elsewhere. The managing down initiative required much balancing and diplomacy. We struggled to keep first asylum open when harsh *asylum-country* pressures threatened to restrict or close it.

Asylum-country *humane deterrence* schemes were not always humane. They sometimes confined refugees to closed camps, frequently guarded and austere with almost no freedom of movement. Subsistence services were kept to a minimum to discourage more refugee arrivals. By setting up refugee camps in remote sites and often close to war zones, asylum countries added to the security concerns and challenges. The *resettlement countries* insisted that the *first-asylum countries* make *improvements* in *camp conditions* and allow *resettlement countries access* to the refugees; *this insistence* sometimes met with reluctant or delayed acceptance. The dialogue remained open and compromise was usually reasonable.

Between 1975 and 1987, the State Department achieved significant programmatic and budgetary realignments in keeping with evolving refugee situations in Southeast Asia and the rest of the world. Overall, the United States contributed around $4 billion to global refugee programs during that period. Budget allocations for highly expensive refugee resettlement programs—primarily Indochinese resettlement—consumed a significant proportion of these resources in the early years. They reached a high of nearly 80 percent in 1979 before declining to around 30 percent in 1983 and later (*see* Table 3). This allowed the redirection of freed-up resources to solutions outside resettlement and the augmentation of relief assistance to growing worldwide refugee populations, up by over 300 percent during those years.

These and similar subjects usually formed the agenda for RP negotiations among asylum, resettlement, and donor countries. The United States had the largest *third-country resettlement* program, and we used it to leverage influence, particularly in Southeast Asia.

The signal I wanted to pass became clear: "If you want American help on resettlement, help us on security, humane first asylum, and abuse issues." We were not always successful, but we kept US influence high and the most egregious threats countered.

Direct Negotiations and Mutual Challenges

One important vehicle for employing American leverage was direct negotiation on mutual challenges with a range of donors and asylum country officials. An example, our relations with the Thai squadron leader, Soonsiri Prasong, also chairman of Thailand's national security council.[2] My first meeting with Prasong was at the UNHCR executive committee meeting in Geneva in 1982. I knew he was in charge for the Thai Government on refugees and exerted influence with the other first-asylum governments. He was well known to the American Embassy in Bangkok.

I learned much from our annual meetings. Prasong gave a good brief on how the ASEAN asylum governments planned and coordinated their actions, similar to the Americans and other major resettlement governments. He informed me that in October 1981, ASEAN governments, following Thailand's lead, had introduced restrictive measures called *humane deterrence*, designed to reduce the magnet effect they believed first asylum and resettlement created. Their waning faith in the resettlement and donor countries was clear.

The Thai Government had closed nine camps and announced that only refugees arriving before a certain date would be considered for resettlement. Others would be supported in austere camps and denied access to resettlement countries. The remaining four refugee camps were set up by refugee *country of origin*: Laotian refugees had two camps, Ban Vinai and Ban Na Pho; Cambodians were kept in Khao I Dang and Vietnamese in Sikhiu.[3]

Prasong reported that the number of first-asylum refugees in Thailand fell by over 35 percent, 1981–82, due to the new deterrence policy, combined with increased resettlement and reduced arrivals.[4] Other asylum governments announced similar results. In Hong Kong, the UK Government announced the establishment of "closed camps," as opposed to previously "open camps." So, refugees were denied access to resettlement. Refugee flows to Hong Kong likewise decreased.[5] The United States had many discussions with the UK and Hong Kong Governments about taking a more humane approach. *Humane deterrence* was announced for Laotians, Cambodians, and Vietnamese to quell the new flows of people, some of whom believed camp asylum was the route to permanent resettlement.

Prasong and I met at least yearly in Geneva, Bangkok, or Washington to negotiate, argue, and, sometimes, agree. (He once joked that his goal in life was to be resettled as a Lao refugee to El Paso, Texas.) We always tried to work toward eventual agreement on plans that each could trust. Proposals advanced by both sides sometimes found resistance elsewhere. When mutual commitments were made, however, we tried never to renege. In return for US resettlement assistance, I received Thai help on other fronts, such as access to sensitive populations and cases, nonresettlement solutions, moving camps from endangered locations with security provided, and antipiracy efforts. We kept open the process of talk and negotiation until permanent agreement came into view. Comparable results were achieved with other asylum governments.

Over the years, asylum governments made many exceptions, compromises, and harsh decisions. All actions, they maintained, helped the deserving, the true refugees, while simultaneously discouraging the adventurous, those mainly seeking a better or different life. Where possible, they tried to be receptive to our requests to pull the identified groups or individuals out of the *humane deterrence camps* for compassionate resettlement processing. RP learned how to use the large US resettlement program for maximum leverage.

Above all, the asylum countries were concerned that their openness and generosity to refugees not be allowed to harm their own stability, economic development, and relations with neighboring countries.

We also attempted to keep open communication with the origin countries. We were convinced that an important way to stop dangerous, clandestine boat departures from Vietnam was to negotiate with the SRV, to reenergize the *orderly departure* program. This reform, started in 1979, took time and patience, but it happened, eventually.

Orderly Departure Program

Even after the shaky start of the Orderly Departure Program (ODP), in 1979 (*see* chapter 15), the Americans maintained clear expectations going forward. ODP's future success would be measured by the degree to which refugees leaving Vietnam used the program rather than risking boat departure. We wanted to see ODP departures equaling clandestine departures then exceeding and eventually replacing them, over time.

But we continued to see little progress in the early Reagan years. By the end of 1982, slightly over twenty-three thousand Vietnamese had left via ODP, and only about six thousand (27 percent) of those resettled in the United States. Over that same period, many hundreds of thousands left clandestinely. We did not find this situation acceptable.

ODP's slow pace was troubling for three reasons: first, unless accelerated significantly, it could not provide the safe alternative we envisioned for refugees; second, we would need a smoothly functioning ODP if we got the Vietnam Government, SRV, to release two particularly vulnerable refugee groups: the Amerasian children (and their immediate family members) and the Vietnamese political prisoners; and third, a well-functioning ODP would be necessary if we could ever redirect increasing numbers of family reunion cases through normal immigration channels. Therefore, it became urgent that new and stronger understandings be reached with the Vietnamese Government.

Direct US Negotiations
Socialist Republic of Vietnam

The RP leadership team decided we could no longer depend solely on UNHCR's discussions with the Socialist Republic of Vietnam (SRV) to resolve ODP problems. We needed direct talks with the SRV. Secretary Shultz agreed, and we asked the UNHCR to present this request to the Vietnamese. With apprehension, they agreed to the bilateral talks in Geneva.

To represent the United States with the SRV's deputy foreign minister, I selected the deputy assistant secretary Bob Funseth. I had great regard for Bob's diplomatic skills, and I knew him to be steady and disciplined. We could depend on him to represent American interests with skill and resolve. For a staff aide, he chose Doug Hunter, then at RP in Washington.

The discussions got off to a good start and resolved many technical problems, such as the composition of future departure lists. Before adjourning, both sides agreed to continue annual meetings to allow more direct contact. We hoped this would lead to further improvements made even more urgent by the continuing scourge of pirate attacks on boat refugees.

In 1983, ODP brought out sixteen thousand refugees, of whom seven thousand were admitted to the United States. This result was still fewer than we had hoped, but the trend was slowly moving in the right direction. Less encouraging was the report that the antipiracy program relaunched two years earlier had arrested no suspects.

UN officials reported the orderly departure program was an important alternative for many Vietnamese. Of those who came out in 1983, a third said they had tried clandestine departure, a third said they had considered it, and another third said they had ruled out clandestine departure.[6] The mindset was moving in the right direction, though results were still unsatisfactory.

UNHCR reported that in the eight years from April 1975 to the end of 1983, nearly 530,000 boat people arrivals in first-asylum countries had been recorded, over 200,000 during the peak year of 1979 alone. By comparison, only forty thousand had left under ODP in the program's four-plus years. Orderly departures from Vietnam increased 1984–85, when thirty thousand departed each year. Those departures exceeded boat arrivals for the first time in 1984.

United States and Socialist Republic of Vietnam talks took on greater political significance in 1984 when President Reagan and Secretary Shultz announced American initiatives regarding Amerasian children and Vietnamese political prisoners. They would depart Vietnam via ODP.[7]

The SRV was critical of these initiatives yet eventually agreed to help with the Amerasian children. No immediate progress could be made on the political prisoners, whom they regarded as traitors. The SRV became more obstinate over orderly departure issues, especially the composition of future departure lists. The SRV wanted to use ODP to rid itself of ethnic Chinese, whereas the United States wanted to reach other known humanitarian cases. The differences became so heated that in late 1985, the SRV announced unilateral cessation of processing for new orderly departure cases by January 1986 unless the American side relented about future lists. We did not back down, and the suspension of the Orderly Departure Program went into effect.

While regrettable, this suspension did not stop departures in 1986, as there were enough approved cases in the pipeline to maintain the previous year's level. Since we had no choice but to accept this unilateral suspension, we kept trying to persuade the SRV to resume the processing on agreed standards before permanent damage was done.

When I left RP in late 1986, almost 160,000 Vietnamese had left Vietnam safely through orderly departure, including eight thousand four hundred Amerasian children and family members. Half of ODP refugees went to the United States. By the end of 1986, only 752 former prisoners and their families could leave. The significant movement of political prisoners would not occur until later.[8] The composition of people leaving Vietnam under the ODP in 1986 favored immigrants over refugees. Intense negotiations between the UN and the SRV in 1987 led to the resumption of the program; over 170,000 Vietnamese had departed via ODP by the end of that year.

These developments gave evidence to our earlier contention that a functioning Orderly Departure Program would become a major vehicle for stabilization through steady, regulated movement of people from Vietnam to America and other receiving countries in the years ahead.

26

PHASE 2. PROTECTION

IN REFUGEE ORTHODOXY, *DURABLE SOLUTIONS* ARE grounded in *protection*. Within the refugee protection phase under President Reagan, the RP team gave sustained attention to the people most vulnerable to dangers in Southeast Asia: piracy victims (especially women and children) and other refugees in distress on the high seas; Kampucheans on the border and in Thailand; vulnerable Laotian and land Vietnamese; Asian American (Amerasian) children in Vietnam, and former South Vietnamese political prisoners forced into reeducation camps because of close ties to the United States.

Rescue at Sea and Anti-Piracy

Nowhere was protection for Vietnamese more imperative than for those leaving by sea. It was difficult for RP to separate the two intertwined dangers of the unsafe vessels and the ruthless pirates. For clarity, they are dealt with separately here.

By 1983, upwards of half a million Vietnamese had left by boat. How many perished? No one knows for sure, as no reliable data are available for the 1978–81 period. The general wisdom in Vietnam was that about half the boats that set out finished their journeys. And asylum countries were reluctant to allow disembarkation or acceptance of refugees rescued at sea. UNHCR introduced two programs in August 1979 to address that problem.

Rescue-at-Sea Resettlement Offers, or RASRO, and Disembarkation Resettlement Offers, DISERO efforts (*see* chapter 15) showed typical slow, sporadic results. Some progress was seen in the early 1980s, due to increased public awareness, especially among ships at sea.

One freighter crew that helped in 1983 was serving on a mammoth American commercial vessel, the *Rose City*. The ship's crew heroically rescued endangered small-craft survivors in the South China Sea. The UNHCR awarded the *Rose City* crew the annual Nansen Award in 1984 to commemorate the event. In refugee work, the Nansen Award is equivalent to the Nobel Prize. Captain Lewis Hiller and two of his seamen, Greg Turay and Jeff Kass, were made official members of the American delegation in Geneva that year to receive this award at a well-attended UNHCR executive committee meeting, where I gave the American statement highlighting the remarkable rescue by the ship's crew.[1] The media reported the *Rose City*'s experience extensively.

The RASRO and DISERO programs had to be ended a decade later as countries in the region proved unwilling to disembark more rescued boat people. However, by that time, the normal programs of concerned governments and international organizations could deal with the continuing, but smaller, boat departures.

Formal antipiracy efforts were on life support when Reagan became president. An emergency meeting in late 1981 between UNHCR, the ICRC, and interested governments breathed new life into UNHCR's almost defunct 1980 antipiracy program. Following this meeting, UNHCR made a formal appeal, garnering almost $4 million from twelve countries. The provision of large and small patrol boats, decoy boats mimicking refugee craft, and two spotter planes helped restart the antipiracy program in July 1981.

Because UNHCR did not collect piracy data and statistics until late 1981, no data are available for the heavy boat flows of earlier years. But in the first reporting year, 349 of 452 boats (77 percent) that arrived in Thailand were attacked an average of three times each. UNHCR reported that during those attacks 578 women had been raped, 228 women abducted, and 881 people were killed or missing.[2]

RP noted in congressional testimony that the United States frequently discussed piracy with Thai officials, maintaining that a more effective piracy solution might lie in Thailand's ability to apprehend, prosecute, and imprison convicted pirates. If pirates operated with impunity, they would not stop. While the Thai Government agreed to consider punitive policy, the record was spotty. Between 1979 and 1982, only fifty-three fishermen were arrested for alleged crimes against Vietnamese boat people. Of these, just twenty-seven were tried and convicted of charges ranging from gang robbery, gang rape, and murder.

Victims' unwillingness to take part in lengthy court proceedings, primarily fearing delay in their resettlement, thwarted prosecutions. Innocent Thai fishermen feared their compatriots that had turned to piracy.

To encourage more aggressiveness by the Thai Government, Rep. Stephen Solarz, (D-NY), chairman of the House Foreign Affairs Subcommittee on Asia and Pacific Affairs, earmarked $5 million of RP's 1982 and 1983 budgets to combat piracy in the Gulf of Thailand. His plan included larger blue-water ships to be acquired by the Thai Navy and used in piracy area patrols.

The piracy problems continued, with RP under pressure from the Congress and NGOs. NGO official Roger Winter's "nuisance factor," as much as anything, led Gene Dewey to bring in Bob Gersony to work on antipiracy.

Consultant Gersony traveled to Southeast Asia and talked with scores of survivors among rape victims and those abducted and later saved, local governments, and UNHCR officials. These included the US consul general Pancho Huddle in Songkhla, the UNHCR's Graham Lean, and RP's Carl Harris. Clear ideas emerged: pay for information about piracy events and encourage victims to identify assailants.

While in Bangkok, Gersony heard about a DEA agent, a fluent Thai speaker and former Peace Corps volunteer in Thailand, Tex Lierly. Tex had two decades of narcotics trafficking intelligence-gathering, and action experience. He began to put pieces in place with Thai Maritime Police in Bangkok for an informant network to get information from crew members of offending ships and to collect survivor testimonies. Arrests, prosecutions, and convictions increased. Zealous Thai prosecutors got more convictions the next year than in all previous years.

The system worked because Tex Lierly and the Thai Maritime Police identified repeat offenders and gave highest priority to the collection of intelligence and evidence of their crimes. According to Tex, the number of attacks plummeted soon thereafter, although occasional opportunistic attacks by random fishing vessels still occurred.

Another success factor was my ongoing contact with the Thai squadron leader Soonsiri Prasong, mentioned previously. In annual meetings with him, I stressed our piracy concerns: "We request that you order Thai Navy apprehensions, using evidence and information the team is collecting. Bring offenders to trial and apply long prison sentences. Deterrence."

Prasong wanted our help on resettlement, and we wanted Thai help on antipiracy. A bargain seemed in sight. However, unhappy with our demands, he would not say a clear "yes" or "no." But, we began to see that apprehensions, arrests, and prosecutions had gone up dramatically. Witness intimidation was suppressed. News about trials and long sentences became commonplace. Pirate attacks diminished.

Following the reinvigorated team's lead, the antipiracy program shifted increasingly to land-based operations. Thai police units and harbor officials registered fishing boats, photographed crews, and conducted public awareness campaigns on the penalties for piracy. Concerted efforts were made to link piracy victims with police and prosecutors, to monitor court trials, arrange witness transfers from abroad, and provide interpretation services for investigations, arrests, and trials. By 1987, only 8 percent of all boats arriving in Thailand had been attacked, a 96 percent drop from 1981. There were no deaths from pirate attacks; some rapes were reported. After virtual containment for a few years, pirate attacks renewed briefly in 1989, but the sophisticated investigative techniques introduced earlier gave them a quick end by 1990.[3]

An earlier RP initiative that may have set the table for this positive outcome was a 1984 papal visit to Thailand. Gene Dewey had worked with Cardinal John O'Connor when he was the US Navy Chief of Chaplains. Gene called O'Connor and described how we needed Pope John Paul's intervention in his upcoming meetings with the Thai prime minister and king. We wanted him to urge maximum sentences for pirates We were never privy to the substance of the pope's meetings. But his visit gave greater public attention to refugee issues.

When the antipiracy initiative launched, we feared that relying on survivor testimony would lead pirates to kill victims before throwing them overboard. To address this concern, the new strategy primarily relied on crew and dock informant testimonies; survivor statements were used sparingly. We were relieved to see that over time the death rates among kidnapped women did not increase.

Reports showed that the land information and prosecution strategies helped reduce pirate attacks, which fell by as much as 90 percent overall and saved many lives. Later, Soonsiri Prasong insisted that factors other than land-based enforcement led to these results. The Vietnamese were discouraging boat flight, there was a noticeable shortage of boats, and pirates were on to other ventures. But we were convinced that our efforts had paid off. In December 1991, I attended the closing of the Anti-Piracy Center in Bangkok, no longer needed. This was good testimony for broad humanitarian efforts to combat piracy.

Khmer Populations of Special Humanitarian Concern

The Khmer were a vulnerable ethnic population requiring special protection and assistance when President Reagan came into office. Some 230,000 were encamped along the Thai border and 160,000 were at the Khao-I-Dang camp inside Thailand.

After closing their open door to Khmer people in February 1980, the Thai added their *humane deterrence* policy to Vietnamese and Laotian refugees in early 1981. This meant that all new arrivals from the Indochina Triangle would be incarcerated in special camps under austere conditions. They would receive food, shelter, and medical care from UN agencies, but would be ineligible for resettlement. Thailand was concerned about the "pull" factor of resettlement.[4]

In late 1981, these conditions set the stage for Director Dick Vine's first visit to Southeast Asia, where he met with Soonsiri Prasong. The Squadron Leader explained Thailand's new humane deterrence policy and pressed for US endorsement and support. He told Vine that his government believed the new humane deterrence policy for the Vietnamese and Lao was working well. Indochinese refugee arrivals had declined by almost 90 percent in the past year because, in Prasong's view, new restrictions limited eligibility for third-country resettlement.[5] He neglected to mention the deteriorating plight of refugees then in Thailand, especially Kampucheans, or the constant security threats they faced.

Dick Vine returned to Washington perplexed about the American response to Prasong. He sought advice. RP deputies Gene Dewey and Richard English, EAP's Paul Wolfowitz, John Mongo, Dan O'Donohue, and I provided views and recommendations.

Khmer Inside Thailand

I had concerns about every Indochinese ethnic group and advocated for help targeted for each one. The Khmer inside Thailand and on the border were in especially severe conditions. Resolving their dilemmas would take extreme, passionate, and complicated efforts by different parties.

Khmer living conditions in Thai camps involved difficulties such as tenuous protection and security. At almost any point, they could face violence from the Vietnamese or Kampuchean forces, and there were no durable solution efforts underway. Repatriation and regional settlement attempts had proven unsuccessful.[6] The Thai maintained that Khmer resettlement to the United States from Khao-I-Dang ran risks for both Thailand and Kampuchea. Unless handled carefully, resettlement could encourage new surges to Thailand, the magnet effect, and risk collapse of safe asylum, generating more forced returns.

The changed situation of the Kampucheans in Thailand since my September 1981 consultations testimony to the Judiciary Committees was troubling. In that testimony, I had said:

> … additional callouts of Khmer from the holding centers in Thailand were not being proposed at that time because we did not want to endanger ongoing negotiations between UNHCR, the RTG (Royal Thai Government) and Phnom Penh authorities regarding voluntary repatriation of a substantial number of the Khmer. However, … if those negotiations did not produce a timely or successful repatriation program and the continuance of these refugees in Thailand began to

threaten first asylum, steps would have to be taken to relieve that problem.[7]

Early in 1982, the UN high commissioner for refugees Poul Hartling wrote to Secretary Shultz to make plain he could not repatriate all the Khmer in the *holding centers* in Thailand. He asked the United States to resettle fifty thousand. While suggesting that the global call for Khmer resettlement was ill-timed (because of the potential magnet effect), the United States left open the door for a limited program. (As repatriation was not under consideration, the Thai changed course and pressed for greater international Kampuchean resettlement.)

After considering these elements, I urged that we leverage our support for small and selective resettlement programs for the Khmer in Thailand and for targeted improvements for other groups. I endorsed a renewed UN presence on the Thai border to safeguard the border Khmer until permanent return arrangements could be made. Director Vine agreed.

On April 27, 1982, the US Government made a formal policy announcement that after April 30 refugees from Vietnam, Cambodia (Kampuchea), and Laos arriving in Thailand or other Southeast Asian countries would be considered for resettlement in America *only if* they could demonstrate close US ties.

While RP did not endorse *humane deterrence*, we would tolerate rational restrictions by the Thai in return for limited and targeted resettlement. This tougher policy did not go as far as the Thai wanted. But Soonsiri Prasong praised our statement and said it would help eliminate the "pull factors" that had been attracting refugees to Thailand and to other countries in the region. This tougher policy signaled that escape to Thailand was not the route to resettlement.

I insisted we clarify that the new resettlement restrictions would apply only to refugees arriving in Thailand after April 30, 1982. Those already in Thai camps or arriving before then were eligible for resettlement processing. For the 160,000 Cambodians in the Thai refugee camps prior to the cutoff date, UNHCR was now in the picture. By mandate, UNHCR could then pursue durable solutions.

From the six priority *refugee resettlement* categories, we called out (from the holding centers) only those fitting into categories I to III, meaning close relatives (spouses and siblings) of refugees already admitted, former employees of US entities, and key Lon Nol followers associated with the United States before 1975. This limited our resettlement program to those only in imminent danger or with close US family or professional ties. We thought there might be a thousand in the first category, three thousand in the second, and about fourteen thousand in the third. As most of the Khmer in Khao-I-Dang fell into ineligible categories, we believed our recommendation were targeted and restricted.[8] Refugees eligible for resettlement were transferred to Kamput, a nearby processing camp.

A key consideration was whether this action required advance consultation with Congress under the 1980 Refugee Act. We had just completed extensive consultations and agreed on resettlement numbers and budgets for each region. Even Congress had avoided country-by-country breakdowns for Southeast Asia to provide greater flexibility. As Khmer were Indochina refugees, I was confident of our authority to act without further consultation. However, the 1980 Refugee Act was new, and Congress had an important interest in executive branch interpretations. They expressed special concern for the Khmer at the hearings and could rightly say they signaled a desire to be involved. Also, their confidence in State had been shaken by the recent September surprise episode.

Director Vine was adamant that Congress could not interfere with the president's prerogatives. Our legal advisor agreed with his general contention but thought the 1980 Refugee Act gave Congress more input than would normally be the case. I preferred prior consultation. Because of the urgency, however, I suggested immediate processing and simultaneous notification of the committees. Dick Vine reluctantly agreed, but even simultaneous notification would expose us to congressional criticism. I thought the fallout could be managed.

The processing began in April 1982, and Dick Vine simultaneously requested personal meetings with Rep. Mazzoli and Sen. Simpson. The meeting with Mazzoli did not go well. As reported back, Dick was argumentative, gruff, dismissive, and seemed to question the committee's prerogatives. In reaction, Chairman Mazzoli wrote to Director Vine criticizing the department's approach and accusing me of misleading them regarding Khmer at the previous fall's hearings. His letter quoted from the hearing's transcript and was harsh and accusatory.[9]

Dick brought this letter to me.

"Guess I really pissed him off," he said.

"Yes," I replied, "it looks like you did, and I'm the one on the spot. We must repair the damage or RP will live with it for years. Because I'm the one under attack, why don't you let me do damage control."

A lengthy response to Rep. Mazzoli's letter pointed out how he had taken two lines from my previous testimony out of context and constructed a spurious argument. Next, I repeated and reiterated my statements during the hearings about the need for flexibility to deal with Khmer, Vietnamese, and Laotian refugees to maintain safe first asylum.[10]

Committee staff understood what we had done. But Vine had offended Mazzoli. He must apologize, or Mazzoli wouldn't let go. I included profuse apologies in the letter I prepared for Vine's reply to Mazzoli.

Dick liked the substantive part of my draft but said: "I will not apologize. I have nothing to apologize for."

Dick and I argued constantly about the letter over the next few days. Finally, I said:

"Dick, you're stubborn and you're wrong. You insulted the man. Simply apologize and we're done."

He delayed several days, then relented:

"OK, send the letter."

Afterwards, I talked with the Mazzoli, Simpson, and committee staff, who were flabbergasted that we would have risked such an unnecessary confrontation. The fire was extinguished, but the committees were still displeased that we had initiated Khmer processing.

Processing commenced under the 1980 Refugee Act, but it did not go well. INS was not enthusiastic about extending to Khmer the leeway it had earlier given the highly publicized Vietnamese boat people. As required by the Act, many could not demonstrate individual persecution. INS was also concerned that some applicants might have been former Khmer Rouge. That would render them ineligible for US resettlement.[11]

Dick Vine left in early summer 1982. By August, I was back in the acting director chair, and INS denial rates for Khmer continued to climb higher than for any other Indochina group. Arguments between State and INS were heated and antagonistic. State believed INS was denying the legitimate claims of some of the world's most persecuted people. INS thought that State was undermining the law's requirements and wanted to resettle Khmer for foreign policy reasons. The debate became so contentious that INS asked me to summon the Bangkok staff of both organizations to Washington. We met around my table and heard both cases. I became irritated with both sides.

"You folks want us to tell you how to do your job," I said. "You can't sit down and discuss like rational people, so you push things upstairs. Go back, do your job. If things don't improve in short order, we will replace the whole team." Both teams returned to Bangkok dissatisfied.

Upon reflection and later discussion with our Bangkok staff and other trusted allies, however, I concluded things were not as clear as they could be. More guidance was needed. Working with INS's Doris Meissner, we clarified the legal standing of the Khmer awaiting resettlement and issued joint guidance on ties to Pol Pot's brutal Khmer Rouge regime. INS prepared new refugee processing guidelines. They also provided further operational guidance in correspondence referred to collectively as the "Kamput Cables."

The National Security Council's Richard Childress worked with RP and Justice to further clarify refugee processing guidance, issuing a National Security Decision Directive (NSDD-93), May 1983, accompanied by a personal statement from President Reagan.[12]

NSDD-93, a national security decision directive, had a dramatic impact on processing of Khmer for US refugee resettlement. Whereas the Refugee Act of 1980 required individual determination of persecution, this directive additionally allowed persecuted classes of applicants to be considered by the INS. Persons within approved categories did not need to prove individual persecution. With new guidance, Mac Thompson, JVA officer at Kamput, supervised additional reviews of Khmer cases.

The processing continued for the next several years; it was never easy. Richard English. prepared additional legal guidance pertaining to Khmer refugees. Lacy Wright, Bangkok refugee coordinator, was RP's point man for administering the resettlement program during this difficult and conflictive period. Interpretative difficulties remained, often requiring the intervention of Washington's INS and RP leaders. President Reagan, Secretary of State Shultz, and I received more letters and criticism on Khmer processing than any other refugee issue of that time. Many critics (including scores of senators, representatives, NGO officials and concerned individuals) believed that US processing was too rigid and that many bona fide refugees were unfairly denied. They wanted case reviews, rereviews, and then more reviews of denied cases.

No critic was more sincere, vocal, or persistent than Kitty Dukakis, wife of Massachusetts Governor Michael Dukakis. Kitty was a member of the Massachusetts Governor's advisory committee on refugee resettlement, a board member of Refugees International, and a leading NGO refugee advocate. She visited me regularly to lobby on behalf of numerous rejected Khmer cases of interest to Massachusetts, usually accompanied by Peter Pond, a New England activist and philanthropist with a passion for the Khmer refugees. His concern led him to be arrested in 1980 for opposing Thailand's forced repatriation of thousands of Khmer refugees and imprisoned "in a shack filled with human excrement." When Thailand's Queen Sirikit heard about his treatment, she ordered him released and granted three wishes. He responded by identifying three Khmer orphans to bring to the United States. Devoutly religious, Pond was at different times a Lutheran, a Congregationalist, a Unitarian-Universalist, and a Roman Catholic. Throughout his career, he founded or directed the Inter-Religious Mission for Peace in Cambodia, the Cambodian Crisis Committee and the Thai Friends Relief Foundation.[13]

In early 1985 Kitty Dukakis encouraged Refugees International's chairperson Susan Goodwillie to invite me to a board meeting where the rejected Khmer cases would be discussed. This highly advertised meeting attracted most of the State Department's critics. At the head table with Goodwillie and me was "The Killing Fields" actor Sam Waterston, who had become a Khmer refugee advocate. I faced a barrage of questions, criticism, and little sympathy as I explained the government's policy and position. Few minds were changed.

Continuing criticism led Rep. Stephen (Steve) Solarz to call a July 1985 hearing on Khmer refugee processing.[14] I was the main government witness, with EAP Assistant Secretary Paul Wolfowitz. Other important witnesses were Sen. John Glenn (D–OH) and many leading advocates including Kitty Dukakis and Libby Mitchell, a Maine legislator, attorney, and foster parent of a Khmer child. (Libby and I were also fellow Furman University alumni.) Chairman Solarz invited members of the Khmer community to participate. So many were present they had to be rotated periodically between the hearing room and the outside hall. This hearing was a landmark event in that it brought national attention to this sensitive issue and as satisfactory a public/private understanding as was possible.

Due to the absence of other durable solution alternatives for the Khmer in Thailand, I eventually extended US resettlement processing to all six priority categories for eligible Khmer at the holding centers. In early May 1985, Doris Meissner (INS) and I were happy to send this message by diplomatic cable to our respective Washington and overseas establishments:

> With the processing of the current caseload of Cambodian refugees from Khao-I-Dang now approaching completion, it is the appropriate time to recognize the historic achievements that the processing of this Cambodian population is. The cases of approximately 165,000 Cambodians will have been examined, and 90 percent will have been given resettlement in the United States and other countries. These cases have presented, in a variety of forms, some of the most difficult problems in the application of the Refugee Act of 1980, and the accomplishments of processing this population could never have been attained without the contributions of energy, effort, and hard work of many dedicated individuals. Moreover, this work has been performed under continuously difficult and often dangerous conditions.[15]

Resettlement processing for eligible Khmer refugees was completed the following month, an astounding result. As the Reagan administration ended in 1989, RP could look back and say that the United States accepted over 144,000 refugees from Kampuchea (over fifty thousand resettled by other governments) since the start of the crisis in 1975. The approval rate of those the United States considered was exceptional, one of the highest in the US–Indochina program. Australia, France, Canada, and other Western nations also resettled significant numbers.

Border Khmer

Beyond resettlement, RP worked for a new UN presence on the Thai border to assist those known as *border Khmer*. Over 230,000 Khmer trapped on the border were confined to narrow, conflicted zones vulnerable to annual Vietnamese military offensives and Southeast Asian weather fluctuations.[16] They were denied refugee status and not allowed to live in the UNHCR camps in Thailand. There had been no designated international lead organization responsible for their needs since the ICRC–UNICEF arrangements broke down in 1980.

Nowhere was the Dewey team's initiative on multilateral reform more necessary than for the border Khmer. The Thai Government adamantly opposed a leadership role for UNHCR, fearing that its protection and durable solutions mandates would lead to heightened resettlement demands and more refugee arrivals. In January 1982, the UN established a new agency, the UN Border Relief Organization. UNBRO was to oversee relief and assistance needs of the border Khmer but was denied protection and durable solutions mandates. As the organization was being set up in Bangkok, Gene Dewey came to know of Sir Robert Jackson from Australia. Due to medical issues, the young Robert had not attended university and at age eighteen joined the Australian Navy. He later became a development expert and served under several UN secretaries general, including Norwegian statesman, Trygve Lie, the first.

Gene Dewey studied Sir Robert's earlier work and thought he possessed the right skills to run UNBRO's complicated operation, and he would be acceptable to the Thai. Sir Robert's unparalleled field leadership in post-World War II reconstruction, sharpened in a score of major multilateral operations, was needed to help the Khmer trapped on the border. We recommended him, and, to its credit, the UN agreed.

For years, UNBRO distinguished itself by efficiently managing assistance needs and assuring safety for the border Khmer, especially during the annual Vietnam dry season offensives against the Khmer resistance.

These offensives generally were of short duration and the human displacement limited. In 1985, however, the Vietnamese drove the resistance off the border and into Thailand but blocked their return. Under Sir Robert's guidance, UNBRO organized the temporary relocation of 238,000 Khmer and negotiated their stay until return to the border became possible.[17] This brave action earned considerable credit to UNBRO and its leaders.

The border relief organization would develop into one of the UN's most innovative agencies, a multilateral model the US refugee bureau team in the State Department would attempt to replicate in responding to other world problems. Even absent a formal mandate, UNBRO was a protection force to be reckoned with. Keeping the border relief organization alive and sufficiently funded, however, proved a formidable challenge for the US team, requiring RP to bring the full force of the US Government to support this unique organization and its leader.

Gene Dewey later said it was fascinating to analyze the "Sir Robert Crisis Management Technique." He could be harsh or sensitive, as the situation required. Dewey chaired the advance meetings before New York donor conferences with UNICEF and WFP (World Food Program), and other donors to arrive at common positions on UNBRO programs and funding. This provided him an opportunity to leverage sizeable US contributions with other donors, magnifying our influence.

The sluggishness of UN responses occasionally left Sir Robert Jackson scratching his head in puzzlement, knowing from experience that better reactions were possible. A good example was the pressing need to address a serious outbreak of malaria in the border camps and the UN's inability to launch a rapid response. Jackson was disappointed but understanding when Dewey had to bypass the UN and bring in the Centers for Disease Control to combat this problem.

Dewey often ran interference for Sir Robert by serving as his man in court in New York. As a no-nonsense field operator with limited patience for bureaucracy, Sir Robert railed against what he called "the eunuchs" in the UN secretariat constantly nipping at his heels and trying to get at him by lobbying the secretary general to retire him because he was over the mandatory UN retirement age of sixty-five.

Over time, the escalating threats to the border Khmer led the United

States to consider more formal protection arrangements. A permanent protection-and-security presence was needed as the problem moved toward resolution. RP acknowledged that both UNHCR and UNBRO would be unacceptable to the Thai, and Gene Dewey and I had extensive discussions on this issue with Paul Wolfowitz and EAP colleagues John Mongo and Dan O'Donohue.

In May 1985, Paul Wolfowitz and I recommended to Secretary Shultz that the United States propose the UN secretary general's special representative for the Kampuchean people Dr. Tatsuro Kunugi of Japan as designee responsible for protecting the border Khmer. Secretary Shultz agreed to sound out other countries. The idea found favor and this arrangement was formalized by the secretary general. The consulting governments clarified to Dr. Kunugi, however, that his protection responsibility was limited to the immediate welfare of the border Khmer pending a *durable political solution* acceptable to the Thai.[18]

This arrangement worked as we expected. In 1991, the UN established the United Nations Transitional Authority in Cambodia (UNTAC) to administer Kampuchea's pending elections. From March 1992 to May 1993, UNHCR returned over 360,000 Khmer home from Thailand in time to participate in the peaceful elections. Those elections resulted in the return to power of Prince Norodum Sihanouk, who came back to a capital he had been forced to abandon almost twenty years earlier. The UN's envoy Sergio Vieira de Mello supervised the returns and then brokered and implemented the ensuing peace agreement.

From 1975 until 1992, the year mass returns to Cambodia began, over 235,000 Khmer refugees resettled overseas, including 150,000 in the United States. Many years later, Gene Dewey and I nominated Sir Robert Jackson for the Nobel Peace Prize for his splendid humanitarian work in UNBRO and on behalf of the border Khmer. He remained high on our list of global heroes, regardless of any prize.

In the name of the US refugee programs and our partners at home and abroad, I accepted a Save Cambodia award in 1986. The strategy to keep the vulnerable Khmer as safe as border conditions permitted, until they could return home, had worked.

In 2014, almost thirty-five years after these events, a special UN Tribunal (the Extraordinary Chambers in the Courts of Cambodia) brought leaders of the Khmer Rouge to justice. Khieu Samphan, the regime's former head of state and Nuon Chea, chief ideologist, received life sentences. Prison director Kaing Khek Iev, also known as Comrade Duch, had been sentenced earlier. Pol Pot was dead, as were Ieng Sary, former foreign minister, and Ieng Thirith, wife of Ieng Sary and formerly a social affairs and economies minister.[19]

Cambodia is currently considered an emerging Asian economy.

Vulnerable Montagnard, Hmong, Land Vietnamese, and Lowland Lao

About a million ethnic highland people known as Montagnard remained in Vietnam when American forces withdrew in 1975. They remained for the next decade and continued their guerilla war against the new communist government. They were nearly forgotten by the United States until 1986, when 212 Montagnard people arrived in Thailand. This brought them to the attention of some of their former US military colleagues, especially Green Berets, who pressed for their resettlement in America.[20]

Knowing of their history and community cohesion, I believed that all Montagnard people should be resettled in a single US resettlement location. Several US resettlement agencies had prior contact with them and wanted to be their resettlement sponsor. I requested proposals from agencies wishing to participate. We received several thoughtful proposals and settled on the Lutheran Immigration and Resettlement Service (LIRS), which proposed to resettle Montagnard people in Greensboro, North Carolina. The Greensboro resettlement worked well, and numerous community groups and individuals contributed. One was a Lutheran cousin of my wife who took great pride in her Montagnard flock, helping them to adapt culturally, find jobs, and, in one case, obtain a home mortgage.

In 1992, a later group of 400 Montagnard people was resettled in Raleigh, North Carolina. Over nine thousand eventually resettled in the United States.

Hmong

The situation of Hmong hilltribe refugees from Laos has been discussed earlier. Their resettlement began in small numbers in 1975 and did not increase. These nomadic agriculturalists did not adapt well to industrialized countries. In the 1980s, Thai Squadron Leader Prasong told me often that Thailand would accommodate them until they could return home. In the early 1980s when resettled Hmong feared coming out of the downtown Detroit buildings, where they were temporarily housed, RP brought refugee officer Jerry Daniels from Thailand to reassure them. On another occasion, we invited the Hmong leadership to the State Department to disabuse them of the idea that the United States would sponsor a military return to Laos to uproot the communists. We urged the younger Hmong leaders to give up any false hopes of return and instead devote their attention to assimilation into American society. We believed they should balance respect for their elders with preparation of their young for life in an industrialized society.

Many Hmong resettled in Minnesota, where the 3M Company worked hard to assimilate them throughout the state. In 1983, I received a letter from Sen. David Durenberger (R-MN) complaining that Hmong resettlement in his State was causing problems.[21] He announced publicly that he wanted it stopped. Within days, the NGOs and faith-based groups in Minnesota vehemently objected to his announcement. The senator was forced to retract his earlier objection; and he showered praise on the Hmong, declaring Minnesota open to receive more.[22]

More than a quarter-century later, former RP official Lionel Rosenblatt received an honorary degree from Concordia University in St. Paul, Minnesota. At the ceremony, the Rector of Concordia said,

> … without the Hmong infusing new talent and energy, St. Paul would be a dead city. They have a farmers' market, and they have established refugee businesses and restaurants around the city. They have done extremely well and have turned around the capital of Minnesota.[23]

Lionel Rosenblatt pronounced the Hmong "one of the most successful of the Indochina groups. They have an academic bent and, even though poor, saw that education was the key to success in America." Over 140,000 were resettled in the United States during the thirty years following the 1975 Saigon Fall.

Land Vietnamese and Lowland Lao

Of the Land Vietnamese, a small group of perhaps ten-to-twelve thousand made the torturous overland journey across Cambodia to Thailand. Lowland (ethnic) Lao refugees in small numbers made similar journeys. Both groups received targeted attention and response from RP.

27

PROTECTION—POLITICAL PRISONERS AND AMERASIANS

MEDIA INTEREST WAS HIGH REGARDING REAGAN ADMINIStration achievements for refugee protection, highlighted by its initiatives for the release and relocation of South Vietnamese political prisoners and Amerasian children.

South Vietnamese Political Prisoners

The Socialist Republic of Vietnam, SRV, the unified Vietnam Government, opened communist reeducation centers within days of the US withdrawal. US intelligence reports said the SRV confined large numbers of low-ranking officials for short periods in April and May 1975.

By June 1975, higher-ranking officers were being jailed. The Vietnamese word for "studies," meaning "reeducation" in common parlance, was replaced by the word for "reconstruction" (used by the North to describe prisons). The United States and the other external observers continued to use the term *reeducation* for these abusive camps. Over time, as many as one hundred reeducation camps were in operation after the war, and up to one million or more persons were sent to them.

By 1978, low-ranking officers were released. Military officers from colonel up were moved farther north. In 1980, new arrests were reported, and US officials speculated that they might have resulted from resistance speeches by the influential Vietnamese in the United States.

No one knew how many political prisoners Vietnam still held by the mid-1980s. Intelligence reports noted at least 20,000 mid-level and high-ranking allies were punished cruelly for past association with the Americans. Refugee and intelligence reports characterized their imprisonment in stark terms: torture and abuse, hard agricultural labor, near-starvation rations, and no visits from relatives for months, if at all. Outspoken dissenters received punitive treatment, including confinement in cages, or were executed. Through deaths, emigration, and assimilation into communist society, that number had been probably reduced up to half by the mid-1980s. The survivors were of special humanitarian concern, and their stories were eloquently passed on by journalists like Barbara Crosette.[1]

Hanoi's Foreign Minister Nguyen Co Thach suggested that probably about ten thousand people remained in camps by the mid-1980s. In addition, there were tens of thousands of other former camp inmates. Many might try to obtain an exit visa because they had been imprisoned, even though SRV policy denied exit permits based solely on camp confinement.

Near the end of the Carter administration, attempts had been made to obtain the release of US former allies. The deputy secretary of state Walter Stoessel had gone to Vietnam to discuss a negotiated release. Foreign Minister Thach responded by offering the release of "everyone in reeducation camps" if the Americans wanted them. Given experience with the Cuban Marielitos, Stoessel declined. After that experience, the Vietnamese showed no interest in discussing the subject.[2]

But US military and diplomatic colleagues convinced me there was no group of more compelling humanitarian concern to the United States. We don't leave allies behind.

If RP focused on high priority cases in the American interest (especially former South Vietnam officers, government officials, and diplomats), we might call the SRV's bluff. The large Vietnamese community in America by then estimated at almost 700,000 could absorb and support them all and had indicated a strong willingness to do so. I asked the RP team if they thought a deal possible now.

"Without the president's involvement, it wouldn't get any traction," they said.

"So, if we need to, we'll get Reagan involved."

Amerasian Children and Families

Just as intractable as political prisoner treatment was the persecution suffered by Amerasians, as offspring of American servicemen and contractors in Vietnam were called. For ten thousand or more Amerasian children, life was hell. They were harassed as "children of the dust" in their homeland and in the United States. People often forgot they were no longer infants and toddlers but teenagers and young adults. Soon emigration would be impossible for those children. The mothers had survived through determination to protect their children.[3]

Because many children looked Western, because Americans were despised in Vietnam, and because the mothers were considered prostitutes, the Amerasian children were treated as pariahs.

In 1982, I had visited Phanot Nikhon Transit Center in Bangkok, where I first learned of their plight. In an area crowded with refugees awaiting medical examination was an obviously nervous young boy. He spoke and dressed Vietnamese, but his physical appearance was Western. My colleague told me the boy was Amerasian, the offspring left behind by his American military father. I was told there were many thousands more, but the Vietnamese authorities said they would not let them out or could not find them. I wrestled with how to find a way for these children and made a note to investigate further on return to Washington.

Denton–McKinney

The administration and Congress had been trying to address the plight of Amerasian children and their families. Congress had attempted a legislative remedy, the Amerasian Immigration Act of 1982, PL 93–359, written and sponsored by Sen. Jeremiah Denton (R-AL) and Rep. Stewart McKinney (D-CT). Sen. Denton was a war hero, among those held longest as prisoners of war in Vietnam. The proposed legislation created an immigration category requiring petitioning fathers of Amerasian children to file visa applications for those still in Vietnam, Korea, Laos, Cambodia, or Thailand. The plan excluded the Indochinese mothers and siblings. Mothers had to sign an irrevocable custody release for their children's applications to be approved.

Under Denton–McKinney, Amerasian children admitted to the

United States could later petition for family members to join them when they reached majority age. The bill passed with strong bipartisan support. Yet no Amerasian child was resettled under Denton-McKinney during the two years following enactment. Vietnamese families refused to split up, even to resolve persecution circumstances. According to the international refugee definition, although still technically within their country of habitual residence, these Amerasian children—plus mothers and siblings in the immediate family—had as great a claim to refugee status (maybe even more) as others we admitted. Serious concern led to a new plan.

At a staff meeting, I reasoned, "Since we need to go to the secretary and the president for the political prisoners, why not also seek agreement to declare Amerasians as refugees according to the 1980 Refugee Act? We could use the Orderly Departure Program to bring them here."

The deputy assistant secretary Richard English chose John Campbell, a bright and capable young Foreign Service Officer, to produce an RP decision memorandum, seeking Secretary Shultz's agreement to classify Amerasians as refugees and to bring them to the United States under the ODP. After initial reluctance by State's Consular Affairs bureau and the refugee coordinator, the endorsed proposal was forwarded to the departments of Health and Human Services (HHS) and Justice. They concurred.

On behalf of the administration, Secretary Shultz approved this dramatic measure. Regulations were changed, and our field staff and the NGOs were notified that Amerasian children and immediate family members (mothers and siblings) would henceforth be eligible for refugee resettlement. Relevant congressional committees were consulted.

This change did not immediately produce as many Amerasian child applications as hoped, because the Vietnamese authorities kept dragging their feet. Considerations of Amerasian resettlement bounced around, and the secretary of state's resolve was tested in a dramatic way.

State's Leader in the Spotlight

I invited Sen. Al Simpson (R-WY) to Southeast Asia.[4] It was late 1983; I hoped the trip might better inform this key legislator. After the senator's return, Secretary Shultz prepared to attend a meeting at the US Capitol to hear Sen. Simpson's report on his trip. He asked me to join him for a meeting in minority leader Bob Dole's office, right off the Senate floor. From the beginning, Al Simpson expressed clear displeasure about facts learned on his trip. His first target was what he saw as abuse of the Orderly Departure Program (ODP). He expressed ire that the ODP director was using the program to bring out members of his Vietnamese wife's extended family. I had investigated this case earlier after a request to the US ambassador in Thailand and to me. Owing to the severe persecution of the wife's family, we had approved the request. We would not discriminate against a persecuted family member of an employee of the US Government.

Next, Sen. Simpson revealed the real reason for the meeting. He said, in effect, to Secretary Shultz, "George, they are totally ignoring this wonderful piece of legislation (Denton–McKinney) that was intended to bring these Amerasians in as immigrants, and now they are declaring them all to be refugees? This is a distortion of the law."

The senator was correct. No Amerasian child had come to the United States, but that was due to the law's rigidly defined criteria; families rejected the law's tightly defined eligibility requirements, particularly regarding separation from close family members, i.e., mothers and siblings.

Sen. Simpson told us he had been one of the Senate floor managers for the bill. He made his arguments passionately, while others in the meeting were silent. Secretary Shultz was expected to respond, and he looked at me. "Jim, what do you say to the Senator?"

It was time to make a compelling argument on an issue that I had studied and agonized over for many months. I could not hold back:

> Senator, with all due respect, the Denton–McKinney bill was flawed. It set up requirements that made it impossible for any Amerasian child to come to this country. It required splitting the children off and leaving their mothers and siblings behind. No one has applied for entry under Denton–McKinney, and we believe this pattern will continue.
>
> In my view, it is not right to split these families, especially since the children are getting older and the

> mothers are suffering severe persecution. No one questions that they meet all the requirements specified in the new refugee act. They're undeniably subject to persecution and harassment based on race and nationality. They have no protection from their government. These are exactly the persecuted people the 1980 Refugee Act was supposed to help. Under existing authority, the administration has declared Amerasian children, their mothers and immediate family members in the household to be refugees ... for purposes of admission to this country.

Finishing, I realized how still the group had become; and I clearly remember how no one moved or uttered a sound. Obviously, no one had wanted to dispute Al Simpson, the powerful minority whip in the Senate. And neither had I. The senator was highly respected and a friend to many of us. He had helped secure my nomination for the RP director position.

He seemed startled by the frankness of my remarks; abruptly, the meeting broke up, and Shultz and his team left. I stayed behind to talk to Sen. Simpson and Dick Day. We had been through much together over the years. And now I could hardly believe how fervently I had spoken on this subject so dear to my heart.

The senator looked at me. "Jim, I really blew it this time, didn't I?"

Surprisingly, my nerves remained calm. "Yes, Senator. This won't work, can't work, and we're not going to stop processing Amerasians because of a piece of faulty legislation."

"Go back, I'll call George, we'll try to make up," he urged.

I returned to the State Department, sure that I had committed an unpardonable sin. Later that day, I attended a seventh-floor reception for a foreign dignitary. In the receiving line was the deputy secretary John Whitehead, who knew of the developments and shook his head as he looked at me.

When Secretary Shultz shook my hand, he asked, "Jim, what was that all about?"

"I'm sorry it had to come to that. But we had to set the record straight because we hope to put forward a major initiative for Amerasians and political prisoners. We'll probably need the ODP for both. We had to clear the air for these initiatives to have a chance."

"Good job, Jim."

I left still full of gumption for the day and comforted that we were on the right track. My faith had demanded a bold response.

Bob Funseth soon traveled to Geneva to continue the ODP discussions with Vietnamese foreign ministry officials. These discussions about Amerasians and political prisoners were taking on new urgency.

Major Initiatives for Amerasian Children and South Vietnamese Political Prisoners

Work began in spring 1984 on an initiatives package to cover Amerasian children and Vietnamese political prisoners. We knew what we wanted to do, but the "how" was still a question. Planning assumed ten thousand prisoners and ten thousand Amerasians and family members (we had no way to know how many mothers and family members) and their admission as refugees under the Orderly Departure Program (ODP).

Resource Questions

We had to tackle how to (1) accommodate sizeable new resettlement programs within static or declining refugee budgets and resettlement programs (likely to be hit even harder soon by federal cutbacks) and (2) reorganize the ODP to accommodate these new priorities without undermining its primary purpose (as a safe alternative to clandestine boat departures) or losing asylum countries support.

Asylum countries were far less interested in orderly departures from Vietnam than in the increased resettlement from their countries. Clearly, they feared a zero-sum game that they might lose.

A Nimble Approach

We would be lucky to keep our FY 1984 budget, about $340 million. Our job was to accommodate these initiatives within existing resource constraints. Trying from many angles, we could not find a way. Then, Ann Morgan, the ESL/CO chief, offered a solution at a budget meeting:

"Jim, I understand what you're trying to do and why you can't fit prisoners and Amerasians into present budget and allocation planning. But, we're thinking in a static way. We need to think differently. Let me suggest a way that might work."

Since most refugees had to remain in camps more than one year to complete their language training and orientation to life in a new home. Ann's proposal was complicated. It involved multi-year, rather than single-year, planning. A light went on as Ann described her proposal. We had to rethink how we factored new arrivals into our budget, into our financial schemes, into our resettlement schemes! Accustomed to annual appropriations, we had to upgrade our thinking to multiple year planning. We needed to assure the Philippine Refugee Processing Center (PRPC) in Bataan remained open and other support mechanisms remained operational. But for possible new arrivals, we needed to use budgeted allocated admission numbers only in the year the refugees departed. Numbers freed up (planned and budgeted) could then be used for initiatives.

The pre-entry training program had already evolved by creating components within it to deal with groups with special needs. Training no longer targeted only the potential wage earners and had broadened to include the children bound for elementary and secondary schools. Fortuitously, planning was also underway for an additional component, to address the challenges facing the young adult refugee. Most would enter the workplace with no training while trying to go to school—many for the first time. It was a training component tailor-made for Amerasians, most of whom spoke no English and had only a few years of education. Also, having suffered severe discrimination in Vietnam, most were withdrawn and had little motivation to succeed. Directing Amerasians to the young adult program would provide education and counseling to a vulnerable group.

Grateful, I told Ann Morgan to run the numbers and develop a comprehensive plan incorporating new requirements into existing resettlement and budget structures. After many revisions and debates, Ann came back with a plan.

I called the leadership team in and said, "I want Ann to describe this plan in detail because I need you to understand it and know where we are going. Try to poke holes in the plan. Ask questions, press Ann, make her defend these numbers."

They did, and at the end of that discussion, we had unanimous agreement on a workable plan.

Decision Time

The deputy assistant secretary Richard English supervised staff work for the initiatives, and his resettlement team—Bruce Flatin, Peggy Barnhard, Don Ellison, and John Campbell—immediately produced the Orderly Departure (ODP) restructuring to accommodate them. Work accelerated at a breakneck speed, including a decision memorandum for the under secretary for political affairs Michael Armacost.[5] This memorandum, sent forward in August 1984, requested approval for new initiatives and structural changes in ODP. With Ambassador Armacost's immediate approval, the memorandum's decisions were endorsed by interagency partners and incorporated into congressional testimony for the secretary.

Amerasians and Political Prisoners

On September 11, 1984, the date of the first consultation hearing that year, my secretary, Andrea Long, rushed into the office.

"Secretary Shultz's office is on the phone and he wants you to go up now and review arrangements for today's hearing! He also wants you to ride with him to the Hill."

Refugee consultation hearings with the House Judiciary Committee would begin that day in the Rayburn Building, with Secretary Shultz as the lead-off witness.[6] He would announce presidential initiatives accelerating aid that had been delayed too long for Amerasian children and Vietnamese political prisoners.

When I arrived at the secretary's office, his manner seemed stern.

"Come in, Jim, and let's go over this one last time and make sure I understand the rationale for these special programs." He motioned me to take a chair. "I have a couple of questions."

I had assumed the secretary would be pleased with these developments.

However, he expressed concerns. He asked how I knew the Vietnamese Government would work with us on these initiatives. They'd shown no interest so far. In fact, some were worried that they might want to use the political prisoners and the children as leverage in dickering for trade benefits, diplomatic recognition, or a freer hand in Kampuchea. How would we avoid the Mariel effect where they try to force us to take everyone in reeducation custody, an attempt they had tried with Walt Stoessel? That was what had discouraged the previous administration. Could we even afford these new programs?

Taking in the secretary's apprehensions, I said that we had no way of knowing whether they would agree now or in the future.

"But to me," I said, "that's beside the point. They would probably disagree, stall, or cloud the issue with extraneous concerns. But our moral obligation trumps everything else."

Our misadventures in Vietnam had caused problems that played out in these people's lives every day. There was no one else to help if we turned away. RP was convinced that our diplomacy would be strong enough to avoid the Mariel syndrome that the principled diplomat Walt Stoessel had confronted.

We'd been urging the Vietnamese to allow the ICRC access to the camps. Access would result in accurate census data on the inmate population. Equally important, it might push the Vietnamese to improve the deplorable conditions. With a reliable census, we'd be able to submit to Vietnam a list of camp inmates (including their families) of US humanitarian interest.

Although we had not made ICRC access a pre-condition of our proposal, we believed it was is a humane and important first step to a regularized, expanding program. Thus far, all ICRC requests for access have had been denied. We should not let Vietnamese intransigence block this initiative.

"We can accommodate the increased refugee admissions," I said, "within the FY 1985 budget and 1986 budget awaiting congressional enactment. Also, we have reconstructed the ODP program to accommodate the physical movements from both programs. We are ready to go."

At that, Secretary Shultz said we really should get going, and we left to meet his car. On the ride up to the Hill, he was grim, stony-faced, and said little other than to ask a few questions about arrangements for the hearing.

We arrived and were escorted to the large committee hearing room. Because the secretary was testifying, the room was packed. After greeting and shaking hands with committee members, he took his seat at the witness table and asked me to take the chair to his right. He opened his briefing book to review his statement.

He noticed a last-minute change RP staff had made in one concluding sentence that contained some duplicate language. (I was mortified; nobody does that to the secretary of state.) Secretary Shultz took his pencil, crossed out the repeated sentence, glanced at me, and smiled.

The chairman called the hearing to order and read a statement. He welcomed Secretary Shultz and gave him the floor. I still did not know what to expect, as I had gleaned no definitive reaction from the secretary since our earlier discussion.

Once he began to speak, I knew we had nothing to fear. The secretary was committed. He gave an expressive and impassioned statement and answered questions with verve and enthusiasm. He clarified that as a country we would not shirk our moral responsibility. It might take time, but we would not let Vietnamese intransigence obscure this humanitarian concern. He hoped to visit the region soon to add impetus to this growing movement.

The congressional response was quick and overwhelmingly positive. On the ride back, I remarked on his performance and members' appreciative and supportive tone.

He smiled and only said, "Jim, tell your folks that I really appreciate their work. We're on our way."

I returned to my office and called the staff together. They were overjoyed by the news and the secretary's commending remarks.

When they left, I sat alone and reflected on these momentous developments and gave silent thanks for the team's hard-fought battle. I renewed my pledge to assure their work would not be in vain.

Media reports for the next few days gave the administration glowing kudos.[7] This achievement was welcome news, as the president's team had been taking serious media hits in other parts of the world.

Soon, both houses of Congress endorsed the president's initiatives. Over the next three years, almost five thousand Amerasian children and seven thousand relatives came to the United States as refugees.[8]

Amerasian Homecoming Act

In September 1987, the United States and Vietnam signed a bilateral agreement to facilitate and accelerate Amerasian emigration from Vietnam. Two months later, as part of the FY 1988 Continuing Resolution, Congress passed the Amerasian Homecoming Act of 1988 (PL 100–200), allowing all Amerasians born in Vietnam between January 1, 1962, and January 1, 1976, and their immediate family members to apply and be processed as immigrants with full refugee benefits if admitted.[9]

Author Trin Yarborough reported that thirty thousand Amerasian children entered the United States as immigrants between 1988 and 1994 under the Amerasian Homecoming Act, with perhaps eighty thousand accompanying family members.[10]

The release and admission of political prisoners began as I departed in 1986. The numbers were small. Then, in July 1989, the United States and Vietnam agreed on the emigration of former political prisoners and their families. Departures increased dramatically under that accord. By 1991, 21,500 reeducation camp detainees and family members departed under the orderly departure program (ODP).[11]

As Ann Morgan had urged, the team pushed through boundaries and got the results so eagerly sought.

28

PHASE 3. REFORM

AMERICA'S LEADING ROLE IN INTERNATIONAL REFUGEE matters had become disproportionate to other nations' in the 1980s. Making matters worse, the refugee bona fides of some Indochinese were coming into question. The congressional budget reductions under the Gramm–Rudman–Hollings Act in 1984 and 1985 posed dire consequences for the Bureau for Refugee Programs.[1] They multiplied pressures on budgets and programs previously skewed toward costly resettlement programs.

US refugee programs had to adjust priorities to free resources for *relief and assistance* for surging global refugee populations. The times needed donor governments and multilateral organizations to share burgeoning resettlement and financial burdens. But a major US concern was that a weak and overly-bureaucratic multilateral system allowed less committed governments to sidestep their responsibilities and shift their share to the "traditional donors," of which the United States was the most prominent.

RP reform initiatives looked toward (a) achieving more equitable burden-sharing among governments, (b) assuring that the changing profile of many asylum seekers did not lead to abuse of refugee designations, and (c) forging multilateral reforms and solutions.

Burden-Sharing, Summer 1983

Gene Douglas asked me to go to New York with him one Sunday. "I've set up a meeting about refugee burden sharing with the Canadian immigration minister and a couple of his staffers. We'll have brunch at the Waldorf Astoria at eleven."

This request came Friday evening as we were closing for the day. I reflected on it. 'How can it hurt to go with him? Maybe we can clarify our developing partnership and learn more about Canada's refugee plans.'

We flew to New York on Sunday morning and met Lloyd Axworthy, Canada's minister of immigration.[2] As I had been led to believe, he was personable, articulate, and clearly focused on reassessing Canada's role in Indochina refugee programs. With him (as I recall) were James "Joe" Bissett, career senior Canadian immigration official, Terry Sheehan, and Raf Gerard from external affairs. Joe was my Canadian counterpart, and I regarded Terry and Raf as colleagues.

Gene Douglas was a gracious host, profuse in his praise for Canada's role in the Indochina programs. Only the United States had resettled more refugees than Canada (Australia was just a flicker behind Canada).

"The US is under extreme funding pressure from the Congress," Gene Douglas said, trying to find out what added surge capacity the Canadians might have.

The Canadian minister said Ottawa was raising questions about how much further the main countries like Canada could or should go. And he sensed that UNHCR's financial and resettlement projections for coming years far exceeded Canada's, and possibly America's, ability to fund. Many other governments that spoke eloquently about the need for greater international solidarity, but left others to carry the lion's share of the burden. By 1983, a handful of nations had borne most of the burden—the United States, Canada, Australia, Japan, and a few Nordic and European governments. The list of financial contributors was long, yet most donors' contributions were comparatively small. If UNHCR's requirements remained high for the next few years and others did not step up, we would all come under increasing pressure to do more. Without more equitable burden-sharing, we might all be forced to retrench.

We agreed on the immediate steps: first, the United States and Canada would coordinate their respective Indochinese refugee programs and set the outer parameters for future financial and resettlement commitments; second, we would communicate at earlier stages than before on our future contributions; and third, we would insist that greater burden sharing be high on the agenda of future international meetings.

The meeting's results were about as expected from an unplanned diplomatic gathering. But it was a start. Reviewing with Canadian counterparts the next week, we parlayed New York ideas into hypotheticals: What if the major donors to the Indochina refugee programs met regularly to size up the issues from their perspectives and set the agenda for intergovernmental cooperation going forward, including resettlement and financing? If we continued to provide most of the wherewithal, then it would be reasonable for us to clarify from the outset the outer boundaries of our participation.

In further talks, a consensus developed on an approach. We called for a next meeting, to be hosted by the United States. Secretary Shultz liked the strategy. We would invite Australia, Japan, and the deputy high commissioner for refugees Dick Smyser, a former RP director. The Japanese were invited because they contributed 50 percent of UNHCR's budget for care and maintenance programs in Southeast Asia. They did not have large resettlement programs because cultural norms made that difficult. They compensated with generous financial contributions.

The enlarged meeting agenda was based on common realities, perceptions, and opinions that Canada and the United States had shared in New York. The Informal Consultations Group on Indochinese Refugees, known as ICG, was born, including the United States, Canada, Japan, Australia, and the deputy UN high commissioner.

Consultative Group on Indochina Refugees

Over the next few years, the Informal Consultations Group (ICG) met at least twice annually to coordinate policy, financial, and operational parameters to guide our respective governments' involvements in Indochina. Through our respective information networks, plus the presence of the UNHCR deputy, we always had a good sense of present and future requirements. Based on these assessments, we used these meetings to establish how far we could go to meet needs and, if still more was required, how to insist other governments take on a commensurate role.

This setup led to a role reversal. Rather than the international organizations telling us what they expected, we told them what we agreed and could provide. They would be required to operate within those constraints.

The first working ICG meeting was in Hawaii at the headquarters of the US Pacific Command, the United States hosting. Gene Douglas and I attended with my executive assistant, Phil Chicola. I opened the meeting with a Power Point briefing, laying out background and policy issues.

For the next two days, policymakers from these four major donor governments took apart existing programs and put them back together in a rational fashion. Without ignoring existing or vital new needs, the participating countries specified the resources our governments could bring to bear and framed them in ways that our publics and legislatures could accept. We would look to other governments to fill remaining gaps.

Future ICG meetings were held in Canberra, Tokyo, Washington, Ottawa, and Geneva. As in Hawaii, these meetings were analytical, probing, hard-hitting, adaptable, and action oriented. As we hoped, the UNHCR used the information to push other governments to share more of the burdens. They were pleased to see the major governments taking such an active interest.

Frank discussions in the ICG advanced the policy and operational aspects common to our countries. We all noted that an increasing proportion of people coming out of Southeast Asia as refugees had profiles more befitting ordinary immigrants. If true, significant changes would be needed.

The ICG proved to be the most useful instrument conceived up to then to connect like-minded governments and encourage sharing in policy, leadership, operations, and financing for Indochina refugees. The ongoing impetus for the ICG proved to be a small group of committed professionals: Terry Sheehan, Raf Gerard, Mike Malloy, and Joe Bissett from Canada; Ian Simington and Rodney Inder from Australia; Bob Funseth, Gene Dewey, Richard English, Bruce Sasser, and me from the United States; and Dick Smyser from UNHCR. This group, plus a few other participants from our respective governments, set the framework and guided the actions that led the international community to look seriously at endgame measures to resolve the long-running Indochinese crisis.

Maintain Integrity of Refugee Programs

In 1985, I was approaching my last year with State's refugee programs, although I did not know it yet. My mind was focused on where refugee resettlement was headed in Southeast Asia, about which I felt uneasy. Operations under the 1980 Refugee Act had revealed a growing number of refugee claimants with weak bona fides. Many believed the profiles of a growing number of recent Vietnamese arrivals had characteristics more akin to immigrants than refugees. Khmer processing had proven to be especially conflicting with INS. These realizations posed concerns. Persecution had been used in the past by the three communist nations as a weapon against enemies of the state. That was undoubtedly continuing for some, but there were questions about others. Resettlement governments needed to stay on guard. If we processed refugee resettlement cases with weak or fraudulent persecution claims, our publics would be outraged.

Early in 1985, I flew to Hong Kong to visit the Jubilee Camp, where I conducted my own refugee interviews.

One Vietnamese family—husband, wife, two young children—had been living in the camp since the previous year. Their lodgings were in an old factory where accommodations climbed three levels. Ladders gave access to the higher levels. The family lived in about twenty square feet of clean space arranged efficiently. I noticed a television in the corner. My overall impression was that they were comfortable, despite the cramped space.

Through an interpreter, I learned they were from North Vietnam. The husband was a farmer. He had not been in the army or the war, and he said he had no previous political involvement. Farming had always been hard and was more difficult now than before, but they could survive through long hours and hard toil. He reported no persecution against his family or himself, but life under the new regime was far more difficult than before. His wife had never been off the farm before their Hong Kong journey.

I was interested to know why they had left home. The interview went like this:

"Why did you come all this way if you weren't at risk?" I asked the husband through an interpreter there to help both of us.

"We wanted a better life," he answered. "We could not advance if we stayed on the farm. Also, we wanted a family, and we thought we could do better by going where my wife and the babies could get professional medical attention. We heard stories about the refugee camp and decided to take a chance. And, our country has been at war for most of our lives."

"This is a refugee camp," I reasoned, "and you folks are not refugees. You're not fleeing persecution. Your side won. Return home and try to qualify for immigration to another country's program. It will take longer, but that's all you qualify for."

The father laughed, "No, we'll stay because living here is just so much easier. Neither the British nor the Americans would dare send us back to Vietnam now. The new Vietnamese government won't allow anyone to return. And who knows, maybe we'll get lucky and some resettlement country in the West will take us."

I left, thinking, 'He's right. We can't send them back because the act of leaving Vietnam, regardless of persecution, has made them unacceptable as returnees.' Until we could do eligibility screening and make better return arrangements, families like this would be home free.

On the one hand, such cases must be corrected. On the other hand, the notion of *forced return* highlighted a serious policy difference the Americans often had with the UK's and Hong Kong's first-asylum policy. Forced returns of refugees, we maintained, contradicted our obligations under the 1951 Convention and were detrimental to our joint efforts to assure safe first asylum. While the United States favored safe voluntary return, we opposed forced returns in any guise.

I learned later that the Vietnamese family I had interviewed at Jubilee Camp was subsequently included in a camp closeout and resettled abroad, just as the father had predicted. The Refugee Act of 1980 had established guiding principles, yet execution remained confusing. US refugee policy had not kept up with changing conditions throughout Indochina.

There was also the Khmer processing experience. True, we had resolved many thorny processing issues over the previous couple of years and the Khmer resettlement results were remarkable, with over 90 percent INS approvals. But it had taken presidential involvement to force through some of the more sensitive processing compromises. Congressional advocates on both sides of this controversy had been livid, directing most of their anger at the State Department, and RP's congressional relations took a major hit. INS blamed State and the NGOs for trying to skew the results toward political decisions. RP objected strongly. We were at almost irreconcilable odds, and relationships suffered. However, the only solution track available was still refugee processing, because immigration solutions did not exist.

In an ideal world, and as the executive branch bureaucratic architecture had originally envisioned, these problems were precisely the kinds of systemic issues that an effective US refugee coordinator should have addressed. Alas, that was not to be the case here. Finding answers to these philosophical disagreements and to the conflicting processing demands threatened the US refugee programs going forward and could only be resolved by the highest levels of our government.

In late 1985, I took the issue to John Whitehead, the deputy secretary of state.[3] He agreed with my concerns and suggested that we had to go outside the system for help. An independent blue-ribbon commission was urgently needed, and Whitehead and I set about organizing one. It was to be called the Indochina Refugee Panel, and it needed notable experts to serve. After wide consultations, an outstanding five-member blue ribbon panel was appointed, headed by former Governor Robert D. Ray (R-Iowa).[4]

The Ray Indochina Refugee Panel

In early spring 1985, I briefed the first meeting of the Ray Indochina Refugee Panel about policies, problems, and reforms the United States might consider for Indochina. RP was facing issues unlike those of the earlier exodus-emergency and stabilization-protection phases; many new arrivals and first-asylum populations now came for family reunion or economic reasons; some had unimpeachable cases of persecution; some had mixed motivations. We needed a new strategy to reorient resettlement to prevailing conditions.

The Ray Panel's charge was to form proposals to accomplish specific aims:

- Reflect the changing nature of first-asylum populations
- Focus our efforts on bona fide refugees, through screening
- Prevent erosion of domestic support for the refugee programs
- Avoid the perpetuation of refugee resettlement as an "entitlement"
- Meet family reunification and economic needs through non-refugee means
- Consider the return of non-refugees to origin countries

The panel members reviewed interagency and global refugee programs in depth over several months. They met with involved public and private agencies and talked at length with the relevant congressional committees, NGOs, and interested citizens. They traveled in Indochina to meet with leaders and refugees.

The Ray Panel Report and Recommendations

The historic Ray Panel report was delivered to Secretary Shultz in April 1986. It recommended that the United States, with other resettlement countries, provide for a *two-tiered system* for the movement of persons from Indochina, i.e., a strictly-defined refugee resettlement track geared to bona fide persecution and other special humanitarian concerns. Separately, an expanded legal immigration track would be created. After a two-year transition period, immigration procedures should replace refugee procedures for all Indochinese with qualified relatives as sponsors in the United States.

The panel noted that the "great majority" of Southeast Asians admitted as refugees since 1975 had been in the United States for over five years, the minimum residence requirements for citizenship application. It recommended that steps be taken to encourage those residents to seek citizenship and predicted that, as the number of naturalized citizens increased, a correspondingly sizable percentage of Indochinese relatives would become eligible for immigrant visas.

Recalling the massive number of refugees already accepted by the United States, the panel called on other countries to share the burden.

The report recommended eligibility screening to decide the proper channel for refugee and immigration applicants. Those disqualified for either channel, including nonqualifying long-stayers in first-asylum countries, should receive "safe" repatriation. Whenever safety was deemed questionable, the United States and other governments should accept for resettlement, on a *one-time,* shared-out basis, some long-stayers who had remained in first asylum since their rejection.

The report endorsed the concept of regional settlement, that is, countries of *first asylum* allowing certain refugees to remain indefinitely (to apply to Thailand and the Hmong, specifically).

Innovative repatriation and local integration mechanisms for Vietnamese and Lao should be devised, principally by UNHCR. The United States and other countries should provide economic support and other assistance to encourage *safe repatriation* and *local integration.* The report supported *humane deterrence* measures in Thailand and other first-asylum countries, if implemented safely.

Current programs for legal orderly departures should be expanded and new ones developed. The report specifically endorsed the Orderly Departure Program for resettlement of Amerasian children and political prisoners from Vietnam. They endorsed and supported the nearly completed rereview of Khmer refugee applications rejected in Thailand.

The coordinated and phased implementation of the Ray Report would bring the refugee programs in Southeast Asia to a "steady state" desired for a long time and put them on the way to conclusion. All governments were expected to take part in these solutions and share the costs.

Other recommendations for reforms in legal immigration and refugee processing included suggestions for dealing with camp populations in first asylum. Regarding the border Khmer, the report recommended this group be ineligible for further large-scale resettlement. But it supported enhanced care and maintenance services, education, and formal protection pending return to Kampuchea. Eventually, that happened.

Only the maintenance and skillful implementation of the report's strategy could avoid domestic political pressure or the potential for overreaction by first-asylum countries. Advocates expressed pleasure over the

Ray Panel's recommendations and hoped the State Department would implement them promptly.[5] The results validated RP's present course. As I was close to departure from RP, the timing was exactly right.

Informal Consultation Group Contribution

The Ray Panel report also suggested special meetings of the Informal Consultations Group (ICG) to coordinate the new approach with other resettlement countries. Expanded membership would also encourage greater contributions. The purpose of the first expanded ICG meeting in Tokyo in 1986 was to consider the findings and recommendations of the Ray Panel at an international level.

Over a Decade of Detailed Planning at Every Level

The Ray Panel's multilateral initiative paved the way for a successful Indochina refugee durable solution several years later, led by UNHCR. A salute belongs to Chairman Bob Ray, the first US governor to offer his state's continuing acceptance of refugees at a critical, skeptical time, 1979.

29

PHASE 4. SOLUTIONS

THE GUIDING PRINCIPLES OF THE EARLY INDOCHINA STRATegy were safe first asylum and help to vulnerable groups in exchange for generous *third-country resettlement*. They had worked as envisioned from the time of the Geneva Conference in 1979 up to about 1983. Then the strategy began to unravel; resettlement countries were increasingly afflicted with "compassion fatigue" and ASEAN governments, sensing declining interest, retreated and started pulling in the welcome mat. To make matters worse, many people still fleeing Indochina countries had characteristics more befitting immigrants but were drawn because of the attractiveness of the resettlement program. The donors and the resettlement governments had little incentive to keep up past generosity.

A new strategic approach was needed to continue aid to victims, as needed, yet also aimed at bringing the long-running humanitarian programs to a humane and respectable end, taking account of the existing environment and the needs and capacities of helping countries. Those governments wanted to resist the temptation to pull up stakes and leave but leaving was what they faced unless a more rational Southeast Asia humanitarian strategy was devised and put in place, quickly. Shoring up public support for governments' refugee undertakings through expanded and committed burden-sharing was crucial. Rather than running away from these new realities, *governments came together in unprecedented cooperation to forge a refugee paradigm for the future.*

Southeast Asia Solutions Compact

The faltering resettlement program needed to be reenergized. The Informal Consultations Group (ICG) deliberations gave opportunity to bring the lengthy resettlement saga to a humane end. During ICG discussions, I described a new framework we were constructing to solve this crisis, "the informal solutions compact," or simply, "compact." The approach featured enhanced cooperation and compromises among asylum, donor, resettlement and, eventually, the origin governments, the multilateral organizations and NGOs, and the other partners jointly focused on agreed outcomes. These hoped-for outcomes were endorsed and incorporated into the next round of international discussions aimed at Indochinese solutions.

Durable Solution for Refugees

At an expanded 1986 Tokyo Informal Consultations Group (ICG) meeting, endgame proposals achieved consensus and culminated in the design of the architecture of an Indochina refugee solution. Accordingly, the international partners proposed to maintain safe and secure first asylum; inaugurate eligibility screening for applicants; provide refugee status for deserving cases; make immigration systems and procedures available for non-refugees; channel potential Vietnamese asylum seekers through the Orderly Departure Program (ODP), where possible; share-out resettlement in third countries when no other solutions were available; and negotiate with origin countries to accept the safe return of non-refugees. Every hard-fought, hard-won discussion, decision, and creative piece needed approval across powerful governmental systems.

Future ICG meetings looked to refine and reorient the Indochina program along those lines. The ICG and the Ray Panel report predicted that a comprehensive and durable solution for Indochinese refugees would diminish future flows from Vietnam, a significant destabilizing problem.

To its richly deserved credit, the UNHCR used this groundwork to begin discussions with the origin, asylum, resettlement, and donor countries (including Vietnam and UK-Hong Kong), geared toward a durable solution. UNHCR issued an informal note to governments in June 1988 explaining the complicated arrangements that ensued.[1]

As a priority, they reactivated ODP—whose new cases had been halted in 1986. The United States continued bilateral ODP discussions with Vietnam, and UNHCR undertook multilateral talks with Vietnam in December 1986 and in February and September 1987.

After September 1987 talks, Vietnam provided the UNHCR a written assurance.

> The humanitarian policy of Viet Nam consists of authorizing all Vietnamese citizens who may have legitimate reasons to do so, to leave Vietnam. With the UNHCR's help and cooperation, the government of Viet Nam is ready to discuss this problem directly with the receiving countries.[2]

This statement signaled openness to the ODP's reactivation and was, of course, directed primarily to the Americans. The next development was UNHCR-initiated discussions with the Socialist Republic of Vietnam on acceptance of returning non–refugees.

UNHCR's informal note reported that by mid-1988: "... the SRV attitude on the issue of 'return' may not be inextricably rigid. Given the right approach, the SRV may see ... its longer-term interests to be accommodating on this subject."[3]

The UN's perseverance and strengthened diplomacy led to agreements that made assisted returns possible, including the SRV (a) viewing this concession as a means of confidence-building in the ASEAN region, and (b) accepting that the return of non-refugees would impose no undue economic burdens on its struggling economy. A decisive driver of this strategy was the agreement of the SRV's foreign minister, Tran Quang Co, to send a delegation to Geneva in mid-1988 to discuss these matters further.

The informal note of June 1988 reported on the inter-governmental consultative group Ottawa meeting:

> ... (this) approach has been the subject of extensive informal discussions among the major receiving/donor countries within the framework of the Inter–Governmental

Consultative Group on Indochinese Refugees. At its last meeting in Ottawa on 7 and 8 April, broad support for the main elements of this approach, i.e., improved ODP, eligibility screening mechanism and approach to Viet Nam was expressed. The Ottawa meeting also reaffirmed the intention to continue resettlement and supported the principle of first asylum. UNHCR has since moved to intensify its dialogue with the SRV.[4]

Kuala Lumpur, Durable Solution Achieved

An expanded Informal Consultations Group (ICG), meeting called by UNHCR in Kuala Lumpur in 1989, focused on gaining international agreement on a Comprehensive Plan of Action (CPA) for Indochinese refugees. The CPA, as explained below, was a complex set of understandings, steered to consensus approval by UNHCR Associate High Commissioner Sergio Vieira de Mello. Jonathan Moore, a former Ray Panel member (my successor by then as RP director), RP's Bob Funseth, Doug Hunter, and Alan Jury (US Mission in Geneva) were active in these final deliberations.

The CPA had profound achievements:

- Reducing clandestine boat departures through official measures, including information campaigns aimed at organizers of boat departures
- Promoting legal migration through the Orderly Departure Program (ODP)
- Providing temporary asylum to all asylum seekers until their status was established and a durable solution found
- Determining the refugee status of all asylum seekers under international standards and criteria
- Resettling in third countries those recognized as refugees and all Vietnamese in camps prior to the regional cutoff dates
- Returning those found not to be refugees and reintegrating them in their home countries[5]

Implementation of the Comprehensive Plan of Action ended the continuing stream of Vietnamese asylum seekers. Whereas seventy thousand Vietnamese sought asylum in 1989, the number reduced to forty-one persons by 1992 and remained negligible thereafter. There were about fifty thousand pre-cutoff date Vietnamese refugees in Southeast Asian refugee camps during the CPA conference. A quarter had been rejected and about the same number were low priority cases. By 1991, virtually all had resettled. Of Vietnamese at the post-cutoff date, thirty-two thousand were resettled, in comparison with eighty-three thousand three hundred whose rejected claims meant their return to Vietnam.[6]

Orderly Return to Vietnam

The ASEAN asylum countries eventually signed Orderly Return, OR, agreements with Vietnam. Under these agreements, UNHCR covered transportation and logistical support and maintained it could participate only in voluntary returns. Over time, however, violence in the camps, including in Hong Kong, blurred the distinction between voluntary and forced returns. Repatriation accelerated after 1992 and over 109,000 Vietnamese eventually returned home under CPA arrangements.[7] One of the important by-products of the Indochina learning experience was a revitalized multilateral system enjoying active support by a wide range of the governments and international organizations. This revitalized architecture was replicated often in the coming years to address humanitarian crises around the world.

Southeast Asia Log

For some of the most grueling years of the Refugee Programs bureau, from 1979 to 1987 and coinciding with my tenure, Southeast Asia was a compelling theater for one of modern history's most dramatic escape and rescue operations. Courage was a hallmark of those hunted for punishment or death. Courage marked the multitudes of people and entities that stood with them and helped. Their lessons and solutions set the stage for Indochina *durable solutions* and, significantly, were replicated in unique ways in other world crises.

By 1987, approximately 1.2 million asylum seekers from Vietnam, Laos, and Cambodia crossed the frontiers of the ASEAN member states and Hong Kong seeking safety and help (border Khmer considered separately). During that same period, slightly more than a million people departed the ASEAN area, mainly through third-country resettlement and leaving about 150,000 in the area). Some additional 710,000 refugees were caught up in these tragic events in non-ASEAN areas during this period (*see* Table 6). These figures exclude the large unknown numbers of asylum seekers who drowned or were killed by pirates as they attempted to escape or the unknown number whose escape plans failed, forcing them to return home. Informed observers estimate the perished in the hundreds of thousands.

Excluding those settled in China and the border Khmer, the State Department reported that nearly 60 percent (about 850,000) of refugees permanently resettled in third countries during this period went to the United States. Refugees resettled permanently in the United States, 1975 to 1987 (*see* Table 2) resulted from the work of three presidential administrations:

Three US Presidents and Permanent Resettlement 1975–87

Gerald Ford	1975–76	150,000
Jimmy Carter	1977–79	267,894
Ronald Reagan	1981–87	431,568
Total		**849,462**

This permanent resettlement population can be attributed approximately to two solution phases mentioned earlier: 1) exodus and emergency (625,000) and 2) stabilization, protection reform, solution (225,000).

Beyond the one million people who fled into and through the ASEAN area by 1987 and were resettled, an additional 250,000 made the same journey with the same results over the next decade. The Orderly Departure Program (ODP) quadrupled (*see* Table 7).

Over the full life of the Indochina program, 1975–97, UNHCR reported that almost two million refugees were in third-country resettlement, two-thirds in the United States. More than 750,000 more were repatriated or relocated by UNHCR. When unsuccessful escape attempts are factored in, this means that more than three million people were caught up in the Southeast Asia's extensive refugee crisis (*see* Table 7).

Over the years of the Indochina refugee program, American efforts, beginning in 1979, were guided by leaders unafraid to put Indochina victims in a central place in their thinking and action. The resulting *solution framework* guided the United States and the international humanitarian efforts, with appropriate situational revisions, to historic durable solutions.

Anchor for Durable Solutions, 1979–97

Continuing to anchor cooperation through secure first asylum was the key solutions ingredient throughout the hectic phases of the Indochina program, allowing time and space to explore and implement a full range of solutions. This approach was undergirded by unprecedented cooperation, planning, and implementation over the life of the Indochina refugee programs. The *informal solutions compact* of the ICG deliberations was an important contributor. Although not a legal arrangement, its informal and agreed understandings between partners set the tone and guided joint efforts to agreed outcomes.

National approaches over those years often differed and were not always traversed in straight lines. Results came through melded efforts. Examples of successful intergovernmental cooperation throughout the Indochina refugee programs include the following:

- 1979 Geneva Conference (International Conference on Indochinese Refugees)
- Anti-piracy cooperation
- Resettled refugees (record numbers in key partner countries)
- The Ray Indochina Refugee Panel
- Informal Consultations Group (ICG) and
- Comprehensive Plan of Action for Indochinese Refugees (CPA)

Common goals like these were achieved by a true "coalition of the willing."

30

THE MEANING OF VIETNAM

AMERICA ROSE FROM THE ASHES OF WORLD WAR II FEAR and indifference with a desire to put a painful era quickly behind it. The United States underwent a dramatic reawakening as it faced up to the post-war Vietnamese refugee crisis that roiled Indochina and the world. The State Department refugee team directly engaged in these transformative changes.

The Historic Humanitarian Role of the United States, 1975–1987

Origin, asylum, transit, donor, and resettlement countries established exceptional cooperation to protect refugees in flight, in regional asylum, and those in resettlement as they progressed toward enduring durable solutions. Each phase had to be devised, negotiated, and realized over years of learning.

The United States gave all endangered groups—Amerasian children, South Vietnamese political prisoners, land and boat Vietnamese, Cambodian holocaust survivors, and Laotians (Hmong and Lowland Lao)—special care and attention through very torturous years. Pirate attacks in Asian waters and other dangers were significantly reduced over time. Refugees bound for the US took part in language, acculturation, and vocational skills training, allowing them to quickly assimilate in welcoming places which, eventually, could become their own places to call home. They left the refugee status and labels behind and became valued permanent residents and American citizens.

There were costs and gains in lives, time, relationships, and resources. RP reprioritized, reoriented, and stabilized its budget—at times static, declining or under attack—to assist many more refugees around the world than ever before. This happened as UNHCR reported that the world refugee population more than quadrupled, the largest proportional growth throughout turbulent years of the twentieth century.

As security conditions in Vietnam and Laos improved, RP redirected many economic and family migrants into new and more appropriate immigration channels, relieving pressure on refugee admissions programs and budgets and leaving refugee regimes for the most deserving.

America's worldview was undeniably enriched by Indochina refugee programs. This was especially important as events beyond Southeast Asia appeared over the horizon. The early policy decision to use the private sector as its major refugee resettlement partner brought about dramatic cultural shifts in the United States: anyone visiting a church or parish during the 1980s would see the Indochinese refugees worshiping alongside new friends helping them integrate in their communities. The same spirit could also be seen in the resettlement managed by secular organizations. Through family life, education, and hard work, the Indochinese refugees and immigrants succeeded in America far beyond expectations.

There were many problems to overcome, but America was rewarded for opening its arms and embracing war-ravaged people. The American global outlook expanded in more positive ways than perhaps any other time in recent history.

Indochinese resettlement begun by the State Department in the late 1970s had significant start-up problems. The cultural shifts were evolutionary, as America and its new citizens needed time to adjust to each other, as illustrated by this anecdote:

In the early years, our desks at the State Department were piled with call messages from complaining governors, mayors, social service providers, congressional staff, and others each morning. Common grievances included: "The refugees are sick, speak no English, take jobs away, and are costly." Also, "they drain state and local treasuries," or "They're dangerous."

Several years later, the same people were calling with different messages: "How do we get more Indochinese refugees and immigrants? They are hard workers, industrious, good citizens, and are renewing and revitalizing our communities."

Historical Perspective

The State Department and RP decided to change course on *durable solutions* for the Indochinese, away from resettlement as the almost exclusive durable solution. There was a wider range of possibilities. The historical assessment from UNHCR bears out this conclusion:

> Western countries were no longer prepared to make open-ended commitments to resettlement as a durable solution. Even within UNHCR, one 1994 assessment noted that 'the disenchantment with resettlement' brought on by the Indochina experience, 'has had a negative effect on UNHCR's capacity to effectively perform resettlement functions.' … From the vantage point of a new century, it may be possible to look back at UNHCR's experience with the Indochinese refugees and see that resettlement was not the problem. On its own, it was not the solution either. The legacy of the Indochinese program is that the international community and UNHCR stayed engaged over a long and challenging period to find a combination of solutions that eventually brought the crisis to a relatively humane end.[1]

Secretary of State George Shultz delivered a speech, "The Meaning of Vietnam," at the State Department in April 1985 on the tenth anniversary of America's withdrawal from Vietnam. He summed up the Indochina refugee experience:

"The work of people in this Department has saved countless lives. Your dedication to the refugees of Indochina marks one of the shining moments of the Foreign Service."[2]

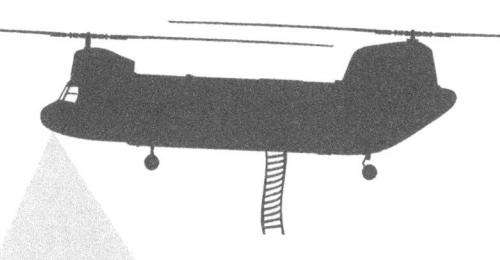

BOOK THREE
"WE ARE HERE"
The World in Danger

31

EASTERN EUROPE AND THE SOVIET UNION

IT'S THE LAST QUARTER OF THE TWENTIETH CENTURY AND the old communist USSR system is breaking down in Bucharest, Warsaw, Sofia, Budapest, Moscow, Kiev, and St. Petersburg. In its weakened and declining years, that harsh system punishes religious minorities, political activists, and other dissenters caught in its sights. Unless the scapegoated classes swear allegiance to the state and the governing elites, they stay in danger on the fringes of society. Repression wreaks havoc and denies basic human rights and often forbids emigration.

This was the background: post-war agreements between the United States, USSR, and Great Britain had split Germany into East and West, dividing Berlin and giving the Soviets control over Eastern Europe. In May 1955, a mutual defense agreement, the Warsaw Pact, was signed between the USSR and its European satellites—Albania, Bulgaria, Czechoslovakia, East Germany, Hungary, Poland, and Romania. That key event propelled scores of people in the countries of the so-called Eastern Bloc to try to escape the repressive Soviet system. The Warsaw Pact followed the North American Treaty Organization (NATO) creation (1949). The Warsaw Pact put the Soviets in command of a unified military structure designed to counter worries of a power rebound by one NATO member, West Germany, and to provide a buffer against imagined threats from the West. Emphasizing national security worries, the Pact compelled satellite governments to subordinate national interests to those of the Eastern Bloc, through military force if necessary, and to pledge loyalty to the USSR. This construct was also known as the Brezhnev Doctrine.

The resulting refugee situation in Europe (1945 and immediate years following) had no parallel elsewhere in the developed world. Europe's massive disruptions required large-scale capacities to process refugees for *third-country resettlement*, in and outside Europe. US refugee operations in Western Europe worked through NGOs (nongovernmental organizations) that had operated for years in each country apart from US consular or diplomatic officers. This was unlike the Joint Voluntary Agency (JVA) approach used elsewhere from 1976. There probably was greater refugee burden-sharing in Europe than anywhere else, since the aim of the NGOs was to resettle refugees to any destination, without regard to other considerations. NGO diversity in Europe also allowed them to respond to the refugee flows that changed markedly in size and composition year after year.[1]

Resettlement to the United States

Crises of the 1950s would reverberate for decades. From early efforts to resettle displaced persons after World War II, Eastern Europe faced successive crises requiring Western assistance through an expansion of US and international resettlement systems. For the United States, its diplomatic mission in Geneva handled refugee processing operations in the field in conjunction with INS, NGOs, and Western European countries, until the creation of the State Department's Bureau for Refugee Programs, RP.

In 1979, RP incorporated the former US Resettlement Program (USRP) into the new RP bureau's mandate, making RP responsible for US resettlement of the refugees fleeing persecution in the Soviet Union and its satellites, Warsaw Pact countries. The major Eastern European countries originating refugees were Romania, Poland, Bulgaria, Czechoslovakia, and Hungary.

RP was also charged to strengthen ties between the United States, UNHCR, and the Intergovernmental Committee for European Migration (ICEM), which later expanded beyond Europe and eventually was renamed the International Organization for Migration. Interestingly, 1978–81 refugee resettlement to the United States (RP's primary measure of humanitarian action in the region) was heavily skewed for refugees from the Soviet Union, which accounted for 82 percent of all resettled refugees versus 18 percent from European countries. However, from 1982 to 1987, the trends reversed. This flip resulted when Soviet reactions hardened after world condemnation of their invasion of Afghanistan.

Refugees numbering 200,000 from Eastern Europe and the Soviet Union were resettled in the United States from 1979 to 1987 (*see* Table 2).

From the first resettlement efforts for displaced persons after World War II, successive crises in Europe every decade or so required rapid expansion of the assistance and resettlement system (Hungary in 1956, Czechoslovakia in 1969, Romania from the 1970s on, and Poland in 1981).

Hungary

On October 23, 1956, tens of thousands of Hungarian citizens revolted against USSR–Warsaw Pact control. After twelve days of revolt, Hungary was free, and negotiations were underway in Budapest for the withdrawal of Soviet forces. Suddenly, the Soviets dispatched large-scale military forces into Hungary and the citizen flight began. Between October 1956 and April 1957, over 170,000 Hungarians fled to Austria. In early November, the director of the Intergovernmental Committee for European Migration (ICEM) sent an international refugee organization official, James Carlin, to Vienna to oversee Hungarian refugee selection and processing for resettlement.

Hungary was the first major refugee crisis addressed by the international community after the immediate post-World War II era. Thirty thousand Hungarian refugees were resettled in the United States and 100,000 in twenty-nine other countries.[2]

Czechoslovakia 1968

For eight months, January to August 1968, the Prague Spring revolt against Soviet oppression brought a period of political liberalization to Czechoslovakia. On January 5, 1968, a few days into the revolt, the reformist leader Alexander Dubcek became First Secretary of the Communist Party of Czechoslovakia.

On August 21, 1968, five Warsaw Pact countries—Soviet Union,

Bulgaria, German Democratic Republic, Hungary (forced to remain in the fold after its revolt), and Poland—invaded Czechoslovakia. Romania and Albania did not take part. The invasion force mobilized over 200,000 troops and five thousand tanks. Seventy-six Czech and Slovak citizens were killed and over 700 wounded. More than 300,000 Czechs left their country, becoming refugees. Czechoslovakia reinstituted the system in effect prior to Dubcek and installed a new leader, Gustav Husak. Continuing unrest led to the "velvet" or "gentle" revolution, November 1989. Top communist party leadership resigned, and the single-party apparatus was abolished. Warsaw Pact effects remained, however, including invasion fears, until November 9, 1989, the day of the fall of the Berlin Wall.[3]

Jean and I were in Prague for migration meetings in December 1990 and saw the first public commemoration of Christmas after many years. Large numbers of people had gathered around stalls in the downtown market square to see a reverent depiction of the Christmas story with patient actors. This was a very emotional time for them and for us. The cold, the piles of rocks at intersections, and the abandoned tanks scattered throughout Prague could not dampen the warm good cheer of celebration afterward.

Romania

According to RP's Margaret Carpenter in a landmark 1982 critique, Romania posed the most glaring anomaly in the European refugee programs, with its unique Third Country Processing, or TCP, regime. In the early 1970s, Romanian immigration to the United States was handled differently because of dual US objectives (occasionally conflicting) to encourage close political and economic ties with the Soviet-controlled nation while aiding victims of the brutal regime of dictator Nicolae Ceausescu.[4] (*See* Appendix B.)

The perplexing dilemma of Romanian resettlement hit me squarely between the eyes in 1983 at one of Secretary Shultz's senior staff meetings. I had finished a global overview of RP programs and initiatives in each region, including a decision to put a moratorium on refugee processing for Romanians until the government agreed to reforms. I had mentioned the State Department counselor Ed Derwinski's work on reforms with Romania, and I said we wanted to put a revised program in place soon.

The moratorium decision for Romania had already affected Rick Burt, the assistant secretary for Europe, and he challenged my hardline approach in that meeting. He argued that restricted US resettlement of Romanians posed an irritant to United States–Romania relations and made it hard to obtain Most Favored Nation (MFN) trading status for Romania. Burt was responsible for keeping relations with European countries on an even keel, including those controlled by the Soviets, opposing potential threats to their and US interests. I was responsible for overseeing a worldwide humanitarian program that operated within binding legal constraints, regardless of political considerations. As so often happened, the two objectives collided.

Romanian Third Country Processing (TCP) was one of RP's most technically complicated and abused programs. I knew it would be impossible to explain the complexities further in the staff meeting, especially since I had just referred to TCP complexities in Romania and its abuses by the Romanian leader Nicolai Ceausescu. I assumed Secretary Shultz's awareness of the complexities, yet given Burt's alarming outcry, I scheduled a meeting to brief the secretary. I would focus on resettlement processing, MFN trade status, the 1974 Trade Act, the Jackson–Vanik bill in Congress, and the proposed RP reforms.

Jerry Hoganson served as the RP director for Europe and the Near East and knew the problems well. In April 1982 he had prepared a memorandum to director Dick Vine that highlighted the dysfunctions and proposed that the United States undertake negotiations with Romanian authorities and insist that they stop issuing passports until resettlement applicants cleared all the legal requirements.[5]

Director Vine approved Hogenson's reforms, but the Romanian government slowed implementation. In winter, 1982, the third-country processing caseload was skewing and overwhelming RP's Eastern European program and depriving more deserving cases. Back in the RP director's chair in early 1983, I decided to place a moratorium on new cases until the Romanians cooperated with Hoganson-type reforms. That moratorium had led to Rick Burt's strong objections during the secretary's meeting.

In the next meeting with Secretary Shultz, I briefed him on the background details, although he knew the major substance already. His nod signaled his continued support for RP reforms. Ed Derwinski, State Department counselor, continued to work with Romanian authorities on improvements to TCP (Third Country Processing). (*See* Appendix B.2 for TCP background notes.)

Derwinski's negotiations with Romania paid off in 1984, and the Romania program subsequently evolved into a legally authorized admissions program that met diplomatic necessities. Congressional and State Department concurrence for reforms was assured. Ed Derwinski, a former member of the House Foreign Affairs Committee with strong contacts in Romania and Eastern Europe, had been a natural for that sensitive role.

Poland

In December 1981, Poland's prime minister General Wojciech Jaruzelski declared martial law and outlawed Poland's independent trade union, Solidarity, in a Soviet-inspired takeover. He arrested Solidarity leadership, claiming these moves would prevent a Soviet invasion.

The crackdown followed the Soviet invasion of Afghanistan, and President Reagan was publicly upset about events throughout the communist world, including in Poland. He decided the USSR and its satellite states should be made to pay for continuing aggression. His administration imposed stinging economic sanctions on the USSR and its Eastern Bloc allies.[6] As expected, United States–Poland–Soviet relations became more antagonistic.

Following the Solidarity trade union suspension, Poland's communist leaders harassed and imprisoned union leaders and dissenters, forcing many to flee. Trade union leader Lech Walesa led a successful, peaceful revolt, becoming a heroic figure throughout the free world. He received the Nobel Peace Prize in 1983. By that time, world outrage against communist repression was so vociferous that most Solidarity leaders were released from prisons or jails, although Solidarity remained illegal.

When large US *resettlement* programs for Poles started, I asked

Jim Carlin, director general of the Intergovernmental Committee for Migration (ICM), to establish a facility at Bad Soden, Germany, to assist the Polish dissenters. Through ICM, Poles received temporary asylum with housing, language training, and cultural orientation as they awaited resettlement. European NGOs helped many to relocate to Western Europe and the United States. Some returned home.

The American government unrelentingly supported Lech Walesa and the Solidarity unionists. An unforgettable demonstration of this occurred in early 1987 during a trip by the deputy secretary of state John Whitehead to Eastern Europe. When informed that Lech Walesa could not meet him in Warsaw because Solidarity had been declared illegal and Walesa was restricted to Gdansk, Whitehead balked:

"If Walesa is not permitted to come to Warsaw, I will fly to Gdansk instead of meeting here in Warsaw with General Jaruzelski."[7]

The communist leader quickly folded and flew Walesa to Warsaw to meet with John Whitehead.

In 1987, US Rep. Stephen Solarz, a humanitarian legislator and a former Peace Corps volunteer, concluded that the 1981 sanctions on Poland had succeeded and led a congressional initiative to lift them.[8]

In a historic 1989 roundtable agreement between Poland's leaders and Solidarity, Polish authorities allowed the first free and fair elections since the end of World War II. Solidarity, which by then had been legalized, won in a landslide. Lech Walesa became president of Poland.

Not surprisingly, many tried and tested organizations, personalities, practices, and operational concepts of earlier refugee programs in Europe were carried over to the founding of the new Bureau for Refugee Programs, RP, and the US Refugee Act of 1980. Their impact and influence have endured.

32

SOVIET RELIGIOUS MINORITIES

FEW TWENTIETH CENTURY GEOPOLITICAL CRISES WERE more exasperating to US administrations than the USSR emigration bans on Soviet Jews. It was one of the most intractable problems the refugee programs inherited during the refugee decade, 1979–89; it was also one of the least susceptible to solution. The USSR tried to erase knowledge of Judaism entirely from its citizenry, including withholding vital information about Jewishness. Natan Sharansky, a Jew who experienced that repression, gained freedom to leave the Soviet Union after years of punishment, including imprisonment, for his efforts to confront the repressive system. In *Defending Identity*, he wrote, "…a society without a strong identity is also a society imperiled …. The right to live a unique way of life is a right worth fighting for and if necessary worth dying for."[1]

Over centuries, the fate of the Soviet Jews worsened. When communist leader Vladimir Lenin led the Bolsheviks to take control in the 1917 (October 31) Revolution, three centuries of Russian rule by Romanov tsars ended. The change at first offered hope to Russian Jews, when anti-Semitism was officially condemned. Many young Jews moved to the cities and were educated to become the USSR's needed technocrats. Many Jews worked in government, the communist party, and the universities, as well as serving in the Red Army at a rate disproportionate to their percentage of the Soviet population.

This respite, however, was short-lived. By 1921, massive Soviet pogroms killed about thirty thousand Jews in over two thousand massacres. Over one million were left homeless. Vladimir Lenin, founder of the feared Red Army, was angered by Jews and other ethnicities and feared that their unique identities threatened the USSR. He appointed Joseph Stalin as the commissar of nationalities and created structures and mentalities designed to emphasize the primacy of Soviet identity. In 1924, at age fifty-three, Lenin died, and the dictatorial Stalin rose to power. He commenced the great purges of the 1930s, affecting about 80 percent of the communist party. Few older party leaders survived. To restrict Jewish travel in 1932, he revived the internal passport that tsars had used to restrict Jews. The passport revealed Jewish nationality as "Yevrei," meaning Jew, and prevented their emigration and temporary travel within the Soviet Union.[2] In 1948, Israel's first prime minister appointed Kiev-born Golda Meir, who had lived in the United States, as Israeli ambassador to the Soviet Union. She remained in that position for only a brief time, but long enough to begin informing Soviet Jews about Israel.

This period of Stalin's rule, the so-called Black Years of Soviet Jewry, was stained by the murder of countless dissidents and intellectuals and the notorious "Doctor's Plot," under which noted Jewish physicians were brought to trial on fake murder charges. Stalin's fearful rule was adapted from Hitler's playbook.

In 1953, upon Stalin's death, Nikita Khrushchev rose in Soviet power. This brought renewed hope among Jews, including the possibility of emigration. In 1956, Khrushchev exposed Stalin-era crimes, and he promised reforms. However, the situation for Jews hardened. By the 1960s, repression under Khrushchev worsened, and his rule inspired political trials of Jewish activists and intellectuals. The Soviet Union's repression was becoming widely known and reported by Jews in other regions. Yet, fear continued to dominate the hearts and minds of the Soviet Jews, who were warned against contact with foreigners visiting the USSR. Although the isolated Soviet Union controlled information and denied wrongdoings, my generation recalls hearing about the Soviet State's newspaper, *Pravda*, and its dissemination of propaganda.

Rescuing Soviet Jews

The first crack in the Soviet wall of silence and misdirection occurred in Latvia in 1963 at Rumbula, the site of the notorious 1941 German massacre of the Latvian Jews. Living in a Soviet satellite country, Jews from Riga defied Soviet law and gathered at the massacre site, posting a sign: "Here were silenced the voices of 38,000 Jews of Riga on November 29–30 and on December 8–9, 1941."[3] Thereafter, annual gatherings commemorated the Rumbula massacre.

"Free Soviet Jewry" was a resounding activist theme during the last third of the twentieth century. The worldwide campaign to liberate persecuted Jews from the Soviet Union was a Cold War phenomenon. It was a clear link between the Cold War and Jewish history. When American and Soviet relations were good, the Soviet Jews and other religious minorities could emigrate. When good relations faded or turned poor, the emigration doors began to close. Soviet Jews became bargaining chips to be played at the whims of their oppressors.

Soviet Jewish Emigration Trends

Soviet Jewish emigration in the last half of the twentieth century paralleled significant evolutionary events and the developments of that era (*see* Graph):

1. Low emigration, 1963–67, as the Soviet government denied the existence of Jewish problems
2. Near cessation of Jewish emigration from the USSR following the 1967 Arab-Israeli "Six Day War"
3. Significant increases in emigration 1972 and 1973, as the Soviets tried to dampen world outrage over trials like the Leningrad dissidents' trials of December 1970
4. Stabilization of emigration, 1974–78, as Soviets attempted to defeat the American Jackson–Vanik legislation and the human rights provisions of the CSCE's Helsinki Final Act
5. Record emigration in 1979, as the Soviets allowed increased emigration for trade, wheat sales, and high-tech investments
6. Record low emigration, 1980–87, as the Soviets reacted to world condemnation of their invasion of Afghanistan in late 1979
7. End of the Cold War

8. Record high emigration, 1988 to the early 1990s, as Reagan and Gorbachev reached unprecedented agreements on arms control, trade, and human rights

Soviet refugee admissions to the United States during many of those crucial years are shown in Table 2 and the Graph.

Prior to 1990, the only Soviet Jews approved for emigration were those who secured an invitation letter and a Soviet-issued exit visa for family reunification in Israel. They left Russia via overnight trains to Vienna and then traveled directly to Israel. FSO John Buche was based in Vienna in the 1990s and reconfirmed the accuracy of the history of that period. The Soviet Jews choosing to settle in countries other than Israel were called "drop outs." America-bound Jews were shifted from Vienna to Rome for visa processing. In Rome, two American Jewish organizations assisted: the American Joint Distribution Committee (AJDC) handled housing and financial support, and the Hebrew Immigrant Aid Society (HIAS) handled visa processing; US immigration officials had their first opportunity to interview applicants about their refugee bona fides.[4]

Since Jews could not be repatriated to Russia, they were considered "presumptively eligible" for refugee status. The *well-founded fear of persecution* requirement of the US Refugee Act of 1980 was not enforced until the late 1980s. The United States adopted a freedom of choice policy (to country of resettlement) on behalf of the Soviet Jews, and RP articulated it often before Congress and other audiences.

Major Developments between Rivals

Four crucial human rights and emigration-related developments fueled Soviet–American antagonism and led to significant policy changes during the last half of the twentieth century: (1) the US Jackson–Vanik Trade Agreement, (2) Helsinki Final Act Basket III provisions of the Commission on Security and Cooperation in Europe (CSCE), (3) the Soviet invasion of Afghanistan, and (4) US and USSR leadership changes.

(1) Trade Legislation

Early in the 1970s, the US Congress discussed linking Soviet–American trade to human rights, especially Jewish emigration. The proposed vehicle was the Jackson–Vanik amendment to a US trade bill authored by Sen. Henry Jackson (D-WA); Rep. Charles Vanik (R-OH) introduced a companion bill in the House of Representatives, October 1972. I discussed these events in 2015 with Elliott Abrams, former congressional aide to Sen. Jackson, who had been close to these events and aware of the Nixon administration's vigorous opposition. It was feared that Jackson–Vanik would damage détente with the Soviet Union. The Soviets feared it might impede negotiations on their Most Favored Nation (MFN) trading status.[5]

The Soviets increased Jewish emigration to show flexibility and that this legislation was unnecessary. Emigration levels increased and remained high in 1972 (thirty-two thousand) and 1973 (thirty-five thousand) during Jackson–Vanik consideration. President Nixon asked Israeli Prime Minister Golda Meir to help him oppose the bill, and she responded: "I cannot tell Jews in the United States not to concern themselves with their brethren in the Soviet Union."[6]

Aware that some form of Jackson–Vanik would become law, the secretary of state Henry Kissinger shuttled between Washington and Moscow to negotiate future emigration levels. His efforts resulted in an exchange of letters setting emigration at sixty thousand annually and identifying waivers that could be granted if all terms of the compromise were honored. Both parties signed the letters in the fall 1973. Congress passed a trade bill with the Jackson–Vanik amendment in December 1973. The Soviets immediately pulled out of the agreement, handing Nixon a huge defeat. The USSR complained there had been too many changes in their understandings since the original negotiations. Bad feelings were left on both sides and would last far into the future.[7] Even though this process had placed Jewish emigration at the top of the US agenda with the Soviets, it had no significant impact on actual emigration, which declined from thirty-five thousand in 1973, to twenty-one thousand in 1974, and finally to thirteen thousand in 1975. Elliott Abrams told me that Jackson–Vanik helped the Soviets understand that the trade–emigration imbroglio would face them every time they dealt with the West.

(2) Helsinki Final Act—Commission on Security and Cooperation in Europe (CSCE)

The USSR signed the Helsinki Final Act in August 1975 with thirty-two other governments. This Act had three interconnected "baskets" (sections), including (I) arms, (II) trade, and (III) human rights. Basket III provided for the free movement of people and information across borders and regular compliance reviews. The signatory governments understood that Basket III's main objective was free emigration for Soviet Jews. After objecting to free movement for so many years, the Soviet Union now seemed to reverse course. The strategic reason was clear: Baskets I and II provided international recognition for the post-war Soviet empire by formalizing European borders established after the war. The Baltic States and Eastern Europe were within these redrawn borders. By supporting Baskets I and II, the West hoped to gain influence through Basket III monitoring.[8]

The Soviets were not concerned about human rights. As previously, they would honor only what favored them. That knowledge led some in the West to believe they had given away too much. Therefore, they emphasized Basket III's monitoring, trusting that it might counter dismissive Soviet behavior on human rights.

(3) Soviet Invasion of Afghanistan

The State Department Refugee Programs bureau was in its early months when a Soviet force of about one hundred thousand invaded Afghanistan in December 1979 with tanks and heavy artillery, ostensibly to combat threats from radical Islamic fighters. These radicals were the ideological predecessors of the present-day Taliban (*see* "Afghanistan and South Asia" in Chapter 35). The RP team watched these events closely, understanding they meant another refugee crisis, as US and USSR détente was halted. In retaliation, President Carter cancelled everything in the works with the Soviets: participation in the Moscow Olympics (sixty other countries also withdrew); the sale of grain, computers, and other high-tech resources; and cultural and educational exchanges. President Carter also pulled the SALT II agreement from Senate ratification.[9]

Soviet tempers rose against Jews, whose emigration took a nosedive and stayed low for the next eight years. Dissident leaders were forced out of Moscow and the remaining *refuseniks* (those refused permission to emigrate) went underground. Arms control talks were dormant. Relations between the two superpowers plunged, and they were beyond the power of existing leaders to influence. Only a new relational framework could change those dynamics. It took almost a decade for that to happen.

(4) Leadership Changes

In 1980, Americans elected Ronald Reagan to be the president. He was best known as an actor, television spokesperson, and the former Republican governor of California. The new president pulled no punches and incensed the Soviet leaders. He called them "the Evil Empire" and asserted his belief "that communism is another sad, bizarre chapter in human history whose last pages even now are being written," and "the quest for human freedom is not material, but spiritual. And because it knows no limitation, it must terrify and ultimately triumph over those who would enslave their fellow man."[10]

The Soviets bitterly resented President Reagan's words and actions. They arrested dissidents and drove them further underground. They launched anti-Zionist campaigns. The movement to aid Soviet Jews stalled. No progress had been made in recent years, and emigration was near its last breath. According to Fred Lazin, in *The Struggle for Soviet Jewry in American Politics*, most informed observers estimated there were hundreds of thousands of long-term *refuseniks* stranded in the USSR; up to 400,000 had requested invitations from Israel.[11] RP continued to make contingency plans for the resumption of Soviet Jewish emigration, as both sides moth-balled diplomacy.

At September 1981 consultation hearings before the House and Senate Judiciary Committees, one of many hearings I would attend during the refugee decade, I testified that "American policy remains 'free choice for Soviet Jews'." This meant that the refugee program would welcome and assist any Soviet Jews who wanted to come and could somehow get to America. The under secretary for political affairs Walter Stoessel accompanied me to that hearing, and he endorsed that policy on behalf of the State Department and the administration. Although actual US refugee admissions were minimal, we kept the official refugee ceiling for

Soviet Jews high as a way of communicating US intentions to the Soviet government. Congress gave its full support.

Shocking news in the spring months of 1982 came from the US refugee coordinator Gene Douglas. He told American Jewish leaders that the president wanted to pursue a contrary policy, to curb refugee admissions to the United States, including Soviet Jews.[12] Rep. Hamilton Fish (R-NY) got wind of those discussions and was irate, since they were at variance with testimony he had heard from me earlier.

Douglas had told the Jewish leaders that the White House believed it was in the interest of both Israel and the United States that most Soviet émigrés settle in Israel and thereby reduce the financial burden on the United States. Douglas had not informed RP or others in the State Department of this significant policy change. The result was damning consternation within the administration and the American Jewish community for several weeks.

Finally, when reality settled, Douglas was forced to write to Rep. Fish on August 23, 1982, saying he had no intention to go ahead with the proposed changes. He said that it would be unthinkable to precipitate any action that might impede the ability of Jews to leave the Soviet Union.

◊

On July 16, 1982, President Reagan appointed George P. Shultz as his second secretary of state. A former Nixon administration official, George Shultz had served as secretaries of Labor and Treasury, and as White House budget director (OMB). He brought policy and business experience, having been a successful businessman and educator. His leadership at the State Department would profoundly affect the Soviet–American relations. In August, Shultz appointed me as the next director of the Bureau for Refugee Programs (RP). My portfolio contained assistance to Jewish dropouts from the Soviet Union who chose American resettlement.

Breakthrough with the Soviets

In the second term, the rival leadership teams were set: US President Reagan and Secretary of State Shultz for the Americans and President

Gorbachev and Foreign Minister Shevardnadze for the USSR. For his part, Reagan wanted to move beyond right-wing orthodoxy.

A strong human rights advocate, Secretary Shultz had used his influence to move Reagan's Soviet agenda quietly forward in the president's first term. Preferring private diplomacy, he organized Reagan's first meeting with a Soviet official in 1983, a White House chat with Ambassador Anatoly Dobrynin. Reagan dominated the meeting, talking about human rights, *refuseniks*, and religious freedom. He complained about a small group of Christian Pentecostals that had taken refuge in the American Embassy in Moscow five years earlier and still could not practice their religion or emigrate. President Reagan asked for Dobrynin's help with the Pentecostals and any other human rights cases needing attention and vowed "simply to be delighted and ... not embarrass you by undue publicity, by claims of credit for ourselves, or by crowing," according to Secretary Shultz years later.[13] Secretary Shultz and Ambassador Dobrynin worked personally, without fanfare or publicity, to move the Pentecostals to the United States. The secretary commented to me, later, that he felt this simple unpublicized venture brought considerable credibility and trust with Ambassador Dobrynin and his Soviet colleagues.

Early in his second term, President Reagan instructed Secretary Shultz to seek more opportunities with the Soviets. Following four years of almost no contact, Shultz traveled to Geneva to open the arms reduction talks with the Soviet foreign minister Andrei Gromyko, hoping to encourage Premier Gorbachev to be more forthcoming. From the outset, Reagan and Shultz tried to clarify that freedom of emigration for Soviet Jews and other minorities was a prerequisite for détente.

Reagan and Gorbachev Policy Summits

Over the next three years, events moved quickly as leaders on both sides sought improvements in their relationship. In November 1985, George Shultz and Anatoly Chernyaev (one of Mikhail Gorbachev's trusted advisors) realized they were pursuing mutually reenforcing goals: to move their bosses beyond existing problems and obstacles, in the direction they both wanted to go. Both sides agreed and began preparations for a summit in Geneva. (Later, according to Andrew Roth, advisor to Soviet leader

Gorbachev, Shultz hoped that Gorbachev might also be ready to jump-start a new relationship.)[14] The precipitating venues for profound relational changes were four summits between November 1985 and June 1988.

First Summit, Geneva

The 1985 summit in Geneva brought the president to his first official meeting with a Soviet leader. Also significant was the presence of Avital Sharansky, wife of the renowned Jewish dissident Anatoly Sharansky.

The National Council on Soviet Jewry president Morris Abram, former president of Brandeis University and later US ambassador in Geneva (during my time there), urged President Reagan to place freedom of emigration for Soviet Jews squarely in the center of the Geneva negotiating table. Raising the subject of Soviet Jews at the outset was a distraction to Gorbachev. He had hoped to keep the talks focused exclusively on arms control. Star Wars, President Reagan's missile defense system, was troubling, as Gorbachev feared it might lead to an accelerated arms race. If President Reagan could be convinced to abandon Star Wars, Gorbachev would consider dismantling intermediate-range nuclear warheads in Europe. Talk of Soviet Jews and emigration diverted their attention, as far as the USSR president Mikhail Gorbachev was concerned.[15] The two sides reached no significant agreement at the Geneva summit and decided to hold further talks.

"Meet at the Glienicke Bridge"

In the Soviet Union, arrests and harassment of dissidents continued, but a sense of change was apparent in Moscow and Washington. In February 1986, Secretary Shultz called Avital Sharansky to tell her that her imprisoned husband was to be released. She could meet him on February 11, 1986, at the Glienicke Bridge, linking West Berlin and Potsdam.[16] By releasing their most prominent Jewish prisoner in such a public way during the Cold War, the Soviets took a gigantic leap forward. They also provided the Soviet Jewish advocacy movement its most dynamic leader.

That year, Gorbachev's reform message to the Twenty-Seventh Congress of the Communist Party highlighted two reforms: *perestroika* and *glasnost*. The first represented a move toward a more enterprising economic system, and the other called for greater Soviet openness, including human rights. Gorbachev made clear his strong preference for dialogue over confrontation.

Second Summit, Iceland

An unscheduled second summit in Iceland, early October 1986, was designed as a business-only meeting. It included two working groups, one for arms control and one for human rights.

From the arms control group came major Gorbachev concessions: elimination of all intermediate-range nuclear missiles from Europe; the USSR would agree to a mutual cut of both countries' strategic weapons, and possible elimination of all nuclear weapons. But even while President Reagan essentially agreed, he would not abandon Star Wars. This impasse brought the summit to a screeching halt.

An especially significant breakthrough initiative on human rights formed in the second working group was lost.[17] Yet both parties agreed that human rights should remain on their agenda.

⋄

My tenure as director of the State Department's Bureau for Refugee Programs (RP) ended in August 1986. As I departed, the Soviet admissions program was still on life support, in the Afghan-invasion mode. Nevertheless, we had kept the Soviet admissions ceilings high to signal American intentions to assist Soviet refugees choosing to settle in the United States. Mikhail Gorbachev had been the Soviet secretary general for just over a year, and his *glasnost* and *perestroika* policies had just been announced. Emigration was low, and his regime continued crackdowns on Jewish cultural life. Gorbachev personally opposed unrestricted emigration, as he believed the Soviet Union could ill afford to lose the energy and brain power of the Jews and other minorities. The Soviet economy was tanking, and the Cold War isolated the Soviet Union from the help it needed. Particularly after the second US-USSR summit, however, Soviet attitudes and polices had begun to swing toward freer emigration.

Later inspiring events (following my RP departure) revealed ice-breaking cooperation, notably under President Reagan's firm leadership and the Soviet secretary general Gorbachev's willingness to face up to an otherwise bleak USSR future. They began to unfold in Washington, DC, at the third summit.

Third Summit, Washington

To cap the positive developments of the Iceland summit, a third summit in Washington, took place on December 8, 1987. I had left RP by then and followed news of the third summit closely, due to my closeness to the emigration desires held by many Soviet Jews.

Remarkably, at the third summit, US President Reagan and Soviet Secretary General Gorbachev signed a treaty of two important dimensions: a major deescalation of the global arms race *and* the launch of a historic exodus of Soviet Jews. President Reagan included these words in his post-summit address to the American and the Soviet people:

> ... the American philosopher, Ralph Waldo Emerson, once wrote that there is properly no history, only biography. He meant by this that it is not enough to talk about history as simply forces and factors. History is ultimately a record of human will, human spirit, human aspirations of Earth's men and women, each with the precious soul and free will that the Lord bestows.[18]

Restrictions were relaxed by the Soviets and the emigration of Jews and others soared. At the urging of Morris Abram and other National Congress on Soviet Jewry leaders, and as a sign of goodwill, Sen. Phil Gramm (R-TX), led Congress to withdraw restrictive economic sanctions directed at the Soviet Union.

Fourth and Final Summit, Moscow

President Reagan and General Secretary Gorbachev held a fourth and final summit in Moscow, June 1988. (My wife and I were preparing our minds for our move to Geneva, Switzerland, where I would serve as the director general of IOM, the International Organization for Migration.)

At the final summit meeting, the Americans argued for free emigration for all the Jews who wanted to leave, including provision for direct flights, and full cultural, religious, and educational rights for those who remained. To highlight the importance of this demand, President Reagan hosted the Zieman family, *refuseniks* who had been trying to emigrate since 1977, and another 98 *refuseniks* at Spaso House (the US ambassador's residence) during the first day of the Moscow talks.

This summit led to a substantial increase in exit visas and liberalization in the cultural and religious life of Soviet Jews. Despite bureaucratic problems in matters of emigration, the stage was set for a massive exodus and a revival of Jewish cultural and religious life in the Soviet Union.

Even as this success was being celebrated, some informed observers, including the assistant secretary of state for human rights Richard Schifter, predicted that a major change in American policy toward Soviet Jewish émigrés might become necessary, since there was another country of refuge, Israel.

From Geneva, on November 9, 1989, I watched with the world as international TV news covered the fall of the Berlin Wall. The Cold War was over.

Soviet Emigration Surge

Many reliable American and Israeli sources expected multitudes to leave the Soviet Union during the next few years. But if high dropout rates continued, the sizeable proportion coming to the United States would quickly outpace resettlement openings. For both the American government and Jewish leaders, these developments created serious concerns:

- Limited US resettlement places and funding
- Competing worldwide resettlement needs
- High United States versus Israel resettlement costs
- Demands to resettle Soviet Jews in Israel

The need for a fresh approach had been signaled in August 1988 when US Attorney General Edward Meese wrote to the president's assistant for national security affairs Colin Powell that "current practices in processing Soviet émigrés appear not to conform to the requirements of the Refugee Act of 1980. Thereafter, Soviet Jews applying for refugee status must prove a 'well-founded fear of persecution'."[19]

Secretary of State James Baker noted at his confirmation hearings: "... we have more refugees at our gates than resources to accept them."[20]

An old argument surfaced: 'Does the United States have a moral right to reject Jewish refugee applicants who suffer from both religious and ethnic discrimination?' The government's reaction was quick and clear: Soviet Jews now have options, and the United States has no automatic responsibility to resettle them all.

New Soviet Refugee Processing Approach

Clearly, the United States needed a new Soviet refugee processing approach geared to evolving developments. Surging demand for Soviet Jewish admissions required the Bush administration to initiate emergency consultations on refugee ceilings for FY 1989. In June 1989, President George H. W. Bush signed Presidential Determination 89-15, increasing the annual refugee ceiling from 94,000 to 116,500 and increasing the ceiling for Eastern Europe and the Soviet Union to 50,000.

As expected, refugee applicant rejections processed under the terms of the 1980 Refugee Act created backlogs in Moscow and Rome. The attorney general agreed to use his parole authority on a limited basis during the transition to assist certain rejected cases. These temporary solutions, however, did not solve the overriding problem.

The reality of the new situation hit on July 4, 1989, when the American Embassy in Moscow stopped processing visa applications for all Soviet citizens until October 1989. Officially, the suspension was imposed because State's "reception and placement" money was exhausted. Also, there were significant concerns about the refugee bona fides of many of the applicants, considering liberalizations underway in the Soviet Union. Up to that time, all Soviet Jewish applicants to the United States were automatically considered refugees. Author Fred Lazin argues that the suspension may have signaled that the US government was unwilling to accept them all as refugees.

US Policy Adjustment

Following the inauguration of President George H. W. Bush in 1989, the State Department, under the direction of the RP deputy assistant secretary of state Priscilla Clapp, established an interagency task force to recommend a way forward for Soviet refugees.[21] The work of her task force led to a Presidential Determination in September 1989, to be implemented over the next two years:

- Close the route for Soviet refugees through Europe by October 1989; all processing thereafter would be conducted in Moscow.
- Re-adjudicate some seventy thousand Soviet refugee applicants stranded in Italy because INS determined they did not meet refugee standards.
- Give preference to Soviet Jews with relatives in the United States and to Pentecostals and to inform other potential Jewish refugees and immigrants they had another place to go to seek asylum, namely Israel.
- Temporarily increase the admission numbers for Soviet refugees to ninety thousand in FY 1990 (primarily to accommodate those who had been stranded in Italy) and keep them at roughly fifty thousand thereafter.

Jewish advocates considered these admissions levels inadequate, and they threw support behind the Lautenberg (Sen. Frank, D-NJ) Amendment, enacted in November 1989. This provision lowered the *burden of proof of persecution* for Soviet Jews, Evangelical Christians and members of the Ukrainian Catholic and Autocephalous (autonomous) churches seeking to obtain refugee admission to the United States. Many believed this amendment made every Soviet émigré a potential refugee.

These developments led to negotiations between the administration, the Jewish resettlement agencies, and Congress on future refugee resettlement levels, beginning with FY 1990. The new Soviet refugee policy that emerged from the consultations process was controversial, particularly with key congressional partners, but it signaled an agreed way forward.

The proposal for a two-track system in Moscow, favored by the US

Government and the Jewish organizations, allowed Soviet Jews to apply in Moscow either to emigrate to Israel or to resettle in the United States or other western countries. It resulted in Israel becoming the destination for most. As the US quota filled quickly for the first two years, other Soviet Jews could either wait a few years or go directly to Israel, which offered a quick exodus from the Soviet Union.

Uncertainty about the Soviet Union's future and America's willingness to admit large numbers of Soviet Jews led to an unprecedented exodus. With the opening of the gates, almost 650,000 Soviet Jews went to Israel, the United States, or other countries between 1989 and 1993.

Flexible Soviet–American Relations

The grand bargain and the thaw in Soviet–American relations brought significant procedural changes in the US selection and processing of refugees, beginning in FY 1990. US immigration officials could interview applicants in Russia and, using provisions of the Refugee Act of 1980, determine whether they met enumerated criteria. Those not able to establish persecution could be denied. This important change allowed the processing of the Soviet Jews to be brought into line with worldwide refugee processing procedures. If rejected for US admission, the Soviet Jews could go to Israel

Correspondingly, the Soviet Government allowed in-country refugee approval and departure directly from Moscow and other locations, avoiding the need for US-bound refugees to travel to Vienna or Rome. To arrange their transport, the US Government turned to the International Organization for Migration (IOM), which I then headed. However, as with other international organizations in Russia, IOM did not have enough legal standing with the Russian Government to operate an entity in its territory. An alternative was needed.

Under Priscilla Clapp's direction at State, a commercial venture formally known as the Soviet Pan American Travel Effort (SPATE) was established between Aeroflot and Pan American Airlines. It provided the legal creation of a Migrant Processing Center (MPC) in Moscow—directed by IOM—to oversee the processing and travel arrangements for Soviet refugees destined to the United States.

Exodus

The payoff came quickly as the Israeli Government and IOM in Moscow arranged the movement of hundreds of thousands of Soviet refugees to Israel, the United States, and other destination countries (*see* Graph).

Special arrangements for embattled Soviet Jews, from 1963 onward, allowed almost a million Jews to emigrate from the Soviet Union. It is estimated that 60 percent went to Israel, about a third came to America and slightly less than 10 percent went to other countries.

As the twentieth century ended, the original goal of lawful emigration for Soviet Jews and other minorities needing and desiring it was accomplished. They had secured the rights guaranteed years earlier in the 1948 Universal Declaration of Human Rights for all people.

Policy sea-changes had to happen. Carmi Schwartz, former executive vice president of the Council of Jewish Federations, crystalized this monumental shift:

> Freedom of choice is no longer an item on the American Jewish communal agenda, simply because to have freedom of choice would bring 200,000-300,000 Jews into this American environment. The American Jewish community couldn't handle this number economically, and the Government of the United States doesn't want them to come in these numbers and would not participate, not only in its economics but in the necessary policies related to those kinds of numbers. So, freedom of choice was dropped from our vocabulary and 'destination Israel' was re-inserted into the vocabulary. 'Family re-unification' became the new code word for the arrival of Soviet Jews into the country as opposed to 'freedom of choice' for all.[22]

During most of the last twenty years of the movement to gain unfettered emigration rights for Soviet Jews, the US Department of State's Refugee Programs bureau and the International Organization for Migration (IOM) managed many of the movement's dynamic consequences and helped demonstrate again a striking example of bureaucracy, diplomacy, and law taking high ground to alter, in positive and generational ways, the lives of deserving individuals and families.

> The reason to record and remember how Soviet Jews were saved is to be prepared to act again when the need arises. If we are ever to live in a civilized world, what was accomplished for the Soviet Jews must become the rule rather than the exception. We must not only preach the doctrine of human rights, we must learn how actually to be our brother's keeper.[23] —George P. Shultz

Postscript

Before moving on, let us scroll forward to the year 2017 and listen to the current warnings of Mikhail Gorbachev about new threats to the Intermediate-Range Nuclear Forces (INF) Treaty that President Reagan and he negotiated and signed in 1987, eliminating a whole class of nuclear weapons, land-based missiles, and launchers in Europe. Of significance here is the opening the treaty created for a historic humanitarian achievement. Today, Mikhail Gorbachev is concerned about calls on both sides to scrap the INF Treaty, even while acknowledging, as recently as 2015, that it had led to decommissioning or destruction of 80 percent of the nuclear weapons accumulated during the Cold War. He called for a new, full-scale summit on reducing nuclear weapons and strengthening strategic stability. Superpower meetings on the margins of international gatherings, Gorbachev said, are not sufficient to address the broad range of problems now facing the two super powers.

> We are living in a troubled world. It is particularly disturbing that relations between the major nuclear powers, Russia and the United States, have become a serious source of tensions and a hostage to domestic politics. It is time to return to sanity.... it is time to take the first step.[24] —Mikhail Gorbachev

33

AFRICA

The Africa Refugee Program

FIGURATIVELY, LIGHTS WERE FLASHING AND SIRENS BLARing as I made a startling discovery in the Refugee Programs' earliest days, July 1979: Africa was the region of our largest, most contentious, and fastest growing refugee problems—and we had just two part-time staffers to deal with them. And they would soon depart, leaving nobody knowledgeable about Africa.

At an emergency meeting with the under secretary of state for management Ben Read, I discussed the program's excruciating birthing pains in Africa.

"I cannot overstate our critical situation in Africa. If State does not come through with the help you and Warren Christopher promised, we're doomed from the get-go."

Ben seemed testy about my latest dire prediction. I knew that central personnel (PER) had tried to paint him into an uncomfortable corner because of their irritation with me. I had recently rejected all marginally qualified officers and staff they had proposed for RP. I also had charged that an attempt was being made to slip unqualified officers into our struggling enterprise.

"They'll sink us before we ever take off," I complained.

Ben countered that PER was telling him they were offering the best that was available, and I was refusing to work with them. He asked if I couldn't be more cooperative.

I pulled a map from the papers I carried around and pointed to Africa.

"The twenty-five highlighted countries are hosting 3.6 million refugees. There are probably an equal number of internally-displaced people."[1]

Ben knew why the millions were in flight or in sketchy hiding spots: wars, dictators, apartheid, corruption, drought, poverty, or a combination of reasons. When he remained silent, I pushed, pointing again to the map.

"This continent is weighed down with the largest number of refugee crises in the world, and our Africa programs and budgets are climbing exponentially. Yet, with *no* staff assigned for Africa, PER wants me to take an unqualified, half-time FSO to head it up! I've reviewed the list of available candidates and not one could handle RP/Africa's needs!"

I said I'd found a good outside hire, but PER had balked. "Your approval is needed to go forward," I said. "To build a first-class organization, I need special help now!" I made the case as forcefully as I could, put the Africa map away, and left Ben with a difficult call to make.

The Team for the Job

Ben Read arranged an outside hire for RP/Africa, adding he felt sure I would find the central management offices more helpful going forward. He also advised me to "make peace."

RP/Africa would be a key hub in our new, more vigorous approach to refugee issues. There would be no more episodic, spur-of-the-moment, crisis-by-crisis conceptualizations, with responsibilities spread around State and USAID. We planned to feature a highly professional, comprehensive, and global approach in a revitalized organization.

About that time, at a Secretary Vance staff meeting, the first few issues discussed were significant to RP, and I commented on each.

"That's not ours," I said, when a non-refugee issue finally came up. Everyone seemed relieved.

Talking with Jean at home one evening, I mentioned our staffing woes. "I need really good people who can think on their feet and manage crises. Jim Lawrence mentioned a Peace Corps Africa officer, Karl Beck. Know anything about him?"

"The name rings a bell. I think he's one of Peace Corps' stars," she said.

"Well, his five-year tour of service there is almost over."

"I'd talk to him soon."

I met with Karl and decided he was what RP needed for Africa, and we needed him yesterday. With Ben Read's approval of my outside hire request, I was confident the Peace Corps would help again if the need arose, as they had done for our Jim Lawrence. Before long, director Dick Celeste agreed to a temporary detail to cover Karl Beck's salary for three months.

Karl knew we needed an insider to be his number two person. "I've found the person we need," he said. "Jim Kelley." Karl and Jim had known each other in Southern Africa, and Kelley was already a State Department employee, working in the office of Foreign Buildings Overseas (FBO). He had worked in Africa with Catholic Relief Services and was eager to come to RP. After my impassioned explanation, PER finally accepted to qualify an FBO officer for refugee work.

After considerable convincing, Margaret McKelvey of RP's Kampuchea Relief Group agreed to become an RP/Africa officer. USAID's Office of Foreign Disaster Assistance had detailed her to RP earlier. Margaret eventually became a recognized Africa refugee expert.

We turned to securing the necessary funding and establishing cooperative Africa partnerships. Those were the next vital building blocks.

Refugee Programs and First Africa Budget

The first comprehensive Africa refugee budget, FY 1982, shaped up during spring and summer 1980. The general strategy was to secure the right of first asylum for the refugees in receiving countries, with priority to the first two *durable solutions: voluntary repatriation* and *regional settlement* when conditions allowed.

State approved RP's sizeable budget request for 1982, sending it to the Office of Management and Budget (OMB). After intensive executive branch review, it went to Congress, where we defended it in multiple hearings before the House and Senate Judiciary, Authorization, and Appropriations Committees.

The approved budgets established RP as the leading international donor for refugees in Africa (*see* Table 4). RP/Africa funding went primarily to international and private organizations, including the United Nations High Commission for Refugees (UNHCR), International Children's Emergency Fund (UNICEF), the World Food Program (WFP), and the UN Development Program (UNDP).

Other international organizations included the International Committee of the Red Cross (ICRC), Red Cross National Societies, the Intergovernmental Committee for Migration (ICM), renamed International Organization for Migration (IOM, and a host of American and international private nongovernmental organizations.

We had to deal with some of Africa's most corrupt and incompetent governments and numerous tribal and civil conflicts, plus struggling international organizations. My advice to staff was simple: deal with each problem as it evolves; always keep the United States as an honest broker; identify the glitches and dysfunctions; and gain support to correct them.

"When we get to know all the players and are accepted as a serious dependable partner," I said, "then we can perform an invaluable integrating role."

American voters elected a new administration in 1980. Arthur Eugene "Gene" Dewey joined RP as deputy assistant secretary responsible for global refugee relief programs, including Africa. A West Point graduate, Gene had commanded helicopter rescue operations in Vietnam. Before serving as the White House fellows program director, he had been the US Government's point person on humanitarian assistance during Nigeria's Biafra War. Action-oriented, he was the perfect choice to spearhead RP's international protection and relief efforts. Gene Dewey would be my strong right hand for many years ahead. From that time forward, the turbulent African problems received courageous and determined attention from him and the team.

During early discussions with Karl Beck, I requested a survey and analysis of the greatest refugee challenges, threats, and problems in Africa. Beset by poverty, corruption and wars, African states were significant in the Cold War, where some sided with the Soviets, others with the United States. The region remained rife with gnarly humanitarian issues and geopolitical rivalries.

The Horn of Africa

The toughest issue was the Horn of Africa—Djibouti, Somalia, Sudan, Ethiopia, parts of Kenya—a spearhead-like formation of countries in northeast Africa strategically near the Indian Ocean, Red Sea, Gulf of Aden, and the Persian Gulf. Those waters controlled the headwaters of the Nile River. Regional conflicts and changing external alliances complicated the Horn's political and military situations. Human tensions and chronic drought produced severe hardships for millions of people in or from Ethiopia and Sudan. US humanitarian aid was at the forefront of perennial drought relief.

Somalia

Somalia became an example of Cold War rivalries rampant in much of Africa during the 1980s that added to the region's misery. In 1977, with Soviet support, Somali President Siad Barre successfully invaded the arid Ethiopian Ogaden region near the Somalia–Ethiopia border. When the Soviets switched support to the Marxist Ethiopian President Mengistu, Somalia switched sides to align with the United States.

Beginning in 1978, the Somali troops in Ethiopia suffered a stinging defeat and retreated. Hundreds of thousands of ethnic Somalis that had settled in the Ogaden feared reprisals and fled home. A large number went to Djibouti. In 1979, Somalia appealed to the UNHCR for assistance to deal with a surging refugee and displaced persons population—a humanitarian tragedy in the making. Karl Beck alerted me that up to one million refugees could begin to flee, with no shelter, water, or food available. He feared that even the basics for an accurate population estimate did not exist. We set up the Somalia Task Force for planning action under Karl Beck's direction and provided funding from the president's refugee emergency fund.

In early months of the crisis, Gene Dewey and I were in Geneva for the UNHCR executive committee meeting when I learned that the Somali Government's extraordinary refugee commissioner Abdi Mohamed Tarah had requested a meeting. He wanted US help to provide food, medical supplies, and shelter for a million refugees and many residents affected by the enormous influx into an impoverished region.

I assured the Somali commissioner of US help, as we tried to get exact numbers on the true refugees in the camps. In that regard, we had conducted a surprise camp census in a single pilot camp early one morning. We used an ink stamp on the hand to prevent multiple counting. Although the refugees were surprised, Somali ingenuity quickly developed a way to erase the ink. That led to lines of refugees in orbit, passing multiple times through the counting station. We had to do better, and this need led to use of satellite photography, a more reliable process.

Next, we had the problem of laying out this disparity for the Somali Government without calling their veracity into question: we told both the Somali Government and UNHCR that, while we could not dispute the official Somali refugee estimate, US budget constraints limited our food contributions to only 450,000 persons. We showed Commissioner Tarah on-the-ground photos of US Food for Peace bags of grain being sold in Mogadishu street markets. We emphasized the critical need to stop diversions of costly imported food. Ambassador Tarah became agitated and declared that using our lower estimate would harm the refugees.

He charged that we were part of a Reagan administration alliance with the Mengistu regime to destabilize Somalia by driving starving refugees into the streets of Mogadishu.

"If you believe President Reagan would enter an alliance with Mengistu, Mr. Ambassador, you are sadly mistaken," I interrupted.

We ended the meeting acrimoniously on one hand but with assurances of US help on the other.

RP's emergency program for Somalia continued for several years, after which assistance was continued through RP's regular Africa program. Through the UN, the Red Cross, and other participating organizations, we kept a sharp eye on the Somali Government and refugee camp developments. Not surprisingly, complexity often characterized our dealings with the Somalia Government, which had become known as "Refugees Inc." We knew that, unless checked and caught by donors, refugee relief supplies sometimes bypassed refugee camps and ended up elsewhere.

Ethiopia

In 1981, Karl Beck became counselor at the US Mission in Geneva and Jim Kelley replaced him as RP/Africa leader. In late 1984, drought and famine plagued Northern Ethiopia, putting life-threatening pressure on the Eritreans and Tigrayans fighting the Soviet-backed Mengistu regime. Our Emergency Management Unit director Tex Harris (known for demonstrating courageous use of the dissent channel in a previous Argentine human rights crisis) saw the danger of a long and arduous refugee trek from Tigray and Eritrea into Eastern Sudan. The Catholic Relief Services organization was requesting food from the United States for direct distribution within the affected areas of Ethiopia, aiming to minimize the need for desperate flight. This was a perfect fit with RP's strategy to decrease deaths by anchoring the needy population within Ethiopia.

Ambassador Jeanne Kirkpatrick strongly objected, calling it unacceptable support to the Mengistu regime. Tex Harris asked USAID's Peter McPherson (President Reagan's representative for humanitarian assistance in the Horn of Africa) to call Kirkpatrick. The result was a clear policy statement: "In situations of acute humanitarian need, the United States is politically blind." The president gave this policy a memorable endorsement when he issued his famous dictum: "A hungry child knows no politics."[2]

Mother Teresa became involved with African relief efforts when she visited Northern Ethiopia in December 1984 and saw the needs. Later, she visited the American Embassy in Khartoum to brief the chargé. Father Kevin Doheny, Gene Dewey's friend from Biafra relief days, accompanied her.

Father Doheny later described to Gene what happened. Mother Teresa told the American chargé what she had seen and then asked if she might give President Reagan the same first-hand account.

The chargé responded that he was sure the president would be interested but contacting him would be difficult.

Mother Teresa asked, "Doesn't the president live in a house?"

"Yes."

"Doesn't he have a phone in his house?"

"Yes," again.

"Don't you have a phone in this house?"

The chargé saw where this was leading and put a call through to the White House. President Reagan proved far more inclined to follow his heart to do what the United States could do, rather than heed bureaucratic or ideological warnings against overresponding. He eagerly engaged with Mother Teresa on what the United States should do.

Sudan

By 1984, civil war, drought and famine had driven over two-thirds of Africa's 3.5 million refugees into Sudan from Chad, Ethiopia, and Uganda. During a visit to the Horn of Africa, RP found over 300,000 destitute famine victims spread out over 300 border miles from Kassala in the North to Gedaref. They were settled primarily in two camps, Wad Sherife (North) and Wad Kowlie (South). Eastern Sudan's UNHCR refugee camps then accounted for the highest mortality and morbidity rates ever recorded in Africa, caused mainly by contaminated water intake.

The RP Emergency Management Unit (EMU) director Tex Harris went to the region in October and November 1984, with consultant Fred Cuny and the emergency unit's Don Krumm, veteran of US Forest Service emergency operations in Montana, to oversee operations. UNHCR had no emergency capability then for acquiring food, clean water, shelter, or measles vaccines to mitigate the accelerating death rates.

Krumm arrived at Wad Kowlie and found water and food supplies desperately short. He also found private commercial warehouses overflowing with food stocks. To spur UNHCR to action, Krumm said he had authority to purchase up to $500,000 in local commercial food if they could not solve the food problem. UNHCR then diverted ships, and the food pipeline quickly filled.

He found the scarce local water supply to be contaminated. He and team members Fred Cuny and water engineer Col. Ted Maddry contracted trucks to pull water from nearby sources, purify it in the trucks with a water purification system parachuted in by the Air Force, and distribute it through a pipeline system financed by RP. Empowered with authority and funding, the RP team continued to supply water until UNHCR could take over.

Jerry Weaver, RP's resident coordinator in Khartoum, on detail to RP from USAID, had told me that the refugee situation in South Sudan, where the black Christians and the animists opposed the Muslim government in the North, was a tinderbox ready to erupt. Arrangements were made for an RP Sudan assessment to include Gene Douglas, US coordinator for refugee affairs, his assistant Harry Fornoff, RP/Africa's Jim Kelley, and Jerry Weaver, and me. We left from Dulles International Airport in Virginia on a March weekend in 1984. The Washington, DC, area was almost blinded by a snowstorm. We landed in Khartoum's enveloping heat the next day. Karen AbuZayd from UNHCR joined us to board a small plane to Juba, a South Sudan town where conditions were quickly deteriorating. There was no electricity or petrol in a society that appeared to stand still.

Throughout the Juba area, Ugandans who had fled the Obote regime filled refugee camps. We saw people camping out in the bush and visited a small NGO hospital where wheelbarrows, oxcarts, or the arms of family or neighbors transported the sick or injured.

I got to know RP's representative Jerry Weaver on that trip. He cast a formidable presence in Sudan. Jerry, a Ohio University alumnus, had built strong relations with the Sudanese interior ministry and military. His big-game hunting and card-playing talents helped him gain favor among Sudanese officials.

Douglas and Fornoff returned to Washington a few days later, and the rest of us flew on a small plane to Gedaref, where we met drought-plagued Ethiopians in refugee camps in the North and East. As Jerry directed us through the desert, I noticed the Sudanese military escort, always present on the fringes. That night, a Sudanese soldier kept guard outside my room. 'Is he keeping me in or others out?' I assumed this was customary protocol for government visitors.

Several days later, we arrived back in Gedaref for return to Khartoum by small plane. In Khartoum, I learned why armed militia personnel had traveled alongside us. Egyptian and US intelligence had detected plans for a surprise attack on Khartoum by Libya's Colonel Gaddafi. The Libyan Air Force had dropped five bombs on Omdurman (Sudan's second largest city) a few days earlier and returned to a base in the Kufra Oasis of Libya. While we had traveled away from news zones, Egypt had readied its Air Force to counter the Khartoum attack, and the United States had warned Libya of "serious consequences." American General Vernon Walters, representing Secretary Shultz, had come to Sudan to organize US military responses, if needed. Gaddafi apparently learned that his plans had been detected and called off the attack at the last minute. Back home, my wife had heard news reports and updates about the plan. My mother had called her soon after.

◇

I had known nothing of these events that caused a Sudanese military guard to be with us, at the ready to and from the desert.

Our first night back in Khartoum, our group met with people from the American Embassy in a hotel restaurant. During that dinner, Jim Kelley leaned toward me: "I think I see some familiar faces over there." His eyes directed me to a nearby table.

I sensed that Jerry Weaver also felt uneasy. He must have seen my questioning expression.

Jim Kelley explained: "They are Jewish NGO officials. From Canada."

Jerry Weaver and Jim Kelley feared these were Canadian NGO activists trying to stimulate Ethiopian Jewish refugees in Ethiopia's Gondar region to flee to Sudan in hopes of relocation to Israel. The US Government did not favor mass movements of Ethiopian Jews to Israel via Sudan, considering such movements to be political dynamite, logistically hard to organize, and likely to cause deaths.

As dinner wound down, we wandered over to casually introduce our team to the other group. They described themselves as organizers of boat excursions down the Nile. We smiled. All knew their true agenda. We opined that their plan was a serious mistake, rife with potential to create major problems with the Sudan Government. We emphasized, "You have no solid preparations, which makes it extremely dangerous for the people you want to help!"

What we did not know, what they did not tell us, was that their secretive mission to move Ethiopian Jews was already underway.

Details of Ethiopian Jews' movements remained highly-sensitive and unexposed for years. As time passed, however, the subject received considerable public attention and exposure, much of it inaccurate or incomplete. RP had a critical perspective and played a significant role in this unfolding historical drama. My aim here is to complement the present record and advance understanding of actions taken to rescue and relocate as many Falasha as was possible.

Rescue Logistics for Ethiopian Jews

Ethiopian Jews, sometimes called the Falasha (or Beta Israel), are an ancient Hamitic people claiming descent from Menelik I, son of the Queen of Sheba and King Solomon. Not knowing of the Talmud, their practice was to use an ancient scripture and a prayer book written in Ga'ez, the ancient Ethiopian language, and to follow the Jewish traditions including circumcision, observing the Sabbath, attending synagogue, and following ancient dietary, purity, and burial laws.

In 1975, the Chief Rabbinate of Israel officially recognized Ethiopian Jews as eligible for the Law of Return. Later, Israeli Prime Minister Menachem Begin obtained clear rulings from Chief Sephardic Rabbi Ovadia Yosef saying they were Jewish descendants.[3]

Starting in 1978, the State Department had worked with the Israeli Government, the Jewish Agency, the Mossad, and trusted officials in the Sudanese Government to arrange monthly escapes of small numbers of Ethiopian Jews to Sudan. This risky adventure was described as "very secret stuff, moving in very small groups, ranging from six to twenty (at a time) and numbering only in the hundreds over a year's time."[4] With fictitious visas, they went by boat from Port Sudan or by air from Khartoum, destination Israel by way of Europe.

Early 1984 cable traffic from Khartoum alerted us to small but increasing numbers of Ethiopian Jews crossing into Sudan in horrible physical condition. The cables raised new fears that American and Canadian NGOs had applied pressure on Ethiopian Jews to move en masse. Prime Minister Begin talked with President Reagan to request American help.

In 1984, UNHCR assigned growing numbers of Falasha to camps like the one near Um Rakuba, about fifty miles from the Sudan–Ethiopia border. As larger arrivals continued, living conditions deteriorated, and the United States and Israel undertook further contingency planning.

Noting Sudanese Government sensitivities, we wanted the refugees to be moved out of Sudan fast, without raising suspicions.

During his August 1984 home leave, Jerry Weaver came to RP headquarters in Washington for consultations on Ethiopian Jews. Charles Powers of the *L.A. Times* got wind of it:

> ... the meetings were going on at a high level, involving the top officers in his own bureau, [director] James N. Purcell, Jr. and [deputy assistant secretary] Arthur E. (Gene) Dewey ... as well as Princeton Lyman, the deputy assistant secretary for East Africa; Elliott Abrams, assistant secretary for human rights; and the US refugee coordinator.[5]

We were displeased about publicity regarding those meetings.

An idea emerged from those consultations: *airlift*. But how would we do it in those precarious circumstances? Sudan urgently needed American aid. Maybe the State Department could leverage RP assistance for Falasha rescue.

The breakthrough came in September when Jerry Weaver met with a mid-level Sudanese Government counterpart and learned that travel documents were the major obstacle to Falasha evacuation, not the immigration or refugee restrictions as feared. Jerry urged his counterpart to arrange a meeting between the American Embassy and Sudanese state security.

Ambassador Hume Horan met with General Omar Tayeb, also Sudan's first vice president. He laid out the problem, and General Tayeb eventually agreed to the plan to move the Ethiopian Jews from Sudan to Israel. But, he said, the operation must be conducted with extreme secrecy. Ambassador Horan agreed and cabled Washington that night. Approval came quickly, and planning accelerated.

Coordination from Khartoum would involve the Jewish agency, Mossad, and Jerry Weaver. The American Embassy in Khartoum was to lead and keep all involved parties informed. Washington and Tel Aviv would give logistical and financial support as needs became clearer. In

Washington, key players in early planning were RP, the refugee coordinator's office, and State's Africa bureau.

Cut Out

A few weeks passed after our planning decisions, and RP heard nothing but routine refugee reporting from Khartoum. We felt sure the evacuation plans were moving forward quietly, as agreed. Then, as Gene Dewey was about to return to Washington from Khartoum, Ethiopian refugee matters began to take a weird turn. Jim Carlin of ICM, the Intergovernmental Committee for Migration headquartered in Geneva, intercepted Gene on the airport tarmac. Carlin said ICM field people were reporting acute life-threatening conditions in the Falasha camps in eastern Sudan. New camp arrivals seemed too frightened to leave their huts. Also, they were malnourished, sick, exhausted from the long trek, and unknown numbers were dying. There were no signs of special UNHCR help for them. The lack of field reporting on this development led Gene to alert me.

"We should not need to learn such vital information from people outside the State Department!" I blurted.

We soon learned more, such as the Falasha interpretation of Jewish law, which caused them to eat a strict age-old diet and refuse medical care and camp sanitation procedures. American Jewish groups confirmed this report, including that there were up to fifteen deaths a day.

I called UNHCR in Geneva for their assessment. Oddly, UNHCR field staff saw no difference between Falasha conditions and many thousands of others in Sudan, saying all refugees were treated equally and nothing was especially concerning about this population.[6] Gene Dewey passed this assessment to our contacts in the Jewish community.

They responded loudly, "No," and the conditions, if anything, were worsening.

We alerted UNHCR that its report conflicted with what we were hearing. They checked again and provided the same assessment.

As no reporting on these developments had come from the field, we became suspicious, our concerns rising. Gene Dewey approached State's

Africa bureau, which shed no light on this sudden communications gap. As Gene continued to check with Jerry Weaver in Khartoum, it became clearer that RP had been cut out from vital information about the Falasha.

We vowed to find out who was behind this blackout, and why.

As we tried to solve the puzzle, Gene and I received a weekend luncheon invitation from Maury Atkin, an important Jewish partner and refugee advocate. He also invited a RP program officer, Judy Chavchavadze, to join us on his boat on the Chesapeake Bay.

It was a beautiful, sunny Saturday, and Maury offered a fantastic lunch shared while we talked, reminisced, and went for a swim. Later, as we relaxed, Maury shot a serious statement toward me:

"One of the reasons I invited you is that we are surprised that RP seems to be disconnected, out of the picture, regarding recent developments in Sudan. The Jewish agencies are concerned and wanted to know why. We know how active RP has been in solving refugee issues in other regions."[7]

I explained there'd been no special reporting to us from Khartoum about the problems described; we'd just learned about perceived communications gaps, Khartoum to Washington:

"We're investigating. We're waiting to hear from Jerry Weaver and the embassy about the medical and nutrition problems," we all said, "and they will be fixed."

Maury told us other news that his sources had picked up in Sudan and Washington, adding, "Your attention is needed immediately."

"Most of the information you're providing has never reached me," I said. Gene and Judy acknowledged the same.

"I was afraid that might be the case," Maury said. He thought we should know more: "I've heard that RP has been eliminated from distribution of cables from Khartoum, regarding the Falasha. We're concerned that the response will be hampered unless you get involved."

That RP had been deliberately cut out was staggering news, although it confirmed troubling suspicions Gene and I had after Jim Carlin's comments a few days earlier on the Khartoum tarmac. That this catastrophe had happened was beyond the pale.

"This is incredible," I said to Maury. "You're telling me that the addressee list on cables regarding one of the most serious refugee problems in the world excludes RP? Believe me, we'll get to the bottom of this!"

A fast call to the State Department worldwide office of communications got the answer: "... a revised distribution was ordered, and it *excluded* RP."

Given that Secretary Shultz had designated Ed Derwinski, seventh-floor counselor, for urgent contacts, I called Ed. He got back to me with what he'd learned, that "special need-to-know arrangements" had been ordered to restrict information on the Falasha issue. He did not know how or why RP had been left blind on major refugee developments.

This was unbelievable. I pushed: "Why restrict RP, the department's main refugee arm?!"

Territorial end runs on shared humanitarian needs made no sense. RP had been through many in-house battles over the years, but none quite so potentially harmful as this one. On its face, it was beyond comprehension; it was also dangerous, and I wanted the message to be clear to those involved.

"Ed, if the State Department wants regional bureaus and the coordinator's office to run refugee programs, then you don't need RP! The Jewish agencies and a friend in Geneva had to bring this backhanded nonsense to my attention. The agencies are blaming RP, specifically me. They've been wondering why we were 'ignoring desperate Jewish refugees'! Those are their words!"

I was on the verge of resigning on the spot, and Ed knew he had to address the problem immediately. He also knew that RP was central to each contentious refugee crisis in other regions. He asked me to be calm and steady while he worked on this problem.

Ed called back soon, saying that RP was back in the picture. He did not explain, yet I concluded from his demeanor that the seventh floor was now troubled by this revelation.

Khartoum cables immediately came flooding into RP. I told Ed Derwinski that we would immediately assume responsibility for our mandated refugee responsibilities. Ed realized I had lost confidence in our in-house colleagues.

I went immediately to the refugee coordinator's office and got assurances they would cease interference with RP's work on this issue, although they denied responsibility for the information blackout. One of that office's staff members had recently made a dangerous blunder by sending a message to one of our Sudan contacts through the Sudan Embassy in Washington. It had jeopardized the life of our contact by exposing what was supposed to be a covert channel. Gene Dewey had heard from Sudan's key refugee official, Ambassador Mohamed Al Ahmadi, who demanded help to avoid such problems.

Gene talked again to State's Africa bureau about the information blackout but received no clarification. He called Jerry Weaver in Khartoum, who pleaded innocence. He said it was a Washington problem. I instructed Dewey to keep a sharp eye on Jerry and to remind him he worked for RP.

Our suspicions were at high alert, but we agreed to set our concerns aside while the crisis was underway. The urgency required all State Department organizations to devote full attention to the problem at hand. No further information came to light on the separate communications track, how and why it was created, or who ordered it. The lid was on tight.

Immediately, we worked with Jewish organizations in Israel and the United States to organize and send specialized medical and nutritional experts to treat health and nutrition problems in the camps.

Gene and I were in Geneva later, attending a UNHCR meeting. While there, we met in the basement of the Hotel InterContinental with officials working on the secret airlift: Princeton Lyman from State's Africa bureau, RP/Khartoum's Jerry Weaver, plus agents from the United Israel Appeal (UIA), and the Israeli Mossad. That meeting put Operation Moses in play.

Operation Moses

As the executing agent, Jerry Weaver needed substantial funding to hire buses, planes, equipment, and other logistical parts. The Israeli government provided black bag funds. Prime Minister Menachem "Benny"

Begin was informed that Ethiopian Jewish refugees would arrive in Israel soon in large, yet unknown, numbers.

"They're our brothers and sisters, we welcome them; they are part of our Diaspora. Whatever number comes, we'll make sure that they're welcome." So said the unswerving prime minister of Israel.

The action began late one night as the refugees from Um Rakuba boarded Jerry Weaver's prearranged convoy transports and traveled to Khartoum. Waiting in a far corner of the Khartoum airport, a Swedish airliner arranged by Gene Dewey through ICM/Geneva, took on its special cargo, destination Israel. Between November 21, 1984 and January 6, 1985, Operation Moses proceeded in that manner, moving almost eight thousand people of an endangered and ancient culture to safety in another ancient homeland.[8]

Operation Moses was to be conducted with extraordinary secrecy at every level, including its existence, destinations, routes, schedules and assisting staff. Human and political catastrophe could follow any information sabotage. Yet, Israeli contacts detected violations of the operation's secrecy. They told us of leaks in Israel and perhaps in the Washington. Learning that some US reporters had picked up strands of information about Operation Moses, the State Department, particularly the Africa bureau and RP, contacted numerous news organizations to hold off their reporting. Most complied, but word was still leaking.

In early January 1985, Operation Moses was brought to a premature end. After public disclosure, Sudan's President Jaafar Nimeiri announced that any Jewish refugees in Sudan would be denied help from his government. If they wanted to leave on their own, that was their business. Sudan's Vice President General Omar Tayeb was removed from office and later imprisoned.

One journalist's work on events surrounding Operation Moses was as informative, yet sensitive, as any I could have hoped for in those strange days. It was Wolf Blitzer, Washington correspondent for the *Jerusalem Post*, who wrote of the concluding events in an evident tone of dismay. He mentioned unnamed sources that wanted recognition more than protection for Operation Moses.

"If ever there was an example of defeat being snatched from the jaws of victory—with damage yet to be calculated— it was the sudden end to the rescue of starving Jews from Ethiopia by the State of Israel," Blitzer wrote.[9] He credited "premature publicity" for ending the operation, possibly permanently. Meanwhile, he reported that "thousands of Ethiopian Jews still in Ethiopia or the refugee camps in Sudan" needed help.

For *Jerusalem Post* readers, Blitzer called out different actors including Israeli political parties and Jewish organizations. He specifically mentioned Jewish Agency comments on the airlift and other organizations and publications that picked up and expanded on their comments. Other public commenters included reporters Bernard Gwertzman (*New York Times*) and William Beecher (*The Boston Globe*), ABC News, and new Prime Minister Shimon Peres, who discussed the operation in the Knesset, based on assurances it was already public knowledge.

Blitzer acknowledged that the Reagan administration had been ready to help and had been disappointed about leaks.

"There are critical but obvious lessons for all concerned to be learned from this incident. If the airlift should resume, they should not be forgotten," he wrote.

RP estimated that about 500 Falasha people remained stranded in Sudan. We held out hopes to resurrect and enlarge the earlier clandestine route to evacuate them. However, Jewish organizations in Washington and in Canada again applied political pressure, saying that thousands would be slaughtered without an immediate resumption of the airlift.

About that time, Chet Crocker, assistant secretary for Africa, invited me to go with him to brief Vice President George Bush for an upcoming trip to Sudan. The situation of Ethiopian Jews was an issue the vice president would bring up with President Nimeiri. I told the vice president there were so few left, we could get them out using the earlier clandestine route. I did not see a need to relaunch the airlift, and State's Africa bureau agreed. We believed a new airlift would be afflicted with the same problems as Operation Moses, whose premature exposure presented an incredible political problem for the Nimeiri government and dangers for the Falasha and helping staff.

The vice president's staff, particularly Don Gregg (later ambassador to South Korea) disagreed and said there were thousands, not hundreds, left and a second airlift was the only way to get them out. The vice president overruled our objections, and planning for a second airlift commenced, to be conducted this time by the CIA. It was to be called Operation Sheba.

Operation Sheba

Chet Crocker invited me to join the vice president's team to Sudan. I declined on the grounds that critical funding arrangements for the Operation Sheba airlift had to be set, and I needed to remain behind to organize them and deal with refugee crises in other regions. And, I was still uneasy about the cables debacle.

I went to the State Department's budget office, the OMB, and the NSC for authorization to use the president's refugee emergency fund for Operation Sheba. I told officials this was a secret foreign policy operation I could not yet describe, assuring them of its highest urgency, with specifics to follow as soon as possible.

In early March 1985, Vice President Bush was still in Sudan when the White House sent the US ambassador in Sudan the news of a presidential order for the evacuation of the remaining Falasha refugees within the next seventy-two to ninety-six hours.[10]

Jerry Weaver flew with two Air force pilots to the planned evacuation site. The pilots paced off its 900 meters surfaced in rough, red, and laterite gravel and graded slightly uphill, west to east. The flights were doable.

From that point, Jerry was not directly involved in the evacuation. While in Khartoum, Vice President Bush presented him a distinguished service award, as proposed by the American Embassy in Khartoum. A Weaver colleague who had helped in Operation Moses was called back to Khartoum to screen and prepare the refugees for departure under Operation Sheba.

The White House three-day timetable could not be met; it took twelve days to formulate and refine evacuation plans. Meanwhile, Sudanese state security rounded up anyone thought to be a possible leak, no explanations given. They kept such people, including reporters, away from the evacuation zone.[11] Nevertheless, rumors flourished. *Los Angeles Times* correspondent Charles Powers was in Khartoum working on a Falasha article during the runup to the second airlift. He did not have the full story but had been piecing it together over many weeks.

On March 23, 1985, four US Air Force C-130 aircraft landed in desert secrecy outside Gedaref, the first at about six a.m., and fewer than 500 evacuees were whisked away and flown directly to Israel. The entire operation was over by nine that morning. When Sudanese state security soldiers returned to barracks, correspondent Powers observed they were covered with red dust, laughing, and joking. Curious, Powers asked about this and was told, "that was from the big American airplanes that just left."[12] He put it all together.

Ambassador Hume Horan met with Gene Dewey in Khartoum for a postmortem the morning after the extraction. Gene remembered commenting on this as a model for crisis management and the ambassador being puzzled by the notion of managing a crisis.

The Sunday after the evacuation, I drove to a convenience store close to home to buy the morning's *Washington Post*. The front page laid out the entire secret operation in glowing detail, including RP's involvement through Gene Dewey, Princeton Lyman, Jerry Weaver, and other players. My role was highlighted. I was livid about the report, written by none other than *LA Times*' Charles Powers.

On Monday morning I told Andrea Long, my secretary, to call Jerry Weaver and get him in. "Jim," she said, "that won't be necessary. Jerry is sitting in the reception area. He's driven all night to be here this morning. He knew you would want to see him."

Jerry began by telling me that he and his staff had left Sudan under personal threat, due to the publicity that had gotten so intense. The American Embassy had received serious threats against his life.

I was furious. "And how did Powers get the story, Jerry?"

Jerry said he had been feeding small increments of the story to Powers, aiming at misdirection. He'd known the reporter was trying to pull it together, and he'd thought bits of information might keep Powers away from the main story.

I said, "He had the whole story the next day, including all details."

Jerry said Roman Polanski had approached him about a movie on this story.

"Not a word is to get out," I said. "There will be no further talk until we are assured no other lives are at risk. We gave our word to collaborators, and we cannot let them down."

Jerry pulled back while we considered the matter further. These intense and unfortunate events in Sudan led to his decision to leave federal service. He would keep his personal account in his safe and never reveal it unless needed to straighten the record.

Unauthorized leaks came from sources in Washington and Israel. The story was pieced together by news and reporting services and the gist of it became widely available. We could not put the genie back in the bottle, but I embargoed public discussion of this sensitive RP operation. I believed we still had plausible deniability, because no reputable government official had confirmed any reports.

In his reporting on Operation Sheba, reporter Charles Powers had mentioned that the planning had taken place in Purcell's office and included Dewey. That caused State Department concerns for our safety, including that we not leave Washington for several months. We doubted we could meet a request that would keep us both grounded.

I had strong feelings that Operations Moses and Sheba had been successful humanitarian maneuvers that saved the lives of thousands of otherwise doomed refugees. Operating in a hostile environment where human lives are at stake requires risks where unconventional approaches become the norm. Jerry Weaver deserves much credit for outstanding operational performance under pressure, and I regarded these operations as truly remarkable in their results.

Nevertheless, the sloppy execution that characterized these noble efforts appalled me. Executing the plan had unnecessarily involved self-serving actors (in Israel and the United States) with devious motives, desiring to publicize and glamorize their own roles. Usual loyalties, reporting practices, and security standards were ignored or bypassed. Lifesaving programs had to be cancelled and then resurrected through intervention by the highest officials of our government. Their involvement had become necessary to straighten out disarray caused by bureaucratic intriguers.

State Department Caper

In the middle of Operation Moses, a separate information track was put into play for a time. As previously mentioned, persons within the State Department excluded RP and other parties from cable traffic and involvement in active policy and operations. They not only cut off access to information but even tried to block us from learning we had been the cutout. Later, our best estimate was that this went on for a couple of weeks. RP, like any other operation, relied on a continuing flow of accurate, up-to-date information. The embargo of cable traffic harmed our operations for a while, and no one "owned up." Blanket denials blocked our efforts to find the source.

Only recently I learned missing details about the unofficial cable embargo. My original decision to avoid using this book to settle old scores prevents me from further discussing this disturbing episode. It is a relief, however, finally to know the full story. Mainly, I was satisfied that RP handled the disruption well in a highly professional manner.

At the time, questions circled in my head: Why secretly exclude RP from vital information about a sensitive refugee operation it was part of? Why lead us to believe all was going well?

The attempt had been bound to fail, as it did, when Jewish agencies and ICM brought the case to my attention. They were legitimately questioning why RP was so quiet on such a critical refugee issue. State Department leaders, once aware, had to intervene, and no one wants an issue to rise to that level.

Going forward, RP positioned itself better to avoid future leaks and any attempted cutouts. Our team would remember the warnings of the Falasha experience. We made operational improvements afterward.

Operation Solomon

In 1991, Israel launched Operation Solomon, the last, to rescue over fourteen thousand Ethiopian Jews endangered in Ethiopia's Gondar region. Operation Solomon departed from the Israeli Embassy grounds in Addis Ababa. Small numbers were thought to be remaining in Ethiopia, yet not in danger.

This new refugee population had to bridge a two-thousand-year gap in Israel. When Gene Dewey later visited a summer camp near Caesarea that included new Falasha arrivals and Israeli children, this was vividly dramatized. The Israeli children were shocked to see how far behind modern practices their new population was, when Falasha children adamantly insisted on their ancient version of the Seder meal. This conflict illustrated the complications of integrating into an unfamiliar culture, as well as the complications of helping others integrate.

Continuing Disappointments in Sudan

While untangling Falasha mix-ups, constant reminders of multilateral organizations' poor performance in eastern Sudan were magnified by extensive drought and famine. We were especially concerned that UNHCR was at near paralysis over the outbreak of a major measles epidemic. RP's nearly real-time reporting system, attuned to the risks of unvaccinated children in overcrowded camps, recorded forty children dying each day in Wad Sherife camp. Meanwhile, UNHCR had difficulty acquiring adequate food, clean water, shelter, and measles vaccines to mitigate the soaring death rates.

For the Ethiopian Jews' camps, RP dispatched direct aid and Israeli agencies sent medical doctors and nutritionists to prepare acceptable Jewish food and see to severe medical needs. The United States intervened with air-shipped measles vaccine, cold chains (supplies needing temperature controls), and US medical teams. We later learned that in Khartoum UNICEF had in stock all the vaccine and cold chains needed, but either UNHCR staff had not asked for them or UNICEF had not suspected the obvious need and volunteered.

RP's experience in the Horn of Africa brought to light that UNHCR and the other international organizations in Africa were not prepared to deal daily with severe life-and-death emergencies. RP initiated work with UNHCR colleagues to develop emergency management training. Its application was tested in real time in Africa (proving the training's value) and was later adopted by UNHCR for global training (*see* chapter 37).

October 1984, Famine

Simultaneous to the Falasha operations, there were worsening civil wars, antagonisms, and drought across the Horn of Africa in 1984. The Ethiopian famine that year became one of the most widely publicized humanitarian crises of that era.[13] Over a million Ethiopians died, and reports from other countries were as dramatic.

As conditions in Sub-Saharan Africa spiraled further downward, Gene Dewey and I had two certain beliefs, (1) that many multilateral agencies like the UNDP, UNICEF, UNHCR, and the World Food Program (WFP) were responding in a business-as-usual fashion, and (2) they were concurrently disorganized, turf conscious, and not cooperating. Their lethargy, we believed, put dependent people in severe jeopardy.

RP's Emergency Management Unit reported another UN disaster in the offing, as 150 million people in Africa lacked adequate nutrition and some thirty million suffered in acute hunger. Brad Morse, head of UNDP, called it "… the most massive catastrophe that has been visited on the planet."[14]

Our staff agonized over the situation and almost concluded that our expectations for UN improvement in this Africa crisis were unachievable. In frustration, I thought maybe a bypass of the UN was called for. I had already directed Dewey's team to do a workup about other partnering possibilities, and we believed other multilateral and private agencies could develop competencies for addressing these humanitarian disasters.

I told Dewey, "We can find other multilateral organizations to work with us and we can use NGOs. It would be good for the UN to see that it has lost the confidence of its major donor."

Dewey remained unusually quiet. It seemed I could hear the mental wheels turning. Eventually, he spoke up, his voice calm:

"What if we force the secretary general to set up an overarching and powerful coordinating organization that can direct and integrate the contributions of the various multilateral agencies? Look at what Sir Robert Jackson and UNBRO were able to achieve in Bangkok for the border Khmer."

I pondered the idea for a few minutes. "It might work, but what are the chances we could get something like that fast enough? It's needed now. Could we bypass the bureaucracy here that would try to coordinate it to death?"

Business as usual, I feared, would assure that this initiative would never see the light of day.

"Let's give it a try, Jim." Gene looked at me with an expression I knew well. "I'll volunteer to see the secretary general tomorrow if I can get in and lay the matter before him. I'll suggest UNBRO as a model and someone to head it."

"If he doesn't agree, we'll tell him the Americans will go bilateral."

"Can you deal with things here in Washington, the critical sell?" he asked.

As we tossed the idea around some more we saw the need to work undercover—and with great speed—if we were to have a chance for success.

"Gene, Secretary Shultz has given me fairly wide berth in multilateral refugee diplomacy," I said. "Because the issues are so grave here, I am willing to test the outer limits and proceed as we discussed. Maybe you can co-opt some of our friends in New York to help. I can probably look to the Africa Bureau of support. Regardless of the odds, let's move forward. I'll let Shultz know where we're headed. You should go to New York, and unless I call you off before you see the secretary general, proceed as we discussed. Maybe you can get UNICEF's Jim Grant to partner with you."

I understood the ramifications. The State Department's International Organizations bureau (IO) and USAID would be livid over my authorization for a unilateral approach to the secretary general regarding refugees and Africa. IO considered the UN its exclusive province, and USAID believed it was the lead US agency for Africa emergencies; it would likely view RP's initiative as a threat and try to block further action.

Gene and I conversed more about salient facts. Jim Grant, UNICEF executive director, had more influence than anyone we knew at UN headquarters. We had earlier argued with Grant, disagreeing with his view that the Horn of Africa famine was confined to Ethiopia. We believed the crisis extended into other parts of the Horn. We also disagreed that his plan to replace UNDP's ineffective resident representative in Ethiopia would solve the problem.

When RP's plan was ready, Dewey immediately got a flight to New York. On the plane, he spotted a news article about children dying in Omdurman (a suburb of Khartoum, Sudan).

When Dewey got to Jim Grant's UN office, he waved the headline upon entering and announced, "Those are your kids, Jim, and they are not in Ethiopia!"

Grant had to admit it. "I know. I've seen those reports. We've got to prepare for something bigger."

Quick to react, Dewey warned that absent decisive action the UN and the secretary general might be the next to appear on front pages unfavorably.

Jim Grant and Gene Dewey agreed to propose a new organization to lead the multilateral famine response in the Horn, modeled after UNBRO. It would be called the Office of Emergency Operations in Africa, or OEOA. Grant and Dewey were concerned that Secretary General Perez de Cuellar would not act unless credible names headed the new organization. Grant agreed, and was set on naming UNDP's Brad Morse, who had proven skills and the standing needed for this job. Also, Grant's intervention in Ethiopia had infuriated Morse and put Grant heavily in Morse's debt. Dewey and Grant also agreed to propose Canadian diplomat Maurice Strong as the deputy. OEOA was literally "done" in one afternoon (and formally inaugurated shortly thereafter).

By the time Gene called me about the New York events, I had alerted Secretary Shultz. He seemed excited about the initiative and left me to figure out the bureaucratic details. We must plan for international organizations' reactions, expected to be negative.

Giving birth to OEOA was painful, and perhaps explains why it represented the clearest example of RP's "tough love." We had to venture out on a wing and a prayer, trusting that our efforts would succeed and be understood. When Dewey returned from New York, we regrouped.

"Good job, Gene. It's been a good day," I said. "This initiative would never have happened if RP had not gone outside the box."

Office of Emergency Operations in Africa, OEOA

The criticisms were far more severe and accusatory than expected. Many on the UN's thirty-eighth floor (equivalent to State's seventh floor), inside State's International Organizations (IO) bureau, and both State and USAID offices were puzzled and bewildered. They questioned why I took such action, sidestepping bureaucratic boundaries without clear authority. Perhaps the most upset was the IO assistant secretary who barged into my office threatening consequences. My explanations did not satisfy him, but, as I told him, this emergency plan was already in place.

That OEOA was officially set up in one afternoon probably spared me further criticism. That OEOA would start to work as quickly as we envisioned was imperative.

Gene Dewey later wrote,

> ... if we had used traditional US channels to get UN action, the OEOA idea would never have reached the secretary general. ... As you knew when to take a courageous risk in Washington, Jim Grant also understood this was the time to act in New York. But, we had to approach UN Secretary General Perez de Cuellar directly and personally, bypassing his naysaying chef de cabinet and director of economic affairs.[15]

After the UN decision for OEOA, we insisted on RP's usual follow-through. Our team met with Brad Morse and Maurice Strong nearly every week. We described to them our version of their job descriptions. OEOA specified human needs, response scenarios, and partnerships needed. It garnered resources and directed and integrated responses.

We asked Maurice Strong later about how OEOA got the job done.

He answered, "At the outset, Brad and I sat down to determine the handful of critical elements of information we needed each day."

Maurice added, "We insisted on feedback from the field as to whether we were asking too much, or too little; and we put the field on notice that it must make every effort to keep us from being surprised."

Later, he reminisced further:

Having visited Ethiopia a number of times, I was appalled at the scale of death, dislocation, and suffering that had affected all the Ethiopian people by a combination of internal conflict, compounded by recurrent drought and devastating famine. The international community had been slow to respond until the television cameras revealed the shocking dimensions of the unfolding tragedy.[16]

After the OEOA decision, UNHCR called an emergency conference in Geneva amid rising questions about its work in eastern Sudan. Gene Dewey and I attended and planned to highlight the need for more reliable refugee protection, as called for by the US Government. We wanted the entire UN system, including UNHCR, to make emergency response systems a higher priority and develop better capabilities.

We also wanted to give the high commissioner room to regain lost ground with the United States, UNHCR's major donor. The high commissioner was Poul Hartling, a Dane, a former foreign minister, and an Anglican priest. His UN-mandated term would end the next year, and he was seeking reelection. Key to his reelection would be American support. Poul and I had become friends over the years.

Thus began another gut-wrenching time. Gene and I arrived in Geneva for the UNHCR executive committee meetings and checked into the InterContinental Hotel. In our rooms were briefing books from the US Mission and Poul Hartling's invitation for dinner that evening, to include the US delegation and UNHCR leadership. *He's going all out.*

That week, my ears stayed tuned for any mention of recent gaps in emergency response. It didn't happen at briefings, in speeches, or even in social gatherings. At midweek, I reviewed the draft statement Gene Dewey and Karl Beck had prepared for my delivery on the last day. There it was, in stark terms, where the draft highlighted our concerns about recent emergency response deficiencies and called out UNHCR leadership.

We knew that such a statement by the head of the American delegation would quickly be factored into the upcoming UNHCR elections. I fretted the next few days and discussed my unease with Gene and Karl. They were convinced of the need for a strong American statement.

"That's fine for you, but you don't have to carry the weight of this decision," I said, and called the full American delegation to meet in the US Mission cafeteria.

"You all know what's in my statement. It will be devastating to the high commissioner. I want honest reactions from each of you about whether this is the right thing to do."

I explained our options and went around the room soliciting opinions. There were no objections to the draft. One of Karl's staffers tried to avoid offering an opinion but joined the consensus after I would not let him off the hook.

"Then, let it be." I went up to Karl's office, made a few changes, and had the statement retyped and printed for final distribution. The executive committee chairman recognized me as a final speaker.

The room was packed, as most delegations were anxious to hear the US statement. It pained me to call out the UNHCR for failing to assist and protect refugees most at risk, especially in the Horn of Africa. Yet, it had to be done. I made a broad call for protection reforms, regardless of political or other considerations. Urgent change was needed to improve the multilateral system's deficient emergency response capabilities, including UNHCR. I attributed deaths to their failings.

Occasionally, I stole a look at the dais. Many heads were shaking, "No." When it was over, only the Japanese and Dutch delegations supported what I had said. Others said I had insulted the organization. Many questioned if I spoke for my government. I felt confident. Lives had hung on the thread of hope that help would come immediately. Secretary Shultz had authorized me to do what I thought best. I knew he was not inclined to avoid a tough line where needed.

Office of Emergency Operations in Africa Performance

OEOA became one of the most successful UN operations of its kind and set the standard, with UNBRO, for multilateral crisis response of that era and an example of the acute urgency those times demanded. As OEOA was ending in October 1986, the UN observed, "While Africa's worst famine of the century is by no means over, the drought has subsided and the number of people in danger of starvation has dropped dramatically: from 150 million people in early 1985 to current estimates of fourteen million persons."[17]

For people in danger and dependent on the world's active compassion, fourteen million of them, the work would continue, having reached a point where regular agencies could continue the famine relief. While the United States agreed that upwards of 150 million in two-dozen sub-Saharan countries were at risk in 1984, the State Department estimated that about eight million people faced starvation in 1985, and the rejuvenated international response saved over six million lives most notably at risk.[18]

In 1986, the State Department's International Operations (IO) assistant secretary Alan Keyes testified before the Senate Foreign Relations Committee about the positive contributions of OEOA; he confirmed and praised the UN's lifesaving contribution and leadership through OEOA, in coping with the famine of the century. I felt that RP was vindicated by the testimony, since previous IO leadership had been severely critical of our actions.[19]

International Conference on Assistance to Refugees in Africa (ICARA)

In the early 1980s, record African refugee flight caused hospitable asylum countries to question whether to allow refugees to cross their borders. They feared the worsening of a dependency mindset that was developing among some long-staying refugee groups. I was telling Congress that RP was shifting emphasis in Africa "towards engaging with them (refugees) in community self-reliance projects and integrating long-staying refugees into local societies." Job creation was critical, and the link between relief and development became obvious.

The UN called the 1981 International Conference for Assistance to Refugees in Africa (ICARA). [20] The pledging conference in Geneva was to bolster the efforts of overwhelmed asylum countries. The United States was usually opposed to pledging conferences; they added pressure on the usual donors: Americans, Europeans, Japanese, and a handful of other steadfast contributors. Yet, since the African asylum nations had pushed hard for the meetings, the United States wanted to keep faith with them and agreed to attend and endorse the ICARA concept, along with other major donors.

UN Ambassador Jeanne Kirkpatrick led the American delegation. As RP deputy assistant secretary for programs and budget then, I arranged a respectable US financial response. We accumulated reports from other federal organizations about programs and budgets planned or devoted to Africa. RP aggregated and packaged these plans with respectable results, although we produced little new funding.

Governments' ICARA pledges totaled several billion dollars and brought renewed attention to African refugees. But the conference did not tackle infrastructure impacts in asylum countries almost collapsing under the weight of large refugee populations in asylum a long time, known as *long-stayers*. For example, Sudan, population twenty million, had around two million refugees crowding its cities, needing homes, schools, and jobs. This affected infrastructure at every level. To keep first-asylum doors open, countries like Sudan needed urgent help.

Since the first ICARA meetings had not addressed these needs, the UN called an ICARA II conference for July 1984. This time, international development agencies would help identify projects to assure infrastructure and economic advancement in countries with high asylum population. Although hesitant at first, the United States thought this conference had greater potential than the first.

Significantly, the UN Development Program, UNDP, chaired the planning mechanism. Economic development arms of relevant multilateral and national governments participated. A steering committee included influential people like the Organization for African Unity secretary general Dr. Peter Onu, the UN under secretary general Abi Farah, and the deputies of the UNHCR and UNDP. The US attorney general William French Smith led the American delegation.

Fourteen African governments highly affected proposed 120 infrastructure projects needing $120 million. Planning projects were presented to donors.

The ICARA II Conference results were respectable, yet follow-through was difficult, as donor interest waned with other emerging crises. ICARA II did provide a model to address the developmental impacts of large, extended-stay asylum populations.

Uganda—The Luwero Triangle 1980–1985

Uganda in the 1980s illustrates the violent challenges RP confronted in refugee *protection* in Africa. From 1980–1985, the oppressive Obote regime fought the insurgents, the National Resistance Army (NRA), headed by Yoweri Museveni. Obote forces wanted to drive the NRA out of the Luwero Triangle, one of the most prosperous regions. Before the violence, over 1.5 million people had called Luwero home.

The International Committee for the Red Cross (ICRC) and Save the Children/UK access to Luwero began to be curtailed in Spring 1984. Gene Dewey assigned RP consultant Bob Gersony to Uganda. The ambassador Allen Clayton Davis and the deputy chief of mission John E. Bennett in Uganda quickly recognized Gersony as a secret weapon and asked him to prepare the Uganda section of the annual refugee consultations report to Congress. Bob Gersony's review acquainted him with the Luwero Triangle, and it became the major focus of his remaining six-month contract.

Gersony proceeded in stealth fashion. With formal avenues blocked, a Ugandan advisor risked his life to sneak Bob into the Luwero Triangle. What they saw was grisly. In one day, they found four concentration camps where Obote's minions systematically starved and beat thousands of people to death. There were rapes of small children, ten to twelve years old, after which their limbs were severed with machetes. Bob stopped one evening along the road near Ugandan soldiers mustering out for an evening operation. He overheard them bragging on orders "to go to *X* village and murder everything that moves, man, woman, child, dog, you name it."

We learned from Gersony that Obote's forces included advisors from North Korea, and the goal was to destroy the opposition through a combination of attacks on their villages followed by roundups into displaced camps where no food or medical attention was allowed.

For five years, the people of the Luwero Triangle had suffered immeasurable horrors inflicted upon them by the Ugandan Army. One observer compared the 1,900 South African deaths in the two previous years with the Luwero Triangle over the same period, where Gersony estimated that over 100,000 people had been slaughtered or starved to death.[21]

When Bob Gersony's reports came through to Washington, Gene Dewey had them distributed widely throughout the government. Gene also assigned RP's Emergency Management Unit to help Gersony get the word to people at the State Department like Chet Crocker, Princeton Lyman, and Dick Bogosian of the Africa bureau; Elliott Abrams in Human Rights; relevant White House officials, and Congress. The Anglican archbishop of Uganda met with Vice President George H. W. Bush, and State's Africa bureau made sure that Uganda's human rights abuses and their crimes were on the agenda.

Caryle Murphy of *The Washington Post* quoted Elliott Abrams in her front page Sunday article in August 1984, "New Uganda crackdown said to kill thousands."[22] When the paper hit the streets, it sparked outrage. A congressional letter with over seventy signatures asked President Reagan to act (the kind of advocacy needed in crisis situations). World attention was suddenly focused on Uganda as never before and condemnation poured on its government. Elliott Abrams later told me of a prearranged international radio broadcast in which he elaborated on Uganda's abuses.

Bob Gersony reported to us that within a week of the public exposure of Obote's abuses the killings stopped, and ICRC and Save the Children were allowed back into the Luwero Triangle. They quickly restarted feeding programs and provided medical care in the camps. Wounded children were evacuated to hospitals in Kampala. The situation began to normalize.

Chet Crocker flew to Kampala shortly thereafter and walked with Obote, holding hands in Ugandan style, in the presidential gardens. Although US disclosure and condemnation of the murderous conduct of Obote's army in Luwero negatively affected US relations with Uganda, Ambassador Davis reported Crocker's full and unflinching support of RP's actions.

When Obote was overthrown in July 1985, NRA leader Yoweri Museveni became president and called an early meeting of the diplomatic community. As reported by the newly-arrived US ambassador Bob Houdek, the new president expressed great appreciation for the US role in exposing the vast human tragedy and acting to end it. And he gave overly cautious embassies a tongue lashing.

Gersony later told us, "I was scared out of my mind during the whole thing. It was way beyond my ability, but RP backed me up in everything."

Bob Gersony Assessment

As "an affirmative actor on the scene," Bob gave his evaluation of our bureau.

> Not just providing money to UNHCR, RP's idea was to play a proactive role being a part of the solution; that was kind of the way things were; that's why there was an emergency unit and I felt kind of at home in RP. I came from more of an action-oriented background. So, we came out unscathed, a few enemies and a few people resenting RP on the margins, but basically knowing that we had done the right thing, that the research and the solutions they led to were right. We learned.[23]

Regarding his results, Gersony could have added, "Many lives were spared."

◆

Sad to say, even now as a historic famine ravishes lives in South Sudan, Nigeria, Yemen, and Somalia, the world community falters; six months after the UN's urgent February 2017–2018 appeal, less than a third of the needed resources had been provided by donor government. Carolyn Miles, Save the Children president, and David Beasley, World Food Program (WFP) director and former South Carolina governor, have lamented donor inattention to this disaster.

34

THE MIDDLE EAST 1979 AND FORWARD

THE MOST EXPLOSIVE HOT POTATO IN WORLD POLITICS FELL into our hands in 1979 when Middle East refugee issues came under the new Refugee Programs bureau's watch. "Middle East problems" then meant Israel and Palestine: one contested land, two names, and two peoples. Their linked pasts, unresolved wars, displacements, and grabs for self-determination were bound to affect RP and bring into question both sides' connections to one of their major benefactors, the American government. I sensed a unique role we might play in this embattled region and made an early strategic decision, that RP should not tilt. I would keep programs in the region as non-partisan as possible. Jews and Palestinians would receive equal caring and firmness. I did not realize how difficult that would become, until the fireworks started.

To reinforce an evenhanded policy, I assigned Israel and Palestinian portfolios to Judy Chavchavadze, also RP's most experienced officer. The value of that decision would become startlingly clear.

For Israel, our refugee program would remain a major partner to help return the Jewish Diaspora to Israel, under its Law of Return, and would offer other assistance elaborated elsewhere in this book. All efforts were part of a historic and enduring Israeli-American relationship.

For the Palestinians, we would continue to aid over two million refugees annually through financial and programmatic support for the UN Relief and Works Agency for Palestinian Refugees (UNRWA). The agency gave health and education support to Palestinian refugees and helped make it possible to keep their unique identity. We would become one of the organization's most dependable US allies.

Nothing done in the region or between these two perennial combatants had ever been easy. Unforeseeable was the heat that conflicting and powerful interests would put on the refugee programs in the next years, not only in the Middle East, but also from within the State Department, wider Washington, and New York.

Palestinians are proud of their long history, their origins traced to a period well before the birth of Christ. Jericho, for example, goes as far back as 10,000 years before Christ, staking its claim as the oldest continuously-inhabited city in the world. It sits at the crossroads of three continents and contains sites of holy reverence for more than half the world's population.

Over the centuries, Palestine has been ruled by the Canaanites, Egyptians, Philistines, Israelites, Persians, and a few others. The British Empire was the last to rule over Palestine.[1] Prior to 1948, many Palestinians and Jews enjoyed times of harmony there. But in 1948 and later, relations became strained and, at times, toxic. The Palestinians came to refer to the events of 1948 as "The Nakba," when the Arabs and Israelis were at war. The Arabs lost, the State of Israel was born, and hundreds of thousands of Palestinians fled or were expelled from their homes, becoming people of a diaspora (living even today as refugees throughout the Middle East and many other regions). Thereafter, the Palestine Liberation Organization (PLO), gained strength as a shadow government for the Palestinians in South Lebanon, under a charismatic political and military leader, Yasser Arafat. Initially, the public had little awareness of, and governments had little interest in, the PLO. But Israel, ever wary, kept a watchful eye.

United Nations Relief and Works Agency, UNRWA

During the first briefing session on the Middle East, Judy Chavchavadze provided comprehensive written and oral reviews of the American refugee involvement in the Middle East. She informed us that an organization mandated by the United Nations, the UN Relief and Works Agency (UNRWA), was created in 1949 exclusively to assist Palestinian refugees. The number of Palestinian refugees increased with every Arab-Israeli conflict. The Six-Day War of June 5–10, 1967, resulted in Israel's occupation of the West Bank and Gaza, The October 1973 Yom Kippur War created more refugees. By 1980, Palestinian refugees numbered approximately 1.8 million.[2] (*See* Table 8.)

UNRWA served a vital US political objective in the Middle East as a demonstrable example of American even-handedness in Palestinian-Israeli disputes. Sustained political and financial support was a principal element.

The plight of Palestinian refugees would be relieved, leaders thought, through a peaceful integration into nearby Arab countries or in their former homeland. The UN General Assembly passed repatriation or compensation resolutions as part of a settlement of "the Palestinian question." Large scale relief and medical programs under UN auspices aided health and prevented epidemics.

The "works" part of UNRWA's original mandate never made much headway. Projects were costly, and Palestinians distrusted them. Therefore, international assistance through UNRWA shifted emphasis to medical care, schooling, and vocational training for a rural population deprived of its land and needing training for available jobs in adjacent communities or countries. UNRWA was incomparably more professional, more productive, and less political than its PLO-managed counterparts in Gaza and West Bank. It was by far the best bet for creating an atmosphere of moderation needed for a future peace.

In the Middle East, the State Department's Refugee Programs bureau occupied a unique position; it was the only official entity with ongoing humanitarian and diplomatic contact *and* operational programs with both sides. Many others dealt either with Israel or Palestine, and only RP maintained ongoing operations and dialogue with both. This was important because each side saw the American government as the only power able to harness and control the other.

Israel Invades Lebanon, 1982

Following its expulsion from Jordan after bloody battles in the late 1970s, the Palestine Liberation Organization (PLO) established its headquarters in Beirut and based its combatants in wider parts of Lebanon. On June 3, 1982, the PLO shot and critically wounded the Israeli ambassador to Britain, Shlomo Argov. In retaliation, the Israelis bombed targets in Lebanon The PLO responded with artillery attacks on northern Israel. On June 5, the UN security council, meeting at Lebanon's request, issued a unanimous call for a cease-fire. But on June 6, Israeli tanks and infantry crossed into Lebanon, supported by air strikes and sea landings.[3]

I had just arrived at work when Gene Dewey rushed into my office, shouting: "Jim, have you heard? Israeli Defense Forces have invaded South Lebanon, and it's all-out war!"

A former military officer, Dewey had been following Israel-Lebanon dynamics closely. We both had seen months of television coverage of Lebanon shelling Jewish settlements in the border area, the rhetoric on both sides continually ratcheting up. Israel's warnings had not stopped the bombardments.

Ariel Sharon, Israel's Army chief, led the retaliatory invasion. His military objectives were clear—eliminate Lebanon's ability to launch further rocket attacks on Jewish settlements, disrupt PLO military capabilities in Lebanon, and clean out hot spots. Finally, Sharon intended to teach the Lebanese an unforgettable lesson, to go as far as to occupy and destroy their crown jewel and capital city, Beirut.

Sharon's army headed north, making a clean sweep on the ground and from the air. We knew that more refugees would be a result. Lebanon was a major UNRWA activity area, and this invasion would likely have operational implications for relief programs in the region.

"We need information and intelligence, and we need it now," I told Dewey. He'd been talking to Peter McPherson, administrator of USAID and the president's personal envoy for Lebanon, about a trip to Lebanon. Dewey and McPherson flew out the next day. Soon after they arrived, Dewey called.

"Jim, you're not going to believe this, but Peter and I are shadowing the Israeli Defense Forces in their moves through Lebanon. I've got first-hand information. Sharon is going to break them this time. He's marching as fast as he can to Beirut. He's taking everything in his path. He's out for blood."

"That's good intelligence, but you and Peter have gone beyond the call of duty. I worry about your safety. Get back when you can and let's plot strategy."

Dewey and McPherson returned to Washington and began monthly commutes to Lebanon during the crisis, forging a sound working relationship. USAID concentrated on the Lebanon economy and the central bank, and RP handled the humanitarian and refugee problems. However, once on the ground, MacPherson and Dewey found little action on the economy or the central bank; the center of gravity for Lebanon was RP, through Dewey, and the growing refugee issue.

Siblin Vocational Training Center

UNRWA Commissioner General Olof Rydbeck called from Vienna to report that the Israeli Defense Forces had entered UNRWA's Siblin Vocational Training Center in Lebanon, just twenty miles south of Beirut.[4]

"I'm distraught to report this," Rydbeck said, "but during the invasion IDF found substantial PLO armaments—knives, guns, all kinds of explosives. Those have been collected and are under guard."

Rydbeck explained that the PLO was using the Siblin school as a PLO military training center. "This is a major problem for UNRWA, and I knew you would want to know."

"Not only for UNRWA," I said. "If it proves true, it would be a substantial problem for us. US law forbids providing funds to any facility used for training combatants in the Middle East, especially the PLO. Please give me a full report as soon as you can."

Rydbeck sent photographs and documentation about substantial arms caches at Siblin. I told him to make sure the arms were kept secure and not released under any circumstances. Then I informed Secretary Shultz and our congressional oversight committees.

Unfortunately, these revelations coincided with my appearances before the committees handling RP's annual appropriation requests. My first stop was the office of Sen. Bob Kasten (R-WI), chair of the Senate Appropriations Committee and a staunch supporter of Israel. With us was Jim Bond, his chief of staff, whom I considered a friend *and* antagonist. Knowing both gentlemen well, I was expecting the third degree. The senator was not an UNRWA supporter. At a later hearing before his committee, Sen. Kasten's first question was, "What was the outcome of this incursion into the training center?"

He spoke rhetorically, for he knew my answer. I had photos that showed an arms cache had been seized and was under lock and key. I told him everything we had learned. "Well," he said, "you know this is a violation of US law. I'll now need a written letter from the secretary, indicating what has been uncovered and the steps being taken to address this violation."

I promised to comply and assured him we took this matter seriously and would keep the committees in both houses up to date.

The situation became worse when I learned that PLO soldiers had refused UNRWA staff entry to Siblin. From then on, a new American policy was instituted, cutting US funding immediately from any UNRWA school or facility if its staff members could not monitor operations and prevent misuse. Olaf Rydbeck agreed to this policy. RP staff also would make periodic inspections.

RP's Emergency Management Unit developed spreadsheets showing evolving situations in UNRWA camps, almost driving Rydbeck to distraction. But they kept the agency on mission with significant help for corrective actions. The Siblin problem was contained for the moment, but I feared more from this episode. The Siblin Center closed for security reasons from 1982 to 1987.

The Siege of Beirut and Bitter Negotiations

When the Israeli Defense Forces reached Beirut in July 1982, Alexander Haig was ending his tenure as the secretary of state and George Shultz was awaiting Senate confirmation. As the war in Lebanon broke out, the president's special envoy to the Middle East Phil Habib was on his way to Lebanon. Ariel Sharon and the IDF reached Beirut, decimated the Lebanese resistance, surrounded the city, and began a struggle that threatened its destruction. Ambassador Habib talked with Ariel Sharon at length and learned that he wanted all PLO forces out of Beirut immediately. It was urgent. Otherwise, the ambassador and others feared that Sharon would destroy Beirut.

Habib contacted Secretary Shultz to communicate his conviction that Sharon would destroy Beirut. Sharon had been heard to say that he once had Yasser Arafat in the cross hairs and letting him off had been his biggest mistake ever.

Intense diplomatic negotiations aimed at removing the PLO from Lebanon involved the president and top foreign policy officials at State, as well as Defense, CIA, the Israeli prime minister, foreign minister, and defense minister, as well as top PLO leadership.[5]

During negotiations, the opposing sides angled for advantage by attempting to disrupt any forward progress. Sharon repeatedly launched military strikes while cease-fires were being discussed or in effect. The PLO made unreasonable demands, as did the Lebanese Government. Each threat and setback was overcome by American diplomacy. By August 20, 1982, the negotiated evacuation of the PLO from Beirut, Lebanon, was ready to proceed. The UN had authorized a multinational force composed of French, Italian, and American forces, in place to secure Beirut during PLO evacuation. What remained was to get PLO forces out safely, which was Secretary Shultz's job.

Evacuation Urgent

Secretary Shultz turned to under secretary for political affairs Larry Eagleburger to organize the PLO evacuation. In my view, Eagleburger should have turned to the Department of Defense, because of its relations with the multinational force being organized for Lebanon. But he knew that involving DoD would take too long and would be too expensive. Instead, he looked within the State Department for an office with capability and experience to evacuate people quickly and likely to offer less resistance. He contacted his old State/EUR friend and colleague, the recently-appointed RP director, Dick Vine.

Eagleburger told Vine the secretary must move PLO fighters out of Beirut by the weekend. "Can you do it?"

"Certainly, we will get it done," Vine said.

Then he called me. He was new on the job and understandably did not want to disappoint Eagleburger or the secretary. Without seeking advice from RP staff, he'd said yes. I was flabbergasted.

"How can *we* do it? We operate under specific legislative authorities!" I began to fill him in about the Migration and Refugee Assistance Act of 1962 and the Refugee Act of 1980.

"We have authority to help refugees, people fleeing persecution. We are *not* authorized to move armed combatants! It's not within our mandate! They should call DoD!"

I could hardly restrain myself. Sen. Kasten and the Senate Appropriations Committee were at the front of my mind. This would never sit well.

"If we use our authorities inappropriately," I warned Vine, "Congress will be so upset that this program could be in jeopardy for years!"

Vine insisted the opposite, saying I didn't understand. He'd already agreed with Larry and, thereby, with the secretary, that we'd do it. Vine said, "Now we have to find a way!"

I decided to talk with RP lawyer Andre Surena, very much a stickler for the rules and the letter of the law. I also knew him to be creative and flexible. If we needed to do something and there was any legal way, Surena would find it.

Andre got back to me the next day.

"There is one far-out possibility. It involves a little-known provision of the Migration and Refugee Assistance Act," he said. "It relates to authorities pertaining to the International Committee of the Red Cross. They are so respected and trusted that Congress gave RP authority to fund any activity or program the ICRC proposes. If you could get ICRC to say they are undertaking this as a humanitarian action and request US funding for it, you could then allocate funds from the president's refugee emergency fund for this purpose. ICRC could then undertake the work on RP's behalf. I realize it's far-fetched, but it's the only legal possibility I see."

ICRC. I let it sink in for a minute.

"That really is a stretch," I said. "It's such a weak reed. I can't see Jim Bond or any of our congressional committees falling for it. I think it could get us in a lot of trouble. But, it is what it is. I'll pass the information to Dick Vine."

I told Vine our lawyer's caution, and I thought this dangerous course could cost RP dearly. He ignored the advice and reported at once to

Eagleburger that a way had been found. He advised Secretary Shultz, and word was passed to Ambassador Habib in Beirut.

Vine also ignored my suggestion to inform RP's congressional committees prior to the action. He was fearful they might object and delay the evacuation.

Gene Dewey assigned the PLO evacuation action to Alan Van Egmond, his assistant. They contacted ICRC in Geneva and called in some favors.

After a lot of hand-wringing, ICRC came around.

At every step, the threat, the need, and the urgency had been too great to ignore. "We," meaning RP, would execute the plan as hazy as it was. The pieces began to fall into place, starting at the highest levels.

Ambassador Geoffrey Swaebe at the mission in Geneva alerted the Intergovernmental Committee for Migration (ICM) director Jim Carlin. He set the wheels in motion, starting with formation of a task force and alerting missions in Athens and Nicosia.

Dewey and Van Egmond asked ICM to find ships for evacuation. ICM thought it risky and problematic, but when informed of the momentous importance, they agreed to search for a ship; it would be expensive, especially on short notice and to move combatants.[6] We estimated 8,500 combatants to be evacuated by sea, plus arms and other equipment.

An additional 2,500 Palestinian Army forces and 3,600 Syrians from the Arab Deterrent Force would be evacuated overland or by air.[7]

ICM chartered ships and arranged for them to lie off Beirut port by first light Saturday. At the arranged time in Lebanon, UNRWA staff and multinational forces escorted the PLO combatants to the ships on Saturday. Arrangements were made for PLO forces to be received in Latakia, Larnaca, Tartus, Port Said, and Iraq. Yasser Arafat later went to Tunis to set up PLO headquarters.

The total price tag for this expensive weekend campaign was $7 million. The bill was increased substantially because of the need to evacuate PLO armaments. We withdrew funds from the president's refugee emergency fund and informed Phil Habib of the arrangements, including estimated arrival and departure times.

After the PLO evacuation, Ambassador Habib reported that Israel's Ariel Sharon was satisfied and would spare Beirut.

Jim Bond, majority staff director of the Senate Appropriations subcommittee, was far from happy. He had read in the Sunday papers about the combatant evacuation and its implementation by RP. On Monday morning, Bond summoned Director Vine to his office to explain.

I told Vine, "This is your baby."

"Don't worry. Our lawyer said it's legal. I don't fear these guys." Vine cavalierly went to the Hill, thinking to smooth things over with an explanation. I heard a recount later about the brief and rough meeting after Vine arrived at Bond's office.

Bond was prepared. "Okay, Mr. Vine, what did you do and under what legal authority did you do it?"

Vine described the evacuation urgency and added, "Our lawyer said it was legal."

"No, that's not my question," Bond retorted. "I want to know *which* specific legal authority you used."

Vine and Bond sparred for a few minutes. Vine became increasingly antagonistic, and Bond responded in kind.

Bond realized Vine did not know which specific authority RP had used. He only knew State's lawyer said it was legal. Bond exploded, and Vine got mad. They parted in anger.

Within minutes Bond was yelling into the phone at me. "I want you up here immediately to explain what's going on down there!"

I rounded up legal counsel Surena. We had been expecting this call.

When we got there, Bond was furious. He was legitimately angry with the State Department, RP, Vine, and increasingly with me. Andre Surena and I carefully explained the authority and the rationale we used. We had gotten ICRC, the International Committee of the Red Cross, acquiescence, with strong reservations, to agree this was their program. We allocated funding to ICRC, which transferred these funds to ICM to pay the shipping agent. It was done. It was urgent. It was legal, and about that there could be no disagreement.

Bond reacted curtly, "This is not right. Senator Kasten and the other members of our committee will not agree with this misuse of RP authorities. We will highlight this issue at the upcoming appropriations hearings with RP."

"Okay," I said, "I'll pass that word to my superiors."

The hearing was well publicized. Sen. Kasten chaired and every committee member attended. I represented the administration, describing the evacuation in full detail. I emphasized that using RP's legal authorities for the evacuation had resulted in saving the city of Beirut and avoiding a major foreign policy disaster. I highlighted the need and the urgency of the operation and explained that the secretary thought this was a justifiable use of RP authorities and funding.

When told the bill was $7 million and it came from RP's emergency fund, Sen. Kasten was outraged. He wanted to know who would reimburse these funds.

Learning that we had no plan for reimbursement, the Committee ordered the State Department to arrange for interested Arab governments to pay. While the chairman did not say so expressly, I knew there was an implied threat if this did not happen soon.

Gene Dewey was designated as RP's contact point, and he provided regular status briefings for the Committee staff over the next year. State Department leaders sensed a big mistake had been made: The refugee apparatus had been put in jeopardy.

It took almost a year, but Ambassador Richard Murphy finally convinced Saudi Arabia to reimburse the $7 million. With the money in hand, I went back to Sen. Kasten's committee, and said, "Now look at what we did. We avoided a major foreign policy disaster in the volatile Middle East, it did not cost the US Government a single penny, and we saved the city of Beirut. That's a fairly good bargain."

The Committee did not appreciate my attempt at levity, but we mutually decided this incident probably could pass into history.

Throughout the administration's discussions about the Beirut evacuation, Secretary Shultz had fended off strong suggestions by other powerful government officials to link these Beirut discussions with broader Middle East peace initiatives. The secretary convinced President Reagan they were separate issues.

Sabra and Shatila Refugee Camps, Lebanon

American, French, and Italian troops making up the multinational force that guaranteed security during the Palestine Liberation Organization evacuation withdrew from Lebanon in early September 1982. In his May 1990 oral history for the Foreign Affairs Oral History Project, Ambassador Robert S. "Bob" Dillon recalled:

> ... the whole deal with the Palestinian leadership included solemn promises, bolstered by pledges from both the Maronite militia and the Israelis, that there would be no reprisals and no violence visited on the Palestinian civilians who remained behind after the withdrawal of the PLO forces.[8]

But weeks later, reports appeared that just after the withdrawal of the multinational forces, Lebanese Phalangists had attacked the Palestinian refugee camps of Sabra and Shatila in West Beirut, September 16–17, 1982. As these attacks took place, Israeli Defense Force units occupied key positions surrounding the camps. The massacre was rationalized as retaliation for the assassination, just days before, of newly-elected Lebanese President Bashir Gamayel, leader of the Kataeb Party. It had been assumed, wrongly, that the assassination had been carried out by Palestinian militants.[9]

In the aftermath of the killings came eyewitness reports of massacres, including women and children. They said that Israeli bulldozers had come in to push rubble over the bodies. The Lebanese Army chief prosecutor's investigation concluded that at least 460 people, and perhaps double that number, had been killed. Israeli intelligence estimated at least 700 dead, while the Palestinian Red Crescent Society claimed two thousand.

From the outset, it was clear that Israeli Defense Minister Sharon and his forces were complicit in these attacks. World outrage was instant and overwhelming: Someone must be held accountable. Reagan was ready to send the marines back into Lebanon. The McBride Commission, established by the Israeli Government and chaired by Sean McBride (then assistant to the UN secretary general and later president of the UN General Assembly), concluded that Israel, as the camp's occupying power, bore responsibility for the attack, considered genocide.

US intelligence at first did not tag the IDF directly for the massacre and objected to the genocide label. It indicated, however, that the IDF appeared to provide cover and perimeter security for the Phalangists. Under international humanitarian law, as the "controlling power" in West Beirut, the Israelis were responsible. They did not have to pull the trigger; they didn't even have to be in Shatila. They controlled it, and whether they facilitated the attack did not matter. They were accountable. (This same argument was used years later by US officials when confronting Radovan Karadzic over his complicity in the Srebrenica and Zepa safe area massacres in Bosnia. When he said, "But I wasn't there," the US response was, "It doesn't matter. You were in control. You are responsible.")

Less than a week after the Sabra and Shatila camp massacres, Israeli Prime Minister Begin gave in to pressure and appointed a judicial commission of inquiry. The chairman of the commission was the chief justice Yitzhak Kahan. In February 1983, the Kahan Commission issued its report, recommending disciplinary actions and the dismissal of top Israeli officials, including the defense minister Ariel Sharon. In response, the Israeli cabinet voted sixteen-to-one to accept the report of the Kahan Commission. Accountability was established and accepted.[10]

Many compelling human tragedies were embodied in the Sabra and Shatila massacres, but one continues to haunt me. In fall 1982, early in Gene Dewey and Peter McPherson's commutes to Beirut, they flew commercially into Nicosia, Cyprus, and were then ferried by US Marine Corps helicopter directly into the largely nonfunctioning Beirut airport.

A week before the massacres, Dewey visited the Shatila refugee camp, just before having to rush to the Beirut helipad for liftoff to Cyprus. An old Palestinian man approached him and an embassy escort in a narrow alley in one camp.

The man carried a tray of steaming coffee and insisted Dewey stop for a cup. Dewey repeatedly apologized that he couldn't accept, lest he miss his flight. He promised the man he would look him up on the next trip. The old fellow was not to be dissuaded, insisting he at least drink a cup as they walked along. Dewey finally had to just dash away to make the schedule.

Just after the massacre, Dewey was on a weekly conference call with the American embassy when he heard words that made his heart sink.

"You remember the old man with the coffee in Shatila?" asked the contact. "Well, he didn't make it. He was dashing down one of the alleys for safety when gunmen cut him down."

There would be no "next time" for the old man.

"This story may be apropos of nothing, except for me," a devastated Dewey shared with me. "But for me it placed a haunting question mark on all my protestations that I was about the ordinary people, that I was always on the side of, and had time for, the victims, no matter what procedural or bureaucratic situations might stand in the way, and that I would never be accused of being a 'drive-by' humanitarian. I will forever be haunted by that kind, elderly man."

For firsthand reporting on camp conditions during these developments, Gene Dewey dispatched EMU chief Tex Harris to Lebanon while we considered strategy options. Harris frequently visited the Sabra and Shatila camps and places elsewhere in the region. His was a face of American concern. He assured adequate UNRWA support to keep necessary protective measures in place.

Around that time, the UNHCR executive committee was debating a resolution that would prohibit "armed attacks against refugee camps," a burning issue not just in the Middle East but also in Central America and many parts of Africa. The United States had influenced governments that opposed this resolution—based on fears that unarmed or unprotected refugee camps could become magnets for armed elements. US reasoning about the potential harm was powerful: a seemingly good resolution could cause harm because refugee camps could become *de facto* sanctuaries for lawless elements.

As head of the US delegation when this issue was under reconsideration, I had to lay out the weighty concern. Such a resolution would put civilians in the camps into more danger, not less. It would expose them rather than protect them and a more appropriate course of action would be for all governments to respect, voluntarily, the neutral status of refugee camps and prohibit military personnel from entering them.

The attacks at Sabra and Shatila tragically substantiated those worries. Unfortunately, consensus could not be reached by the executive committee on a resolution prohibiting armed attacks on refugee camps.

United States Threats to UN Relief and Works Agency for Palestinian Refugees

Of all RP team battles waged to preserve UNRWA as an evenhanded force in the lingering Palestinian-Israeli dispute, probably the most disconcerting were the challenges we faced within the US administration to keep UNRWA viable, or even alive. Some on the political right wanted it dismantled. Quick to pounce when opportunities arose, they seemed to believe that antagonizing UNRWA gave added weight to their pro-Israel views. They maintained, incorrectly we thought, that UNRWA interfered with the US-Israeli relationship. We asserted that UNRWA undergirded America's balanced approach in the Middle East and was our single thin red line of evenhandedness in the standoff.

The right-wing revolt came to a head in 1984, when RP was dealing with that year's funding for UNRWA. There had been times in the past where other governments' funding for that agency was slim, and the US contributed up to 50 percent of the budget. The United States proposed to contribute slightly over one-third that year, which UNRWA insisted was critical to their survival. The issue was so sensitive that he queried RP just before the New York pledging conference to assure we were still firm. Dewey reassured him. We were unaware that the US Mission to the UN in New York had stacked the American delegation to the pledging conference with anti-UNRWA officials.

Ambassador Jeanne Kirkpatrick would head the delegation. She added Sen. Bob Kasten, the refugee coordinator Eugene Douglas, and her deputy in New York. Without coordinating with RP, the delegation decided it was time to begin defunding UNRWA. They planned substantial reduction of the pledge for that year and further reductions ahead. Such a unilateral decision at that time would be devastating to UNRWA.

Gene Dewey got wind of this revolt through a staff member at the US Mission in New York and immediately called the commissioner general of UNRWA Olof Rydbeck, who warned him: "A reduced American pledge will undercut everything I'm trying to do and make it impossible to get money from other donors. It would be better to pledge nothing at all right now, to say the American pledge is still being considered."

Dewey assured Rydbeck that we would do everything possible to maintain a respectable pledge.

I had no choice but to take up this matter with Secretary Shultz. I told him a revolt was taking place, and its goal was to destabilize UNRWA.

"We need to send guidance immediately to New York," I said, "and tell them to pull back. We could make no pledge now and say we are still considering. However, they'll only listen to you."

Secretary Shultz, appalled at this turn of events, quickly agreed. A cable was prepared from me, with Shultz's approval, to Douglas and Kirkpatrick, saying the United States was to make no pledge, and we were still considering.

Assuming there would be resistance, Gene Dewey sent his assistant, Alan Van Egmond, to New York with a copy of the cable and instructions to position himself at the door to the UN conference room. He was to block the door and not let the American delegation in until they read the message.

That's exactly how it happened.

"This is from Secretary Shultz, it's his direction!" Van Egmond shouted when the delegation arrived.

They hesitated. They would not go up against George Shultz.

Sen. Kasten perceived it was a lost cause and said, "I'm not even going to stay around."

The revolt was temporarily defeated, and we were relieved to confirm America's full pledge the next day.

"I'd always expected to fight dragons trying to gobble up UNRWA," Rydbeck said, as he reflected on the events. "I just never thought they would be from the United States."

"I hope you accept from this experience that you have many American friends," I said, "who will stand by you and the Palestinians."

He grudgingly agreed. But it was clear that my reassurances were getting harder for him to accept.

Palestinian Quality of Life

In Jerusalem in November 1983, Israeli Prime Minister Begin's minister without portfolio, Mordechai Ben Porat, announced a "quality of life" plan for *voluntary relocation* of 30,000 Palestinian refugee families from twenty-eight UNRWA camps in the West Bank and Gaza. This plan would settle the families in decent new homes over the next six years. At a cost of $1.5 billion, it would be financed by foreign sources, including the United States. The new homes would be built near their old homes or in nearby towns, and the existing camps would be demolished as families left.[11] The West hoped to demonstrate its commitment to a positive durable solution.

President Reagan and Secretary Shultz were already concerned about the Palestinians' quality of life and agreed to give the plan serious consideration. It would counter accusations that the international community, the Israelis, or both were in collusion to keep the Palestinians in poverty.[12]

As part of the US review, Gene Dewey traveled to the region to conduct a "market survey" with the refugees. In one of his discussions, he asked a group of bearded Palestinian elders:

"What do you think of the quality of life idea?"

There was dead silence. Finally, an elder gently pulled a little boy, probably five years old, from the crowd behind them.

"Let me tell you about quality of life," the elder began. "This little boy knows where his home is in Palestine. He knows the town name, the street name, and the number of his house. But the Israelis won't let him return to his home. Don't tell us any more about quality of life until he is permitted to go home."

This story dramatized the great divide between Israel and the Palestinians. True, many or most Palestinians were not likely to return to their former homes, even if offered the chance. It was also beside the point that some Palestinian leaders wanted their people to wallow in camp squalor, so their plight would continue to be dramatized to the world. The powerful image of a little boy who couldn't go home was a narrative with the right political ring for the Palestinian extremists, and it was unlikely to change soon.

But on the same day that the elders trashed the Ben Porat Plan, Dewey visited one dilapidated shack in the mud and misery of a refugee camp. A Palestinian mother with six children was inside. She had heard about the plan and it seemed to spark her hopes for a better life.

"I would love to get my children out of here and into a decent apartment," she said excitedly. "That would be my dream come true."

Sadly, she was one of thousands of powerless Palestinians who would not see such dreams fulfilled.

These contradictions were magnified when the US refugee coordinator inserted himself into the issue. In a 1983 trip to the Middle East, he made confusing and contradictory statements to both Jordan's Crown Prince Hassan and to Israel's prime minister regarding the American support for the Ben Porat Plan. The American ambassador in Amman requested and received clarification from Washington.

"If these dissimilar positions become known to either the Israelis or the Jordanians, and there is a strong likelihood they will," he said, "then we are in trouble."[13]

To keep the world focused on their perilous living conditions in the Middle East, the Palestinians decided they could not accept the Ben Porat Plan. Consequently, in 1983 the Arab States persuaded the UN General Assembly to denounce it as a "violation of the (refugees') inalienable right of return, a basic right guaranteed by international agreements."[14]

Conclusions

These examples illustrate the virtually insoluble and politically-entrenched problems and how the State Department team dealt with crises that engulfed the Middle East. In other regions, defining root causes, trouble-shooting obstacles, assessing options, and finding *durable solutions* were fundamental to RP's work. But in the Middle East we were forced into a containment policy, trying to keep alive a legacy of American evenhandedness toward what is arguably the world's most intractable problem.

We were pleased with the Reagan administration's support for bringing Palestinian civil and human rights into the light and making them accepted US policy, highlighted by ambitions to support the goal of an educated, healthy, and economically self-sufficient Palestinian population in the Middle East.

As crises mounted, UNRWA had become an increasingly necessary and vital stabilizing presence in the volatile Middle East. The siege of Beirut threatened the destruction of Beirut; it was avoided only by American diplomacy. That episode, plus the massacres at the Sabra and Shatila refugee camps, ignited passions and became tragic milestones that raised global consciousness of the appalling circumstances of the Palestinians.

RP's staff fought the good fight to balance American support for Israelis and Palestinians with steadfastness and resolve. We trusted that an assessment of our help to both sides during that era would conclude, "They did not tilt."

◇

Years later, I was involved in yet another Israeli-Palestinian peace process in a different capacity. As an international official, I shuttled between Yassar Arafat in Tunis and Yitzak Rabin in Geneva and both in New York to review return possibilities for Palestinian refugees, as discussed in President Clinton's 1993 Oslo Peace Conference with his Israeli and Palestinian counterparts. We were making progress after our last discussions in New York (for UN's fiftieth anniversary celebrations in 1995), but things fell apart abruptly with the assassination of Prime Minister Rabin. I have often speculated about "what might have been."

35

AFGHANISTAN AND SOUTH ASIA

ON APRIL 14, 1979, THE AMERICAN AMBASSADOR TO Afghanistan Adolph "Spike" Dubs was carjacked by four men and taken by force to the Kabul Hotel. He was immediately assassinated. Disputed reports said some or all abductors wore Afghan police uniforms and demanded release of one or more religious or political prisoners. The true circumstance of the kidnapping and assassination were never clarified, but Soviet and Afghan security agents were implicated. National Security Advisor Zbigniew Brzezinski denounced Ambassador Dubs' death as "a tragic event which involved either Soviet ineptitude or collusion." An outraged Carter administration immediately started pulling back from Afghanistan and expressed sympathy with the Afghan regime opponents. By the time the Soviets invaded in late December 1979, the American Embassy was down to a skeleton crew.[1] I learned these details a few years later from Bruce Flatin, who served as political counselor in the American Embassy in Kabul when these events transpired.

Bloody Invasion

In December 1979, five months into RP's life, our attention was mainly devoted to Southeast Asia, with an occasional eye on disturbing signs in other regions. I was in my office the day after Christmas hoping for quiet catch-up time. I spotted unusually heavy cable traffic from Kabul and was shocked to read that the Soviet Union had invaded Afghanistan, wanting it securely back in the communist fold. The weak Afghan Government and military were no match for the USSR. Yet, they resisted through local insurgents, an Islamist group known as the Mujahideen, a name unknown to me before then. Heavy fighting was underway with initial reports of significant casualties on both sides.

Seeds of the Trouble

The Democratic Republic of Afghanistan had been established the previous year, April 1978, after a Marxist coup d'état overthrew and killed President Mohammad Daoud, named Noor Mohammad Taraki president and prime minister and installed Babrak Karmal as deputy prime minister.

The State Department's historian and other public affairs reporting provided comprehensive accounts of the ensuing events.[2]

President Carter, hoping to steer Taraki away from Moscow, recognized the new government against the advice of National Security Advisor Zbigniew Brzezinski and appointed "Spike" Dubs as the ambassador.

When plans had leaked to Moscow that the deputy prime minister Karmal was leading a plot to overthrow Taraki, they replaced him with Hafizullah Amin. Moscow was concerned that continuing internal strife was damaging the Kabul government's plan to bring the communist revolution to the Islamic tribal areas beyond the capital. Taraki and Amin traveled to Moscow to sign an agreement that invited direct Soviet military assistance if an Islamic insurgency threatened the regime. Civil war, however, caused Moscow to become critical of Taraki and Amin, and they dispatched Soviet combat troops to the Bagram Air Base outside Kabul. These developments prompted the Carter administration to supply non-lethal aid to the Afghan Mujahideen insurgents.

The ambassador had been assassinated in April, and by August 1979, a high-ranking Soviet military delegation went to Kabul to assess their situation. Fearing this mission's purpose was to strengthen Noor Mohammad Taraki, forces loyal to Hafizullah Amin executed Taraki.

Faced with mutinies and uncertain leadership, the Afghan army was by winter 1979 unable to provide basic security for the government against advancing Islamic forces pushing toward Kabul. As a precaution, Moscow amassed combat units along its border.

On Christmas Eve 1979, the Soviet invasion of Afghanistan began.

Soviet troops killed Amin and installed Babrak Karmal as the head of a puppet government. It appeared that Kremlin leaders hoped for a quick military takeover to reinforce the Brezhnev Doctrine, which held that countries within the Soviet communist orbit could never withdraw.

Widening War

An outraged President Carter wrote to Brezhnev denouncing Soviet aggression. In his January 1980 State of the Union speech, he vowed to protect Middle East oil supplies from Soviet encroachment. He imposed economic and trade sanctions, called for a boycott of the 1980 Moscow Olympics, and increased aid to the Afghan insurgents. Nearly 100,000 Soviet troops took control of major cities and highways. Rebellion was swift and broad, and the Soviets dealt brutally with the Afghan rebels. They leveled entire cities to deny haven to the rebels. Foreign fighters poured in from Pakistan, China, other Middle Eastern countries, and the United States and Europe to support the rebels. The Mujahideen declared Jihad, "holy war." A nationwide insurgency against the Soviet invasion and the Democratic Republic of Afghanistan was underway.[3]

The Mujahideen was composed mostly of two insurgent alliances called the Peshawar Seven and the Tehran Eight (Shia). The Peshawar Seven received military training in Pakistan and China and weapons and billions of dollars from the United States, the United Kingdom, and Saudi Arabia. The Shia groups of the Tehran Eight received support from the Islamic Republic of Iran.[4]

The morale of the Afghanistan Mujahideen forces was high, and they put up stiff resistance. They had old rifles but knew the mountain terrain and the weather around Kabul. As the war progressed, the Mujahideen fighters received access to American surface-to-air missiles (though not through direct sales).[5]

The Soviets used napalm, poison gas, and helicopter gunships against the Mujahideen, yet they experienced mounting losses of troops, supply convoys, helicopters, and fixed-wing aircraft. The Mujahideen proved to have more capable and dedicated fighters than expected. The Soviets bogged down, as their army could not maneuver in the difficult Afghan terrain. It became clear this would be a long, drawn-out war, and the Soviets would pay a heavy price.

Afghan Refugee Flight

Upon news of the Soviet invasion of Afghanistan, the United States, through RP, sprang into action to help the Afghan refugees caught in the ensuing maelstrom. We set up an Afghan Task Force to oversee initial American involvement in this new refugee tragedy. (That brought the number of emergency task forces in the Refugee Programs to four, after the Horn of Africa, Cuba and Haiti, and Kampuchea (Cambodia). Simultaneously, we were putting the newly-established bureau on its feet.

In the first post-invasion years, the Afghan refugees surged mainly to Pakistan and Iran. The estimated number of Afghans in exile quickly exceeded 3.5 million, about 20 percent of the 1979 Afghan population, and they became the world's largest and most complex refugee problem (*see* Table 9). Having been focused on Southeast Asia, the international refugee community, under the leadership of UNHCR, hurried to adjust to another region's needs.

United Nations Action

In January 1980, the UN General Assembly overwhelmingly approved a resolution calling for a negotiated political settlement in Afghanistan based on four principles: complete withdrawal of Soviet troops, restoration of an independent and nonaligned Afghanistan, self-determination for the Afghan people, and the return of refugees with safety and honor. Russia vetoed a UN Security Council motion calling for the withdrawal of its forces.[6]

In June 1982, the UN secretary general undertook indirect negotiations for a political settlement in a first round of talks in Geneva. The fifth round ended in August 1985. Talks included the Democratic Republic of Afghanistan and the Government of Pakistan, with the Soviets unofficially involved. Pakistan refused to negotiate directly with the Kabul government, and the UN under secretary general Diego Cordovez shuttled between the two delegations as agreement remained beyond reach.

Throughout this conflict, the United States opposed the Soviet occupation of Afghanistan, and this issue remained a major irritant in East-West relations. Soviet withdrawal would be key, and the United States argued that a settlement must also provide for the three other principles in the UN Afghanistan resolutions.

US Refugee Strategy

As a key member of the international coalition for assistance to Afghan refugees, the United States addressed four complex strategic issues:

(1) Bolstering Pakistan's commitment to continue asylum for Afghans, despite Soviet threats of retaliation and the social, economic, and environmental costs to Pakistan of the huge refugee influx

(2) Keeping Pakistan's compensation claims within reasonable bounds and monitoring the donor food and non-food items Pakistan claimed it needed to support the refugees

(3) Supporting the World Bank's ambitious reforestation and job creation program to deal with the effects of hosting millions of refugees

(4) Using significant US financial contributions to leverage generous inputs from other donors and extracting maximum operational performance from both UNHCR and the government of Pakistan, its implementing partner

The international donor community organized itself around the UN high commissioner for refugees Poul Hartling.

Regional Impacts

The Afghan refugees were mostly ethnic Pashtuns seeking refuge in Pakistan's Pashtun-dominated areas. UNHCR established over 300 'refugee villages' in Pakistan that accommodated most of them. The Afghan refugees in Iran were largely ethnic Tajiks, Uzbeks, and Hazaras lodged mostly in Iranian cities and towns.[7]

The presence of up to 3 million refugees had a major impact on Pakistan, which, as a good neighbor, pledged to let refugees stay. Pakistan expected international help to provide shelter, food, health care, and employment. They also wanted help to address infrastructural impacts.

The northwest frontier province governor Fazle Haq was frank in describing to a visiting congressional delegation some of the calculus Pakistan was using. Because nearly all the male refugees were armed, many keeping their guns under their camp bed rolls, and all were potential jihadists, there was fear of Soviet hot pursuit into Pakistan or an even broader invasion of parts of the province.[8] Pakistan willingly took on this burden, notwithstanding the high vulnerability it brought to the country.

To show solidarity, RP worked with Pakistani authorities to identify specific areas for direct bilateral assistance to help relieve refugee impacts on the country. This was in addition to the US role as the principal partner and financier of the multilateral relief effort. Under Jerry Hoganson's lead, RP spearheaded the US Afghan refugee team that provided Pakistan special and unique assistance to promote continued *safe asylum* to the world's largest refugee population.

Food Aid

Pakistan's state-controlled logistics system became UNHCR's chief partner for delivering food aid. Rather than transporting the huge wheat tonnages (Pakistan requested about 400,000 tons per year, usually getting somewhat less from the United States) all the way from the Karachi port to the refugee camps in the Northwest Frontier province, the government of Pakistan used a pragmatic exchange system. It provided local wheat for the camps in the province, and we agreed that they use the US wheat for Pakistan's own domestic consumption elsewhere. While we were not always clear on the modalities of this exchange program, it was accepted on the grounds of Pakistan's logistics efficiencies, and the avoidance of huge transport fees to the camps.[9]

Health and Medical

The refugee program staff were diligent in measuring mortality, morbidity, and communicable disease incidence in the camps. We did this largely through Centers for Disease Control (CDC) field visits and through height/weight/nutrition status monitoring. This practice maintained the integrity of assistance and preserved a constructive and workable relationship with the Pakistan authorities.

The refugee camps in Pakistan were difficult for UNHCR to manage. Many male inhabitants were combatants using the camps for rest from fighting the Soviets. Many brought their battlefield injuries back into the camps, and the international medical personnel faced many severe injuries. It eventually became necessary to establish an Afghan medical program under the auspices of an international organization whose mission was to fly out of the region the critically injured who could not be treated locally. Rehabilitative treatment was included.

Environment—Pakistan Reforestation Program

The Pakistan Government was concerned about its growing domestic vulnerability due to land, crop, and environmental damage caused by refugees occupying large tracts of their territory. Their citizens complained that refugees cut the trees for fuel, denied land use to Pakistani citizens, and competed for limited jobs.

RP broached this problem with the World Bank staff and discovered similar concerns. Within a brief time, our advocacy plus the World Bank support led to an innovative tree-planting and job-creation program. In several meetings with the World Bank president Barber Conable, Gene Dewey found him seized with this initiative, and it paved the way for the creation of the bank's first NGO liaison office. This breakthrough for RP and the World Bank led to high donor support. At each donor conference, the government placed these issues at the top of its priority needs list. This tree-planting initiative was the foundation for UNHCR's income generating program, created in 1984 in partnership with the World Bank.

The environmental program for Afghan refugees in protection in Pakistan extended over the next twelve years, with $85 million invested for 300 projects in three heavily-impacted provinces. The projects included reforestation, watershed management, irrigation, road repair and construction. Similar projects were undertaken in Iran through the International Fund for Agricultural Development project, although donor contributions were minimal.[10]

Logistics and Transport

The Pakistani Government requested help to augment its transport system to deal with its massive influx of refugees. The number of refugees and their wide dispersal throughout the country used up Pakistani trucks to haul supplies, equipment, and people.[11] Gene Dewey and I agreed this might be another opportunity for the United States to demonstrate partnership with Pakistan.

Assessing truck needs and capacities was not an RP area of expertise, but we thought we might find an American business to supply the trucks. Gene assigned this task to our new program officer, Paula Lynch, who settled on International Harvester in Seattle. They met our requirements and their cost was competitive. We authorized Paula to make a deal.

Then a cultural concern came into play when the question arose, "Who will we send to Islamabad to assure the trucks arrive undamaged and present them to the Pakistani Government?" This should not have been an issue. We normally would send the assigned program officer, in this case Paula Lynch. The problem was that females were not being sent to Muslim countries, particularly war zones.

I decided not to decide for Paula. When we had a job to do, anywhere, we were expected to do it. So, I asked Paula to travel to Pakistan. I thought her facial expression seemed leery until she said, "Sure, I'll go."

After word got out that Paula Lynch was going to Pakistan, I got one call after another, mainly from our male staff, saying, "Jim, you can't send a female to Pakistan. It's just not done." I considered all comments and decided, 'I'm not going to make that call. I'm going to support her follow-through.'

Paula's experience proved beneficial to her and to RP. It showed when we had dangerous work to do, officers would do it without regard to gender. Today, such assignments for women are routine in the Foreign Service.

Afghan Census

To get a correct census of the Afghans in camps was problematic. The men came and went, and the veiled women mostly stayed inside their tents when strangers were present. Muslim custom did not allow outsiders, particularly men, to enter tents if women were present. However, estimation techniques were developed without the availability of a precise census, and special programs were set up to address the problems the Afghan women and children faced in daily life.

Durable Solutions for Afghan Refugees

Throughout these dangerous years for the civilians, the international community maintained the original consensus that the Afghan refugees in Pakistan and Iran should be maintained in *safe first asylum* (in the region) until conditions would permit their return home. We resisted suggestions to launch a large *third-country resettlement* program for Afghans, as had been done for the Vietnamese and the other Southeast Asians. We found a few urban refugees whom we included in the resettlement program. Overall, we saw the real solution was to stabilize these refugees' lives in *safe regional asylum* until return was possible.

The *stabilization* plan happened over many years. From 1980 to 1987, 40,000 Afghans from the region were resettled in the United States (less than 1 percent of all the Afghan refugees). Of those, approximately 40 percent were selected from refugee sites in Pakistan, 50 percent from Iran, 8 percent from Iraq, and small numbers from Libya, Saudi Arabia, Syria, and Lebanon (*see* Table 2). Most camp refugees eventually returned home or settled spontaneously in the region.

In those times, the Afghan refugees were the biggest refugee problem with political and military implications. The US administration believed the international humanitarian community's strategic approach for the Afghan refugees was correct; it helped Pakistan, a friendly and cooperative government, provide *safe asylum* for many years, until the right *durable solution—safe repatriation—*became possible.

Protection Reality

The RP team was sometimes uncomfortable about an inconsistency in our worldwide camp-*protection* policy. In the Salvadoran and Nicaraguan refugee camps in Honduras (where two insurgent ideologies were at work), we wanted strict exclusion of weapons and insurgent uses of them in camps, consistent with UNHCR rules. We actively opposed armed refugees in the UNRWA facilities in the Middle East and in the UNHCR and in the UNBRO camps in Southeast Asia. But in the Pakistan camps for Afghan refugees, we tolerated the widespread presence of weapons and use of camps as support bases for the anti-Soviet insurgents. How did we reconcile this contradiction?

The simple answer is that we could not. The Pakistan Government was in charge. We concluded that possessing a weapon under the bedroll was integral to the Pashtun culture and that absent their men, the women and children could not have taken refuge there either. Trying to enforce a ban, particularly in vast open camps, could have led to open revolt. If Pakistan could live with it and still avoid the Soviet hot pursuit into its territory, the international community pragmatically accepted this reality. To serve the refugees, we had no other choice.

Soviet Withdrawal from Afghanistan

After ten long years of grueling war, the Soviet forces failed to suppress the Afghan resistance or to establish the authority of the Babrak Karmal government. Facing increasingly effective opposition and a weak and ineffective Afghan army partner, the Soviets had to rely increasingly on their own troops. Their brutal tactics included saturation bombing, willful destruction of crops and livestock, and reprisals against the noncombatants to wear down the civilian resistance.[12] Mikhail Gorbachev brought the war to an end (1988–89). He realized the Soviets could not win and the war costs were crippling their already weak economy.

The UN estimated that the United States provided more than $2 billion in aid to the Mujahideen during the war years, 1979–89. The war caused about one million civilian deaths. Ninety thousand Mujahideen fighters, eighteen thousand Afghan troops, and fourteen thousand five hundred Soviet troops also perished. The Soviets left behind a shattered

Afghanistan. The long-running conflict has been called "the Soviet Union's Vietnam War."[13]

After Soviet military withdrawal from Afghanistan in February 1989, the victorious Afghan Mujahideen morphed into the infamous Taliban and seized control of the insurgency, providing Osama bin Laden a training base from which to launch terrorist operations worldwide, including against the United States. The Taliban story that played out in Afghanistan during the refugee decade, 1979–89, was another tragic episode in world affairs during that volatile period.

Nineteenth-century events, including outside, or foreign, influences in South Asia had caused disillusioned madrassas to return exclusively to Koranic teachings, "stripping out anything Hindu or European from the curriculum."[14] Almost 150 years later, the Taliban emerged in Pakistan and Afghanistan, a time later agreed to have been the nexus of al-Qaeda's rise.

36

CENTRAL AMERICA AND THE CARIBBEAN

IN 1979, DEATH SQUADS IN EL SALVADOR AND GUATEMALA and human rights violations in Nicaragua produced floods of refugees and *internally displaced persons* (IDPs). Right-wing elected governments and military dictators in El Salvador and Guatemala were attempting to contain left-wing insurgencies. In Nicaragua, Contra rebels were at war with Daniel Ortega's Sandinistas. Elements in the American and European religious and NGO establishments, opposed to the right-wing tendencies witnessed in Central America, came close to encouraging revolution. The US–Soviet influence magnified the conflicts. The Cold War was hot. Central American civil wars uprooted two million people. Most of them were *internally displaced* or became *undocumented aliens* in other Central or North American countries. Around 150,000 persons were recognized as legal refugees, and they resided in the *first-asylum* camps in Honduras, Costa Rica, and Mexico.

These were dangerous times in the Western Hemisphere as governments acted to address throngs of people on the move.

The Cartagena Declaration on Refugees

African governments had successfully broadened the UN Refugee Convention definition of refugees in 1969, to include

> ...persons who flee their country because their lives, safety or freedom have been threatened by generalized violence, foreign aggression, internal conflicts, massive

violation of human rights or other circumstances which
have seriously disturbed public order.

Similarly, the Central American and Mexican governments and civil society representatives met in Cartagena, Colombia, in November 1984 to adopt the Cartagena Declaration on Refugees, which expanded the refugee definition for their region to include *economic privation* and *(economic) persecution*.

The United States and the other major refugee resettlement countries did not support or apply the expanded definition for either Africa or Latin America, reasoning it would bestow legal refugee benefits and protection to most of the world's poor and go far beyond the definitions for *politically persecuted* or *victims of war*. If applied for Central America, most of the two million people who fled *economic privation* and *(economic) persecution* during the 1980s would receive refugee status.

The next year, 1985, I headed the American delegation to Geneva for UNHCR's executive committee meeting. The head of the Colombian delegation, Ambassador Hector Charry-Samper, approached me about American support for the Cartagena Declaration. I explained our disagreement to the proposed expansion of the refugee definition and our belief it would render meaningless the international commitment to refugees; the result would be less protection for refugees, rather than more. We continued to apply the accepted, world-wide definition.

Refugee–Immigration Impacts on the United States

A small fraction of the one-half million people who fled to the United States from Central America were awarded *refugee status*. Lacking the viable possibility to achieve *political asylum*, most of the others went into an irregular status and faced the omnipresent fear of deportation. Some went to Canada.

The uniformly low rates of approval for *asylum* in the United States were higher for the Nicaraguans than for the Salvadorans or the Guatemalans. The administration took a hard line favoring the quick return of rejected asylum-seekers, although a limited number could stay longer (until conditions improved in their country) through a process known as Extended Voluntary Departure, or EVD. Eventually, they too had to return.

The US policy regarding EVD for Central American asylum-seekers was articulated by the assistant secretary of state Elliott Abrams at an April 1985 House Foreign Affairs Committee hearing. I attended that hearing as another principal administration witness. Abrams was asked to comment on a proposal by several subcommittee members (Reps. Weiss, Jeffords, Conte, and Frank) for expanded EVD for Guatemalans.

> ... this administration has not favored EVD for nationals of any Central American country for a number of reasons. But I think the primary one, which would be true for Guatemala as well as El Salvador, is that, given that this is a region of tremendous flows of illegal immigrants to the United States, the EVD is likely, therefore, to encourage larger flows and induce people knowing that they cannot be deported, induce more people to come.[1]

Large numbers of *economic migrants* were also moving northward, and it was often difficult to distinguish them from asylum seekers. The ongoing problem with illegal Central American entrants added fuel to this flammable mix. Sanctuary cities sprang up across America. Right-wing reactionaries attempted to indoctrinate fear through warnings of a "brown horde" invading the United States; they argued for more restrictive policies.

In Cuba, within five months of RP's startup, Fidel Castro opened the Port of Mariel and forced out over 125,000 people he described as "undesirables." The Haitians seized this opportunity to launch simultaneous boat flotillas.

United States Refugee Policy

The US refugee policies for Central America and the Caribbean, Mexico, and Cuba attempted to follow internationally-accepted *durable solution* priorities. The United States considered most refugee cases to be solvable through *repatriation* or *regional settlement*. Therefore, refugee programming and funding emphasized the maintenance of *safe regional asylum* to allow time for *permanent durable solutions* to develop.

The American refugee policies for Central America and Cuba posed many perplexing issues for RP. How were we to craft humane US policy true to international refugee obligations, including *durable solutions*, while facing widespread, often combative left-wing opposition to anything but US *resettlement*. How to protect the victims from death squads and intimidating governments, how to assess their needs, and how to help an entirely new class of victims displaced within their own countries—these were the new challenges.

Compared to the US generosity displayed in other regions, policies in the Western Hemisphere were seen by many critics as hard-nosed, restrictive, and detached. These critics came from many corners: politicians, clergy, civil rights advocates, academicians, liberal NGOs, and international organizations. They often united in opposition to the Reagan administration's support of the conservative anti-communist military regimes in Central America.

UNHCR and US Flip-Side

The United States discovered in Central America what every helping nation faces: concerns on borders can be more difficult to address than those in distant places. Nowhere was this clearer than in our refugee and immigration relationship with UNHCR in Central America. We were at loggerheads. In most other regions, we agreed on overall strategic policy goals, even during occasional disagreements on tactics.

The motives for much of the Salvadoran flight, for example, were questioned by the Reagan administration and *targeted solutions* were insisted upon. On the other hand, UNHCR granted (Cartagena-type) *de facto refugee status* to all Salvadorans fleeing the civil war (a blanket measure commonly applied in Africa but a first in Latin America).[2] Seeing this practical difference, many other multilateral and NGO players, already opposed to President Reagan's Central America policy, became even more hostile to its management of *refugee policy*.

UNHCR contemplated similar group refugee status designations for the people fleeing violence in Guatemala, Nicaragua, Haiti, and Cuba. However, they eventually stayed with individual refugee determinations in keeping with the 1951 Refugee Convention. The level of violence in Guatemala and Nicaragua could have justified a different decision, they concluded, but the affected populations were much smaller. Cubans were a special case and most Haitians were eventually found to be *economic migrants*.[3]

Innovative Solutions for Salvadoran IDPs

Diverse Latin American programs of the refugee decade, 1979–89, are best demonstrated by focus on major categories with their own stories. Central America was one of the most politically volatile for US policy makers, although the region had fewer than 150,000 *registered refugees*, the smallest of RP's regional programs in resettlement and financial expenditures. Even as the international community addressed the plight of large numbers of Salvadoran *asylum seekers* fleeing to *regional asylum* countries, a problem of equal magnitude was erupting inside El Salvador. By 1981, 165,000 people fled village and community violence by moving elsewhere within the country, thereby entering *displaced persons* status. Isolated rural families moved into nearby villages; villagers moved to larger towns; and small-town families fled to the big cities, all seeking greater security. These extended families were in refugee-like situations. But, as they were *internally displaced*, they had not crossed an international border, and they did not fall within the refugee definition for assistance or *protection*, or within the charters of UNHCR or the US Bureau for Refugee Programs (RP). This represented a big gap in the global humanitarian system then, and it has persisted. No international network or agency had, or has, a clear mandate for the *internally displaced persons*.

To meet the 1981 challenge in El Salvador, USAID's Office of Foreign Disaster Assistance hired consultant Bob Gersony to lead a team to El Salvador for in-depth assessment of the conditions and needs of displaced persons and a proposal for operational response. The result was a cooperative IDP program involving unprecedented cooperation between OFDA and RP.

In response to a question from Sen. Dennis DeConcini (D-AZ) at a September 1983 congressional hearing, I testified that RP had contributed to the IDP jobs program and that, despite budget strains, was committed to continue. I acknowledged this was done even though *displaced persons* fell only tangentially within our area of responsibility. In a March 1984 Senate Appropriations Committee hearing (chaired by Sen. Robert Kasten (R-WI), I reported that refugee programs were helping the ICRC to assist about 90,000 displaced persons and helping the government of El Salvador (through its agency and partners) to serve almost 270,000 displaced.[4]

As the IDP project in El Salvador was well into implementation by that time, we sent a joint RP–USAID team, including staff from RP's Emergency Management Unit (EMU) and the CDC, to field-check the effort. They validated and endorsed the IDP jobs approach and recommended its expansion, also urging the strengthening of public health efforts.

In future years, as more global crises erupted, IDPs would become the paramount concern of the international humanitarian community. RP's early experience in Central America set the tone for what was to come. In retrospect, the joint USAID–RP initiative in El Salvador was ground-breaking and precedent-setting for this vulnerable category.

Relocating Salvadoran Camps Away from Borders

Reports of Salvadoran death squad murders and massacres of entire villages generated worldwide alarm and condemnation; most survivors fled into safer in-country locations or into Honduras.[5] They began arriving in Honduras in 1980, spontaneously settling in the border communities, particularly La Virtud. The Honduran government regarded the arrivals with suspicion as potential guerrilla collaborators. The ongoing conflict forced more to flee, and by 1981 the Salvadoran refugee populations at the Honduran border areas reached 30,000. Recurring conflicts caused Honduras to start resettling the refugees from La Virtud to Mesa Grande, further inland. The refugees and some NGOs protested. The government had UNHCR agreement to continue.

In 1983, RP proposed that the Honduran Government relocate a controversial refugee camp at Colomoncagua away from the border to a site further inside the country. Salvadoran insurgent groups were using border camps for resting from the civil war, to pilfer donor supplies, and recruit. Some US sources loudly alleged that Colomoncagua was being used as a transit camp for arms and a staging area for military operations. The United States was among the strongest advocates for UNHCR to prevent misuse of this and other refugee camps.

To add complications, inertia in Tegucigalpa continued as the embassy in El Salvador maintained a drum beat, that the war could not conclude if the refugee camps remained near the border. RP's Gene Dewey sent consultant Bob Gersony to Honduras with a mission to "move those camps." Bob remembered Gene saying, "Don't come back to Washington until Colomoncagua is moved."

In his report three months later, Bob Gersony confirmed that insurgents were using the refugee camps for R & R breaks and pilfering. But the real problem was a radical Khmer Rouge-style Farabundo Marti National Liberation Front, FMLN, faction in Colomoncagua that ruled all aspects of camp life through intimidation and violence. And UNHCR and NGO staff in the camps, some of which were not supportive of insurgent goals, felt compelled to cede camp control to this brutal faction to maintain their own presence and ability to help endangered refugees.

Contrary to Gene Dewey's expectation, Bob Gersony concluded that insurgents would resist any attempt to move the camp and would guarantee the murder of some camp inhabitants, to give a "black eye to the US." Bob suggested a potentially safer solution. The Honduran Government could implement perimeter controls and law enforcement to protect camp inhabitants and to stop resource diversions. The belief was that better external perimeter security would assist UNHCR and the NGOs to maintain camps for humanitarian purposes.

Bob's next challenge was to change the minds of officials already committed to camp relocation. First, there was Gene Dewey, then me, then Elliott Abrams, finally the US Embassies in El Salvador and Honduras. After hearing and understanding Bob's rationale for this new approach, almost all of us came to agree. To do otherwise would mean catastrophe for the refugees, UNHCR, and the US Government. The ambassador and the staff at the American Embassy in Honduras backed Bob's plan. But a strong objection came from the deputy chief of mission Shep Lowman. Speaking for himself, he gave Gersony a tongue-lashing.

But the harshest American objections came from El Salvador, where Ambassador Ed Corr and DCM David DeLouie strenuously accused Gersony and the embassy in Tegucigalpa of minimizing the degree to which the camps were used by insurgents and for abandoning previous relocation plans. The border camps were the reason, they insisted, that efforts to end the war were failing. They did not seem concerned about the threat of violence if the camp residents were moved. Supported by Elliott Abrams of State's Inter-American Affairs, RP defused these objections and maneuvered around the obstacles. The camps were not moved and the Honduran Government fulfilled the security role envisaged by Bob Gersony. UNHCR strengthened its work in the camps. I was encouraged that facts and solid analysis still played an important role in the decision-making.

Rescuing Targeted Guatemalan Leaders

As the Guatemalan civil war raged, it was common practice to target leaders that opposed repression (politicians, legislators, judges, media figures, academics) for retribution by the Guatemalan Government. To address these death threats, the country's Human Rights Commission set up an escape route using friendly and supportive organizations.[6] As explained to me, the escape scenarios went something like this. A party of ten or more would enter a restaurant for dinner. Mixed within the party would be the person targeted. After a long and pleasant dinner, a party of nine would leave. A local representative of a major international organization, funded by RP, would surreptitiously escort the target out the back door. Later, they would meet up with the organization's representative from a neighboring country, who would escort the targeted official into political asylum. This route to safety kept many officials alive.

Protecting Miskito Indians

The Miskito Indians of Nicaragua were independent farmers who took care of their own. They were strong and fearless anti-communists and joined the Contras in taking the battle to the Sandinistas on Nicaragua's Atlantic coast. They were feared and hated by the Sandinista regime, and their defeat, or elimination, was a goal of the Nicaraguan government.[7]

About 22,000 Miskito Indians fled into Honduras in the mid-1980s and about fourteen thousand were housed at UNHCR's Mocoron receiving camp. The remaining eight thousand resettled spontaneously along the Coco River in a familiar environment. Many had been permanent residents of villages on the Nicaraguan side of the river.[8] Their aim was to remain close to home to achieve self-sufficiency. There were reports that the Contras used the Mocoron camp for small-scale R and R. Bob Gersony reported that insurgent training and operations centers were pervasive in the Mosquitia, but had nothing to do with UNHCR and its refugee camps.

At one point, Sen. Bob Kasten asked how RP could arrange for the Miskitos to stay in Honduras while funding a program by the Intergovernmental Committee for Migration to identify the refugees who wished to return to Nicaragua. Were these contradictory solutions? My response highlighted this was how refugee programs were supposed to work. They assured *safe asylum*, but worked on *durable solutions* as soon as possible.

An American relief and development organization, World Relief, had been working with the Miskitos since they first migrated to Honduras, long before UNHCR arrived. In addition to work in the camps, they provided some subsistence support to self-settlers. It was little wonder that World Relief had developed something of a proprietary claim on the Miskito program. Though it was engaged by UNHCR as its implementing agency for the Mosquitia, it had trouble accepting guidance from UNHCR regarding the refugees living along rivers not served by UNHCR. Don Krumm of RP's emergency management unit went to Honduras to help clarify the program logistics and parameters.

Don contacted all parties and reported that UNHCR and World Relief were experiencing friction. UNHCR insisted on going strictly by the book regarding the Miskitos. The regional director in Geneva, Robert

Muller, argued that it was inconsistent for World Relief, an implementing agency, to assist both registered refugees in the camp and populations resettled spontaneously along rivers at international borders outside their purview. World Relief thought this view was bureaucratic nonsense and fought back.

I had a special relationship with World Relief, having brought them into the refugee resettlement world early. Wishing to prevent the issue getting out of hand, I asked Bob Gersony to go to Honduras again to investigate.

Following a thorough review, his recommendation was to accept UNHCR's position, as it was legally and technically correct. To ease the discomfort, Bob went to World Relief's headquarters in Wheaton, Illinois, to explain the situation to the executive director, Jerry Ballard. After considerable anguish, Bob brought World Relief around and, later, the UN high commissioner for refugees, as well.

Castro's Marielito Expulsions

In late spring 1980, I received an urgent weekend call from Chris Holmes, director of RP's Cuba-Haiti Task Force. Chris was at the Indiantown Gap Camp in Pennsylvania, and he faced a serious security dilemma. Several dangerous Cubans had broken out of their confined section of the camp and were threatening the children and young peoples' sections. What should we do?

Chris and I agreed he should contact the military police and the local police to apprehend and confine these men. They should make a sweep of their barracks, confiscate any weapons found and bring charges against these troublemakers. I told him we would locate a more secure and permanent holding facility for violent offenders and return them to Cuba soon.

Fidel Castro's expulsion of over 125,000 Cubans from the Port of Mariel proved difficult to address; its law enforcement implications carried forward into the Reagan administration. Without question, some Mariel Cubans were among the most violent and disruptive groups RP assisted during these turbulent years.[9]

It took several years of negotiations, but in December 1984, a United

States-Cuba Immigration Agreement was announced.[10] Both sides won: the United States would return 2,800 Mariel criminals and other *excludables* (a US immigration term for those not legally eligible for US entry) to Cuba. Normal immigration suspended since the boat-lift crisis of 1980 would resume, a remarkable achievement given the bitter relations between the two countries.

Enter Radio Marti. Those of us involved in Cuba matters then, at the departments of State and Justice, were dumbfounded that anyone could have failed to see that establishing a radio station to beam American views hostile to Castro into the heart of Cuba would inspire Castro to retaliate with the nearest available instrument, the immigration agreement. To our relief, Castro did not cancel the agreement outright; he suspended it. However, there was a price. More innocent people would suffer.

As one observer opined, "The pity is that Florida politicians in Congress, Cuban-American hardliners, and communist-bashing voices in the administration won their radio station at the expense of great personal hardship for thousands of individuals."[11]

Following a two-year suspension, the bilateral Migration Agreement of 1984 was resumed in November 1987.[12] American refugee NGOs continued to assist deserving Cubans, while law enforcement identified and dealt with the criminals. It took time, because of our protective justice system. But those with legitimate claims for refugee status got help, and the criminals and disrupters were eventually returned to Cuba.

America's Interdiction-Return Policy for Haitians

The Mariel Cuban exodus prompted large numbers of Haitians, who had been waiting in the wings, also to set sail in early 1980 in a parallel outflow of poor emigrants, or economic migrants, toward the United States. Confusingly, the US policy for the Haitians was the exact opposite of its policy for the Cubans. The Haitian migrants were turned around if apprehended at sea and deported as undocumented economic migrants if they made it to our shores. Only the legitimate political refugees, whom US immigration decided were nonexistent, could enter. Haiti-US relations on this issue had a long and sad history. Now juxtaposed with the simultaneous Mariel crisis, this problem was to play out in media frenzy again.

I was never comfortable with the severe US–Haitian policy. But, as the Haitians were not considered refugees, I had little policy influence. This law-enforcement matter fell under Justice Department jurisdiction.

Given concerns about Haitian returnees, we arranged a contract with the Haitian Red Cross to assist and monitor the returnees and report back. Monitors were also sent to the Krome refugee camp in South Florida, where the United States incarcerated the apprehended Haitians until they could be returned home. While these efforts mitigated some of the negative impacts on rejected or incarcerated Haitians, they did nothing to alter the US policy on Haiti. We found that the Haitian returnees melded back into poverty-stricken society and no harm came to them. They just planned their next escape.

While this exodus was underway, I represented the State Department at a congressional hearing before the full House International Relations Committee where Haiti was a major focus. Over twenty members showed up, so each had only five minutes to question witnesses. Most Haiti-related questions went to the Justice Department representative. But Rep. Gary Studds (D-MA) focused on the foreign relations aspects of Haitian movements, and he went at me about the seaworthiness of the Coast Guard vessels used to return Haitians. I tried to deflect his question to the Justice Department witness, but he insisted that I answer. I said I did not know and there followed about thirty more "did you know" questions, with the same answer. Clearly, Studds was setting a record at my expense.

A year later, the UNHCR representative in Washington, Fiorella Capelli, informed me they were joining Father Gerard Jean-Juste, founder of the Haitian Refugee Center in Miami, in a suit against the US Government and me, as RP director, over our Haitian interdiction and return policy. The suit alleged *refoulement,* or *forced repatriation* prohibited by the 1951 Refugee Convention. I knew the suit would gain little traction in US courts, but certain highly placed Reagan administration officials became irate when they heard about UNHCR suing its major donor. I assured the White House of our awareness of the problem and stressed that UNHCR had no choice but to join the suit.

The United States signed a bilateral accord with the Haitian

Government in 1981, under which the latter permitted the US Coast Guard to repatriate all the migrants interdicted on the high seas; Haiti held to its commitment not to prosecute those who returned. As I was departing RP in mid-1986, just over six thousand migrants had returned to Haiti since the beginning of the interdiction program.

Reacting to American Immigration Reform

The United States was unprepared to handle Central American immigration crises during the 1980s. Besieged from all directions, the US administration had difficulty agreeing on desperately needed immigration reform parameters. Policy makers faced an important strategic question: *Are national interests best served by keeping most immigrants out or by letting more in?*

When legal immigration channels clogged or were unavailable, victims of economic and security breakdowns in Central America and elsewhere felt their only choice was to seek mercy from the political asylum system. That phenomenon explained why so many seekers of US asylum were from El Salvador, Nicaragua, Guatemala, and Honduras. All other regular migration avenues were blocked. The absence of consistent and effective American immigration policy for Central America put such added pressure on refugee systems for that region that the humanitarian community became one of the loudest voices for immigration reform.

During a high point in the Cuba-Haiti immigration debate, I spoke at a well-attended symposium at Georgetown University. As expected, most attendees at the emotional session roundly condemned and denounced US strategy and approaches, especially regarding political asylum. I did not find much support for US policy or actions.

During my testimony to an extensive Senate Foreign Operations Appropriations Committee hearing in March 1984 questions came from Sen. Mark Hatfield (R-OR), Sen. Robert Kasten (R-WI), and Sen. Dennis DeConcini (D-AZ). That testimony highlighted the positive and yet antagonistic relations between the US executive and legislative branches on Central America refugee issues then.

To address US immigration dysfunctions, the Immigration and Refugee subcommittees of the House and Senate Judiciary Committees launched a reform effort. They conducted extensive hearings before producing the Immigration and Control Act of 1986. In a 2013 article, INS Deputy Commissioner Mark Everson noted that the challenges of that era were essentially the same as current ones: a legal system that had failed to keep pace with a changing world, ineffective enforcement, and a large illegal population.[13] The 1986 Act sought to beef up immigration enforcement while offering legal status to several million undocumented people. It did not revise the legal immigration system. A cornerstone of that law required employers to hire individuals legally, with work authorization. This provision (which was resisted by the business community) relied on documents provided by the applicant, leading to much document fraud and identity theft. The law's amnesty program was also generous, particularly for agricultural workers. Overall, about three million people gained legal status. Many believed amnesty was a magnet for the rampant illegal immigration that followed.

I followed the progress of the Immigration and Control Act of 1986, enacted just as I was leaving RP. It proved little value in decreasing the flow of illegal immigrants and asylum seekers to the United States. In the opinion of columnist Charles Krauthammer, the law was a "fiasco where amnesty was granted, and border enforcement never came."[14]

Central America—Conclusion

Manifold criticisms of the 1980s US refugee policy for Central America included

- Doubts about American strategy and tactics
- Low refugee admissions to the United States compared to other regions
- Camp misuse, especially by insurgents
- Hostile relations with host governments, IOs, NGOs, and churches
- Misunderstanding of international organization roles and functions
- Self-sufficient asylum versus continued dependency

In those tumultuous years, RP attempted to stabilize refugee and asylum matters in Central America and the Caribbean. We hoped to keep prospects alive for later peace and reconciliation compromises. Specifically, we combined help with diplomacy.

We handled Cuba's Mariel flows, consolidated and improved relations with friendly asylum countries (particularly Mexico), constrained and rationalized movements within Central America, launched the first IDP assistance program for Salvadorans, and tried to prevent perverse efforts to scapegoat US-bound Central American asylum seekers and immigrants.

During my tenure, US critics in Central America were never fully satisfied, yet most came to see there were two sides to these thorny issues. Perhaps that was all that was possible then. We were not surprised that most countries of the region usually applied the Cartagena Declaration's broader refugee definition.

The Central America peace process that began in Esquipulas, Guatemala, in 1987 fortified regional leaders' resolve to end regional conflicts. The 1989 negotiations to end Nicaraguan conflict resulted in Sandinistas voted out the next year. Formal peace agreements were settled in El Salvador and Guatemala in 1992 and 1996, respectively.[15] I was honored to be invited to and attend the 1996 ceremony in Guatemala City celebrating the treaty signing that ended their long-running civil war.

37

SUMMING UP THE REFUGEE DECADE

WHAT BEGAN AS URGENT POST-WAR HELP FOR SOUTHEAST Asia refugees carried over into the 1980s. As soon as they undertook emergency measures for Indochina, US refugee programs were catapulted into the broader universe of refugee and humanitarian concerns. Overnight, measures had to be carefully tested and adjusted for disasters so large, fast growing, and widely dispersed that RP prepared on the run to help address them.

Again, the role of helping key multilateral agencies gear up was thrust on the United States, and others—Australia, Canada, Japan, and a handful of Western Europe nations. The United States and its allies were ready to respond to these global challenges with a vigor and determination that almost no one foresaw—and to stimulate invention and reform in humanitarian practices.

The UN High Commission for Refugees said world-wide refugee populations grew from three million in 1975 to over thirteen million in 1987, a nearly unfathomable increase (*see* Table 1). The years 1979 to 1989 were such a fluid, fiery, and treacherous time—with multiple crises erupting, addressed, and put on the path to resolution—that domestic and international colleagues began referring to it as *the refugee decade.*

I led the US programs during the first eight years of that decade, during which the United States set new refugee records. Over one million were resettled, due to the generosity of US citizens (*see* Table 2), with another 500,000 resettled mainly in Australia, Canada and France (*see* Table 9). About 75 percent of those resettled in the United States were from Southeast Asia, and another 17 percent were from Eastern Europe and the former Soviet Union.

The *refugee decade*'s humanitarian response required extraordinary financial resources and support, far beyond anything ever needed from the international community. Again, America led the way with financial contributions that fueled the global response machinery. Including the Saigon evacuation, the State Department's refugee programs contributed almost four billion dollars to assist the refugees, globally during that period, an enormous sum for that era (*see* Table 3). American citizens, who made this record response possible, contributed incalculable additional amounts through private charities.

An important priority shift occurred during this period, away from dollar-intensive domestic resettlement toward overseas relief programs. Having reached a high of 80 percent of our budget in 1979, domestic resettlement funding declined to around 30 percent in 1983 and later years (*see* Table 3). Still significant, the remaining resettlement programs were more in balance with evolving imperatives. The surging refugee populations overseas benefitted from this strategic change that freed substantial resources to augment global relief assistance.

The historic refugee achievements of this period would have been impossible without reformed and energized multilateral, national, and private response systems willing and able to deliver the goods and share the burdens.

Why RP Worked at the State Department

The State Department's Refugee Programs bureau became a creature unlike anything I had seen or experienced, shaping a distinctive style made up of complementary attributes revealed at various times; they were aggressive, dedicated, disciplined, mission driven, flexible, field oriented, sacrificial, and devoted to the mission. The people of the team cared about those they served. They put their careers and sometimes their lives on the line. It was clear from my first-to-last day on the job that the US team gathered from the State Department, other government agencies, and the private sector was made up of highly-motivated individuals on a shared mission. And this does not even mention the multitudes of private American citizens and families that deserve mention here, who made it possible for refugees to drop that status and become American residents and citizens.

As I have tried to demonstrate, the United States succeeded in this mission by melding humane foreign policy with a can-do, coherent entity that quickly became one of the State Department's most dynamic organizations. We emulated US leaders that placed the victims of global humanitarian disasters at the heart of foreign policy decision-making and insisted that we find the "cure" as well as treat the symptoms. To ignore or abandon vulnerable refugee populations was unthinkable.

The Refugee Programs bureau, RP, brought demonstrable results and institutional success to the State Department's efforts by (1) unifying State's fractured refugee culture, which RP inherited, and thereby bringing coherence to national and international refugee programs of that era; (2) leading the State Department to accommodate and support the needs of fast-paced programs, and (3) demonstrating that with strategic and firm direction a rejuvenated multilateral system could plan and efficiently manage life-and-death crises without sacrificing America's national interests or integrity.

The Changed Culture

Changing the State Department culture was essential. State Department leadership and program staff had to recognize the refugee function as a permanent feature of the foreign affairs landscape, not just a series of exceptional responses to unanticipated catastrophes abroad. Refugee work became a discipline—an advanced field, a specialty, a branch of learning—rather than an amalgam of recurring heroic improvisations to meet standards of expediency. This disciplinary imperative was driven home early by FSO Chas Freeman and the State Department's under secretary for management Ben Read. They made clear their aim, in RP's formative years, to stress the high value of discipline and trust that is necessary to professions, including proto-professions like diplomacy.

The Improved Competencies

Like all bureaucracies, the State Department had its share of mediocre backwaters, and that kind of placement would not do for refugees. State's attitude about refugees had to evolve into a more hospitable environment to recognize RP's mission and its unusual character and needs—and to stretch to meet the challenge. Reliable support beyond the top tier would be needed. That support came slowly at first, and over time it rose to the required level.

Reciprocal rewards came from RP's acquired competencies: budgeting, fiscal management, contracting and procurement, human resource management, information technology, evaluation, and other critical program management skills. RP's learning years gave State a laboratory to experiment and learn to manage programs, not a usual State function. These competencies were harnessed and tested in ensuing years, as more programs fell under State's jurisdiction.

One crucial step forward, mentioned earlier, highlights the significance of RP's transformation in attracting high-quality Foreign Service Officers (FSOs). The bureau's first formal recruitment announcement of FSO positions produced no applicants, not one, from the worldwide system. I well remember my dismay upon learning that refugee work was considered unimportant and even detrimental to a successful FSO career, at that time. This deficiency was overcome, and it required State leadership and involvement. Over time, State's central management began to promote refugee work throughout its foreign and civil service systems. RP jobs became eagerly sought after, as many of the best and brightest took a hard look at humanitarian work. By 1984, *State Magazine* featured the Refugee Programs bureau as one of State's most challenging and rewarding places to work.[1] The reversal was so positive that contemporary Foreign Service Officers' careers lacking a humanitarian component were viewed as deficient. Refugee work moved out of State's backwaters. One critical element remained, to change the understanding and use of the *multilateral system*.

The Rejuvenated Use of the Multilateral System

The third reform was just as difficult: the Refugee Programs bureau had to prove that effective planning and management of crisis programs could occur in a *multilateral* context without sacrificing national interests or smothering passion, drive, or empathy. History is replete with unsuccessful attempts to reform the multilateral system. But this was exactly what we had to accomplish for RP's strategic goals—with cost-sharing by the international community.

The task of multilateral humanitarian system reform fell to Gene Dewey as deputy assistant secretary. In 1982, I charged him to lead a reform to assure that refugee relief, emergency, and protection needs were promptly and humanely addressed. He would speak for RP. His team would identify longer-term solutions, make political and financial burden sharing more equitable among governments, and test the adequacy of crisis recognition and response capabilities, starting with our own government.

Dewey found that multilateral deficiencies were more pronounced than we feared. The UN had gotten so caught up in mandates, legalities, and jurisdictional arguments that action was slowed or nonexistent in many areas. For example, during two of the most critical years (1980–1982), no lead UN agency had responsibility for the vulnerable Khmer while many were barely surviving on the Thai border. Under strong US urging, the UN Border Relief Organization, UNBRO, was established in 1982.

RP challenged the multilateral system to respond boldly to the survival needs of vulnerable refugees and encouraged partners to focus from the outset on root causes and solutions. Foreign and civil service officers assigned to RP were empowered to go beyond the norm to seek solutions. Their mandate included to identify, anticipate, mitigate, deter, address, and solve problems to every extent possible. Establishing creative and reliable solutions was primary. Quick fixes would be unacceptable. No vulnerable refugee population was to be ignored or abandoned. Under this reform mandate, humanitarian allies stayed in close touch with the diplomatic/political/military arms of their governments to assure that victims were placed and remained central in decision-making. As the record confirms, the reforms launched by Gene Dewey's team reinvigorated the multilateral system of that era, going far beyond even lofty expectations.

Leading by example, US Refugee Programs influenced UN agencies to review and incorporate strengthened emergency response capabilities into their arsenals. Refusing to accept continued UN failure, RP's assessment of deficiencies in the Horn of Africa led to the creation of OEOA (*see* chapter 33), and to the creation with UNBRO of a new model for critical emergency response. According to Dewey in 1985, many regarded OEOA's formation as perhaps the UN's finest hour. The *multilateral agencies* showed eagerness to improve their emergency response abilities if given essential tools.

United Nations High Commission for Refugees Emergency Training

UNHCR and other multilateral agencies lacked training or equipment for the refugee decade's crises. Rather than continually pondering the problem or criticizing, RP led corrective reforms. Shocked over the UN's poor handling of refugee emergencies during 1983–85 in Africa's greater Horn region, the US Government announced that its future support would depend on UNHCR and other UN agencies developing response capabilities and performing to high expectations. Existing deficiencies threatened lives and could not be tolerated.

Because of these concerns, relations between RP and UNHCR leadership reached an all-time low. This breach between partners alarmed UNHCR Chef de Cabinet George Gordon Lennox and UNHCR's Emergency Unit Chief Phil Sargisson, and they began an intense search for common ground with the US Government. Phil Sargisson knew funds would likely be unavailable within UNHCR and contacted Diana Morris at the Ford Foundation to propose they provide funds for emergency response training. Phil's call led to a Ford Foundation decision to provide $300,000, on condition that the US Government at least match their grant. The US commitment through RP was $600,000; the government of the Netherlands committed $50,000.

The United States wanted to prove to UNHCR leadership that training was essential. Therefore, one year the government earmarked (through RP and over strong UNHCR objections) a percentage of each regional contribution for training. Momentum was increasing, as Phil Sargisson and UNHCR's Omar Bahket flew to Washington to work out the details with Tex Harris and Don Krumm of our team.

Within a short period, training was inaugurated at the University of Wisconsin's Disaster Management Center, known as DMC. Working with Intertect consulting firm's Paul Thompson and Fred Cuny, the DMC agreed to expand its curriculum from natural disaster response to include UNHCR emergency refugee relief concerns. Soon scores of staff had received technical training in emergency water, sanitation, public health, and shelter techniques.

Thus emerged the ubiquitous blue emergency handbook, a step-by-step guide to life-saving services co-written (1980, '81) by Mark Malloch Brown and Nicholas Morris of UNHCR. The handbook was continually improved and more widely distributed. The training program enhanced UNHCR's emergency capacity, as its later performance demonstrated. Later, the program included organizational development and sectorial management courses. Staff sought training opportunities to sharpen skills and enhance career advancement. Training for implementing partner NGOs and asylum country officials was also added.

These changes instilled an institutional culture of emergency response and training that endured long after our time. By 1990, eighty UNHCR staff had completed the advanced "training of trainers" program. There were twenty-seven training "focal points" in Geneva offices and over thirty training coordinators in the field. An organizational evaluation a decade later highlighted the value of the program to UNHCR's development as having helped develop and forge stronger relationships with private organizations helping refugees. The credibility of UNHCR had been enhanced. "And the high quality of some of the training programmes has certainly helped improve services to refugees."[2] That assessment expressed achievement of our goals in this matter.

When Gene Dewey became the deputy UNHCR high commissioner in 1986, the training unit under Phil Sargisson came under Dewey's direct supervision and received even more high-level attention. It became clear that partner organizations should not assume the UN to be unable or unwilling to do a better job; the key lay in working with them to provide staff training and other resources needed for first-class work.

Emergency Management Capabilities

The Emergency Management Unit (EMU) in the Refugee Programs bureau was an innovation staffed with enterprising officers to anticipate and spot emerging crises. Its mission was to provide RP leaders with crucial early warning alerts to jump-start stalled operations and energize or organize humanitarian action where other actors were absent or unqualified.

Given a successful record of accomplishment during those pivotal years, I was astounded to learn that the EMU was abolished following my departure. The apparent reasoning was that global humanitarian crises had diminished to the point regional offices could handle them. Sadly, unforeseen crises requiring globally coordinated EMU-type action did not diminish.

Leadership and Management Philosophy

The RP leadership style and philosophy were direct: rather than always "leading the charge" or "leading from behind," the team worked alongside partners to assure prompt delivery of lifesaving protection and aid. We had to be confident that (1) the UN and other multilateral agencies stepped forward smartly to lead humanitarian responses under their purview; (2) the governments supported and ceded enough ground for leadership to take root and grow; and (3) the NGOs respected and adhered to the lead role of multilateral teams. Lead agencies were thus pushed to go beyond coordination to integrate partners' efforts proactively, organizing, and sequencing service delivery and assistance for targeted results. Lead agencies and team leaders had to find and end duplication, overlap, and inefficiencies.

Multilateral organizations and teams were incentivized to achieve both operational effectiveness on behalf of emergency victims and financial burden sharing on behalf of taxpayers. They had to assure strict oversight of and guidance to the team members receiving donor funds.

Under no circumstances did donors put multilateral organizations on autopilot. Performance was constantly monitored. Humanitarian political leaders stood up to aggressors, opened doors, and led the way to humanitarian solutions. Two historic examples are President Carter's resolution to forge an Indochina refugee solution and President Reagan's persistent leadership to save the Soviet Jews.

Successful Journey

Secretary of State George Shultz provided an authoritative and cogent summary of the *refugee decade experience* six years into the Reagan administration. Two weeks after my departure, he testified before the Senate Judiciary Committee on Proposed Refugee Admissions for FY 1987.[3] The secretary's starting point was the inauguration of President Reagan after the still-smoldering refugee shocks of the previous decade:

- The massive exodus of refugees from Vietnam, Cambodia, and Laos
- The flood of refugees into Somalia and Ethiopia
- The arrival on US shores of 150,000 Cuban and Haitian entrants in early 1980
- The refugee flight from Afghanistan—3.5 million men, women, and children

He spoke with pride of the refugee and other humanitarian work the United States continued to support throughout Africa, in the volatile Middle East, in the Soviet Union, and in the Western Hemisphere.

Secretary Shultz testified that the pursuit of an international, multilateral approach to refugee solutions was an integral part of this historic accomplishment. America had consistently taken the lead in working to strengthen international mechanisms to deal with the expanding scope of global refugee problems. He named UNHCR, ICRC, and ICM as three international organizations that addressed survival challenges of the world's ten million refugees and stood as their first line of defense. The secretary emphasized the benefits of close cooperation with allies and partners like Australia, Canada, Japan, and Western European countries that had likewise made significant contributions. America was not alone. More than ever, we were part of a well-functioning global system of governments and international and private organizations that multiplied our resources and magnified our impact. These patterns of international cooperation served not only our national and foreign policy interests but also those of the world's refugees.

Significant Priority Shift

Refugee problems are best solved in their *home regions*. Recognition of the fact was a significant development during the *refugee decade*. Limited *third-country resettlement* was reserved for those critical cases where *regional settlement* or *repatriation* was not possible. This strategic shift allowed significant American resources to go to the increasing numbers of refugees surviving closer to their homes, to help them until they could return in safety and dignity. Tables 1–9 and Graph show important US accomplishments during the refugee decade; every number stands for a person who survived, whereas many others did not.

38

CHANGES IN DIRECTION

POSITIVE RP RESULTS HAD ADDED UP MEASURABLY BY LATE fall 1985, showing much had been carried out since the bureau's shaky startup. Domestic resettlement was operating well. Budget and resettlement numbers were finalized for the coming year. The once-menacing Falasha crisis was easing. And, our multiple task forces were adequately staffed and funded for the emergencies confronting them. A contentious relationship with the refugee coordinator had ended when the coordinator left. American influence in international refugee matters stood at an unprecedented high, and the usually reluctant international institutions now consulted regularly with RP on policy and operational matters.

In recent months, Gene Dewey and I had strongly inserted our views into UN decision-making, successfully lobbying for the candidate preferred by the United States to head the UNHCR. And Gene would be asked to be the deputy of that organization.

Sensing a welcomed easing among RP's relationships and accomplishments, Gene and I boarded a flight to New York for UN meetings, anticipating a longed-for victory lap. Within a few hours, I was in my room at a hotel in the relatively calm Turtle Bay area of Manhattan not far from the UN headquarters building. There was a dinner to be held that night.

I answered the room phone as I was dressing to go out. The hotel operator announced a call from Washington, and then came the voice of RP's Bob Funseth. "Jim, have you heard? Jonathan Moore has been named to replace you as head of RP."[1]

... WHAM.
I need a moment to absorb this.

When Funseth and I disconnected, I began to pace and to gather my thoughts. Even though I was ready to hang up my RP spurs, I was saddened to learn of my replacement without even a "heads up" from State leaders. And what did I know about Jonathan Moore? Of course, I knew about his service as a member of the Ray Panel while director of Harvard's Kennedy School of Government. I had been aware of his recent search for an appointment at State with help from a few State insiders. Now, he was set to replace me.

I returned to my Washington office two days later as planned and wanted to meet right away with Secretary Shultz. I felt determined to let him know that I felt let down, even betrayed, by being kept in the dark on this looming change. Except for Bob Funseth's precipitate call, when and how might I have learned of it? At eleven a.m., I showed up at the secretary's office ready for a showdown. There would be a brief delay, so I waited in the reception area.

What happened while I waited I can only call an epiphany. Moving away from stunned displeasure to a sense of unexpected calm, my thoughts sparked. I had been so blessed to have answered the call to set up the bureau and serve refugees. I had accepted long ago that we at RP might never be able to measure the real differences we made in survivors' lives, but I believed it to be substantial. *Why should I now be upset?* I reflected on one of the greatest experiences any State Department officer had ever had. I had helped take the floundering refugee programs bureau through seven years from infancy to maturity, due largely to the growth of a remarkable team.

During most of the journey, I had been with Secretary Shultz after his appointment as State's leader. I respected and admired him greatly. What cause did I have to be angry or upset, given that RP, with his full support, had laid the foundation for a strong and enduring institutional capability in the State Department? A notably committed team had been formed, making RP into a linchpin for what was to come, whatever futures a perplexing world might hold. In fleeting time, waiting outside his office, I realized my present desire. *I want to go out on a high note.*

As those thoughts gelled, I was told the secretary was free and was led into his office. We shook hands, sat, and I began to thank him on behalf of the refugee programs' team and myself for the opportunity to serve.

Characteristically, he listened attentively. In a few memorable moments, I sensed that Secretary Shultz understood even my unspoken disappointment about being replaced so abruptly. He had been led to believe I would demand another high-level assignment.

He responded in his familiar measured, mellow tone, "Your refugee team has done a great job, and America has been the beneficiary."

I did not mention a next assignment, believing I could count on him if or when the time might come. As I left his office, a sense of sweet relief flooded over me.

Reassigned to the Foreign Service Institute's Senior Seminar, I had the opportunity to interact with many public and private authorities and to travel extensively in the United States to learn about major problems facing the country from experts in a wide range of fields. The next phase of my career began.

◊

In 1988, the Reagan administration, through Secretary Shultz, named me as the US candidate for a post I welcomed, director general of the Intergovernmental Committee for Migration (ICM) in Geneva, Switzerland. The organization was about to be renamed the International Organization for Migration (IOM). I was elected to two five-year terms, 1988 (Reagan) and 1993 (Clinton). As more crises arose, Jean and I traveled to many troubled and stimulating parts of the world. We returned home to the United States before Thanksgiving Day, 1998. Readjusting, I advised organizations helping refugees and migrants and was honored with speaking opportunities, including at my alma mater, Furman University: "The Perils of Unresolved Humanitarian Crises: Focus Middle East."[2]

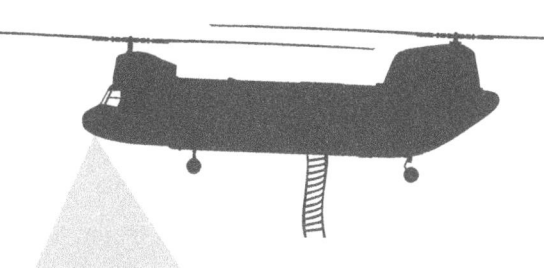

BOOK FOUR
AND NOW ...
A Test of Civilization

39

ABOVE ALL, DO NO HARM

ON SEPTEMBER 11, 2001, AMERICA AND THE WORLD CHANGED. The shaken nation's characteristic openness turned to various degrees of caution and distrust regarding the world beyond its borders. How to prevent future terrorist attacks like September 11 became the main topic of national and homeland security debates and would impact the nation's attitudes toward refugees and migrants for decades to come.

Changes in American concerns about future refugee resettlement did not need to change American empathy and leadership on behalf of refugees and migrants. Sadly, however, it became even more important we never forget that American legal and humanitarian policies could still energize and positively influence international responses to the world's humanitarian tragedies, if we would exert the essential political will to reject fear and move forward.

During the next fifteen years, humanitarian crises tested the international humanitarian system continually, bringing many adaptations to deal with escalating human and security challenges. My passion for humanitarian activism was heightened by a sense of even greater global distress from 2011 forward.

As work on this book progressed, I reflected that in fewer than twenty years the American refugee programs had descended from the mountain top, praised worldwide, to a position feared by some in authority. Suddenly, vulnerable people, refugees from Syria and other places in the Middle East, were viewed as a collective Trojan horse about to release hordes of foreign terrorists to murder and plunder unsuspecting citizens.

Much public consternation arose from perceptions of failed national and international efforts to solve recent humanitarian disasters, particularly in war-torn Syria, and the wider problems these failures thrust on the Middle East, Europe, Africa, South Asia, and the United States.

Why did the humanitarian system that worked so well earlier seem close to collapse at a time of such daunting human need? Why had multitudes of civilians been killed or displaced with impunity, while others remained under threat six years into so-called Arab Spring uprisings?

Syria had become a global concern. Researching the roots and background of that humanitarian crisis and traveling to the region, I came to see multiple reasons for these failures:

- Weak and half-hearted efforts to end the Syrian civil war
- Attention diverted to the nuclear deal with Iran
- Misdirected humanitarian strategies
- Inadequate financing of intergovernmental and private partners
- De facto placement of victims far from the center of allied decision-making (they had, in fact, been exiled to the periphery)
- Low priority or interest in comprehensive solutions
- American foreign policy leaders hugging the sidelines

These failures had allowed a brutal Syrian dictator, vigorous power competitors, and terrorist expansion dreams to keep the regional conflict fueled and expanding. I vowed to better understand the lagging responses to this crisis before proceeding further. This book, after all, had to be more than a history of the earlier refugee decade. To be useful, it also needed to elaborate on that legacy as a guide for current and future humanitarian leaders, especially concerning the historical precedents for their work.

My Mission

It did not take long to spot that, unlike the Indochina crisis, the Syria response had not been guided by strategic partner agreement on the centrality of victim protection and assistance, with its beacon—the quest for *durable solutions*—constantly in view. It appeared to have been guided by impulsive political improvisations that gave scant attention to likely consequences or the considerable support needed to make present approaches successful.

The expanded mission of this book was born, to use the ongoing Syrian crisis to illustrate the essential need for present and future complex humanitarian crises to be guided—from outset to solution—by strategic planning and bold action to keep central the safety and welfare of victims through international attention and action. Documenting the likely consequences of failure to undertake such planning became an important part of that mission.

My observations (ending in February 2019 to meet publishing schedules) contrast present approaches to earlier Indochina responses, which I believe remain a viable model to guide future humanitarian planning and action.

Unless the world changes dramatically, there will be many complex humanitarian crises in the years ahead. Some we might predict now, others are not yet on the horizon. We cannot change what has happened in Syria and elsewhere to date, but we can help launch the search for a "better way" forward and avoid preventable mistakes.

Human and Strategic Consequences

The Syria humanitarian programs were poorly planned, executed, and funded from the outset, in 2011. Consequently, early mistaken strategies propelled the response into a massive crisis four years later: before screening or vetting, victims were allowed to bypass (or leave) Middle East *first asylum* or home locations for *self-selected* countries in Europe. There they requested *political asylum.* Media reports chronicled how more than a million asylum seekers—including migrants from Africa and Asia—surged into Germany and other Western European countries in 2015 (and more continued to arrive). Flawed responses set in motion forces that were beyond the control of asylum governments. They were unprepared and bewildered by the chaotic mass entry of asylum seekers. The political asylum system was quickly overwhelmed, thwarting needed course corrections, until it was too late. Countless lives were shortened, abused, displaced, or disrupted as consequences of earlier mistakes became painfully obvious.

Tragic results mounted, illustrated by the harsh outcomes many experienced. Those who saw media repetition of heart-wrenching photos of three-year-old Alan (Aylan) Kurdi will never forget. His body washed up on a beach in Turkey in September 2015. His family had fled Syria in search of safety. The child drowned in the sea between Turkey and Greece, near the Greek island of Kos. His mother and brother also drowned. All had tried to find a new life. This family became yet another symbol of systemic failures that led to desperation, risks, and tragedies of hundreds of thousands of Syrians, Iraqis, and others.[1]

Syria and the Arab Spring

To understand fully the roots of the crisis in Syria, go back to March 2011, when a group of students in Deraa, Syria, painted on their school's wall the "Arab Spring" slogan: "The people want to topple the regime." The Syrian president Bashar Assad's security forces arrested and tortured them. People across the country took to the streets to support the students, and Assad forces responded with deadly force, shooting into unarmed groups of demonstrating civilians. Many were killed, and thousands were arrested and tortured. Yet a new movement appeared to build.[2]

That Arab Spring event, one of many, had devastating consequences for the Middle East. Civil war and bloodshed soon engulfed Libya. In Iraq, American troops were withdrawn, and the Shiite prime minister turned the US-trained armed forces into a radical sectarian militia. Soon, a deadly Islamic State organization named ISIS appeared in both Iraq and Syria. Unimaginable consequences followed, including a wider war spilling across borders and, as described, "radical jihadists established the faux-state that al-Qaeda could never achieve."[3]

The region was destabilized, and millions were uprooted and on the move. Over the next four years, Syria was devastated by constant war and destruction. The vast movement of people was contained in the region, either through *internal displacement* or, increasingly, in neighboring asylum countries. Unfortunately, the international community provided less than half to two-thirds of the funds needed to humanely accommodate the millions in need throughout this period, and living conditions for most of them rapidly deteriorated.[4] Few returned home and *resettlement* out of the asylum region was almost nonexistent.

By 2015, from a pre-war population of 22.4 million, half the country's citizens either had been displaced within Syria (5.6 million), fled to neighboring asylum countries (five million), or died in the conflict (250,000–300,000). Those in neighboring asylum countries included three million in Turkey, 1.1 million in Lebanon (where they accounted for 25 percent of the population), and the remainder in Jordan, Egypt and Iraq. This massive disruption happened as prominent, able nations failed to comprehend the disaster's reality and arrange for victims.

In mid-2015, a growing number of restless younger asylum seekers became anxious for something better. Because of geographic proximity, their eyes were on European states. Growing numbers planned the next leg of their quest. They self-selected future asylum locations and durable solutions.

When they began to arrive in Germany, Chancellor Angela Merkel surprised everyone by changing course and declaring that the right to asylum in Germany had "no limit." She speculated that 800,000 might come.

The flood gates were opened.

From September to December 2015, four and a half years into Syria's Arab Spring, the aftermath included more than one million Middle Eastern, African, and South Asian asylum seekers fleeing to Europe, quickly overwhelming receiving nations' reception and resettlement capacities. Over four million others remained in asylum in nearby Middle East countries. This was the largest mass movement of refugees and migrants since World War II, and the world's humanitarian system, their last hope, was on the verge of collapse. Who could have imagined 300,000 people slaughtered as the world wavered indecisively, including the United States? Hindsight shows that too many warnings were ignored. And the crisis in Syria, though alarming and newsworthy, represented just a portion of the Middle East under siege.

Late in 2015, the Syrian conflict approached its fifth year and the vast scale of infrastructure destruction foisted on the country came into plain view: some 2.1 million homes, half the country's hospitals, and over seven thousand schools destroyed. The future for a whole generation of Syrians was likely lost; damage was estimated at a staggering $270 billion, and rebuilding could run to more than $300 billion, per a UN expert. That was five times the amount spent on reconstruction in Iraq earlier.[5] Adding insults to injury, Islamic State militants demolished many of the country's archaeological treasures. More victims fled to an overwhelmed and unprepared Europe struggling to cope with over a million asylum seekers, and the EU predicted more to come.

A Paradigm Shift

"We are witnessing a paradigm shift," said a leading humanitarian, António Guterres, then UN high commissioner for refugees and later UN secretary general, in an August 2015 report.[6] Political leaders, the report said, had failed to protect conflict victims when they had the chance and thereby put millions of lives at risk.

The UNHCR report revealed the first signs of a worldwide, shaking, magma-rising volcano. They reported in June 2015 that a global exodus of refugees, *asylum seekers*, and people forced to move within their home country *(internally displaced))* was underway and rising to epic proportions. Only a year after those spiraling population movements surpassed fifty million in 2013 for the first time since World War II, they broke new records when they surged an additional 20 percent in 2014, to sixty million people, a staggering number that included about twenty million *refugees* and forty million *internally displaced persons* and *forced migrants*. The rapidly escalating figures revealed a world of renewed conflict, with wars (at least fifteen wars erupted or reignited in the previous five years) in the Middle East, Africa, Asia, and Europe. Families and individuals were driven from their homes in desperate flights for safety. An average of nearly forty-five thousand a day joined the ranks of people either on the move or stranded far from home.[7]

My fears were confirmed by the public warning of Alexander Betts of the Refugee Studies Center at Oxford University: "There's a real risk that we're seeing the *unraveling* [emphasis added] of the refugee regime that was created in the aftermath of the Second World War on the basis of cooperation and reciprocity."[8] He noted that governments were not stepping up to assist commensurate with the scale of the problem, as they did in previous conflicts, including in Southeast Asia, the Balkans, and Central America.

Problems in Syria and the Mediterranean area did not occur without early warnings of regional disruption, including bloody popular uprisings. Dictatorial powers prevailed, yet warring factions notched up resistance. The Syrian tragedy intensified year-by-year after 2011, as more degradation became known. The clear and disturbing signs were ignored or reasoned away.

Human Suffering Hard to Imagine

"It was hard for us in 2011, 2012 to look this far out and imagine how bad this could actually get," said Julie Smith, a national security advisor to Vice President Joe Biden. "We allowed that optimism (that Bashar al-Assad would fall and the rebels would win) to color our policy decisions."[9]

A national terrorism report in 2015 recounted one important indicator: Iran's ongoing buildup of proxies. "In 2014, Iran continued to provide arms, financing, training, and facilitation of primarily Iraqi Shia and Afghan fighters to support the Assad regime's brutal crackdown that has resulted in the deaths of at least 191,000 people (by the end of 2014) in Syria."[10]

"The Absence of Public Clamor"

There were some warning voices. In a December 2013 article, Morton Abramowitz, legendary ambassador to Thailand during the Indochina refugee crisis and later to Turkey, warned of deadly results if the international community, especially America, remained strikingly detached from the humanitarian crisis in Syria. Unlike prior American leadership and public support to relieve massive human suffering in crises like Rwanda and Cambodia, he warned, the American public and government were complacent about the Syrian conflict. Abramowitz noted American public passivity of over two years, merely watching rather than acting on the continuing destruction of the highly-developed nation of Syria:

> Greater humanitarian assistance is seen as the only way of helping millions of beleaguered people in an uncertain time—an extraordinary admission of political failure … The absence of public clamor had made it easier for the Obama Administration to stay on the sidelines, seeking empty UN resolutions and getting away with providing funds for humanitarian relief without doing more to resolve the underlying issue.[11]

Who cares?

Valerie Amos, outgoing UN under secretary general for humanitarian affairs and emergency relief coordinator, raised a chilling question in April 2015: "Does anyone care about Syria?" As the world looked on, she said, over 220,000 people had been killed and about eight million displaced. Three months later, July 2015, one of the major Syrian opposition parties reported "a death toll commonly estimated at between 200,000 and 300,000 people (though it's certainly higher), more than eleven million displaced and numerous cities in ruins."[12]

During her visits to disaster areas in the region, Amos was asked repeatedly: "Why has the world abandoned us? Why does nobody care?" These questions were not directed at the humanitarian agencies, she claimed, but at permanent UN Security Council members and politicians.

Abramowitz and Amos are savvy humanitarians who came to the same conclusion: action at the political level to place victims at the center of decision-making had been missing. Its absence blocked the path to humanitarian solutions.

Their warnings were ignored.

Policy Blunders

As far back as May 2015, vulnerable populations had been growing, yet still no European policy was in place to handle the increasing reception and integration needs, much less future requirements. On August 9, 2015, the European Commission president, Jean-Claude Juncker, proposed a plan for 120,000 resettlement places (besides forty thousand already pledged) for refugees, shared out among more than two dozen European countries.[13] At the end of October, an emergency summit in Brussels considered increasing the capacity for EU governments to receive about 100,000 more asylum seekers. After lashing out at one another's ineffective handling of the continent's greatest immigration crisis since World War II, they agreed to slow the chaotic flow of people moving up from Greece and provide more shelter as winter approached.[14] (By early 2016, fewer than one thousand slots had been used to resettle refugees.) Pope Francis said those who closed the door to migrants seeking protection should ask for forgiveness from God.

While the world's humanitarian problems continued to accelerate by frightening leaps and bounds—with no sign of abating—the generous spirit of earlier days that led to humanitarian solutions was evaporating. Solutions hostile to refugees and migrants ("blame the victims") gained momentum and support. The divisive issue of religion had entered the dialogue earlier, with the Hungarian prime minister warning Europe against allowing in Muslim families, while other leaders retorted that Christian values demanded helping the less fortunate, regardless of religion. Slovakia, which said it would grant asylum only to Christians, hardened its policy: no refugees. Others followed suit.

The US Holocaust Memorial Museum issued a report in October 2015 about religious persecution carried out by the Islamic State. The report found that ISIS committed crimes against humanity, ethnic cleansing, and war crimes against Christians, Turkmen, Shabak, Sabaean–Mandaean, and Kaka'I people. But it concluded that only the actions against the Yazidis constituted genocide.[15] (In a March 2016 report, the State Department added Christians and others at risk.)

Regarding the Mediterranean boat people crisis in 2015, Director General Bill Swing of the International Organization for Migration (IOM) called for immediate action. The IOM leader compared this "lose-lose" outcome in the Mediterranean with the "win-win" outcome achieved forty years earlier with the boat people of Indochina. Swing said the absence of a coherent migration policy led to a "lose-lose outcome, and he commiserated:

> The sad losers, of course, are the unfortunate migrants shamefully perishing in the waters or deserts each year by the thousands .... Also losing are the citizens and their elected representatives, who watch helplessly as their laws and regulations are flouted by the hundreds of thousands of irregular migrants who do manage to enter Europe, despite the danger .... This is madness.[16]

Reports of rising boat departures in the Mediterranean Sea surfaced, and European policy makers proposed to reinforce naval forces, conduct mass deportations, and destroy smugglers' boats to dissuade boat departures. Human rights groups criticized Europe's focus on a military response to smuggler networks, arguing "that destroying ships will do nothing to ease the surging demand for illegal entry into Europe and may force migrants to take even greater risks. Migrants could become unintended victims of any attempts to destroy smuggler vessels."[17] Human traffickers continued to exploit and profit from this tragedy.

Until early August 2015, Italy had been the top destination country for asylum seekers trying to reach Europe. That distinction then shifted to Greece, a country poorly equipped to receive them. The northeastern Greek island of Lesbos became the most popular gateway to the European Union and earned the reputation as a twenty-first century 'Ellis Island.' Of the nearly one million people who arrived in Europe by sea in 2015, over 800,000 came through the Greek islands and more than half of those landed on Lesbos. Asylum seekers and migrants were using this strategic location to move on to northern Europe, hoping for asylum and work. The Coast Guard operating near Lesbos reported an average four to five rescues a day, as overloaded boats capsized or stalled on the high seas. Approximately 78 percent of arrivals on Greek shores were Syrian. The Italian Coast Guard reported rescuing 1,800 people from seven overcrowded vessels on one July 2015 day. Five corpses were found on a rubber boat. To their credit, both the Italian and Greek Coast Guards continued heroic rescues.

Nightly, large asylum seeker groups in Calais tried to force their way through the rail tunnel linking France and Britain. They severely disrupted the flow of goods and people between the two countries, thereby provoking public anger. After Britain and France enacted tougher security measures at the end of August, Calais became a pressure cooker. Calais had to close the asylum seekers site.

The dangerous voyages continued uninterrupted, and death statistics worsened. Meanwhile, the EU sought reform strategies and agreements.

Overflow to Europe

When human displacements overflowed into Europe, I was saddened by Sunday headlines on August 30, 2015, reporting that the European asylum seeker crisis and the Mediterranean boat people crisis had merged into one. Governments were unprepared when the twin tragedies struck: seventy-one people discovered suffocated in a truck filled with asylum seekers trying to reach Austria, and 117 boat people drowned off the Mediterranean coast of Libya. There were unconfirmed reports of other boats sinking. This meant over 3,500 reported boat people deaths in 2015.

By the year's end the figure would rise to 3,700 (over 5,000 drowned in 2016). Most were from Syria and Iraq and, increasingly, Africa and South Asia. Over one million desperate people ventured out on risky boat journeys in 2015, and we learned that international crime syndicates were (and still are) behind some of these boat schemes.[18]

On Sunday, September 5, 2015, the world awoke to this news: "Asylum-seekers arrive in Western Europe."[19] Refugees previously trapped in Hungary limped across the border into Austria. German Chancellor Angela Merkel said her country expected to take in large numbers of asylum seekers. Canada, Sweden, the United Kingdom, and others said they planned to offer permanent residency to Syrian refugees that year or the next. Pope Francis pleaded with Catholics in Europe to take in refugees. Chancellor Merkel called for mandatory quotas to spread the burden across Europe.

European Union Defensive Actions

European Union (EU) governments suddenly realized the massive and disruptive problems they confronted and took defensive actions to blunt the onslaught. Professor Heaven Crawley of Britain's Coventry University described Europe as plagued by internal division and focusing on keeping people out rather than honestly reckoning what should happen once they arrived.[20] Europe's confusing and increasingly negative responses culminated in a late February 2016 reality check by international media, concluding that doors all over Europe were slamming shut.

Key developments revealed that an alarming relationship was developing between the Middle East and Europe that presaged the dismantling of a historic civilization in Syria and a valued asylum safety net in Europe.

Donald Tusk, president of the European Council, warned potential asylum seekers: "Do not come to Europe. Do not believe the smugglers. Do not risk your lives and your money. It is all for nothing."[21]

Syrians caught trying to enter Europe without authorization would be barred from legal entry. No other nationalities would qualify for sanctuary, including Iraqis and Afghans.

Sunday, March 20, 2016, Chancellor Merkel's brokered deal to curb the flow of the migrants and refugees streaming into Europe through Turkey went into effect. All migrants who attempted to enter Europe via the Aegean Sea—including Syrians fleeing war—were to be sent back to Turkey. In return, Turkey would get visa-free travel to much of Europe, accelerated prospects for joining the European Union, and more financing to support almost three million refugees inside its borders. An unworkable provision of the deal was that Europe would roll out a "one for one" swap, under which one Syrian refugee would be flown by air to Europe for every Syrian returned to Turkey.

Yet, the slammed doors remained shut. Human rights groups were quick to denounce the agreement. They maintained it possibly violated international and EU law and was likely to cause more harm than help. They were concerned that more asylum seekers would be stranded in Turkey, a country that does not abide fully by the 1951 Refugee Convention.

Postulating that the almost incalculable damage to individuals, families, nations, and the humanitarian system could have been prevented (or surely lessened) by calibrated international action at the outset, it is hard to understand why it did not happen or was delayed. When asked about the delay, I point directly to two principal reasons: a desire to avoid distracting from the Iranian nuclear deal and the absence of will to end the Syrian civil war promptly. The lack of action on these fronts kept asylum seekers dangling on the fringes of foreign policy decision-making. They simply were not important enough.

Iran Nuclear Deal

The propriety of the US nuclear deal with Iran is not the issue here, but its timing and relevance to delayed humanitarian action are significant. Clearly, the P5+1 governments—United States, United Kingdom, Russia, France, China and Germany, plus the European Union had their eyes on Iran and sensitive nuclear negotiations. They did not want to rock the boat regarding an Iran deal. David Ignatius of *The Washington Post* wrote that Obama has had the 'slows' in Syria, because he didn't want to confront Iran's proxy force there, the Lebanese Hezbollah militia, and risk blowing up the nuclear talks.[22] Other critics countered that the deal almost guaranteed war, and *The Washington Post's* Michael Gerson called it "Obama's biggest failure."[23] President Obama had maintained that war was the only alternative to the nuclear deal with Iran.

The Obama administration had secured enough Senate votes to avoid defeat of the Iran deal, but Congress required quarterly certification of Iranian compliance. Iran complied with the agreement's requirements to close its nuclear weapons production infrastructure and the shipping of enriched uranium out of the country but continued to exploit agreement loopholes by repeatedly testing ballistic missiles that could carry nuclear warheads. The administration described such actions as violations of UN Resolution 2231, but responded with only minor symbolic sanctions.

Failed Peace Negotiations

In late 2015, the UN Security Council established the International Syria Support Group, ISSG, in Vienna and approved a peace process to end

Syria's civil war. The approving resolution called for negotiations between the Syrian government and the opposition to set up a transition government that would write a new constitution and hold elections within eighteen months. The status of the Syrian president, Bashar Assad, was left unclear, as was the designation of terrorist groups to be left out of the discussion. Staffan de Mistura was named UN envoy for Syria and instructed to guide the parties through these talks. Similarly, a Rome summit on December 13, 2015, endorsed a plan for a cease-fire in Libya, with a national unity government to follow. Diplomats said they wanted to stop Libya from becoming the next Syria.

Through 2016, the civil war tragedies made it nearly impossible to put and keep civilian victims of the conflict in a principal place in decision-making, as diplomatic efforts to end or calm the conflict were weak and ineffective. None of the warring parties in the Middle East conflict—the United States, Russia, Syria, Iran, ISIS, or their proxies—was called to task for their moral failings nor were they sufficiently pressed to rein in the wanton destruction and calamity. The potential victims were not valued or protected as the war dragged on.

After many rounds of combative negotiations among the parties throughout 2016 and 2017, featuring multiple cease-fires, resumption of hostilities, cessation of hostilities, endless rounds of talks between the American and Russian diplomats, little changed.

As civilization dithered on the sidelines, Bashar Assad, ostensibly going after ISIS terrorists, had a free hand to advance the war against opposition strongholds. With Russian and Iranian support, he used barrel bombs, thermobaric bombs and incendiary munitions cluster bombs, that destroyed Syrian hospitals, schools, homes, and the irreplaceable souls forced to flee their destroyed communities. Thousands, including children, were slaughtered.

The opposition was outgunned and militarily constrained, primarily because its major benefactor, the United States, opted both to stay out of the conflict or to provide arms for serious opposition response. Without question, America's reputation and prestige in the region took a big hit when President Obama drew a red line over further chemical attacks in 2015 and then capitulated.

Because of the restrictive parameters western partners imposed on themselves, calls went unheeded for humanitarian corridors or fly-over zones to protect innocent civilians. Each party drew inward, particularly the United States and its allies. They did not press the other side. Who will ever forget President Obama's rejection of proposals from the secretary of state Hillary Clinton, the defense secretary Leon Panetta and the CIA director David Petraeus to arm proxies or create safe zones to protect civilians?

Late in 2016, at least 400,000 Syrian citizens had been killed and one million injured. Approximately six million survivors had fled the country seeking asylum or resettlement, and nine million were displaced inside Syria, where life was no longer sustainable. Syria's largest city and stronghold for the Syrian opposition, Aleppo, was on the verge of destruction. As each new front in the war brought more tragedy, more casualties, hope waned for millions of war victims.

An all too frequent picture emerged, as one party violated peace agreements without fear of consequences and the other side acquiesced.

The slaughter continued, and the United States and Russia traded accusations and barbs and talked past each other. This frightening scenario brought into stark recollection the words of the French ambassador to the United Nations: "… the Syrian regime is continuing to systematically starve hundreds of thousands of civilians. These are war crimes. … There is a strong momentum here in the Security Council … to say, 'enough is enough.'"[24] He said all remember the previous Security Council failures: Guernica, Srebrenica and Grozny (he could also have added the Holocaust, Cambodia, Bosnia, and Rwanda), and that we were then seeing in Aleppo the horrendous repetition of those tragedies. If the international community would not wake up, he said, it would be equally culpable.

Russia sidestepped the calls for investigations, and it became clear there would be none unless the perpetrators agreed to be investigated. On October 8, 2016, Russia vetoed a Security Council resolution aimed at stopping the bombing of Aleppo, their fifth veto in as many years aimed at stopping the carnage. A Russian resolution to withdraw opposition fighters from Aleppo similarly was defeated in the deadlocked Security Council, as they gained only four votes.

Robert S. Ford, former US ambassador to Syria and senior fellow at the Middle East Institute said, "… there is no mechanism that can hold Moscow and Damascus accountable now."[25]

After assuring the capture of Aleppo and the defeat of opposition forces in late 2016, Syria, Russia, and Iran met in Astana, the futuristic capital of Kazakhstan, in late January 2017 to negotiate the terms of a Syrian peace agreement. The United States sat on the sidelines of the so-called peace negotiations.

Humanitarian Conditions, 2017 to early 2018

With entry to Europe through Greece essentially shut down, migrant boat routes switched to the Central European route through Italy, originating primarily in North Africa. But after serving as a safe harbor for hundreds of thousands of desperate migrants, Italy decided in April 2017 to strike a deal with Libya, one of the major North African departure points, to create a de facto migrant blockade. Under the deal, Italy would train Libyan guards to push back and detain migrants and to dispatch land, sea, and air vehicles to aid Libyan patrols.

Until August 2017, authorities had estimated 230,000 migrants were expected to arrive in Italy in 2017; about 70,000 (a 28 percent increase over 2016) had arrived by early June and 2,169 had drowned attempting to cross from Libya. The International Organization for Migration reported in late August 2017 that the number of migrants crossing the Mediterranean appeared to be leveling off, at least temporarily. Slightly over 121,000 arrived in the first eight months of 2017 compared with 273,000 for the same period a year earlier. There was no evidence of drownings in August, compared with 2,400 during the previous seven months.

Humanitarian advocates like Elizabeth Collett, director of Migration Policy Institute Europe, were quick to point out the dangers of drawing quick conclusions from the limited data of one month. She offered several reasons for the slowdown that could change quickly: the revamped Libyan Coast Guard, border changes in Niger (an important starting point for Italy and Europe), and Libyan militias paid by the government to keep migrants in place.

The day after the IOM August report, European leaders from France,

Germany, Italy, and Spain met in Paris with counterparts from Chad, Niger, and Libya (the popular embarkation points for Europe) to discuss plans to stem the flow. They came to several important agreements: expanded development aid for help to curb new outflows, tightened border controls along the African migration routes and the establishment of "hot spots" or reception centers along the way to process asylum claims prior to departure.

Others questioned the new European–African agreements on the grounds of workability, noting that recent experience has shown that the determined migrants continually explore new routes to Europe when other major routes close. The reporting from the International Organization for Migration revealed increasing reliance on a western Mediterranean route, with Spain a main destination, particularly the migrants from Morocco. Reports also noted an uptick in people exploring the dangerous Black Sea passage from Turkey to Romania. Especially alarming was news from the Turkish coast guard of twenty-three migrants drowned and forty rescued in September 2017 when a fishing boat sank off the coast of Kefken, near Turkey's Black Sea coast.

As feared, rescuers reported 23 people drowned in early November 2017. Seven hundred endangered migrants were pulled to safety from the Central Mediterranean, recovered by the European Union's naval mission. Seven people had been found dead and 900 had been rescued two days earlier. The Italian Coast Guard noted November as one of the busiest periods in recent months.

Human rights advocates quickly questioned the propriety of forcing migrants into deteriorating conditions in Libya. Aid groups like Human Rights Watch and other European humanitarian groups pointed out that the Italy–Libya deal would likely trap thousands of migrants in a country made all but lawless in the years since the death of Gaddafi, 2011. Reports in July 2017 had revealed the appalling conditions of returnees to Libyan detention centers. Equally alarming were reported conditions for many who remained in Libya. Since the fall of Gaddafi's government, rival regimes and armed groups had competed for influence and territory. Frequent clashes trapped citizens in their homes and created new no-go zones. Many feared the worst.

On December 12, 2017, Amnesty International charged the European governments with complicity in "grave human rights violations in Libya" due to continuing abuses from the Italy–Libya deal. They said up to 20,000 people were in Libyan detention centers, subjected to "torture, forced labor, extortion, and unlawful killings."[26] The EU statement said they shared Amnesty's concern but noted EU funding with favor. It had helped IOM return 15,000 Africans to their homes safely.

Regardless of the arrival dips, Italy unquestioningly paid a high price between 2015 and early 2018 while migration populations spiked. More than 620,000 migrants went to Italy during those years. Commenting on these developments, including the apprehension of an African asylum seeker for a beach gang raid, Nicola Latorre, chairman of the defense committee of the Italian Senate said, "With this frequency and these numbers, we can easily tell that, soon enough, we won't be able to handle it any longer."[27] Other Italian politicians like the center-left former prime minister Matteo Renzi (*see*king re-election in 2018) continued to feel immigration pressures. He advocated helping potential migrants in their home countries, a position normally embraced by the far right.[28]

In March 2018, the Italian election results were shocking. Two anti-establishment parties, the populist Five Star Movement and the anti-migrant League Party (far right, formerly the Northern League), captured over half the votes in the election and were expected to form the new leadership base. The traditional center-left and center-right parties suffered overwhelming defeats. Matteo Renzi lost decisively and quit the leadership of his party.

The current situation in Germany is almost as precarious. Beyond the unworkable EU–Turkey deal, the government—like other EU partners—was forced to reconsider its open policy for asylum seekers. Reacting to terrorist attacks, including the Christmas 2016 Berlin market attack by Tunisian asylum seeker Anis Amri (under deportation orders), they were forced to consider tough changes to an asylum system that many citizens say has exposed millions of Germans to risk. Typical of the reactions was German lawmaker Stephan Mayer's words, "You cannot apodictically separate security and asylum policy … [Anis] Amri came to Germany disguised as a refugee. The more people come here, the more likely it is there is going to be a villain among them."[29]

Interestingly, the Pew Research Center said more than half the 2.2 million asylum seekers who entered Europe from 2015 to 2017 were still awaiting asylum decisions a year later. About 40 percent, representing 885,000 asylum seekers, had been approved, and 52 percent were still awaiting decisions. The remainder had been ejected or returned.

Adding even more confusion to the mix, 2017 brought two new problems:

First, asylum seekers challenged the German government's authority to adjudicate their right to remain. Commenting on the impact on German courts, one judge told *Der Tagesspiegel* that it will paralyze the courts for years.

Second, the ban on family reunification for asylum seekers in subsidiary status became a political concern for Chancellor Merkel and her ruling Christian Democratic Union (CDU). The consequences of the 2015 surge had caused the German government to restrict family reunification to approved asylum applicants who met the strict *persecution* requirements of the Geneva Convention; and to grant subsidiary protection status to others. Subsidiary status denied entry to family members and imposed more stringent qualifications for obtaining a long-term license to stay in Germany. Subsidiary protectees grew rapidly: 0.6 percent in 2015; 41 percent in 2016; and 60 percent in the first half of 2017.

Efforts by Chancellor Merkel's Christian Democratic Union to form a new German Government after the fall 2017 elections (asylum seekers had been a key concern) with the Free Democratic and Green parties hit a serious snag over the family reunification policy. The chancellor then talked to the center-left Social Democrats about a "grand coalition," but the negotiations were delayed. Family reunification was a sticking point with them, as it had been with the Green Party. The agreement on a new coalition government was finally reached in March 2018, five months after the election.

The debate over family reunification in Germany brought questions about the German migration policy to the fore, like the one raised by Luise Amtsberg, Green Party member of parliament:

> Family reunification is one of the most important and best ways of allowing for legal migration. We always

complain that people are coming illegally over the Mediterranean, but in the case of family reunification, we can determine who comes and from where.[30]

Even though the EU devoted 1.85 billion euros (with 4.5 billion in the pipeline) to the two-year-old EU–Turkey deal, a March 2018 Migration Policy Institute Europe report warned that the European asylum system is still afflicted with many of the chronic weaknesses that "exacerbated the 2015–2016 crisis … and without a fundamental change in its thinking, the European Union risks repeating its mistakes if flows surge anew."[31]

In 2017, the Supreme Court of Greece rejected the arguments of two Syrian men that their return to Turkey be halted because it was an unsafe destination. That paradoxical decision brought into question the fate of thousands of refugees in Greece, as well as others planning to enter Greece to seek asylum.

Equally disturbing was news that only 32,000 people seeking asylum (of the 160,000 that EU nations agreed to relocate from Greece and Italy in September 2015) were resettled in member nations after more than two years. Sadly, in December 2017, the EU referred three members, Hungary, Poland, and the Czech Republic, to the top tribunal, the Court of Justice, for legal action over breaches of their obligations.

The present situations in Germany and Italy suggest that for the first time in recent memory the asylum seekers fleeing war and persecution will face great difficulty entering the major European signatory countries to file asylum claims. A cardinal principle of the 1951 Refugee Convention is under siege.

◇

Reflection on difficulties confronting Germany presently (and other EU countries) recalls similar problems Europe faced in the mid-1980s when I served as IOM director general. Germany was overrun by asylum seekers from many countries, and the German ambassador in Geneva (who served as UNHCR executive committee chairman in the mid-1980s) commiserated that Germany was paying more to house and maintain its unusually large and costly asylum population that year than UNHCR was paying for worldwide refugee care and maintenance.

When asked for help with this unsustainable problem by numerous German authorities, I advised that asylum seekers with mixed motivations had no choice but to try to go to Germany as asylum seekers because that was the only channel open to them. I suggested that legal immigration channels (to meet labor demands or for family reunion) like those used in several other industrialized democracies (Canada, Australia, New Zealand, Israel, and the United States) would take pressures off their asylum regime. But as none existed, they all came as political asylum seekers, regardless of motivation.

The director general of Doctors without Borders Bruno Jochum commenting on the situation in Europe said: "It's part of a general strategy to stop the coming flows at whatever cost… Today, European states are accommodating themselves, and pushing people back into situations of generalized mistreatment."[32]

Unfortunately, the root causes have not been solved, and the search for humane and workable solutions continues. Events of the last seven years make it clear that the failure to set a workable humanitarian strategy at the outset of this crisis has brought unintended yet great harm to millions of Syrians and other victims.

40

MYSTIFYING BREAKDOWN

THE HARSH LIFE IN ECONOMICALLY-STRESSED GREECE HAD killed optimism and caused Rama Wahed, like millions of Syrian refugees, to lose hope.

"We are stuck here," Rama yelled at her mother, Lamis. "Nobody cares what happens to us."[1]

Widowed and driven out by war, Lamis was responsible for her four children at what seemed a dead end in the Diavata refugee camp on the outskirts of Greece's second largest city, Thessaloniki. Daily life in the camp on the grounds of an abandoned toilet paper factory posed questions of human dignity. The housing, feeding, and other subsistence needs of asylum seekers stretched the family and local resources to the limit.

The host government and the camp residents like the Waheds had been led to believe the refugees would be moved soon, elsewhere in Europe. Yet, they remained among the multitudes dangling on a failing promise. The EU plan approved sixteen months earlier had envisioned a resettlement program to relieve Greece and Italy of 160,000 asylum seekers by resettling them across other member states. It had seemed a good plan. But now, in fall 2016, only 20 percent of that pledge had been honored; citing cultural differences and the fear of militants among asylum seekers, EU nations supplied few actual placements. Many European Union governments wanted to drop the pretense and scrap the relocation as completely unrealistic.

Elsewhere, first-asylum countries like Jordan were showing familiar signs of distress. A truck barreling into an army outpost on Jordan's northeastern border with Syria in June 2016 killed seven soldiers. Jordan had in mind to seal the border and deliver aid by crane to over 75,000 refugees at the Rubkan camp. The resource-strained country of 6.4 million was hosting 1.3 million refugees amid concerns that tens of thousands were going to Jordan from long distances, Deir Zour and Raqqa, the Islamic State's de facto capital.[2]

In tiny Lebanon, the lid was about to blow after the murder of a Lebanese, Raya Chidiac, by a Syrian worker in the city of Miziara. Local officials ordered the refugees to leave the town. Fears arose that violence might occur across Lebanon, where refugees are a quarter of the population, the highest concentration in the world.[3]

There was little wonder why Rama Wahed had screamed at her mother, "We never should have left home!"

And Lamis could only respond, "Have you seen the pictures of Aleppo? There is nothing left, my daughter. Go back to what?"[4]

Civilization's Challenge

An *engaged* world community would not tolerate the calamities that befell millions like the Wahed family, caught in the Syrian crisis vortex as it spiraled downward from 2011 on. An engaged world community would act decisively, as in the past, assuming its shared moral responsibility to protect and help the weak, the vulnerable, the persecuted, the "least of these among us." And yet, in the Syrian crisis, previously dependable nations ignored and violated those moral imperatives.

Why? The question and its answer are of existential importance.

In my view, this massive failure lies at the feet of the customarily reliable governments. Failing to react quickly to fast-changing realities, the United States and other countries displayed timidity and recklessness regarding the enveloping humanitarian disaster in Syria. Collectively (with a few rare exceptions), civilized society watched and talked as the disasters piled up for seven years.

This pileup highlighted vast, accumulated evidence of the national and international leaderless drift, including: precipitous withdrawal of US troops from Iraq in 2011 leading to the creation and expansion of al-Qaeda; unresolved brutal and murderous wars in Iraq and Syria, leaving millions dead or displaced; Libya splintered; the red line in Syria ignored; barrel bombs used; schools, hospitals, and historical icons destroyed; the Iran nuclear fiasco; the United States–Russia "reset button" debacle; Aleppo raped; regional first asylum stressed; Europe overwhelmed with non-vetted asylum seekers; "JVs" in Raqqa and Mosul; fruitless peace negotiations; ISIS spreading hate and fear around the world; serial terror attacks; scapegoated refugees and migrants; doors slammed shut; foreigners feared and distrusted; restrictive nationalism rising globally; and the list goes on. The inevitable result of these dysfunctions has been a mind-numbing strategic and political paralysis.

Since the Arab Spring uprisings in 2011, the strategic and political leadership of the world community has been woefully inadequate for its mission in Syria. The victims have been ignored and pushed around like pawns. The governments and citizens tolerated the repugnant and reprehensible crimes against humanity committed by Syria's ruthless dictator, Bashar Assad. Why?

Chemical Weapons Use by Syria

A barbaric chemical attack on August 21, 2013, gassed over 1,400 people in Ghouta, a Damascus suburb. Afterward, Syria joined the Chemical Weapons Convention prohibiting the "development, production, acquisition, stockpiling, retention, transfer or use of chemical weapons."[5]

A later United States-Russia agreement required Syria to dispose of 1,300 declared tons of chemical weapons. But an August 2016 review by the Organization for the Prohibition of Chemical Weapons (OPCW) based in the Hague, found that most of 122 samples taken in Syria contained evidence of potentially undeclared chemical weapons-related activities. Assad has not been held accountable.[6]

New American president Donald Trump was confronted with a chemical weapons attack in Syria within his first two months. Over eighty Syrian citizens were killed by nerve gas, most likely sarin, in the northwest Syria town of Khan Sheikhoun on April 4, 2017. Moved by photos of gassed child victims, President Trump ordered US strikes on Shayrat Airbase, Syria, used to launch the chemical attacks. He cited the "vital national security interest" of the United States and called on "all civilized nations to join us in seeking to end the slaughter and the bloodshed in Syria."[7]

This chemical attack was acknowledged by the UN Commission of Inquiry on Syria in September 2017, as it formally accused the Syrian regime of using the banned nerve agent sarin in the April attack.[8] The OPCW launched a fact-finding mission in February 2018, but acknowledged it could no longer apportion blame. Russia blocked renewal of its authority last year following Syrian government attacks.[9]

Over the next year, Assad's forces conducted more chemical attacks smaller in scale. Since those attacks drew no response from the United States or its allies, and since President Trump announced the imminent withdrawal of American troops, Assad presumed that chemical attacks against civilians could be carried out with impunity. Regrettably, almost a year to the day of the chemical attack at Khan Sheikhoun, Assad forces launched a similar attack on the Damascus suburb of Douma while clearing remaining opposition strongholds. More than 500 people were treated for symptoms of chemical reaction more severe than previous attacks, and almost fifty died.[10]

Five days later, global media reported the United States, Britain, and France had launched over one hundred missiles in coordinated attacks on the Syrian chemical research, production, and storage facilities near Damascus and Homs. Immediately Russia requested an emergency meeting of the UN Security Council to condemn these retaliatory strikes.[11] A familiar Syrian pattern emerged: strike, pull back, retaliate, test the limits of patience, strike again, pull back and retaliate again, always ratcheting aggression up. On April 15, Nikki Haley, ambassador to the UN, announced immediate US sanctions on Russia for the attacks, but the world was left puzzled when the president pulled back from that decision the next day.

Holocaust

Hidden until early 2017 were other atrocities carried out in Assad's name at Syria's Saydnaya Military Prison just outside Damascus. Amnesty International described it as a "human slaughterhouse." Based on a year's extensive research, they reported that between 5,000 and 13,000 Syrians were extrajudicially and brutally tortured and executed there between September 2011 and December 2015.[12]

The Syrian Network for Human Rights maintained in March 2017 that at least 106,727 people were still arrested or had been "forcibly disappeared." Ninety percent were detained in a brutal prison network where abuse and lethal neglect were used for the killing. In May 2017, the State Department reported these crimes continued without pause. The Syrian government had constructed and was using a crematorium to execute and dispose of the prisoner bodies, as many as fifty each day, evoking frightful memories of the Holocaust.[13]

The Abu Ghraib abuses evoked worldwide condemnation; why not Saydnaya?

And reports emerged that even worse torture may have been committed at Syria's military hospitals, like the one known as *601*, just a half mile from President Assad's palace. The victims were primarily the participants in Syria's 2011 Arab Spring uprisings. Investigators say the evidence coming from the military prisons and hospitals may offer some of the most compelling evidence yet uncovered of crimes against humanity.[14]

Consequences of "Leading from Behind"

Coming from the refugee decade era that prized timely and decisive humanitarian action, I could not compute the delayed and weak humanitarian response for Syria. Where were the leaders who would keep victims central in their attention and action and insist on targeted and comprehensive plans to protect them? Where were the leaders who would resist the temptation to dump the problem on the underfunded multilateral system and a handful of regional asylum governments? Where were the leaders who would assure the wherewithal to protect the defenseless?

Unlike the refugee decade, I had to deduce that inept political decision-making led to a troublesome conclusion: governments, including my own, had chosen no longer to lead the world in exceptional humanitarian deeds. Some yet unseen or unidentified leadership with a reinvigorating mindset would be needed to help regain the national and international humanitarian stature like the United States had earlier shown. Otherwise, many fear the unthinkable, a new age of humanitarian timidity.

According to the Islamic State coordinator for the Obama administration, US Marine General John Allen, no less than devastating was failure to act when Syria crossed the "red line" in 2013. If military strikes on Assad's chemical weapons units had been launched, the general maintained, they could have had a decisive impact on the war. Failure to respond, he said, raised a vital existential question for the United States: "Are we engaged enough morally that we are ready to take action ... ?"[15]

I make my harsh judgment about America's declining humanitarian leadership stature despite the evidence that the operational component of the US humanitarian apparatus in Syria performed better than could have been expected under such difficult motivational circumstances. The same is true for the intergovernmental and private organizations that continued to provide heroic lifesaving assistance in the face of daunting obstacles and damaging resource shortages. And who could fail to be impressed with the regional first-asylum hospitality given to millions by Turkey, Jordan, Lebanon, Egypt, and Iraq, usually at great national costs?

I must emphasize, however, that lacking the political will and courageous leadership, the humanitarian outcome of the Syria crisis was plagued from the outset. As the international community discovered in multiple complex human disasters over the years, humanitarian action cannot substitute for political courage and resolve; it depends on it. This perplexing paradox has led many informed participants to fear the global humanitarian spirit of former years has been lost and, unless reclaimed, will damn future humanitarian results to the same or worse outcomes. The decisions and choices made in this present hostile environment will reverberate far into the future.

With these frightening prospects, notwithstanding occasional flourishes, civilization cries out for nations to awaken to the dangers ahead and to work for the renewal of our lost humanitarian spirit and resolve. Civilization must be able again to believe that humanitarian action need not be feared. Who can, or will, lead such a global campaign?

Rather than pursuing multinational cooperation to solve global survival problems like Syria, much of the world is hard at work constructing barriers to renewal, digging the hole deeper. Some of the most egregious offenses have come, unfortunately, from the world's historic global humanitarian leaders. This raises an alarming question: can the world continue to count on the global community's humanitarian leadership, especially America's, going forward?

41

IS AMERICA STILL RELIABLE?

SHOCKED BY THE HUMAN INDECENCIES THAT LED TO ONE of the darkest periods in history and a cataclysmic world war, civilized society made a profound statement in the Universal Declaration of Human Rights in 1948. Led by the United States, the world agreed to create a new order of justice and human rights based on the inherent dignity of all people. Global institutions were created to give expression to this commitment, and they served the world well for more than a half century.

Our commitment to these valued principles is gradually eroding, and civilized societies must again rise to their defense. In many parts of the world, politicians and dissidents are trying to "define nationality based on the dehumanization of cultural outsiders—Muslims, migrants, and refugees."[1] Victims of conflict have been moved to the periphery of attention and decision-making. This cannot—and should not—stand.

As a participant and observer of world affairs, I have experienced the best of such tendencies and the worst, of which the evolving Middle East crisis is a current illustration.

America Adds to Middle East Turmoil

In August 2–4, 1990, the president of Iraq Saddam Hussein invaded US ally Kuwait, situated at the tip of the Persian Gulf. Although Kuwait and Saudi Arabia had claimed Iraq owed and should repay a $30 billion debt, Kuwait had not provoked Iraq. President George H. W. Bush amassed a "coalition of the willing" under UN auspices to counter the invasion and remove Iraqi forces from Kuwait.

President George W. Bush came into office in 2001 fearing that UN weapons inspectors had not been able to remove and destroy Iraq's suspected arsenal of mass destruction weapons. With mixed intelligence findings, he concluded that weapons remained and made the fateful decision to send US troops into Iraq in a pre-emptive strike to remove them. When few were found, it was clear that the US invasion had been precipitous.

After that conflict, America's diplomatic and military leaders inserted an American official into Iraq to guide reconstruction, and he had limited success. Consequently, what was probably an inevitable sectarian conflict accelerated, magnified, and lengthened, and the misery and disenchantment of the Iraqi people continued. In that fertile soil, the seeds of another Middle East disaster were planted, metastasized, and remain the root cause of current Middle East concerns.

When President Barack Obama took office in 2009, he adopted an extremely cautious and de-conflictive Middle East strategy and looked for ways to end American engagement without further losses. In 2011, an Arab Spring opposition revolt in Syria—and the government's harsh responses—set off a civil war. The next year, Assad threatened to use chemical weapons against his own people. In 2012 and 2013, as the civil war continued, reports came that he had, in fact, carried out his threat, injuring and killing civilians in Homs, Aleppo, and elsewhere. Crossing the red line brought no consequences from the Americans.

The civil war continued, and terrorist groups—reacting to the red line inaction—saw a weakness in their enemy, the United States. They multiplied, and the deadly al-Qaeda spread into other countries in the region, as ISIS.

The conflict and human suffering that began in Syria in 2011 displaced millions of civilians from their homes and villages, and many crossed borders for safety. A regional humanitarian crisis was born, and it spread.

Libya was one of the weak and vulnerable countries caught up in this distress.

In a puzzling move, President Barack Obama decided to remove the

Libyan dictator Muammar Gaddafi (2011). Puzzling, because Gaddafi had already removed Libya's weapons of mass destruction and was providing important intelligence assistance against terrorists. Justified on the grounds of human rights abuses, the United States and its allies *again* launched preemptive strikes that removed the dictator. But in doing so they plunged Libya into a black hole of chaos, anarchy, and despair. As happened too often in the Middle East theater—and especially on the humanitarian and refugee fronts—many US decisions (and sometimes indecisions) like this simply made things worse and put far more people in jeopardy.

The next administration inherited this daunting accumulation of past decisions, including the humanitarian and refugee fallout. President Trump and his team in 2017 pledged to radically stem the spread of worldwide terrorism. While given credit for working to help defeat ISIS and for proactively responding to more chemical attacks against civilians in Syria, the administration otherwise pursued limited humanitarian objectives in Syria and the Middle East. It announced a new America-First ("go-it-alone") strategy. Foreign policy adversaries—including Russia, Iran, and Turkey—took encouragement from that disclosure and moved to assume leadership in the Syria crisis.

Though the current administration did not generate today's Middle East problems, it has been thrust into the mix of decision-makers, concerning next steps. The president's December 18, 2018, announcement that US troops would soon withdraw from Syria led to confusion about future American intentions. Hopefully, there is still time to clarify this surprising announcement and set clear policies of concern and cooperation on behalf of the victims of this conflict.

Go It Alone

On the political level, the go-it-alone approach was on full display in the December 2017 announcement of the US decision to recognize Jerusalem as Israel's capital and move the American Embassy there (multiple congressional acts had mandated this action).[2] That decision was not unexpected, but the subsequent threats to "take names" and revoke billions in aid for governments voting for a UN General Assembly resolution opposing the move was unexpected. The Security Council vote was 14 to 1 against, and the General Assembly vote was 129 to 9 against (with 35 abstaining and 21 absent). All of America's important allies voted against the administration's position.

The aid threat was soon carried out, as the administration announced that its contribution to the UN Relief and Works Agency (UNRWA) for Palestinian Refugees was abruptly reduced from $125 million to $60 million for 2018.[3] In September, the US announced an end to its financial support for UNRWA completely and advocated changing the way the UN calculates Palestinian refugee numbers. The proposed recalculation would reduce the population of registered Palestinian refugees by a large percentage, back to the number registered when the agency was created in 1949.[4] Given the desperate plight facing the Palestinian refugees throughout the volatile Middle East, the UNRWA commissioner general was forced to plead with other donors to fill the gap. This was reminiscent of a similar situation RP faced in 1985 (*see* chapter 34).

◇

The consequences of America's go-it-alone strategy have affected many essential foreign policy functions.

Humanitarian Affairs

Nowhere has the go-it-alone approach been more harmful to near-term global engagement than the diminution of the State Department's leadership and management of humanitarian affairs. Since the new administration began in 2017, I have searched diligently to understand its evolving strategies and approaches to the world's humanitarian challenges. Early clues have been disheartening. First, we heard about an isolated and understaffed State Department, plus a proposal to trim its refugee budget by a third and its refugee admissions ceiling by half. Then came reports that State's Bureau of Population, Refugees, and Migration (PRM) might be abolished and its programs sent to USAID or Homeland Security—reminiscent of late-1970s efforts to remove humanitarian issues from State.

It is essential to keep the humanitarian programs linked to diplomacy, closely. This book shows why that is so important.

Human Rights

The global community, including the United States, has been inconsistent in calling attention to human rights abuses around the world (except cases involving endangered nationals). Willing to aggressively call out abuses in certain countries (Castro's Cuba and Maduro's Venezuela), they have been noticeably less aggressive about the serious abuses of citizens in other countries like Azerbaijan, Burma, Cambodia, China, Egypt, the Philippines, Russia, Turkey, and Vietnam. Leaders in those countries have either weakened civil society, undercut fair elections, diminished freedom of speech, ignored the rule of law, or violated the human rights of citizens. Myanmar committed crimes against the Rohingya population, for which humanitarians demanded harsh sanctions.

After Syria, how could the world, especially the United States, continue to ignore the ethnic cleansing and genocide in Myanmar, with almost 750,000 Rohingya Muslims in the Rakhine State forced to flee to neighboring Bangladesh, over 350 villages burned and destroyed, and almost 7,000 men, women and children killed? Only a decade ago the United States led a concerted campaign for democratic governance in Burma, as Myanmar was then called.[5]

Global Migration

The United States further widened its gulf with partner governments in December 2017 by announcing two days before a long-scheduled negotiating session in Mexico, its withdrawal from the efforts to draw up a global compact on migration.[6] The UN initiative was launched in summer 2016 at the first World Humanitarian Summit. Concerned over Syria and other human disasters, governments had agreed to create two international compacts dealing with refugees and migrants. They had hoped to get global agreement on contemporary "rules of the road." But a clear picture emerged. The United States shared few, if any, of its historic allies' (and its own previous) concerns about the global movements of people. The United States was just one of five governments not approving the migration compact at the December 2018 General Assembly session.

◇

Institutional foreign policy has not been the only area of US engagement to face consequences of the *America-first* policy. Consider the other big issues of the day, particularly regarding trade, climate change, and the Iran nuclear agreement. In each case, recent actions separated our nation from traditional allies.

◇

America First

As I understand it, America First is designed to secure the home base as a springboard for higher aspirations. Otherwise, why risk losing the global humanitarian consensus the world community, especially America, worked so hard, over many years, to achieve? The personal relationships the president is developing with key foreign leaders are certainly valuable, yet not intended to replace dynamic US relations with nations at all levels.

In my view, any action that abandons the US partnerships formed in the previous global humanitarian consensus would be counterproductive. It might be acceptable if the bilateral approach had realistic possibilities of working. However, my experience and the formal record inform me that a strictly bilateral approach is imprudent. It is too cautious, dismissive of other parties, expensive, and likely to add to world instability. It offers little hope and creates prospects for self-serving national behavior.

Enlightened Approach Needed

It is painful to admit, but I find that America's performance over the past decade has been irreconcilable with the requisites of global humanitarian leadership. There are dangers involved when humanitarian problems go unresolved or the solutions burdens are not shared, politically and financially, among allies. I challenge current American leaders to "pause, look, see, and understand" that *only global cooperation* can help realize the global humanitarian leadership the world needs and expects. And global cooperation will *not* require diminishing the attention the American government devotes to other national priorities. If not the United States as leader, the world must hope that an ally or allies will step forward courageously and take the mantle. But my preference is, of course, United States quality leadership.

Clearly, the Syria/Middle East crisis has not benefitted—during the last seven years—from the same dedicated American spirit and leadership that brought success in Indochina and other world crises since World War II. But, I see no other player to fill that gap, and US humanitarian leadership to inspire action has been sorely missed. I am hopeful that the American government and people can see the compelling need to remove blinders and work to reclaim our standing as a global humanitarian leader.

My specific proposals for a way forward are in the next chapter, and they provide an opportunity for America to reclaim global humanitarian leadership. The prerequisite is willingness to give certain assurances:

- Steadfast and unapologetic presidential leadership to energize the United States and allies to make conflict victims central to foreign, military, and diplomatic decision-making, as in numerous examples throughout this book of breakout leadership from presidents Ford, Carter, and Reagan
- High levels of international and private partner cooperation sufficient to sustain a viable multilateral team
- A comprehensive and globally supported durable solutions quest to guide planning and operations
- Enthusiastic and generous public and private contributions and partnerships

Present and future administrations must be willing to assure that the US State Department is strengthened and positioned as the primary catalytic agent to work with the domestic and international partners to bring the president's policy guidance into fruition. The current secretary of state Mike Pompeo says that is his goal.

That means the State Department refugee team must be led by administration appointees trusted, mandated, and enabled to plan and guide specific American engagement to (1) assist *refugees and displaced persons in asylum* overseas; (2) document and assist *refugees approved for admission* to the United States, as described below; and (3) arrange safe return home for those not qualified for refugee admission. The State Department takes pride that "the United States provides more humanitarian assistance to refugees than any other nation and maintains the world's largest refugee resettlement program."[7] While the United States has historically been the leading government in these efforts, both have been problematic during the Syria crisis.

Assist Refugees and Internally Displaced People in Asylum Areas

Let me mention here my admiration for the work of our government to keep funding for the international relief programs for Syria at levels sufficient, at least, to avoid catastrophe. As the United States remains *the* leading Syrian relief program donor, its funding, plus equitable contributions from a handful of other governments, has been the difference between life and death for many survivors.

I find it bewildering that the State Department's Bureau of Population, Refugees, and Migration (PRM) appears to have been intentionally kept in a weakened condition in its first year and a half through failure to confirm a permanent assistant secretary. At a time of such heightened humanitarian need in Syria and elsewhere, these inexplicable circumstances make the recent achievements of the bureau's career staff especially significant in the face of an almost 20 percent cut in refugee funding for FY 2018.[8]

The PRM congressional budget for FY 2017 states that the United States has provided over $7.4 billion in humanitarian assistance for this Syrian crisis since its beginning in March 2011.[9] Additional funding is under consideration. With few exceptions, however, other donors have not kept pace.

US financial assistance supports the UN's consolidated appeal for Syria, the 3RP Regional, Refugee, and Resilience Plan. For 2018/2019, the consolidated appeal requests $4.4 billion to support 5.3 million "registered refugees" from Syria and 3.9 million "members of impacted communities in neighboring countries." They are in Egypt, Iraq, Jordan, Lebanon, and Turkey.[10]

International refugee-assistance funding faced severe reductions in the administration's initial plan for the State Department, but hopes remained they would be restored. With massive US budget cuts, the global humanitarian response going forward would remain frighteningly inadequate for upward-spiraling needs in Syria and elsewhere, especially if returns home—with huge reconstruction costs—become possible. Although multilateral teams have stretched limited funding to the maximum since 2011, the poor overall response thwarted efforts to sustain millions of the refugees adequately and safely in regional asylum until permanent (durable) solutions became available.

Admission to Refugee Convention Countries, 2011 Forward

Excepting possibly Canada, the admission of Syrian refugees to Refugee Convention countries has proven to be conflictive, problematic, and laden with fear. As with the EU countries, this also has been the case for the United States, usually the world's leader in this important durable solution.

In 2016, UNHCR estimated that over 1.15 million refugees, globally, needed resettlement, exceeding one million for the first time since reporting of resettlement needs began over thirty years earlier.[11] In recent years, resettlement places have declined, providing only around 12 percent of refugees needing resettlement. It is shocking to realize that global resettlement is being shrunk to virtual insignificance. In 2016, UNHCR's global resettlement was about 126,000, with about 62 percent resettling in the United States and 23 percent in Canada and Australia. The remaining 15 percent resettled in twenty-six other countries. Going forward, planned United States resettlement cuts could further reduce the global effort by one-third or more, depending on the other governments' reactions. Those for whom resettlement is the only viable solution will be endangered further.

As the war in Syria accelerated over the first four years (2011–15) the United States had authority and funding for 280,000 refugee admissions worldwide. Yet, actual admissions of Syrian refugees were fewer than two thousand people. As the end of FY 2015 approached, the secretary of state John Kerry announced a further increase in the global refugee ceilings for 2017 and 2018, devoted primarily to people from Syria and other Middle East countries, up to 10,000 or more each year. These refugees would be selected from neighboring asylum countries.

Whereas only one thousand Syrian refugees actually reached the United States in the first half of FY 2016 (October to March), the Obama administration's "surge operation" in the second half brought the admissions for the year to almost 13,000, bringing to slightly over 18,000 the total number admitted since October 1, 2011 (5 percent of America's authorized global refugee admissions ceilings over those crucial years).[12]

The Obama administration's response was constrained by the time-consuming security screening procedures (eighteen to twenty-four months) required to block the Islamist radical extremists and criminals from entering the country as refugees. The State Department says that refugees of every nationality are subject to the highest level of security checks for any category of traveler. But efforts to bar Islamist terrorists from the United States and to pause or end refugee admissions after September 11, 2001, have turned the US refugee responses (especially for Syrians) into hot-button political and security issues. They have also contributed to perceptions of discrimination against Muslims and excessive costs to the American treasury.

Immigration Bans

The December 2015 terrorist shootings in San Bernardino, California, killed fourteen people. Presidential candidate Donald Trump called for a complete ban on the Muslim immigrants on the grounds of inadequate vetting. After his inauguration, White House advisors drafted an executive order launching a ban, issuing it in late January 2017.

Immediately, the American Civil Liberties Union (ACLU) convinced a Brooklyn judge, Ann Donnelly, to halt deportations and detentions related to the ban. A second entry ban was issued, and the courts immediately blocked it as well. The Supreme Court then fashioned a compromise allowing the ban except for the immigrants with significant US connections (families, jobs). That version expired in the fall, 2017.

A third ban imposed various restrictions on the immigrants from eight countries (Syria, Libya, Yemen, Iran, Chad, Somalia, North Korea, and Venezuela). That version was also challenged.[13] In January 2018, the Supreme Court agreed to consider the ban and in June upheld it.

Vetting Refugee Admissions Applications

Embroiled in that extended debate over bans was a troubling controversy about the vetting of refugee applicants for admission to the United States. While most agree that no one should deny the chief US executive time to consider policy prescriptions, many veteran observers, including myself, believe the executive orders overstated the problem and the solution, at least as far as the refugee admissions to the United States are concerned.

Without doubt, much of the American public and the Congress do not have confidence that existing refugee vetting procedures can detect and exclude potential terrorists from the homeland. Unfortunately, these fears fail to distinguish between the refugees entering under traditional and stringent American refugee vetting and admission procedures and those entering other regions, like Europe, through political asylum. Also, critics fail to distinguish between the refugees and other foreigners entering as irregular or undocumented immigrants. Clearly, the loopholes in the immigration system need urgent attention. The October 2017 New York terrorist attack by Uzbek immigrant Sayfullo Saipov, admitted under the diversity visa lottery system 2011, is a prime example.[14]

In my view, the US refugee resettlement regime has not been at fault. During the refugee decade, for instance, many thousands of questionable applicants failed UNHCR and RP screening, and they were denied refugee status and, therefore, US entry. Under such stringent vetting, the United States vetted, cleared, and admitted over three million refugees over the past thirty-five years *without* major incidences. The CATO

Institute's research confirms that "refugees do not pose a significant threat to American lives" and have lower crime rates than US citizens. Over the past four decades, they found that the refugees have been far less likely than other immigrants or US-born citizens to kill people in the United States in acts of terrorism.[15] No US citizens have been killed by legally-admitted refugees since 1976, yet the refugee program has suffered much from false claims about murderous acts. *"From 1975 through the end of 2015,"* CATO research stated, *"the annual chance of being murdered on US soil in a terrorist attack committed by a refugee was an astronomical one in 3.64 billion per year."*[16]

Unvetted applicants entering under the political asylum system, as in Europe, (Paris, Berlin, Brussels, Nice, Stockholm, London, and Manchester) present serious security concerns. Even there, terrorists represented a tiny fragment of political asylees, however. The United States did not, and would not, allow unvetted refugee applicants admission to our country during the refugee decade or after September 11, 2001, and that practice remains in effect.

The United States employs *careful vetting* of all the refugee applicants, as has been the practice throughout the resettlement program's long history. Over that time, the American program detected and adjudicated serious security challenges fairly and effectively. For example, tailored *vetting* criteria for the murderous Khmer Rouge, African warlords, the Taliban, Central American gang members or the dangerous claimants processed under stringent criteria following September 11, 2001, worked as envisioned. When or if valid corroborating information could not be obtained for conflict countries, the US *vetting procedures* accounted for that deficiency and denied admission.

The claims that refugees are a drain on the American treasury or consume excessive amounts of social welfare are also spurious. Regarding costs of refugee resettlement, an authoritative report issued by the National Bureau of Economic Research (NBER), June 12, 2017, provided convincing evidence that the refugees pay more in taxes than they receive in welfare benefits over the long term.[17] Regarding immigrants as a whole, the National Academy of Science says that on average, they provide $150,000 more in taxes than they receive in benefits, in present value terms, over their lifetime.[18] A May 2018 CATO Institute study found that in 2016 the average immigrant received 39 percent *fewer* welfare state benefits than the average US-born American.[19] The longer refugees and immigrants live in this country, the better their economic outcomes.

A September 2017 Health and Human Services (HHS) report ordered by the president six months earlier concluded that $63 billion more in state and local tax revenue had been contributed by the refugees than the costs of their benefits through the decade ending in 2014.[20]

The president set the US refugee admissions ceiling for 2018 at 45,000 individuals, the lowest in many decades and signaled further cuts in the future (diminished to 30,000 for FY 2019). Inexplicably, these cuts came when the numbers of the world's displaced and those in flight had soared to record levels.[21] I was greatly disappointed at the news of 22,491 US resettlements for FY 2018, which was the lowest annual resettlement since the beginning of the modern refugee admissions program (mid-1970s).[22] Sixty-two Syrian refugees were admitted in FY 2018 compared with 6,557 the previous year.[23] Results of the budget cuts and complicated bans, reviews, and appeals—with inevitable reductions in private sector resettlement capacity—have had confounding consequences.

While resettlement criticisms can be logically refuted, it cannot be denied that the strategic and political blunders that afflicted our past efforts in the Syrian and Libyan crises, compounded by hysteria over refugees and immigrants, have stymied humanitarian efforts *to put the victims at the center of decision-making.*

Prevent Further Harm

The contrast of present US policies to those of the 1980s refugee decade is striking. During that era, the United States and the multilateral system were required to work cooperatively on behalf of the crisis victims and to strengthen each government's stability, including our own. A similar approach was used successfully in the years prior to and after September 11, 2001. Those approaches featured multiple partners sharing massive political, subsistence, and infrastructural burdens. They were also the most cost-efficient strategy for the world community and far less disruptive than alternative bilateral solutions.

The US refugee decade record is plentiful with successful multilateral actions:

- Indochina refugee program, notably the UN Comprehensive Plan of Action for Indochinese Refugees, known as CPA
- Khmer rescue, highlighted by the heroic work of the UN Border Relief Organization (UNBRO)
- African famine relief, especially the UN Office of Emergency Operations in Africa (OEOA)
- African refugee relief and the enduring work of UNHCR and ICRC
- Palestinian refugees, featuring the UN Relief and Works Agency for Palestinian Refugees, UNRWA
- Return of Jewish Diaspora to Israel by public and private agencies
- Afghan refugees and the steady work of the UN High Commission for Refugees, the World Bank, and other partners
- Eastern European refugees and global NGO partners
- Central American refugees and migrants

As an active participant in those refugee decade initiatives and solutions, I can testify that global actions with multiple allies were essential to the success the world community achieved during dangerous times. Bilateral relationships (particularly with faith-based NGOs) were encouraged, forged, and incorporated into most multilateral actions. They were never sole or primary players.

The *multilateral versus bilateral* controversy has affected the present Middle East refugee, migrant, and asylum crises. Germany's high profile has made it a case study in the pitfalls of bilateral crisis resolution. Germany offered political asylum, essentially a bilateral decision, as its preferred solution when confronting massive movements of asylum seekers entering its territory. Several other European nations followed the German lead. Many, including myself, have maintained that if the European governments had opted instead to require and support the multilateral system to lead this crisis innovatively, then the results would likely have been far less damaging for all concerned.

Such deficiencies in current humanitarian strategy by many nations (not only the United States)—as revealed in responses to the Syrian and Libyan crises—have heartbreakingly brought great harm to millions of civilians and all affected states. When these deficiencies are combined with current existential threats—to replace global cooperative action with bilateral initiatives by major nations—the resulting harm to the global humanitarian system is so severe as to bring its future viability into question. In fact, I postulate that these errors are central contributors to spreading populism, xenophobia, and nativism around the globe.

It is imperative that civilization get off the sidelines of today's impending threats and back into the game. We must face the threats directly before it is too late to stop the harm and find common ground. Future cooperative action depends on courageous action going forward.

42

SEARCHING A WAY FORWARD

RECOGNIZING PAST HUMANITARIAN FAILURES IN SYRIA and the Middle East, how do we act to reverse present and prospective harm to crisis victims and to the global humanitarian system? How do we find grounds for future global cooperative action?

Drawing on my experiences leading the State Department's Bureau for Refugee Programs in the 1980s and the International Organization for Migration (IOM) in the 1990s and recognizing that each humanitarian crisis is unique and requires tailor-made solutions, I offer my advice about a viable way forward.

◇

The path to a renewal strategy begins with knowledge of workable solutions from the past as the starting point for three interwoven and essential tasks: (1) recognize mistakes, (2) devise viable strategies useful in existing circumstances, and (3) act with vision and courage to carry them out. Correcting mistakes and moving forward dramatically are civilization's unforgiving and insistent challenges.

First, Recognize Mistakes

Regarding the humanitarian regime for Syria, I believe an incorrect strategy was employed at a critical early stage, and leadership was too blinded by risk averseness and big power competition to recognize the devastating consequences of the mistake. That strategy resulted from failure to draw on the past successes, seek knowledge of workable strategies of the past, anticipate the devastating consequences of spontaneous planning (political expediency), or take corrective actions when mistakes became apparent. The most significant failure of the Syria humanitarian crises was the flawed decision by the European states to employ the political asylum system for admission and integration of the asylum seekers (*see* chapter 39). It is important to examine why and how this failure occurred and what other alternatives might have been considered.

◇

Mass movements of asylum seekers to Europe in Fall 2015 relied largely on *territorial asylum* (distressed individuals reach a self-selected destination state and request [political] asylum, i.e., "refugee" status). Much of the later distress can be traced to this decision. Propelled by chaotic mass entry of large numbers of unvetted asylum seekers, including a few potential terrorists, the results for the transit and receiving states were calamitous. The unsure governments ran for cover. Sadly, the stage had been set for these new flows of asylum seekers by the previous four years' inadequate donor support to maintain safe and secure first-asylum in the Middle East region.

To be fair, however, and acknowledging current humanitarian system lethargy, we must recognize that, scarily, the European governments that were forced to confront this dilemma believed they had no other realistic choice. (At a similar decision point in the Indochina crisis a handful of governments—led by the United States—stepped forward to propose a comprehensive multilateral strategy.) By 2015, the use of traditional *durable solutions* approaches (*repatriation, regional settlement, or third-country resettlement*) had been diminished to the point of irrelevance; there were no outspoken advocates to make the case for them.

There is evidence that as global humanitarian cooperation progressively diminished, and the endangered populations rose to epic levels, use of conventional durable solutions plummeted.[1] Slightly under 150,000 refugees per year had been resettled in *third-country resettlement* globally (most in Canada, Australia, and America) in recent years (approximately 126,000 in 2016), and signs indicated more cuts in the future.

The use of *voluntary repatriation/return*, another durable solution, has likewise been paltry. About 250,000 people were repatriated globally through 2015, with marginal increase in 2016, and UNHCR stated that "not enough refugee-producing countries have established the conditions to allow for safe and voluntary returns."[2] *Regional settlement*, another durable solution, has been problematic.

Given these failures it is not hard to understand why the European nations turned to *political asylum*, a solution they could use immediately and over which they exercised much greater control. A January 2017 Transatlantic Council on Migration (TCM) report bore this out, acknowledging that the *territorial asylum system*, while employed in this crisis response, remains under intense pressure amid record displacement. It concluded, "To this day, territorial asylum does not provide an easy solution for sudden influxes." But it was better than the alternatives, mainly, "third country resettlement," which was "infrequently involved" or "too expensive and cover[s] too few people."[3] The report continued, "... efforts to decouple access to territory and access to protection—either by processing applications in countries of first asylum or at consulates or by resettling people from countries of asylum have remained small in scale and do not provide a workable alternative."

It is ominous that existing *durable solutions* have touched only a miniscule fraction of the global displacement populations in recent times. The growing magnitude of the humanitarian dangers makes those results unacceptable. Some observers believe those poor results gave rise to the overwhelming use of territorial asylum as the only alternative in the Syria crisis, and they rendered *external* or *offshore processing*, as employed in Indochina, unsuitable for humanitarian crises like Syria. With other strategies faltering, *territorial asylum* became the default option.

In recent years, the US Government made another wounding and inexplicable mistake in the Syria–Middle East crisis response: abandoning the traditional leadership role it had played in the global humanitarian system in earlier times. Accordingly, there was nothing like the refugee decade's Informal Consultations Group (ICG) to crystallize creative thinking and spur cooperative action toward humane endgame solutions (*see* chapter 25). No other government could have, in my view, provided the essential "gumption" or "oomph" needed to energize bold initiatives on behalf of conflict victims in ways that created space and muscle for the UN (and its multilateral partners) to step up and lead the global response. Rather than undercutting and handcuffing the multilateral system, as currently, the United States worked in the refugee decade to strengthen its linchpin leadership.

These avoidable missteps left the world with a humanitarian system missing its mobile, willing, and risk-taking quarterback (*sparkplug* might be a better analogy), a position civilization needs some government to fill again.

Another serious and damaging consequence was that substantial donor resources, which historically went to the multilateral budgets for assisting first asylum, were instead diverted to cover (expensive) political asylum costs in European nations. In today's *zero sum* thinking, multilateral budgets never caught up.

Second, Devise More Viable Strategy

I remain convinced that the most viable *future* strategy for addressing complex humanitarian crises could be modeled largely on the international responses to Indochina and other refugee decade crises during the last quarter of the twentieth century. That strategy highlights global cooperation (partner buy in), employs established durable solutions, and builds on the existing structures and mechanisms. It is important to acknowledge that some governments have incorporated or considered aspects/elements of this approach in their Syria responses.

This is consistent with my early conceptual thinking about this book: a *future* humanitarian paradigm would undoubtedly flow from the past seven years' experience in Syria, and I believe it should feature an option using the Indochina strategy. The result would highlight what I earlier called the *solutions compact* (a loose and informal "coalition of the willing") that worked successfully in Indochina (*see* chapter 29). That important multilateral refugee solutions initiative was designed to draw a few close allies (including multilateral partners) and then many others to consensus on durable solutions (trade-offs, compromises, negotiations, action). A similar system was in place after the September 11, 2001, crisis.

In my view, it is the only viable alternative for gaining problem-solving cooperative action in complex global crises. Of course, any future model would be tailored to conditions and situations existing at that time.

However, reflecting on lessons learned from the Syria crisis, I am now inclined to believe the Indochina strategy could also have applicability for the *present*, as well. In 2018, the Syrian crisis was in its seventh year. Humanitarian aid to the region had begun in 2011. That time span parallels the point at which the United States and allies came together during the Indochina conflicts to create a new humanitarian endgame strategy for Indochina.

That invigorated Indochina strategy played out over the next decade and concluded in a compromise that brought the crisis to a humane conclusion and the Indochina states to dynamic takeoff points. It also validated the multilateral system as a competent and humane problem-solver.

This *solutions strategy* employs the *external or offshore processing* regime that requires victims to receive assured protection in *regional first asylum* or *home locations* and to remain there until appropriate *durable solutions* are determined, whether repatriation, regional settlement, or third-country resettlement.[4] Persons in the last category are protected in asylum locations until *third countries* agree to accept them, allowing time for proper vetting, documentation, orientation, and medical clearance prior to departure. Enduring *first asylum* is the anchor.

The resulting paradigm offers the international community a contrasting approach to evaluate in the present and beyond.

Third, Act with Vision and Courage

Cooperation resulting from a mutually appealing "solutions compact" (or whatever it might be called) would encourage and energize like-minded governments, eventually including countries of origin, and multilateral organizations to harmonize efforts and share burdens and contributions. Partners would be enabled to take the long view, encompassing rescue, protection, durable solutions, and humane problem resolution. *No method would be viewed as a singular or isolated solution, but as component stages of a more integrated and comprehensive solution.* But more governments would need to get back in the game.

Given restrictive global attitudes and the rash of multiyear dysfunctions in the present Syria-Middle East regime, it is hard to speculate about likely results. In a best-case scenario I would not rule out significant outcomes. During the refugee decade era, the solutions compact and similar techniques resulted globally in over ten million refugees either being returned home or settled safely in their *home or asylum region*, and about two million resettled safely in *third countries*.

While crisis outcomes were very much in doubt in early 2018, the evolving political/military configurations in Syria, Iraq, and Libya provide fresh opportunities and heightened imperatives to reconsider humanitarian strategies. If my hopes (amplified in the next chapter) for a conclusion to the Syrian War can be realized and the world community can come together in a joint quest for humanitarian solutions, several immediate strategic decisions would face governments participating in the *solutions compact*:

- Confirm the continuing need for active multilateral leadership and engagement
- Reorient mindsets to place victims and their protection central in allied decision-making
- Cooperatively strengthen and maintain first asylum in originating and host regions to accommodate refugees and migrants while durable solutions are determined and implemented
- Provide negotiated and unfettered return, reintegration, and targeted third-country resettlement assistance for designated applicants, through the United Nations
- Implement immigration systems and pathways to complement durable solutions and sustainable reconstruction, development, and opportunity goals
- Provide postwar reconstruction assistance
- Assure requisite funding

Requirements and potential benefits of a *solutions compact* approach for the Syrian crisis are described in *Appendix C*.

By breathing new life and vitality into existing implementation mechanisms, this dynamic approach adds value through (1) expanded cooperation among a wider range of solution partners and (2) action aimed directly at comprehensive solutions and humane endgame results.

It is beyond question that realization of the compact's benefits for contemporary humanitarian crisis solutions would require a sea change in current restrictive attitudes and a greater openness to possibilities. But if equitably supported by governments and the multilateral system, this approach provides civilization's best opportunity to achieve durable solutions for crisis victims and regain its own declining stature.

A Solutions Compact

In a revitalized humanitarian regime, all Refugee Convention signatory governments, especially *solutions compact members*, would be expected to contribute to solutions, as they did for Indochina and other refugee populations.

When the Syrian civil war ends and reconstruction commences, I believe most refugees in the Middle East crisis, excepting possibly ethnic populations targeted for genocide, could be protected and settled in *home regions*. That is a determination, however, to be made later by durable solution practitioners. For others, for whom third-country resettlement would be the only viable solution, equitable sharing of the resettlement burden must be negotiated by compact members, as in the Comprehensive Plan of Action (CPA) for Indochinese Refugees.

As in the past, *repatriation* and *regional settlement* would likely be the primary solutions for the refugees from the Middle East, as they have customarily been for Africa, South Asia, the Balkans, and Central America. While resettlement in *third countries* was important for comparatively small numbers in the past, it was by no means the primary global solution.

The *solutions compact approach* puts significant responsibility on countries and regions of origin. International principles and practices envision *regional asylum* countries offering safe sanctuary, with assured support, while the international community seeks durable solutions. This follows 2017's G20 initiative to maintain refugees in asylum as close to their home country as possible. Just as assured and secure first asylum was essential for building confidence in Southeast Asia, so too will it need to anchor workable solutions going forward.

The UN's Regional, Refugee, and Resilience Plan, 2018–2019,

familiarly known as 3RP, says there are approximately 5.3 million Syrian refugees (3.3 million in Turkey, one million in Lebanon, 600,000 in Jordan, 400,000 in Egypt and Iraq) and 3.9 million host community members surviving, sometimes just barely, in regional asylum countries.[5] Many have been in asylum for four or more years, experience high rates of poverty, and have few hopes for the future. Since 2012, donor governments have given from half to two-thirds of the funding needed for safe and humane asylum, and prospects looking forward are dim.

Given dysfunctions that have characterized efforts to date, the governments that helped in the past have left this gnarly problem with the underfunded multilateral system and regional asylum governments. A *solutions compact approach* attempts to change those dynamics dramatically.

First asylum would no longer be viewed as only a "holding" arrangement, but as a place for preparation of next steps. Donor and resettlement countries would make equitable contributions for *humane solutions*. *Refugee decade* participants gave economic help and assistance to *origin countries* to help prepare for returnees. Compact members would similarly help Middle East and other origin regions prepare for their citizens' return when safety permitted.

The *informal compact*'s partners would determine appropriate *durable solutions*, destinations, and timing for refugees, in concert with partners and beneficiaries. These considerations would take account of the refugee preferences and the absorptive capacities and other impacts on asylum, transit, and destination countries.

In the *solution phase*, an international *comprehensive plan of action* would likely take the humanitarian crisis to a successful conclusion. In the past, in Indochina, even the origin countries gained from a successful outcome. Vietnam participates in the Trans-Pacific Partnership (TPP) and is on schedule to become a top-twenty global economy by 2050; Cambodia and Laos are fast-emerging Asian economies. Similar outcomes could be envisioned for other regions.

Humanitarian Solutions Still Possible?

Notwithstanding the humanitarian successes achieved a quarter century ago in Southeast Asia, many are skeptical that comparable results are realistically possible now in areas like the Middle East. They say lingering effects of September 11, 2001, have made the Indochina solutions approach too dangerous and complex to work in contemporary crises. They say it's too simplistic for contemporary times, when publics are driven by fear, when leaders may be unable or unwilling to guide citizens toward greater openness and cooperation.

In view of this quandary, why then do I advocate this solutions approach for Syria seven years in or for *future* humanitarian crises?

I do so because I recognize that *refugee decade responses* had tested strategic components and a "can do" mindset, both absent currently. Principally, refugee decade crises so troubled US presidents and other international leaders that they mobilized for cooperative global action; they made victims central in deliberations for concerted political, military, diplomatic, and development endeavors; they addressed underlying causes. They collaborated freely with allies and cleared impediments to cooperative action. Leaders insisted that victim protection never be ignored or trivialized. They required allied partners to develop guiding strategies (which today would include terrorism) that kept the search for humane solutions constantly on the front burner. They assured the needed funding. Freeloaders were identified and shamed; dangerous elements were identified and disallowed.

Those responses—and the deliberative process used—have not been at work for the Syrian crisis, and experience has proven that—absent attention to these central strategic ingredients—neither territorial asylum nor external processing is likely to work.

◇

Global engagement and committed leadership remain our only hope to gain the enhanced international cooperation so essential to solving complex humanitarian crises.

43

ENDING WAR AND MOVING AHEAD

BY MID-AUGUST 2018, THE RUINOUS WAR IN SYRIA APPEARED to have almost run its course, but dark clouds were gathering. Bashar Assad had announced plans to bring all areas of the country back under government control in early June 2018, when the Syria–Russia–Iran coalition emerged as the ascendant alliance. Syria's traditional economic hubs came back under Assad's control. Government forces had defeated the opposition in and around Damascus and freed up fighters to take the battle to remaining opposition strongholds: Idlib in the north (near Turkey's border) and Daraa in the south (near Jordan's border). With Russian help, rebels in the southwest were defeated by the Syrian coalition, and that region's conflict was concluded. That allowed Assad to concentrate forces on the Idlib province in the northwest, the remaining opposition holdout. Only Kurdish-controlled areas in the northeast (with US support) were outside the reach of the Assad regime.

Earlier, Assad had warned the United States—a main Kurdish partner—to remove its forces. The United States had warned Assad against attacks on US forces or allies. Israel had said that it would not tolerate Assad's Iranian advisors and Shiite forces near its southwest border.

Meanwhile, Turkey continued to reinforce its position in the northwest as it anticipated Assad's renewed attacks. President Recep Tayyip Erdogan vowed to resist attempts to take the region from Turkey's control, raising risks of yet another showdown with Syrian coalition partners. Three million civilians in the Idlib region could be shoved into the crosshairs if conflict resumed and trigger yet another massive humanitarian crisis. Tensions were so high that the *Washington Post's* Liz Sly reported, the "worst in Syria could be ahead."[1]

◊

Residents around Idlib could again be threatened. Earlier, in Spring 2018, the UN's humanitarian chief had been forced to urge the Syrian government to allow delivery of aid to more than two million people in the areas hard to reach, to avoid a humanitarian disaster. Despite government-imposed limitations and continued fighting, UN convoys delivered food to over two million people in government-controlled areas and 850,000 in rebel areas in April.[2]

Photos of places like Raqqa and Ghouta in 2018 bore out the deadly realities of this civil war: more than a half-million killed, one million injured, more than 100,000 still missing in government jails and prisons, almost eleven million displaced, countries destroyed, more destruction and death likely in coming months, and governments at loggerheads.

◊

Much of Syria had been decimated by the war, but millions desired to return home and begin picking up their lives as soon as security conditions permitted. Renewal prospects were not encouraging with the war continuing, promised international reconstruction funding slim, and an economy showing few signs of recovery.

In this regard, the United States' announcement in March 2018 of a $200 million US donation for the stabilization of Syria and President Trump's request to Saudi Arabia to contribute $4 billion dollars were encouraging.[3] Shortly thereafter, however, President Trump froze the US donation and announced the United States would soon pull forces out of Syria, evoking memories of the disastrous US withdrawal from Iraq several years earlier. In August, the administration redirected those funds ($230 million) away from the stabilization initiative. This decision deprived the emerging stabilization regime of essential funds as hundreds of thousands began planning their returns to areas like bombed-out Raqqa and other locations.

Of course, the combatting sides could continue to pulverize each other until one was forced into complete submission, bringing more death, destruction, and dislocation. Or, they could conclude *it's time to end this horrendous conflict and move to a peaceful restoration.* The latter scenario seemed unlikely, barring a major breakout initiative by regional or global powers.

Ideally, the major global powers—the United States and Russia—would see it was time to stand up their leadership and work to bring hostilities and tactical competition to an end. That would have been my recommendation.

Of course, both Russia and the United States would need to reverse the present policy trajectories that make them distrusted as viable international partners: Russia to end its hostile invasion of Ukraine and the Crimea and its covert interference in other nations' affairs and the United States to stop its resistance to the global order. (These dysfunctions make my preferred course unlikely, even as all parties recognize that the magnitude of the present human crisis calls for extraordinary creativity and cooperation.)

◇

Thus, with the stakes high, an unexpected compromise occurred during the last two weeks of September 2018.

Presidents Putin and Erdogan met in Sochi, Russia, and agreed to establish nine-by-twelve miles for a *demilitarized zone* in Idlib by October 15, 2018, to separate rebel forces from Syrian government troops and head off an all-out battle. Both governments had strong vested interests to stop the fighting: Turkey to avoid new refugee flight across its border and Russia to disentangle from a costly war.

The demilitarized zone would be freed of heavy weapons and more-extreme elements of the insurgency, including militants linked to al-Qaeda. Turkish and Russian forces would patrol the zone.[4] As the deadline passed, monitoring groups confirmed that all of the Turkish-backed opposition's heavy weapons were being withdrawn, but the most extreme militants were still in areas around Idlib. Rebel statements gave tacit acceptance of the agreement but refused to reject armed struggle and continued to voice distrust of Russian intentions.[5]

Additionally, the United States announced a remarkable policy shift: it would remain in Syria until Iran withdraws soldiers and militia forces (the US had earlier announced an imminent withdrawal). Observers and analysts were encouraged because they believed this decision signaled renewed US hope that the long-stalled UN negotiating process might finally be empowered to produce a settlement.[6]

The collaboration of all parties in Syria (including the United States) would be especially important if hostilities were truly ended and energies focused on the next stages: return, reconstruction, and rehabilitation. Given past divisions and competitions in this seven-year war, leadership from the major powers would be critical to break through ethnic/religious barriers and establish confidence among fearful citizens in realistic chances for peace and restoration.

Otherwise, wartime rivalries will carry over and likely continue to dominate, a concern expressed by many Syrian men considering return who questioned the sincerity of the Syrian government's amnesty offer.[7]

I am convinced that it is time to establish policies and strategies that put victim safety and welfare, present and future, central in decision-making—and to bring warring parties and surrogates into line. Such a development could set the stage for the missing ingredient needed to humanely resolve this deadly humanitarian crisis and pave the way for one of the largest and most complex restoration efforts the international community has ever undertaken: *a solutions compact for Syria and the Middle East*. A similar compact performed that role in the Indochina crisis by helping to assure favorable conditions for peace and keeping governments focused on humane outcomes (*see* chapter 29).

These favorable possibilities, however, were thrown into great confusion when President Trump announced on December 19 that American forces would leave Syria, as ISIS had been defeated. Many knowledgeable allies and partners did not agree with this new American approach.[8]

Breaking the political deadlock must start at the top, with the world's superpower leaders. It will be most unfortunate, and sad, if the United

States remains a reluctant advocate for solutions in the Syrian crisis. Its global leadership is needed now.

Thirty years ago, President Reagan and Soviet leader Mikhail Gorbachev faced similar differences, but were able to achieve an unprecedented breakthrough that ended the Cold War, protected the world from nuclear threats for the next quarter century (*see* chapter 32), and paved the way for an unprecedented humanitarian achievement.

Mikhail Gorbachev said recently, "In the final analysis, it was the political will of the two nations' leaders that proved decisive. And that is what's needed now. This is what our two countries' citizens and people everywhere expect from presidents of Russia and the United States."[9]

As the world saw with Reagan and Gorbachev in 1987, engaged leadership sets the tone that allows complementary, supportive voices to rise and be heard. Could breakout leadership occur again, this time for Syria and the Middle East?

Whatever form the next stage takes, I continue to advocate putting victims central in decision-making and trusting that like-minded governments will organize their future political, military, and humanitarian actions to make sure they stay there.

I have not lost faith in the human capacity to empathize and show mercy, even in the face of cloudy confusion and setbacks; but it will take inspirational, engaged leadership to rally doubting publics to rise to defend today's brothers and sisters locked in danger. They are pleading for help. Will we hear them? Who will help? The questions remain.

44

A TEST OF CIVILIZATION

IT HAS BEEN ALMOST A HALF CENTURY SINCE THE WORLD came together in Geneva, Switzerland, to launch a global solution to its most vexing humanitarian problem: Indochina. They put a creative and exciting strategic plan in place at a boat people conference in July 1979 and left the executing governments the job of bringing the problem to a humane and durable solution.

Then, a pulsing world conscience seized on the plight of the doomed and drowning souls and forced governments to act. That conscience would not accept delayed or weak responses and insisted that the Indochina refugees be placed centrally in government planning and action. It took two decades, yet it happened. Results were historic and spectacular.

Since the era of vast human upheaval in Indochina, I have been in positions to observe the rises and declines in global activism on behalf the world's endangered, displaced, and disrupted people. As I have pondered and researched the world's response to the ongoing Syrian crisis, I am left heartbroken and angry. There has been no sustained humanitarian outcry. The world's conscience has been dormant, gone quiet, and governments have been left free to ignore or trivialize their moral obligations to humankind, to look away from the suffering. I have been astounded that the world's humanitarian advocacy community that played such a vital role in Indochina has been so weak as to be barely audible. And millions of innocent people have been killed, driven from their homes, or made destitute while seeking safety and help.

A few advocates have stepped up, but governments have acted mostly with halfhearted indifference, incompetence, or lethargy. They seem to be more interested in self-preservation than in sharing with and helping global neighbors.

Civilization's new test is whether we can help free the world's conscience from the bonds used to tie it down and, once freed, to stir our hearts and minds to regain a sense of moral outrage, purpose, and resolve to face its responsibilities directly, no longer to look away, to act.

I completely agree with author Michael Mandelbaum's description, "There is nothing in our experience that has prepared us for what is going on now: the meltdown of an increasing number of states all at the same time in a globalized world."[1] In that conundrum, corrupt dictators (like Assad and Saddam) plunder resources, weak governments inevitably dissemble, and the remaining citizens are left to look after themselves.

The natural reaction has most often been to flee to places offering safety and better opportunity.

It is troubling, but we must acknowledge that the global volume of crisis victims is expanding far beyond anything experienced before, and the number of places offering safe refuge is shrinking almost to insignificance. The result is a battered humanitarian system, unable to cope with today's major crises in the Middle East and Europe or the broader and surging refugee and humanitarian challenges in the rest of the world.

Caring societies cannot continue to hide from these daunting challenges and shirk their moral duty to endangered brothers and sisters. That does not mean we need to bring all the world's needy to our shores or assume responsibility for all its destitute. Far from it. Yet, as caring members of the international community, we must shape our appropriate and equitable roles in solving the systemic dysfunctions that bring people to the brink of despair. While vigilant to deny entry of terrorists and criminals, let us not let fears blind us to the continuing need to welcome deserving refugees and immigrants.

Above all, we cannot habitually look away from the raw sufferings of others caught up in these appalling circumstances. Civilization demands that we view current survival problems objectively and humanely, understand available options, agree on who is responsible for what, and then act with boldness and resolve. The world, often with US leadership, has experienced that level of multilayered, determined, and rational action before.

But, we will not get there by thrashing the United Nations and other multilateral actors, demonizing refugees and migrants, or by infighting among needed partners and allies. Instead, we need to see the vulnerable as neighbors needing help. Sometimes that help is to save their lives, but most often it's to offer a helping hand to get them back on their feet in or near their homeland. Help to origin governments may be needed to build capacity to aid vulnerable citizens, including through *safe and orderly return*.

Whatever the form of help needed, humanity will be increasingly coarsened if societies continue to turn away; civilization demands that every generation leave room in its collective heart to listen and hear desperate cries of human suffering in displacement.

Civilization at the Crossroads

We must reclaim high moral ground, first by recognizing that civilization is at a crossroads regarding its indispensable protection of the weak, the most vulnerable, and the defenseless. The world is perplexed, wondering why tyrants like Assad that murder and torture their citizens with impunity, are not called to account or made to pay for their actions.

By all objective measures, we are currently failing civilization's test. If the international community cannot come together and resolve Syrian and other global humanitarian crises, including famine in Africa, in a more timely and humane way, the losers will not only be today's victims, but untold future multitudes who will lose confidence and hope in the humanitarian system and accept that they have no trustworthy defenders. And, how can we neglect or overlook that the extremes of today's horrors go by many names, and one is *barbarism*?

Shame on us if we become the first civilized society in contemporary times to say we're afraid, we don't care, we want someone else to do the heavy lifting, or we don't know what to do. We can find a better way. Some specific strategies are included in this book. And surely there are others.

I invite all like-minded humanitarians and nations of good will to join me in a campaign to confront our civilizational crisis, rejecting fear, timidity, and weakness regarding the defense of the persecuted, the voiceless, the "least of these among us."

Henceforth, I trust we will say when tested, "We *will* find a way, together." Perhaps that is what motivated President Trump to defend civilians by responding militarily to the chemical attacks in Syria on April 4, 2017, and a year later. Perhaps that is what motivated Presidents Trump and Putin (on their May 2017 phone call) to discuss the possibility of working toward a cease-fire in Syria.

It is far too early to tell whether those were one-off concessions for the sake of expediency or whether they can endure; but gestures like these are significant. For, as the saying goes, "the proof of the pudding will be in the eating." Until the world's protagonists and combatants can relate with honesty, clarity, and courage, differences cannot be bridged, and innocent civilians cannot be protected. How nations express or fail to express their shared values and fellowship affects their identities as civilized defenders of the world's persecuted and vulnerable.

◊

What I have written is based on the belief that as civilized people, moving forward to better lives for ourselves and others, we can find deep within our souls the courage and wisdom to be keepers and defenders of endangered brothers and sisters. Even as we tend to our own needs, let us not be unwilling to expand our capacities for love and caring for endangered people and keep their needs central in our hearts and attention.

Vice President Walter Mondale led the US delegation to the 1979 Indochina refugee conference in Geneva. At a critically low point, he spoke eloquently for humanity when he challenged assembled governments:

"… Let us fashion a world solution. History will not forgive us if we fail. History will not forget us if we succeed …. Truly, it's a test of civilization."[2]

His words still resonate.

A FRANCISCAN BENEDICTION

*May God bless you with discomfort
at easy answers, half-truths, and superficial relationships
so that you can live deeply within your heart.*

*May God bless you with anger
at injustice, oppression, and exploitation of others,
so that you may work for justice, freedom, and peace.*

*May God bless you with tears
to shed for people who suffer pain, rejection, hunger, and war,
so that you may extend your hand to comfort them and
to turn their pain into joy.*

*And may God bless you with enough foolishness
to believe that you can make a difference in the world,
with His help doing what others claim cannot be done
to bring justice and kindness to all children and the poor.*

Amen[3]

NOTES

BOOK ONE

1. In the Storm

1. White House Press Conference, Transcript, "with Ron Zeigler, Press Secretary and James Purcell, Bureau of the Budget," March 26, 1969.
2. Bureau of the Budget, office memorandum No. 69-41, re: staff changes, April 21, 1969.
3. Parker W. Borg, "Mobilizing for South Vietnam's Last Days," *Foreign Service Journal,* April 2015.
4. Frank Wisner, Lionel Rosenblatt, Jim Bullington, and Tom Miller, Discussions with author.
5. Kenneth M. Quinn, "From the Whitehouse to the White House," *Foreign Service Journal,* April 2015; Larry Clinton Thompson, *Refugee Workers in the Indochina Exodus, 1975-1982.* Jefferson and London: McFarland & Company, 2010, 8-9.

2. Vietnam and Five US Presidents

1. Thomas, Evan, and John Barry. "The enduring lessons of Vietnam," *Newsweek*, November 16, 2009, 35-41.
2. Ibid.
3. Henry Kissinger, *The Complete Memoirs*, (New York: Simon and Schuster, September 24, 2013), 483.
4. Maddow, Rachel, "Congress's blank check," *Washington Post,* June 23, 2014.
5. Gerald R. Ford, address at Tulane University Convocation, April 23, 1975.

6   Gerald R. Ford, Letter to Marine Master Sergeant Colin Broussard, June 15, 2000.
7   Shep Lowman, "Saigon Evacuation," *Foreign Service Journal*, March 1985.
8   Kennedy, Rory, "The Last Days of Vietnam," (documentary), 2015.
9   Jan K. Herman, *The Lucky Few: The Fall of Saigon and the Rescue Mission of the USS Kirk* (Annapolis: Naval Institute Press, 2013), 25–26.

3. Rescue the Perishing

1   Parker W. Borg, "Mobilizing for South Vietnam's Last Days," *Foreign Service Journal*, April 2015.
2   Shultz, George P., "The Meaning of Vietnam," US State Department address, Washington, April 25, 1985.

4. Tragic Triangle

1   *Bulletin*, US Department of State, 79:2031, October 1979.
2   Barry Wain, "The Indochina Refugee Crisis," *Foreign Affairs Journal*, Fall 1979.
3   "Cambodians in Thailand, People on the Edge," US Committee for Refugees, December 1985, 3–4.
4   Becker, Carol A., "Refugee and Migration Affairs," US Department of State, Office of the Historian, March 1984, 2–4.
5   *Bulletin*. State.
6   Larry Clinton Thompson, *Refugee Workers in the Indochina Exodus, 1975–1982* (Jefferson and London: McFarland & Company, 2010), 163.

5. Early Urgent Warnings

1   Van Atta, Dale, "Leo Cherne's Magnificent Obsession," *Reader's Digest*, May 1986.
2   Chandrasekaran, Raju, "Brokered Accord on Bosnia, Sought Peace," *Washington Post*, December 14, 2010.
3   Becker, Carol A., "Refugee and Migration Affairs," US Department of State, Office of the Historian, March 1984, 4.
4   Daniel 5:27, KJV, paraphrase by author.
5   "Refugee Act of 1979," congressional hearing, May 10, 1979, 105.
6   Ibid.

6. Wreckage and Repair

1. Becker, Carol A., "Refugee and Migration Affairs," US Department of State, Office of the Historian, March 1984, 2–4.
2. Chas Freeman, Memorandum to OMB (Office of Management and Budget) on reorganization of refugee functions, April 27, 1979; Peter Tarnoff, executive secretariat, Memorandum to concerned State bureaus on this subject, April 20, 1979; and John Thomas, administration, Letter to congressional committee chairmen, April 26, 1979.

7. From these Ashes, Will I Rise?

1. Clark, Dick, and Leo Cherne, statements at House Judiciary Committee hearings on the Refugee Act of 1979, May 3–4, 1979.

8. Weak Foundations

1. Stephan Bouman and Ralston Deffenbaugh, *They Are Us: Lutherans and Immigration* (Minneapolis: Augsburg Fortress Press, 2009), 43–46.
2. Ibid.
3. Tumulty, Karen, "At home legally—for now," *Washington Post*, November 28, 2014.
4. Bauman and Deffenbaugh, *Lutherans*.
5. US Census Bureau, "1850–2000 Decennial Census," American Community Survey, 2010.
6. Bauman and Deffenbaugh, *Lutherans*.
7. http://historymatters.gmu.edu/d/5078.
8. Bouman and Deffenbaugh, *Lutherans*, 45–46.
9. George L. Warren, "The Development of United States Participation in Intergovernmental Efforts to Resolve Refugee Problems, 1933–1961," Independence: George L. Warren Papers (unpublished), Harry S. Truman Library & Museum, accessed 2016, 15–16.
10. Ibid.
11. Jack R. Fischel, *The Holocaust*, (Greenwood Press Guides to Historic Events of the Twentieth Century, 1998), 28–29.
12. Mondale, Walter, Speech at the UN Conference on Indochinese Refugees, Geneva, July 20, 1979.
13. Warren, "Development," 20–21.
14. Dennis R. Laffer, "The Jewish Trail of Tears: The Evian Conference of July 1938," (Tampa: University of South Florida, thesis, 2011).

15 Diane E. Afoumado, "The St. Louis and the Refugee Crisis in the late 1930s," http://ultimate historyproject.com/the-st-louis.html.
16 Ruth Gruber, *Haven: The Unknown Story of 1000 World War II Refugees* (New York: Coward–McCann, 1983).
17 Randall Hansen, "Constrained by its roots: How the origins of the global asylum system limit contemporary protection" (Washington: Transatlantic Council on Migration, Migration Policy Institute, January 2017), 5–6.
18 Ibid.
19 James L Carlin, *The Refugee Connection: A Lifetime of Running a Lifeline* (London: MacMillan Press, 1989). 30; Bouman and Deffenbaugh, *Lutherans*, 47.
20 Gjelten, Tom, "A bill that changed the face of the U.S.," *Washington Post*, September 27, 2015.
21 Becker, Carol A., "Refugee and Migration Affairs," US Department of State, Office of the Historian, March 1984, 2–4.

9. Durable Solutions Quest

1 George L. Warren, "The Development of United States Participation in Intergovernmental Efforts to Resolve Refugee Problems, 1933–1961" (Independence: George L. Warren Papers, unpublished, Harry S. Truman Library & Museum, accessed 2016), 118–26.
2 Ibid.
3 Refugee definition, UNHCR, http://www.unhcr.org/en-us/protecion/basic/3b73b0d63/states-parties-1951-convention-its-1967-protocol.html.
4 United Nations High Commissioner for Refugees (UNHCR), "Framework for Durable Solutions for Refugees and Persons of Concern," Core Group on Durable Solutions, Geneva, May 2003.
5 Larry Clinton Thompson, *Refugee Workers in the Indochina Exodus, 1975–1982* (Jefferson and London: McFarland & Company, 2010), 162.
6 vanden Heuvel, William, US ambassador in Geneva, Cable (1020) to the secretary of state Cyrus Vance, June 15, 1979.
7 Thompson, *Workers*, 163.
8 vanden Heuvel, Cable.
9 *Bulletin*, US Department of State, 79:2031, October 1979.
10 National Security Council, Memorandum to President Carter forwarding Indochina recommendations proposed by Secretary Vance and Refugee Coordinator Clark, June 21, 1979.

10. Presidential Decision

1. National Security Council, Memorandum to President Carter regarding presidential announcement at the Tokyo summit, July 12, 1979.
2. *Bulletin*, Department of State, 79:2031, October 1979.
3. Brezinski, Zbigniew, National Security Council, Memorandum to President Carter summarizing and forwarding a July 18, 1979 memorandum from Secretary Vance and Refugee Coordinator Clark.
4. Ibid.
5. *Bulletin*, State.
6. Hartling, Poul, UN High Commissioner for Refugees, Opening Statement at the International Conference on Indochinese Refugees, Palais des Nations, Geneva, July 20, 1979.
7. Mondale, Walter, Speech at the International Conference on Indochinese Refugees, Palais des Nations, Geneva, July 20, 1979.
8. Ibid.
9. Ibid.
10. Vice President Mondale's Geneva conference speech outlined seven action areas: 1) Immediate moratorium on the further expulsion of people from Vietnam; 2) asylum governments should continue to provide temporary safe haven for all refugees; 3) resettlement governments should assure first-asylum governments that the refugees will find new homes within a reasonable period; 4) all governments must make greater efforts to contribute to UNHCR; 5) network of new transit centers must be created for refugees destined for permanent resettlement elsewhere; 6) international refugee resettlement fund proposed; governments without the financial wherewithal to offer refugee resettlement must be helped;7) protection for people seeking safety, *Bulletin*, State. July 20, 1979.
11. *Bulletin*, State.

11. Signs of Life

1. Becker, Carol A., "Refugee and Migration Affairs," Department of State, Office of the Historian, March 1984, 4.
2. Department of State announcement, July 30, 1979.

12. Existential Threats

1. Refugee Programs (RP) teams were assigned to review and propose corrective actions:

- a Comptroller Marvin Smith and Financial Management Director Norman Runkles - financial management and contracting;
- b Budget Officer Mary Kavaliunas, budget planning and formulation, and Louise Pope, financial execution;
- c Kitty Kemp, human resources and general services support;
- d Jim Lawrence, information management and computerization;
- e Assistant Director Chris Russell and legal advisor, planning for pending Refugee Act;
- f Program officers, including John Buche, Doug Hunter, and the Geneva Mission staff, global refugee planning.

2 Goldman, Gerald J., Director of Management Planning, Consular Affairs, Department of State, "Organizing the Expanded Refugee Assistance Program in the Department of State," August 1979.
3 "Legal authority for Refugee Matters in DOS and AID," Legal Advisor, Department of State, 1983.
4 Becker, Carol A., "Refugee and Migration Affairs," Office of the Historian, Department of State, March 1984, 4.
5 "Management and Administration of the Office of Refugee and Migration Affairs," Congressional hearings on Foreign Assistance Appropriations for FY 1980, Part 3. (Re: House Investigative Report), April 1979.
6 "Refugee Act of 1979, H.R. 2816," Congressional hearings, Serial No. 10, Washington, May 3–24, 1979, 237.
7 Bill Jordan, Discussion with author.
8 Accomplishments:
- a Largest-ever American refugee budgets to that time, which were endorsed and approved by the Carter administration and Congress (also, the least reduced programs in annual foreign aid legislation);
- b Record US refugee admissions, with strong bipartisan support;
- c Congressional approval of twenty reprogramming adjustments; i.e., formal reallocations of appropriated funds for new or emerging priorities;
- d Successful defense and enactment of the Refugee Act of 1980;
- e Resolution of blistering congressional investigative findings pertaining to the State Department management of refugee programs, leading to abandonment of proposals to transfer the program from the Department;
- f Active participation by all congressional foreign affairs committees (and many individual members) in the landmark July 1979 Indochinese Refugee Conference; bipartisan agreement to sustain safe first asylum in Southeast Asia;

g   Resolution of hundreds of questions and concerns in multiple congressional hearings and hundreds of inquiry letters;
h   Successful revival of US public/private partnerships with advocacy and resettlement NGOs, encouraging domestic and international stakeholders, especially (unprecedented) congressional generosity for refugees.

13. Recalibrating for Global Response

1   "The Refugee Act of 1979," H.R. 2816, congressional hearing, May 3, 1979, Washington, DC, 39.
2   Ibid., 95.

14. Sharpening whilst Salvaging

1   "The Refugee Act of 1979" H.R. 2816, congressional hearing, May 16, 1979, Washington, DC, 222.
2   Ibid., 237.
3   Ibid.
4   Private voluntary agencies (PVOs) involved in US refugee resettlement: American Council on Nationalities Services (ACNS), American Fund for Czechoslovak Refugees, Buddhist Council for Refugee Rescue and Resettlement, Church World Service, Hebrew Immigrant Aid Society, International Rescue Committee, Lutheran Immigration and Refugee Service, US Catholic Conference, Presiding Bishop's Fund for World Relief/the Episcopal Church, Polish American Immigration and Refugee Committee, Tolstoy Foundation, World Relief.
5   Coolfont Conference on Refugee Resettlement, Conclusions. Participants: departments of State, Health, Education and Welfare, Justice, and the private voluntary resettlement agencies, Coolfont, West Virginia, October 1979.
6   Ralie Deffenbaugh, Discussion with author.

15. Survive and Prosper

1   *Bulletin,* Department of State, 79:2031, October 1979.
2   Morgan, Ann, "Urgent Action Report," e-mail to author, January 6, 2014.
3   *Reader's Digest,* "A Tragedy Ignored," January 1986, 91.

4   Mondale, Walter, Address to the International Conference on Indochinese Refugees, Palais des Nations, Geneva, July 21, 1979; *Bulletin,* Department of State, 79:2031, October 1979.
5   Hartling, Poul, UN high commissioner for refugees, Opening speech at International Conference on Indochinese Refugees, Palais des Nations, Geneva, July 20, 1979.
6   *The State of the World's Refugees, Fifty Years of Humanitarian Action,* UN High Commissioner for Refugees (Oxford: Oxford University Press, 2000) 87.
7   Richardson, Michael, "Stormy Weather for Merchant Ships," *Far Eastern Economic Review; News from the UNHCR,* No. 10, October 1982.
8   Barton, Michael, "Orderly Departure from Vietnam," *News from the UNHCR,* No. 13, January 1982.
9   Larry Clinton Thompson, *Refugee Workers in the Indochina Exodus, 1975–1982* (Jefferson and London: McFarland & Company, 2010), 165; *Bulletin,* Mondale.
10   Branigin, William, "Turning Away of Boat People Mars Improved Refugee Situation," *Washington Post,* January 4, 1984.

16. Refugee Act of 1980

1   "Authority for Refugee Matters of the US Coordinator for Refugees, the Department of State, and the Agency for International Development," Legal Advisor, Department of State, 1982.
2   James L. Carlin, *The Refugee Connection: A Lifetime of Running a Lifeline* (London: MacMillan Press, 1989), 102.
3   Ibid.

17. Dark Clouds

1   *The State of the World's Refugees, Fifty Years of Humanitarian Action,* UN High Commissioner for Refugees (Oxford: Oxford University Press, 2000), 92.
2   "Cambodians in Thailand, People on the Edge," US Committee for Refugees, December 1985, 10.
3   Larry Clinton Thompson, *Refugee Workers in the Indochina Exodus, 1975–1982* (Jefferson and London: McFarland & Company, 2010), 184, 198.
4   Tom Barnes, Discussion with author.
5   Thompson, *Workers,* 203, 208–209.
6   Jim Lawrence, Discussion with author.

7 Kenneth Quinn, Discussion with author.
8 William Shawcross, *Quality of Mercy: Cambodia, Holocaust and Modern Conscience* (New York: Simon & Schuster, 1985), 9.

19. From the Management Hub

1 Presidential Directive on Refugee and Migration Policy, Washington, January 16, 1979.
2 Department of State Notice, August 1979.
3 Department of State Notice, December 1979.
4 Minof, Nick, "Anxious Cubans Head for U.S. Soil," *Washington Post*, January 28, 2015.
5 "Report of the Cuban–Haitian Task Force," Washington, November 1, 1980.
6 Loy, Frank E., "Assignment of New Responsibilities and Organizational Changes," memorandum to RP staff, July 28, 1980.

20. The Carter Refugee Record

1 Gil Loescher, *Beyond Charity: International Cooperation and the Global Refugee Crisis* (Oxford: Oxford University Press, 1993), 87.

21. The Significance of Public Service

1 Purcell, James N., Jr., "Administrator Reflects on U.S. Refugee Policy in the 1970s," *The Carter Mondale Letter* (Atlanta: The Carter Center, Fall 2014), 9:2.

BOOK TWO
22. Transistional Leadership

1 English, Richard, 2015 e-mail to author re: Ronald Reagan's extemporaneous conclusion of speech accepting the Republican Party nomination for president, Detroit, 1980.
2 *State Department Newsletter*, Washington, August/September 1981, 27.
3 Ibid., 89.
4 State Department Notice, August 1981.
5 "Oversight Hearings" book, House Judiciary subcommittee on Immigration, Refugees, and International Law, Washington, September 16–23, 1981.

6   Ibid., 202-251.
7   Larry Clinton Thompson, *Refugee Workers in the Indochina Exodus, 1975–1982* (Jefferson and London: McFarland & Company, 2010), 238.
8   House and Senate Judiciary Committees, Consultation letters pertaining to FY 1982 refugee admissions, Washington, October 1981.

23. Struggling to Stay on Course

1   "Assistant Secretaries of State for Population, Refugees, and Migration, 1979–present," Reprinted by the Bureau for Public Affairs, US Department of State, Washington, 2012.
2   State Department Notice, September 1982.
3   State Department senior management meeting, author and key officials on RP staffing, Washington, August 1982.
4   State Department Announcement, June 5, 1982.
5   A Short History of the Department of State (by the summer of 1985, Shultz had personally selected most of the senior officials in the State Department, emphasizing professionalism over political credentials in the process), Washington, 2010.

25. Phase I–Stabilization

1   Sheehey, Gail, "Cambodian Refugees: America's Double-Cross," *Washington Post*, February 6, 1983.
2   Soonsiri Prasong, National Security Council Director, Government of Thailand.
3   de Barrin, Jacques, "Measures to stop the flow of Indochinese refugees," *News from UNHCR*, No. 10, *Le Monde*, Paris, October 1982.
4   Prasong, Thailand.
5   Obrecht, Therese, "Hong Kong: Will closed camps deter future arrivals?" *News from UNHCR*, No.13, January 1983.
6   Branigin, William, "Turning away of boat people mars improved refugee situation," *Washington Post*, February 4, 1984.
7   Funseth, Robert, "Resettlement in the heartlands of America," Multi-State Refugee Conference, St. Louis, MO, June 4, 1986, Reprinted by the Bureau for Public Affairs, US Department of State, Current Policy No. 847.
8   Shultz, George P., "Proposed Refugee Admissions for FY 1987," Statement before the Senate Committee on the Judiciary, released by the Bureau for Public Affairs, Current Policy No. 866, September 16, 1986.

26. Phase 2—Protection

1. Purcell, James N., Jr., "The Challenge of Refugee Protection," Statement at UNHCR Executive Committee meeting, Palais des Nations, Geneva, Reprinted by US Department of State, Bureau for Public Affairs, Current Policy No. 627, October 9, 1984; Purcell, "Piracy Incidents in the Gulf of Thailand," congressional hearing, House Foreign Affairs Committee, subcommittee on Asia and Pacific Affairs, Washington, July 31, 1985.
2. Ibid., "Gulf of Thailand"
3. *The State of the World's Refugees, Fifty Years of Humanitarian Action*, UN High Commissioner for Refugees (Oxford: Oxford University Press, 2000), 87.
4. de Barrin, Jacques. "Measures to stop the flow of Indochinese refugees," *News from UNHCR*, No. 10, *Le Monde*, Paris, October 1982.
5. Branigian, William, "U.S. Changes Refugee Policy to Curb Intake from Indochina," *Washington Post*, April 28, 1982.
6. Purcell, James N., Jr., testimony before House and Senate Judiciary Committees, Refugee Consultations, FY 1982, September 1981.
7. Ibid., Consultations.
8. State Department analysis pertaining to the start-up of Cambodian resettlement processing, March 1982.
9. Mazzoli, Romano A. (D-KY), letter to Ambassador Richard Vine, State Department, regarding Cambodian refugee resettlement in the United States, April 27, 1982.
10. Vine, Richard, response letter to Rep. Romano A. Mazzoli, May 10, 1982.
11. Surtzer, James S., Acting Officer in Charge, "Response to the brief written by Stephen Golub," memorandum to the Officer in Charge (OIC), Immigration and Naturalization Service (INS), Bangkok, May 13, 1986.
12. National Security Decision Directive (NSDD), issued by the National Security Council, regarding refugee processing, accompanied by a presidential letter, Washington, May 13, 1993.
13. *Providence Journal*, "The Reverend Peter L. Pond, 67, (obituary)," June 23, 2000.
14. "Cambodian Refugees in Southeast Asia," congressional hearing, House subcommittee on Asia and Pacific Affairs, Washington, July 31, 1985.
15. Purcell, James and Doris Meissner, Cable to Southeast Asia diplomatic missions, re: Results of Cambodian processing, May 1985.
16. "Cambodians in Thailand: People on the edge," US Committee for Refugees, Washington, December 1985, 13.

17 *The State of the World's Refugees, Fifty Years of Humanitarian Action*, UN High Commissioner for Refugees (Oxford: Oxford University Press, 2000, 95.
18 "USG Policies toward the displaced Khmer," memorandum to Michael A. Armacost, under secretary for political affairs, from Paul Wolfowitz, assistant secretary for East Asia and the Pacific, and James Purcell, Washington, May 23, 1985.
19 Pitman, Todd and Sophang Cheang, "Khmer Rouge leaders convicted," *Washington Post,* August 8, 2014.
20 US Montagnards, http://www.montagnards.org/2012-08-29-04-45-58/us-montagnards.html
21 Durenberger, David (R-MN), senator's letter to the author, March 17, 1986.
22 Berg, Steve, and Tom Hamburger, "Durenberger says Hmong letter was misunderstood," *Washington Post,* April 25, 1986.
23 Lionel Rosenblatt, Discussion with author.

27. Protection–Political Prisoners and Amerasians

1 Crosette, Barbara. "Exiles tell of stark life in Vietnam prisons," *New York Times,* September 16, 1984. https://www.nytimes.com/1984/09/16/world/exiles-tell-of-stark-life-in-vietnam-prisons.html
2 "Initiatives for Vietnamese Political Prisoners and Asian-American Children," memorandum from James Purcell to Michael L. Armacost, State Department, Washington, August 14, 1984.
3 Morgan, Ann, "Urgent Action Report," e-mail to author, January 6, 2014.
4 Alan Simpson (R-WY) was chairman/ranking member of the Senate Judiciary Committee's subcommittee on Immigration and Refugee Policy.
5 "Initiatives for Vietnamese Political Prisoners and Asian-American Children," memorandum from James Purcell to Michael L. Armacost, State Department, Washington, August 14, 1984.
6 Shultz, George P., "Proposed Refugee Admissions for FY 1985," House Judiciary Committee, (Reagan administration lead-off witness, refugee consultation hearings), Washington, September 1984.
7 Editorial, "The thousands still in camps," *Chicago Tribune,* indicative of the numerous editorials and favorable articles reporting on administration initiatives for Vietnamese political prisoners and Amerasian children from Vietnam, October 13, 1984.
8 "To Welcome the Amerasians," Migration and Refugee Services, United States Catholic Conference, Washington, 1988.
9 Ibid.

10 Yarborough, Trin, *Surviving Twice: Amerasian Children of the Vietnam War*, (Sterling: Potomac Booksm 2006)
11 *The State of the World's Refugees, Fifty Years of Humanitarian Action*, United Nations High Commissioner for Refugees (Oxford: Oxford University Press, 2000), 99.

28. Phase 3—Reform

1 Gramm–Rudman–Hollings Deficit Reduction Act of 1985, P.L. 99–177, December 12, 1985.
2 Government of Canada, minister of employment and Immigration, March 3, 1980–August 11, 1983.
3 Deputy secretary of state, July 9, 1985–January 20, 1989.
4 State Department announcement, Introducing Indochinese Refugee Panel members, including: Chairman, Robert D. Ray, governor of Iowa; Members: Edward Schmults, businessman, who served as White House Counselor, Deputy Treasury Secretary, and Deputy Attorney General; Irena Kirkland, Holocaust survivor and refugee from Czechoslovakia, a life-long democracy advocate and a board member of the International rescue Commission (wife of AFL-CIO President Lane Kirkland); former Senator Gale McGee (D-WY), recently retired from the Senate after 18 years and particularly knowledgeable about federal law enforcement; and Jonathan Moore, Dean of the Kennedy School at Harvard. He had served with Attorney General Eliot Richardson at Justice and Defense during the Nixon presidency, and he left Justice in the infamous "Saturday night massacre." Leo Cherne initially served with the Panel but withdrew for health reasons. Staff assistants were Frank Sieverts and Nancy Powell from RP and Joe Schneider from the East Asia and Pacific bureau. August 14, 1985,
5 Kaufman, Marc, "Uprooted: Legacy of Indochina War," *Philadelphia Inquirer*, April 1986.

29. Phase Four—Solutions

1 "Vietnamese Asylum seekers: Current Perspectives for Solutions," Note from UN High Commissioner for Refugees, Geneva, June 14, 1988.
2 Ibid.
3 Ibid.
4 Ibid.

5   *The State of the World's Refugees, Fifty Years of Humanitarian Action*, United Nations High Commissioner for Refugees (Oxford: Oxford University Press, 2000), 84-85.
6   Ibid., 84.
7   Ibid., 85.

30. The Meaning of Vietnam

1   *The State of the World's Refugees, Fifty Years of Humanitarian Action*, United Nations High Commissioner for Refugees (Oxford: Oxford University Press, 2000), 310.
2   Shultz, George, "The Meaning of Vietnam," address at the US State Department, Washington, April 25, 1985.

BOOK THREE
31. Eastern Europe and the Soviet Union

1   Carpenter, Margaret, "The Structure of the Voluntary Agencies in Europe," (plus attachments), memorandum to Ambassador Richard Vine, Washington, April 8, 1982 (*see* Appendix B.1)
2   James L. Carlin, *The Refugee Connection: A Lifetime of Running a Lifeline*, (London: MacMillan Press, 1989), 43-61.
3   "Czech Republic Slovakia: Velvet Revolution at 25," BBC News Europe, Updated November 17, 2014.
4   Carpenter, *Structure*.
5   Hoganson, Jerry, "The Romanian TCP Program," RP internal memorandum to Ambassador Richard Vine, April 30, 1982, (*see* Appendix B.2.).
6   George P. Shultz, *Turmoil and Triumph: My Years as Secretary of State* (New York: Charles Scribner's Sons, 1993), 5, 117.
7   Ibid., 874.
8   Steven Solarz, *A Congressional Memoir* (Waltham: Brandeis University Press, 2011), 189.

32. Soviet Jews

1   Natan Sharansky with Shira Wolosky Weiss, *Defending Identity: Its Indispensable Role in Protecting Democracy* (New York: Perseus Books, 2008), 231–32.

2   Philip Spiegel, *Triumph Over Tyranny, The Heroic Campaigns that Saved 2,000,000 Soviet Jews* (New York: Devora Publishing, 2008), 8–9.
3   Ibid., 96; Gal Beckerman, *When They Come for Us We'll Be Gone, The Epic Struggle to Save Soviet Jewry* (New York: Houghton Mifflin Harcourt, 2010), 20, 31.
4   Buche, John, ADST Oral History, State Department, December 15, 1999.
5   Elliott Abrams, Discussion with author.
6   Beckerman, *When*, 288.
7   Ibid., 302–07.
8   Lazin, Fred A., *The Struggle for Soviet Jewry in American Politics, Israel versus the American Jewish Establishment* (Lanham: Lexington Books, 2005), 52-53. Beckerman, struggle, 325–26.
9   Carter, Jimmy, televised Oval Office presidential address regarding the Soviet invasion of Afghanistan, Washington, December 30, 1979.
10 Reagan, Ronald, Speech to the National Association of Evangelicals, Orlando, March 8, 1983.
11 Lazin, Politics, 215.
12 Ibid., 186–92.
13 George P. Shultz, *Turmoil and Triumph, My Years as Secretary of State* (New York: Charles Scribner's Sons, 1993), 164–65, 452; Author discussion with Shultz, 2015.
14 Roth, Andrew. "Advisor to Soviet leader Gorbachev, Obituary." *Washington Post,* March 16, 2017.
15 Author discussions with Morris Abram.
16 Author discussions with Shultz; Beckerman, Struggle, 478–79.
17 Beckerman, Struggle, 495–96; Lazin, Politics, 220.
18 https://chnm.gmu.edu/1989/archive/files/-speech.
19 Lazin, Politics, 266.
20 Ibid., 266, 272.
21 Clapp, Priscilla, Email to author.
22 Lazin, Politics, 281.
23 Philip Spiegel, George Shultz speech to American Jewish Historical Society (New York: Devora, 2008), xvi.
24 Gorbachev, Mikhail. "Save the treaty I signed with Reagan." *Washington Post,* October 12, 2017.

33. Africa

1. "US Refugee Program," Congressional oversight hearings, chart on African refugee populations provided by the State Department, Washington, May 1979.
2. Arulananthan, Ahilan T., Article reprint in American Constitution Society, June 2008; Teitsch, Kathleen. "U.S. Presses for Increased Relief Aid for Famine." (although the quote is attributed to President Reagan, it appears to have been used first by USAID), *New York Times*, August 19, 1983.
3. "Origins & History of the Tribe of Falasha," April 2005, www.falasha-recordings.co.uk/teachings/res.html.
4. Powers, Charles. "Ethiopian Jews: Exodus of a tribe." *L.A. Times*, July 7, 1985. United Israel Appeal (UIA), briefing to author, 1982.
5. Ibid.
6. Dick Smyser, Discussion with author.
7. Purcell, Dewey, and Chavchavadze lunch with UIA colleague Maury Adkins, Chesapeake Bay, Maryland, August 1984.
8. Powers, Ethiopian.
9. Blitzer, Wolf (Washington Correspondent for the Jerusalem Post). "Imperiling Ethiopia's Jews." *Washington Post*, January 30, 1985.
10. Powers, Charles. "A New Life in Israel for Ethiopians." *L.A. Times*, July 8, 1985.
11. Jerry Weaver, Discussion with author.
12. Weaver, Discussion.
13. *The State of the World's Refugees, Fifty Years of Humanitarian Action*, United Nations High Commissioner for Refugees (Oxford: Oxford University Press, 2000), 113.
14. Morse, Bradford, Administrator of the United Nations Development Program, Head of the UN Office of Emergency Operations in Africa, Press briefing, January 31, 1985.
15. Gene Dewey, Discussion with author.
16. "Relief and Rehabilitation in Ethiopia," www.mauricestrong.net, 1985.
17. Feldman, Linda. "UN aid to Africa shifts focus, closing of emergency relief office sparks controversy over how to meet Africa's needs." *Christian Science Monitor*, October 29, 1986.
18. *GIST*, Bureau for Public Affairs, US State Department, "Ethiopian Famine," December 1985.
19. Keyes, Alan L., Statement before the Subcommittee on African Affairs, Senate Foreign Relations Committee, March 6, 1986.
20. *The State of the World's Refugees, Humanitarian*, 142.

21 Harden, Blaine. "Ugandans resettle after years of terror." *Washington Post*, September 12, 1984.
22 Murphy, Caryle. "New Uganda crackdown said to kill thousands." *Washington Post*, August 5, 1984. https://www.washingtonpost.com/archive/politics/1984/08/05/new-ugandan-crackdown-said-to-kill-thousands.
23 Bob Gersony, Discussion with author.

34. The Middle East

1 Maen, Rashid Areikat. "A deep and rich Palestinian history." *Washington Post*, December 28, 2011.
2 Chavchavadze, Judy, "Palestinian refugees – U.S. refugee Policy: 1975 – 1986," Washington, February 1, 1987.
3 George P. Shultz, *"Turmoil and Triumph, My Years as Secretary of State* (New York: Charles Scribner's Sons, 1993), 43-44.
4 Marvine Howe, *"Palestinians in Lebanon,"* December 20, 2005, Middle East Policy, Wiley Digital Archives, https://doi.org/10.1111/j.1475-4967.2005.00231.x., 149.
5 Shultz, Turmoil, 57-61, 74–76.
6 James L. Carlin, *The Refugee Connection: A Lifetime of Running a Lifeline* (London: MacMillan Press, 1989), 129–30.
7 Shultz, Turmoil, 82-83.
8 Dillon, Ambassador Robert, Oral history, ADST (State Department), May 1990.
9 Noam Chomsky and Avi Shlain, "Democracy Now," Interview with daily independent news hour, January 13, 2014." First Lebanon War: Massacres at Sabra & Shatila," http://www.jewishvirtuallibrary.org/jsource/History/Sabra_&_Shatila.html, September 16-17, 1982.
10 Shultz, Turmoil, 113.
11 *New York Times*. "Israel Announces Plan to House Palestinians." November 23, 1987.
12 Milton Viorst, *"Reaching for the olive branch – UNRWA and Peace in the Middle East,"* The Middle East Institute, Washington, 1989.
13 Cable from American Embassy Amman to Washington, January 1, 1984.
14 Viorst, UNRWA.

35. South Asia

1. Plaque in the Truman Building, Washington, and a memorial in Kabul. Lord, Jeffrey. "Jimmy Carter's Dead Ambassador." American Spectator, October 23, 2012.
2. "The Soviet Invasion of Afghanistan and the U.S. Response, 1979-1980," US State Department, Office of the Historian, October 31, 2013.
3. *GIST*, published by the Bureau for Public Affairs, US Department of State, "Afghanistan," September 1985.
4. The Atlantic, In Focus, "The Soviet War in Afghanistan, 1979–1989," August 4, 2014.
5. History Learning Site, "Russian Invasion of Afghanistan," UK, 2014
6. *GIST*, Afghanistan, History Learning Site, Invasion.
7. *The State of the World's Refugees, Fifty Years of Humanitarian Action*, United Nations High Commissioner for Refugees (Oxford: Oxford University Press, 2000), 116, 118.
8. Gene Dewey, discussion with author.
9. Gene Dewey and Fazel Haq, discussions in 1981–84.
10. The State of the World's Refugees, Humanitarian, 118–20.
11. Gene Dewey, Paula Lynch, discussions with author.
12. *GIST*, Afghanistan.
13. History Learning Site, Invasion UK. Invasion.
14. William Dalrymple, The Last Mughal: The fall of a dynasty, Dehli, 1857 (London: Penguin Group, 2006), 485.

36. Central America and the Caribbean

1. Abrams, Elliott, Congressional testimony, April 1985.
2. Sargisson, Philip, "Central America (February 1980–83)," Note to author, November 3, 2012.
3. Ibid.
4. Author response to question posed by Senator Dennis DeConcini at Congressional hearing, March 7, 1983. Author opening statement at congressional hearing, March 7, 1984.
5. Gene Dewey, Bob Gersony, Tex Harris, Don Krumm, and John Buche, Discussions with author.
6. Author Notes and recollections, International Organization for Migration (IOM), 1988–98.
7. Dewey, Gersony and Buche, discussions with author; Author notes.

8 *The State of the World's Refugees, Fifty Years of Humanitarian Action,* United Nations High Commissioner for Refugees (Oxford: Oxford University Press, 2000), 128.
9 Author recollection.
10 "United Nations–Cuba, Immigration Agreements, 1984–1987; 1994," *Encyclopedia of United Nations and International Agreements,* Vol. 4, Edited by Jan Ozmanczyk and Anthony Mango, 2003, 2546.
11 Meissner, Doris. "Radio Marti: A High Price for Immigrants." *Washington Post,* July 20, 1986.
12 United Nations–Cuba Immigration Agreements, 1987.
13 Everson, Mark. "Tweaking immigration reform." *Washington Post,* June 12, 2013.
14 Krauthammer, Charles. "The trigger and the poison pill." *Washington Post,* April 4, 2013.
15 "The *State of the World's Refugees,* Humanitarian, 131.

37. The Refugee Decade

1 *Newsletter,* "Refugee Boat: The Foreign Service Response (Washington: US Department of State, October 1984), 2–14.
2 Freddie Groot, "A Review of UNHCR Staff Training, Evaluation Report, UNHCR Evaluation Unit, Document EPAU/2000/02), Geneva, June 1999.
3 Shultz, George, "Proposed refugee admissions for FY 1987," congressional (consultations) testimony, Washington, September 16, 1986.

38. Sudden Change in Direction

1 Robinson, Robinson V. "Institute director at Harvard named to U.S. refugee post." Boston Globe, May 24, 1986.
2 Purcell, James N. "The Perils of Unresolved Humanitarian Problems, Focus The Middle East," ebook, 2015.

BOOK FOUR
39. Above All, Do No Harm

1 Raghavan, Sudarsan and Ishaan Tharoor. "My children slipped from my hands.," *Washington Post,* September 2, 2015.
2 Hudson Institute, Seminar, "The Syrian War, Five Months On," Washington, March 29, 2016.

3   Hiatt, Fred. "The price of U.S. inaction." *Washington Post*, November 23, 2015.
4   United Nations, "3RP Regional, Refugee and Resilience Report, 2016/2017," Geneva, December 2015.
5   Sly, Liz. "As tragedies shock Europe, a bigger crisis looms." *Washington Post*, August 30, 2015.
6   UN High Commissioner for Refugees, annual report, "Global Trends in Displacement," Geneva, June 17, 2015.
7   Witte, Griff. "Refugee crisis hits a tipping point, New U.N. report says world's refugee crisis is worse than anyone expected." *Washington Post*, June 18, 2015.
8   Ibid.
9   Epstein, Julie and Morello, Carol. "U.S. is set to take in 10,000 refugees." *Washington Post*, September 1, 2015.
10 Bureau for Counterterrorism and Countering Violent Extremism, Department of State, "Country reports for the Middle East and Africa," 2015, Washington, https://www.state.gov/j/ct/ris/crt/2015/257517.html.
11 Abramowitz, Morton. "Unattended Misery." *Washington Post*, December 6, 2013.
12 Amos, Valerie. "Does anyone care about Syria?" *Washington Post*, April 12, 2015.
13 Birnbaum, Michael. A plan to spread migrants in E.U." *Washington Post*, September 10, 2015.
14 Casert, Raf and Amer Cohadzic. "European leaders agree to add capacity for receiving 100,000 more refugees." *Washington Post*, October 26, 2015.
15 Taylor, Adam. "Islamic State's attacks on Yazidis constitute genocide, Holocaust Museum says." *Washington Post*, WorldViews, November 13, 2015. Morello, Carol and Branigan, William. "Islamic State has committed genocide, Kerry says." *Washington Post*, March 18, 2016.
16 Swing, William Lacey. "We're failing today's boat people." International Organization for Migration, Geneva, April 27, 2015. website article, URL: www.iom.int.
17 Bacetoros, Elena and Nicole Winfield. "European Union: Nations fail to bridge rift over migrant plan." *Washington Post*, June 17, 2015.
18 Missing Migrants Report, International Organization for Migration. Geneva, January 2017.
19 Witte, Griff and Michael Birnbaum. "Asylum-seekers arrive at last in western Europe." *Washington Post*, September 6, 2015.
20 Factbook, World, "Benefits offered to asylum seekers in Europe countries," September 16, 2015.

21 McAuley, James and Karla Adam. "Europe's warning to migrants: 'Don't come.'" *Washington Post*, March 4, 2016.
22 Ignatius, David. "The next challenge with Iran." *Washington Post*, July 17, 2015.
23 Gerson, Michael. "Obama's biggest failure." *Washington Post*, September 4, 2015.
24 DeYoung, Karen. "East Aleppo may face 'total destruction,' U.N. envoy says." *Washington Post*, October 7, 2016.
25 Robert S. Ford, "Diplomatic Dead-End on Syria, there is no mechanism that can hold Moscow and Damascus accountable now," *Middle East Institute*, Washington, October 11, 2016.
26 *Reuters*. E.U. faulted over abuse of migrants in Libya." December 12, 2017.
27 DIGEST, *Washington Post*. "Asylum seeker arrested in beach gang rape." September 4, 2017.
28 Birnbaum, Michael. "Open arms in Italy, many who embraced past migrant waves say this time, it's too much." *Washington Post*, August 26, 2017.
29 Faiola, Anthony. "Beacon for asylum seekers could dim the lights." *Washington Post*, January 11, 2017.
30 Beck, Luisa and Griff Witte. "Asylum rules are key hurdle in Germany's bid to form coalition." *Washington Post*, December 3, 2017.
31 Migration Policy Institute Europe, "Cracked Foundation, Uncertain Future: Structural Weaknesses in the Common European Asylum System," Brussels, March 21, 2018.
32 McAuley, James and Isaac Stanley-Becker. "African, European leaders craft migration deal," *Washington Post*, August 29, 2017.

40. Mystifying Breakdown

1 Faiola, Anthony. "Dispirited refugees left in cold by Europe." *Washington Post*, October 15, 2016.
2 Luck, Taylor. "Jordan may use cranes to deliver aid to 75,000 Syrians across border." *Washington Post*, WorldViews, October 15, 2016.
3 Sly, Liz. "Lebanese turn against refugees after brutal killing." *Washington Post*, October 11, 2017.
4 Faiola, Dispirited.
5 "Trump launches new attack on Syria with 59 Tomahawk missiles," Everett Rosenfeld@EvRosenfeld, NBC/CNBC, https://www//cnbc.com/video/3000608480, April 6, 2017.
6 Ibid.

7 Lamothe, Dan, Missy Ryan, and Thomas Gibbons-Neff. "Firing of cruise missiles comes days after chemical attack against civilians," *Washington Post*, April 7, 2017.
8 Loveluck, Louisa. "United Nations officially accuses Syria of April sarin attack," *Washington Post*, September 7, 2017.
9 Morello, Carol. "Investigators head to Syria as leaders mull action," *Washington Post*, April 11, 2018.
10 Lamothe, et al., Firing.
11 Gearan, Anne and Missy Ryan. "U.S. allies execute retaliatory strikes in Syria," *Washington Post*, April 14, 2018.
12 Loveluck, Louisa and Zakaria, Zakaria, "A journey into Syria's torture wards," *Washington Post*, April 3, 2017.
13 DeYoung, *Karen*. "*Syria using crematorium at prison, U.S. charges*," *Washington Post*, May 16, 2017.
14 Editorials. Syria's 'human slaughterhouse," Amnesty International documents atrocities in a military prison," *Washington Post*, April 3, 2017.
15 Lamothe, et.al., Firing.

41. Is America Still Reliable?

1 Gerson, Michael. "The cost of historical amnesia." *Washington Post*, November 20, 2018.
2 Johnson, Jenna, Morris Loveday, and Carol Morello. "Pence: Embassy will be in Jerusalem next year." *Washington Post*, February 5, 2018.
3 Balousha, Hazem and Ruth Eglash. "'A death sentence': Palestinians decry U.S. decision to reduce aid." *Washington Post*, January 18, 2018.
4 DeYoung, Karen, Ruth Eglash, and Hazim Balousha. "US ends aid to U.N. agency that supports Palestinian refugees," *Washington Post*, September 1, 2018.
5 Diehl, Jackson. "Genocide in Burma, and the United States stands by," *Washington Post*, January 22, 2018.
6 "U.S. withdraws from Migration Compact talks," US Mission to the United Nations in New York (USUN), press announcement, December 8, 2017.
7 Bureau of Population, Refugees and Migration, US Department of State, Diplomacy in Action, Proposed Refugee Admissions for Fiscal Year 2017," September 15, 2016.
8 Bureau of Population, Refugees and Migration, congressional budget presentation, 2018, "Migration and Refugee Assistance."

9 Bureau of Population, Refugees and Migration, US Department of State, Diplomacy in Action, Fact Sheet: US Humanitarian Assistance in Response to the Syrian Crisis, September 21, 2017.

10 United Nations, "3RP Regional Refugee and Resilience Plan, 2018/2019," Geneva, April 4, 2017, and September 24, 2017.

11 United Nations High Commission for Refugees, "Global Projected Resettlement Needs, 2016," Geneva, February 2016.

12 Zong, Jie and Jeanne Batalova. "Syrian Refugees in the United States." Migration Information Source, January 20, 2017.

13 Lowery, Wesley and Josh Dawsey. "In entry-ban fight, a year of chaos." *Washington Post*, February 7, 2018.

14 Merle, Renae, Devlin Barrett, and Westley Lowery. "Vehicle hurtles down bike path in possible terror act." *Washington Post*, November 1, 2017.

15 Nowrastem, Alex, "The Myth of Border Insecurity," CATO at Liberty, Cato Institution, Washington, November 2016. Bier, David, Statement to the House Judiciary Committee on H.R. 2826, a bill to impose an annual statutory limit on the number of refugees of no more than 50,000 [to be admitted to the United States], and other reforms, CATO, email to the author, June 14, 2017. Bier, David and Nowrastem, Alex, "Heritage Report Shows Refugees Are Not a Major Threat," CATO at Liberty, July 13, 2017.

16 Ibid., CATO at Liberty, July 13, 2017.

17 Evans, William N., and Daniel Fitzgerald. "What Happens When Refugees Come to the United States." The National Bureau of Economic Research, Evidence from NBER Working Paper No. 23498, Cambridge, MA, August 2017.

18 Bier, David, "New Rules to Deny Status to Immigrants up to 95% Self-Sufficient," Liberty at CATO, September 14, 2018.

19 Nowrasteh, Alex and Robert Orr, "Immigration and the Welfare State: Immigrant and Native Use Rates and Benefit Levels for Means-Tested Welfare and Entitlement Programs," CATO Institution, Washington, May 10, 2018.

20 EDITORIALS. "A thumb on the refugee scale." *Washington Post*, September 21, 2017.

21 EDITORIALS. "The Trump administration aims low." *Washington Post*, October 3, 2017; Leahy, Michael Patrick, "Refugee Admissions in Firt Fiscal Year of Trump Administration Lowest in History of Program," Breitbart News, October 2, 2018.

22 Leahy, "Refugee Admissions."

23 Refugee Council of America (RCUSA), Statement on the Consultations Process, October 4, 2018.

42. Searching a Way Forward

1. UN High Commissioner for Refugees, Global Trends: Forced Displacements in 2015, Geneva; UNHCR, 2016. URL:http//www.unhcr.org/576408cd7.pdf; van der Zee, Kiki, "Global Humanitarian Assistance Report 2015," United Nations, New York.
2. Bureau for Population, Refugees and Migration, U.S. Department of State, Diplomacy in Action, Proposed Refugee Admissions for Fiscal Year 2018," Overview of US Refugee Policy, Washington, September 2017. UN High Commission for Refugees, UNHCR Resettlement Statistics by Resettlement Country, CY 2016 Admissions, Geneva.
3. Randall Hansen. "Constrained by its Roots: How the Origins of the Global Asylum System Limit Contemporary Protection," (Washington: Atlantic Council on Migration, Migration Policy Institute, Executive Summary, January 2017), 1, 4, 7, 17.
4. "Framework for Durable Solutions for Refugees and Persons of Concern," United Nations, UNHCR/URL: http://www.unhcr.org/en-us/protecion/basic/3b73b0d63/states-parties-1951-convention-its-1967-protocol.html., United Nations High Commissioner for Refugees (UNHCR), Core Group on Durable Solutions, Geneva, May 2003.
5. United Nations, "3RP regional Refugee and Resilience Plan, 2018/2019," Geneva, April 4, 2017.

43. Ending War and Moving Ahead

1. Sly, Liz. "Worst in Syria could be ahead," *Washington Post*, August 12, 2018.
2. Lederer, Edith. UN pleads with Syria to allow aid deliveries," *Washington Post*, May 30, 2018.
3. Sonne, Paul and Karen DeYoung. "Trump sought $4 billion from Saudis for Syria." *Washington Post*, March 15, 2018.
4. Cunningham, Eric. "Turkey, Russia agree on Syria 'demobilized zone'," *Washington Post*, September 18, 2018.
5. Loveluck, Louisa and Ghalia al Alwani. "Syrian militants tepidly back demilitarized zone in last opposition stronghold," *Washington Post*, October 16, 2018.
6. Ryan, Missy, Paul Sonne, and John Hudson. "U.S. Shift on Syria:Stay until Iran leaves," *Washington Post*, October 1, 2018.
7. Loveluck, Louisa. "Syria offers amnesty to military deserters, but exiles have their doubts," *Washington Post*, October 10, 2018.

8   Ryan, Missy and Josh Dawsey. "U.S. to quickly pull troops from Syria," *Washington Post,* December 20, 2018.
9   Gorbachev, Mikhail. "Save the treaty I signed with Reagan," *Washington Post*, October 12, 2017.

44. A Test of Civilization

1   Mandelbaum, Michael, "Mission Failure: America and the world in the Post-Cold War era (London: Oxford University Press, 2016).
2   Mondale, Walter, Address to the UN Conference on Indochinese Refugees, United Nations Palais des Nations, Geneva, July 20, 1979.
3   "A Franciscan Benediction," adapted; differing versions online with same or similar title; (*see* also *Prayer* by Philip Yancey, Zondervan 2007).

APPENDIXES

Appendix A

Intergovernmental Committee on Refugees (in Chapter 8)

Until it was disbanded in 1947, the Intergovernmental Committee on Refugees (ICR), worked in close collaboration with many intervening institutions, including: allied governments, the Red Cross movement, the League of Nations, the Office of Foreign Relief and Rehabilitation Operations (OFRRO), the United States War Refugee Board, the United Nations Relief and Rehabilitation Administration (UNRRA), and numerous nongovernmental organizations (NGOs). During the years 1945–51, the international community created and financed a succession of intergovernmental humanitarian organizations, including: United Nations Food and Agriculture Organization (FAO), 1945 to present; International Refugee Organization (IRO), 1946–52; United Nations International Children's Emergency Fund (UNICEF), 1946–present; UN Relief and Works Agency for Palestinian Refugees (UNRWA), 1948–present; World Health Organization (WHO), 1948–present; UN Korean Reconstruction Agency, 1950–58; Office of the UN High Commissioner for Refugees (UNHCR), 1950–present; and Provisional Intergovernmental Committee for the Movement of Migrants in Europe (PICCME) founded 1951 (later known as Intergovernmental Committee for European Migration (ICEM), renamed Intergovernmental Committee for Migration (ICM), renamed International Organization for Migration (IOM), 1989.) The international community later established several other key global operational organizations, including the Commission for International Tracing Services (CITS) 1955; World Food Program (WFP) 1961; United Nations Disaster Relief Organization (UNDRO) 1965 (natural disasters); and United Nations Development Program (UNDP), 1965.

Appendix B

Eastern Europe and the Soviet Union (in Chapter 31)

B.1 *The Structure of the Voluntary Agencies in Europe,* Memorandum from Margaret Carpenter to Refugee Programs Director Vine, (plus attachments) April 8, 1982. With permission:

Voluntary agencies in Europe, primarily the welfare arms of the Catholic and Protestant churches, were well established by 1951 when the United States began to subsidize them to assist and process WWII refugees. Many private American-supported agencies also predated by many years direct government involvement with refugee resettlement. The German Evangelical Protestant refugee organization, Diakonisches Werk, originated in the nineteenth century. Created during World War II era: The International Rescue Committee, 1937 (to help people fleeing Nazi Germany); The Tolstoy Foundation, 1939; The Polish American Immigration and Relief Committee, 1946; The American Fund for Czechoslovak Refugees, 1948. Over twenty NGOs assisted refugees in Europe in the 1950s, and they aided the resettlement of millions of displaced persons and refugees from Europe, about 800,000 were resettled in the United States between 1946 and the Refugee Act of 1980. In 1962, the US Escapee Program (USEP) became the US Refugee Program (USRP); nine voluntary agencies were operating in Europe with US administrative and financial support. After the first efforts to resettle World War II *displaced persons*, successive crises in Europe (Hungary in 1956, Czechoslovakia in 1968, Romania from the 1970s, and Poland in 1981) required rapid assistance and resettlement expansions.

B.2 Romanian Third-Country Processing (TCP) for full briefing for Secretary Shultz, from *Jerry Hoganson Reform Notes*.

The proposed Hoganson reform notes that Romanian refugees coming to the United States were from two streams: (1) an escape route to Vienna, Belgrade, Athens, or Rome for resettlement processing; (2) a pre-screening route for those approved by the American Embassy in the capital, Bucharest, before final clearance in Rome. In the US Congress, the Jackson–Vanik amendment to the 1974 Trade Act joined trade and immigration to the United States. The Most Favored Nation (MFN) trade status, was linked to freedom of emigration from communist countries.

Appendix C

C.1 Refugee Processing Categories (Chapter 14) for individuals being assessed for refugee status

Category I. Lives in imminent danger (exodus and emergency)
Category II. Close relative of already admitted refugees and unaccompanied minors
Category III. Former employee of US Government entities or allies endangered by past connections
Category IV. Past close association with the United States, including foundations, voluntary agencies, and business firms
Category V. Other specified relative of already admitted refugees
Category VI. Other compelling reasons for granting refugee status

C.2 Solutions Compact (Chapter 42)

Framework Recommendations

UN *refugee camps* and *sites* to be reinvigorated (or established) in *first asylum* areas and protected as *safe areas*. (For Syrian victims, for example, this would not be a new concept for the affected regions as; about five million resided at one time or another in first asylum in Egypt,

Iraq, Jordan, Lebanon and Turkey, although global support has been inadequate);

Establishment of separate refugee tracks and immigration tracks;

Provisions and priority for valid family reunification or especially sensitive cases;

Mechanisms for *safe return* to home countries, *local settlement* or, where necessary, *resettlement in third countries*, including under immigration criteria.

Consideration to *orderly departure* mechanisms (called Offshore Processing) to document and admit refugees and migrants directly from *origin countries*, as done with the government of Vietnam;

New migration pathways running parallel to traditional *resettlement* schemes to "facilitate the mobility of refugees/migrants, whether for work, study, or *permanent resettlement*." Pathways could include existing labor, education, and family reunion schemes offered by governments;

Another initiative receiving attention is the private *sponsorship* of refugees for *resettlement* by individuals, local groups, or faith-based organizations.

Improvements and Benefits

Enhanced recognition that asylum-seeker motivations are mixed, some fleeing war and persecution and some seeking a safer and more secure life;

A needed pause (while in safe first asylum) to allow refugee/immigration motivations and next steps can be assessed;

Honoring *legal rights* of refugee applicants under the 1951 Convention, as they could still request resettlement out of the region (the major difference to involve lodging the request as regional first asylum, rather than as in-country political asylum);

No need to close borders, create questionable programs, or shirk legitimate humanitarian obligations and duties;

Resettlement consideration of new applicants only after they have been vetted and documented in first-asylum countries and approved by authorities;

Each asylum country would be free to set up its resettlement priorities and categories;

All *durable solutions* and *new migration-based approaches* would remain in play (recall that the two systems, as refugee and political asylum, are closely related, differing only in the place where a person asks for *status*; both find their legitimacy in the *1951 Humanitarian Convention*, to which most involved countries are signatories);

Asylum-seekers with a way forward would be free from *life-threatening dangers* on treks to Europe or any other continent.

TABLES

TABLE 1: GLOBAL REFUGEE POPULATIONS 1975–1987, IN THOUSANDS

	1975	1977	1979	1981	1984	1987
AFR	1,617	2,105	3,062	3,026	3,408	3,981
Asia	91	992	1,452	4,678	5,320	6,784
EUR	547	551	559	588	6 76,	1,173
LA/CAR	148	111	117	406	370	338
NAMR	546	714	792	1,099	737	463
OCE	38	50	315	328	105	101
VAR/OTH	5	9	2	70	70	227
Total	**2,991**	**4,531**	**6,298**	**10,194**	**10,685**	**13,069**

Regions: AFR-Africa, EUR-Europe, LA/CAR, Latin America/Caribbean, NAMR-North America, OCE-Oceania, VAR/OTH-Various/Unknown

Data Source: Drawn from *The State of the World's Refugees, Fifty Years of Humanitarian Action* (UNHCR) and State Department annual budgets and refugee consultations reports to Congress.

TABLE 2: REFUGEE ADMISSIONS TO THE UNITED STATES BY REGION, 1975–1987, IN THOUSANDS

	AFR	Asia	E. EUR	USSR	LA/CAR	NE/SA	Total	Consultation Ceilings
1975	0	135	2	6	3	0	146	—
1976	0	15	2	7	3	0	27	—
1977	0	7	2	8	3	0	20	—
1978	0	21	2	11	3	0	37	—
1979	0	77	3	24	7	0	111	—
1980	1	164	5	28	7	2	207	234
1981	2	131	7	13	2	4	159	217
1982	3	74	11	3	1	6	97	140
1983	3	39	12	1	1	5	62	90
1984	3	52	10	1	*	5	71	72
1985	2	50	9	1	*	6	69	70
1986	1	45	9	1	*	6	62	67
1987	2	40	9	4	*	10	65	**70
Total	17	849	83	109	30	45	1,133	

Regions: AFR-Africa, E.EUR-Eastern Europe, USSR-Union of Soviet Socialist Republics (Soviet Union), LA/CAR-Latin America and Caribbean, NE/SA-Near East South Asia

Data Sources: Drawn from admissions reports, 1975-1987, US State Department, Bureau for Refugee Programs (RP) and annual State Department refugee budgets and consultations reports to Congress.

*Less than one thousand.
**Includes 4,000 unallocated by region.

TABLE 3: US STATE DEPARTMENT REFUGEE AND MIGRATION BUDGETS, 1975–1987, IN THOUSANDS

Year	Admission	Relief	IO/Other	Admin.	Total
1975	315,000	14,518	4,726	1,214	333,443
1976	7,435	—	4,668	1,301	15,823
1977	14,625	—	12,771	1,355	28,755
1978	39,390	—	16,450	1,496	57,336
1979	157,316	8,850	29,900	3,052	198,788
1980	269,187	140,742	30,120	5,171	445,220
1981	204,147	167,037	35,150	6,041	412,375
ST	**1,007,100**	**331,147**	**133,785**	**19,630**	**1,491,740**
1982	146,097	233,475	21,870	6,593	408,035
1983	91,443	215,614	24,020	6,976	338,053
1984	98,424	205,826	22,050	7,552	333,852
1985	103,200	204,449	34,500	8,126	350,275
1986	105,342	189,717	21,462	7,720	324,241
1987	108,731	194,725	34,900	8,500	346,856
ST	**653,241**	**1,243,806**	**158,802**	**45,467**	**2,101,312**
GT	**1,660,341**	**1,574,953**	**292,587**	**65,097**	**3,593,052**

Table 3 Recap:

Years	Admissions	Relief	IOs/Other	Admin.
1975-1981	65%	22%	9%	1%
1982-1987	31%	59%	8%	2%

Data Sources: Drawn from Budget of the United States Government, Appendix, 1975-1987; US State Department, Bureau for Refugee Programs (RP) Congressional Budget Submissions, 1975-1987.

Excludes minor technical adjustments.

TABLE 4: OVERSEAS REFUGEE RELIEF AND ASSISTANCE BY REGION, 1975–1987, IN MILLIONS

	EA	AFR	NE/SA	LA/CAR	Other	Total
1975-1978	15	--	--	--	--	15
1979	--	7	1	1	--	9
1980	99	36	4	2	--	141
1981	53	57	51	4	2	167
1982	50	87	90	6	1	234
1983	33	64	95	16	8	216
1984	31	59	95	21	--	206
1985	35	65	90	15	--	204
1986	33	56	85	16	--	190
1987	32	60	88	15	--	195
Total	**380**	**492**	**596**	**96**	**11**	**1575**

Regions: EA-East Asia, AFR-Africa, NE/SA-Near East/South Asia, LA/CAR-Latin America and Caribbean

Data Sources: Drawn from Budget of the United States Government, Appendix, 1975-1987; US State Department, Bureau for Refugee Programs (RP), Congressional Budget Submissions, 1975–1987

TABLE 5: REFUGEE MOVEMENTS TO AND FROM ASEAN REGION. 1975–1987, IN THOUSANDS

	ARRIVALS			DEPARTURES			IN 1987		
	V	L	K	V	L	K	V	L	K
BRU	*			*			*		
HK	113			110			10		
IND	100			99			2		
MAL	226			217			10		
PHIL	40			38			3		
SING	30			30			*		
THAI	99	337	228	85	252	216	15	83	23
Grand Total	**1,173**			**1,048**			**145**		

* Less than one thousand
Countries of Origin: **V**-Vietnam, **L**-Laos, **K**-Kampuchea
ASEAN receiving countries: BRU-Brunei, HK-Hong Kong, IND-Indonesia, MAL-Malaysia, PHIL-Philippines, SING-Singapore, THAI-Thailand

Data Source: Drawn from *"Vietnamese Asylum Seekers: Current Perspectives for Solutions,"* Note from UNHCR, June 14, 1988; US State Department, Bureau for Refugee Programs (and predecessors) annual Congressional budgets and Consultations reports, 1975-1987.

Note: Figures as issued by UNHCR without revision.
Note: ASEAN: Association of Southeast Asian Nations.

TABLE 6: DISPLACEMENTS AND SETTLEMENTS IN ASIA, 1975–1987, IN THOUSANDS

Escapes across ASEAN Borders	1,173
Settlement in People's Republic of China	280
1975 Saigon Evacuation	130
Border Khmer	300
ODP Departures from Vietnam	135
TOTAL	**2,018**

Substantial but unknowable numbers of people perished at sea or gave up escape attempts.

Data Source: Drawn from *"Vietnamese Asylum Seekers: Current Perspectives for Solutions,"* Note from UNHCR, June 14, 1988; US State Department, Bureau for Refugee Programs (and predecessors) annual Congressional budgets and Consultations reports, 1975-1987.

Note: Figures as issued by UNHCR without revision.

TABLE 7. VOLUNTARY RESETTLEMENT, REPATRIATION, AND RELOCATION OF INDOCHINESE REFUGEES BY DESTINATION, 1975–1997, IN THOUSANDS

Settlement in	Cambodian	Laotian	Vietnamese	Total
Australia	16	10	111	138
Canada	17	17	103	137
France	34	34	27	96
Germany	1	2	17	19
United Kingdom	*	*	19	20
United States	150	248	425	823
All other countries	17	9	53	78
Subtotal	**236**	**321**	**755**	**1311**
Orderly Departure	---	---	624**	624
Repatriation (by UNHCR)***	390	27	127	544
Relocation (Ethnic Chinese to China)	---	---	280	280
Grand Total	**626**	**348**	**1786**	**2759**

* Less than one thousand
** Main ODP recipient countries: United States (458k); Canada (60k); Australia (47k); France (19k); Germany (12k); United Kingdom (5k); all others (22k)
*** Many thousands more returned of their own accord or remained surreptitiously in their country of refuge.

Data Sources: Drawn from US State Department Bureau for Refugee Programs (and predecessor/successor organizations), annual budgets and Congressional Consultations reports, 1975-1997; *The State of the World's Refugees: Fifty Years of Humanitarian Action*, UNHCR, 2000, 99. Confirmed by: Courtland W. Robinson, *Terms of Refuge*, UN High Commissioner for Refugees, London: Zed Books, 1998, 270, 276, Appendix 2; Far Eastern Economic Review, June 23, 1978, 20.

TABLE 8: REGISTERED PALESTINIAN REFUGEES, 1950-2008, IN THOUSANDS

	1950	1960	1970	1980	1990	2000	2008
Jordan	506	614	506	716	929	1,570	1937
Lebanon	128	136	176	227	302	376	417
Syria	82	115	159	209	281	383	457
West Bank	---	---	273	324	414	583	754
Gaza	198	255	312	368	496	825	1,060
Total	**914**	**1,120**	**1,426**	**1,844**	**2,422**	**3,737**	**4,625**

Data Source: United Nations Relief and Works Agency for Palestinian Refugees, UNRWA, reports; US State Department, Bureau for Refugee Programs (and predecessor/successor organizations), annual budgets and congressional consultations reports.

TABLE 9. AFGHAN REFUGEE POPULATION BY COUNTRY OF ASYLUM, 1979-1987, IN THOUSANDS

Year	Pakistan	Iran	Other*	Total
1979	402	100	---	502
1980	1,428	300	---	1,728
1981	2,375	1,500	2	3,877
1982	2,877	1,500	3	4,380
1983	2,873	1,700	5	4,578
1984	2,500	1,800	5	4,305
1985	2,730	1,880	5	4,615
1986	2,878	2,190	5	5,073
1987	3,156	2,350	5	5,511

*Primarily India

Data Source: Drawn from *The State of the World's Refugees, Fifty Years of Humanitarian Action, 2000*, UNHCR; US Department of State, Bureau for Refugee Programs (RP), annual budgets and congressional consultations reports.

GRAPH
JEWISH EMIGRATION FROM THE USSR, 1968–1993

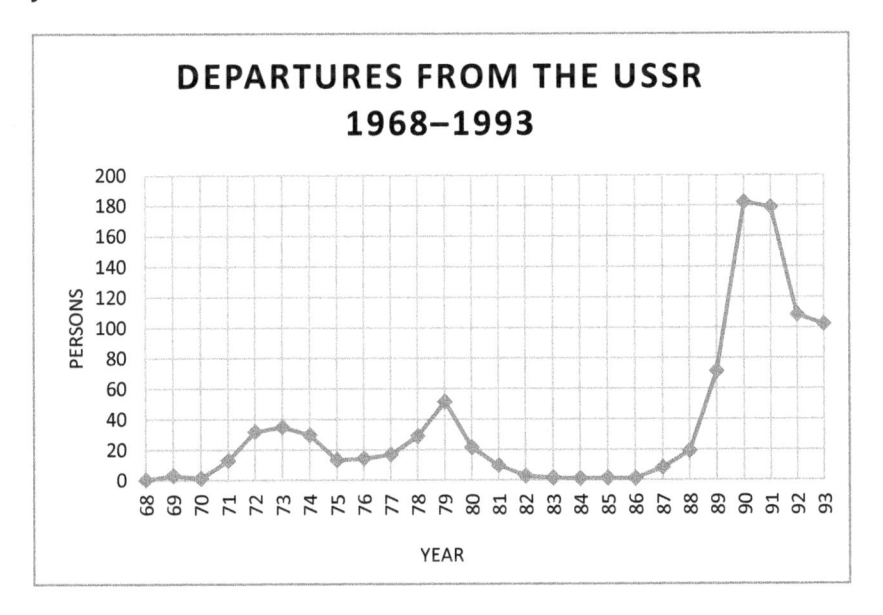

DEPARTURES FROM THE USSR 1968–1993

Graph developed by author from US Department of State, Bureau for Refugee Programs (RP), annual budgets and congressional consultations reports and other confirming sources.

INDEX

ABC News 289
Abram, Morris 263, 265
Abramowitz, Morton (Mort) 31, 69, 75, 124, 125, 129, 130, 184, 185, 373, 374, 448
Abrams, Elliott 179, 258, 283, 304, 338, 342, 343
absence of will 379
Abu Ghraib 392
AbuZayd, Karen 280
access 28, 102
  camps 190, 222
  decouple 412
  information 293
  missiles 327
  seventh floor 125
  State parking 146
  Thai help 190
  Vietnam 222
accomplishments 94
achievement 213
  career staff 402
  CPA 238
  historic refugee 352
  humanitarian 423
  INF Treaty 271
  processing 206
  training programs 357
ACNS (American Council for Nationality Service) 103
acting director
  RP 80, 133, 136, 160, 163, 164, 167, 172, 177, 187, 204
Acts
  Amerasian Homecoming Act 1988 224
  Amerasian Immigration Act 1982 215
  Antideficiency 27, 38, 86, 92, 96
  Antideficiency Act violated 39
  Appropriations 91
  Chinese Exclusion Act 1882 54
  Cuban Adjustment Act 1966 140
  Displaced Persons 1948 60, 61, 118
  Foreign Assistance Appropriations 91
  Foreign Operations Appropriations 45
  Gramm–Rudman–Hollings 225
  Immigration and Control Act 1986 349
  Immigration and Nationality 1952 64

473

Immigration and Nationality
      Act 61
Immigration and Nationality
      Act 1965 62
Indochina Migration and
      Refugee Assistance 17
Indochina Migration and
      Refugee Assistance 1962
      118, 313
Johnson-Reed Act of 1924 55
Kampuchea Relief Act 1979 129
Migration and Refugee
      Assistance 1962 64
Naturalization Act 1790 54
Quota Act of 1921 55
Refugee 1980 313
Refugee Act 1980 41, 50, 69, 85,
      86, 91, 94, 97, 100, 101,
      107, 119, 120, 121, 134,
      158, 164, 185, 186, 202,
      203, 204, 206, 218, 229,
      230, 253, 257, 267, 269
Refugee Act of 1980 32
Refugee Relief 1953 118
Trade Act 1974 251
ACVA (American Council of
      Voluntary Agencies) 20
Adler, Ada 165, 170
Administration
      bureau 46, 81
admission
      and 1980 Refugee Act 185
      applicants 405, 406
      asylum seekers 411
      contentious 167
      denied 406
      from Eastern Europe 158
      from Indochina 21
      legal US 120
      permanent resettlement 90
      persecuted classes 121
      political prisoners 224
      procedures 405
      to Israel 269
      to US 21
      US numbers 18, 188
admissions
      Carter 74
      ceiling 2018 407
      ceilings 404
      cutback 45
      domestic program 101
      emergency authority 121
      funding 93
      G. H. W. Bush 267
      hearings 1981 164
      Indochinese 168
      legislative policy 119
      level 164
      moratorium proposed 169
      negotiations 164
      numbers 137
      or genocide 167
      pause or end 404
      persecuted class 185
      presumptive eligibility 185
      promises 186
      Refugee Act 158
      refugees approved 402
      resettlement 1981 159
      Senate-proposed 1987 359
      September (overage) 171
      Simpson 169
      Soviet Jews 168
      Soviet program 264
      State Department ceiling 398
      Syrian refugees 404
      US jurisdiction 90
      worldwide 404
advocacy 304
      humanitarian 424
advocates 92, 382, 383, 425
Aegean Sea 378
Afghan
      army 326
      census 333

civilian deaths 334
exodus 159
fighters 373
government 325
Hazaras 329
insurgents 327
medical 331
Mujahideen 326, 335
Pakistan protection of 331
population 328
refugees 328, 329
refugees in Iran 333
refugees in Pakistan 333
regime opponents 325
resettlement 333
resistance 334
Tajiks 329
Taliban 335
team 330
troops 334
urban refugees 333
Uzbeks 329
Afghanistan
   1979 259
   crisis 83
   Democratic Republic
      established 326
   DemocraticRepublic of 328
   freedom fighters 157
   invaded 133
   invasion of 256
   Soviet invasion 257
   Soviet invasion of 326, 328
   Soviet occupation 329
   Soviets invaded 325
   Soviet withdrawal 335
   Taliban 335
   UN resolution 328
Africa 81, 356, 368
   analysis 275
   asylum nations 302
   asylum seeker 384

broadened Convention
   definition 336
budget 274
civil wars 83
drought-famine victims 157
famine 426
famine 1984 279
hunger and starvation crisis 295
migration routes 383
multilateral organizations 295
North 382
partnerships 274
programs and budgets 273
refugee relief 275
RP 272
Southern 274
Sub-Sahara 295
top refugee expert on 125
warlords 406
African
   refugees 302
agencies
   international development 302
   Jewish 286
agreement
   contractual 64
   cooperative 106
   El Salvador and Guatemala 350
   European–African 383
   Geneva Conference 98
   Helsinki Final Act 256, 257
   Jackson–Vanik Trade 257
   LIRS 102
Air Force 14
   C-130s 291
   Egypt 280
   pilots 290
   US 279
airlift 128
air patrols 115
AJDC (American Joint Distribution
   Committee) 257
Alaska Air C-130 128

Aleppo 390
    bombing of 381
    capture 382
Allen, John 393
Allen, Richard 159
allies xvi, xxii, 5, 7, 9, 14, 19, 23, 36, 53, 71, 79, 96, 107, 204, 214, 306, 351, 391, 398, 399, 400, 401, 413, 418, 419, 426
allocation 106
    planning 220
al-Qaeda 370, 389, 396, 421
    nexus 335
Alvarado, Donna 169
ambiguity
    constructive 107
Amerasian
    as refugee 216
    children 192, 193, 213, 215, 216, 218, 219, 221, 242
    eligibility 217
    emigration 224
    immigration category 215
    initiatives for 224
    media reports 223
    plight 215
    young adult 220
American
    attitudes evolved 57
    humanitarians 31
    isolationism 20
    leadership 34
    refugee policies 37
    resolve 20
    ships 16
    troops 10
American Embassy
    Bangkok, Thailand 189
    Honduras 343
    in El Salvador 342
    Israel 397
    Khartoum, Sudan 283, 290
    Moscow 262, 267
    refugee operation 32
    skeleton crew in Kabul 325
    South Vietnam 11
    Sudan 283
    Sudan capital Khartoum 278
    Thailand 25
    threats 291
Amin, Hafizullah 326
amnesty
    offer 422
    program 349
Amnesty International
    charged European governments 383
    on Saydnaya 391
Amos, Valerie 374
Amri, Anis 384
Amtsberg, Luise 385
analysis
    refugee staff 77
anarchy 23
anchor
    needy population Ethiopia 278
    workable solutions 416
Angka Loeu 24
Anglican
    archbishop 304
anti-communists 344
Antipas, Andy 125
antipiracy
    center 199
    program 192, 196, 198
    witness interpretation services 198
    witness transfers 198
apparatus
    refugee in jeopardy 316
Appave, Gervais 118
application
    citizenship 232
Applied Linguistics, Center for 112
appointees
    resignation 148

476

appropriations 50, 92
    amendment 45
    emergency 96
    pending 101
    Senate Committee 313
April 30, 1975 22, 27
Arab
    Deterrent Force 314
    governments 316
    Spring consequences 370
    Spring uprisings 368
Arab Spring
    slogan 370
Arafat, Yasser 314, 324
Argov, Shlomo 309
Armacost, Michael 221
Armitage, Richard 15
arms
    cache 311
    control 257, 260, 263, 264
arrivals
    Vietnam and Laos rate 188
    Vietnamese 229
ARTF (Afghan Refugee Task Force) 133
ASEAN (Association of Southeast Asian Nations) 28, 68, 70, 122, 123, 187, 235, 237, 239
Ashe, Robert 128
Asia 111
    asylum countries 68
    budget 70
    camp overcrowding 110
    economies 417
    first asylum 109
    governments 183
    Loescher overview 150
    regional settlement 68
    staff 70, 171
    team 124
Assad, Bashar 370, 373, 380, 390, 391, 393, 419, 425, 426
assimilation 110, 211

pace 186
assistance 102
Astana
    future Kazakhstan capital 382
asylum 57, 413
    Afghan refugees 333
    anchor 414
    and *magnet effect* 190
    applicants 385
    ASEAN countries 70
    ASEAN governments 190
    camps 70, 336
    claims 383, 386
    close to home 416
    Costa Rica 336
    countries 97, 188
    countries and war zones 188
    countries concerned 191
    countries overwhelmed 301
    countries' reluctance 114
    country 357
    country pressures 188
    crises Middle East 408
    expanded 74
    first 393
    first-asylum essential 416
    first regional 390
    first-secure 411
    Geneva pledges 77
    Honduras 336
    impacts 417
    Jordan 388
    long-stayers 302
    maintain first 415
    Mexico 336
    Middle East 371
    misunderstood 190
    moratorium 28
    political 343, 369, 405, 411
    regime 387
    region 371
    regional 340, 403
    regional governments 417

477

rights 68
safe regional 183, 339
seekers 348, 375, 376, 377, 385, 387, 388, 408
seekers Africa 369
seekers and migrants 338
seekers Europe 369
seekers Europe 2015 411
seekers in Central America 338
seekers non-vetted 390
seekers rejected 337
seekers report 372
seekers Salvadoran 340
seekers suffocated 377
seekers to Europe 371, 372
seekers unvetted 411
seekers younger 371
system territorial 412
temporary 253
territorial 411, 412
Asylum
    countries and ODP 219
    seekers Western Europe 377
asylum country 75, 118, 189
asylum seekers 225
    drowned 240
    Vietnamese 236
Athens 314
Atkin, Maury 285
atrocities 78
attacks
    on Khmer 130
attempts
    release former allies 214
attitudes
    American 53
    national 367
    restrictive global 415
Australia 118, 226, 227, 351, 359, 387
    2016 resettling 403
Australian
    concerns 118
    immigration officials 118

Austria 249
baby tossed 15
backlogs
    Moscow and Rome 267
Bagram Air Base 326
Baker, James 184, 267
Baker, John 81, 84, 137
balance
    ethnic 62
Balkans 373
Ballard, Jerry 345
Baltic
    Republics 59
    States 259
Bangkok 128, 129, 204
    border Khmer 295
    refcoord 175
    staff 204
barbarism 426
Barnes, Tom 125
Barnhard, Peggy 187, 221
barriers 422
Barry, John 7, 8
Basket III
    Helsinki Final Act 257
Bassac River 13
Bataan
    ICMC 112
    training recruitment 111
Bataan Island 110, 111
Ba Van Nguyen 15
Bay of Pigs
    Cuba 140
Beasley, David 305
Becker, Carol 63, 64
Beck, Karl 81, 132, 162, 273, 275, 276, 299
Beecher, William 289
Begin, Menachem 282
    on Diaspora 288
Beirut 309, 311
    and Sharon 309
    evacuation 176, 316

helipad 318
   multinational forces 314
Bennett, John E. 303
Ben Porat, Mordechai 321
Ben Porat Plan 323
Berenger, Henry 56
Berlin 384
Berlin Wall 250, 266
Betts, Alexander 372
Biden, Joe 10, 171, 373
bilateral 192, 224, 237, 296, 330, 346, 408, 409
bilateral approach 400
Bird Air 25
Bissett, James (Joe) 226, 228
Blackman, Ann 10
blackout 285
   information 287
Black Sea passage 383
blowback
   spending violation 39
boat
   arrivals 193
   capsized 376
   clandestine 191
   corpses 376
   crime syndicates 377
   decoy 196
   departure 28, 113, 219
   departures 196
   dissuade departures 376
   exodus 133
   flight 199
   Haitian flotillas 338
   Mediterranean 376
   patrol 196
   Port Sudan 282
   refugees 192
   Vietnamese 242
boat people 35, 70, 73, 76, 122, 196, 197, 203
   arrivals 28
   conference 1979 424
   deaths 113, 377
   drowned 377
   Indochina 375
   initiative 46
   Mediterranean 377
   Mediterranean 2015 375
   rescue 78
   Southeast Asia-Cuba-Haiti 157
BoB
   Bureau of the Budget 1
Bolsheviks 254
bombs
   Cambodia 9
   Omdurman 280
Bond, Jim 93, 310, 313, 315
border
   camps 127, 343
   communities 341
   conflicted zones 207
   food distribution 126
   international 340
   Jewish settlements 309
   Kampuchea crisis 124
   Khmer 126, 199, 201, 207, 233
   Moscow combat units 326
   relief 208
   Sa Kaeo camp 129
   Thai 24
borders 19, 367
   asylum 301
   concerns on 339
   danger crossing 27
   redrawn 259
   rivers at 345
Borg, Parker 5
Botti, Anita 187
Bouman, David 53
boundaries
   bureaucratic 298
Bradley, Ed 34
Brezhnev Doctrine 247
Brezhnev, Leonid 327
   Doctrine 327

479

brothers and sisters
    endangered 425
Brown, L. Dean 11, 17
Brown, Mark Malloch 127, 357
Brussels
    logistics 1951 63
    summit 2015 375
Brzezinski, Zbigniew 74, 325, 326
Buche, John 61, 102, 257
budget
    1982 request 99
    allocations 1975-1987 189
    annual international 128
    combat piracy 197
    consultations 92
    cuts 407
    finalized resettlement 361
    FY 1981, 1982 99
    halved 64
    implications 71
    Japan fifty per cent 227
    proposals 98
    reform 98
    refugee 398
    request 2
    RP largest 96
    staff 99
    structures 220
    systems 98
    Vietnam 1
budget and management 166
Building
    New Executive Office 103
Buis, Dale 7
Bullington, Jim 5, 9
burden-sharing 68, 77, 225, 226, 235, 355, 358
bureau
    enormous potential 65
    federal budget 7
    future 176
bureaucracy 18
    bypass 296

diplomacy and law 271
bureaucratic
    channels 52
Burma 399
Burt, Rick 251
Bush, Barbara 184
Bush, George H. W. 184, 267, 268, 289, 290, 304, 395
Byrne, Brendan 35, 75
cable
    distribution 285
    traffic embargo 293
CA (Consular Affairs) 95
Caesarea
    Gene Dewey 294
Calais
    asylum 377
    pressure 377
Califano, Joseph 100
California
    San Bernardino 404
Cambodia 9, 19, 23, 26, 29
    genocide of 24
    holocaust 24
    holocaust survivors 242
    invaded 24
    massive exodus 359
    returns 209
    Save Cambodia award 209
Cambodian
    Crisis Committee 205
    refugees 69
    resettlement 184
Cambodians
    disapproved 184
    Khao I Dang camp 190
camp
    census 277
    closeout 230
    Colomoncagua 342
    Diavata 388
    Indonesia 111
    Khao-I-Dang 123

480

Nong Chan 128
Rubkan 389
Sabra 317
Sa Kaeo 123
security perimeter 342
Shatila 317
Campbell, John 187, 216, 221
camps 97
  border 342
  communist re-education 22
  Cuban security issues 142
  first asylum 28
  for humane deterrence 191
  insurgents pilfering 342
  malaria 208
  overflow 110, 113
  transit 17
  UNRWA 322
  Vietnam reeducation 213
  work 24
Canada 226, 351, 359, 387
  2016 resettling 403
Canadian
  NGOs 282
Can Tho 113
capacities 63, 109, 235, 248, 332, 371, 417, 427
capacity 375, 407, 423, 426
  reception 71
Capelli, Fiorella 347
cargo ship
  Le Goelo 115
Carlin, James 60, 119, 249, 253, 284, 285, 314
Carpenter, Margaret 119, 165, 168, 170, 250
Cartagena
  status type 339
Cartagena Declaration on Refugees 337, 350
Carter Center 152
Carter, James (Jimmy) 33, 35, 39, 71, 73, 78, 103, 114, 131, 144, 148

  administration 32, 36, 40, 45, 84, 87, 93, 98, 113, 115, 117, 131, 132, 134, 137, 140, 143, 144, 145, 148, 149, 150, 214, 325, 326
  diplomacy 144
  foreign policy center 152
  Indochina solution 359
  initiatives 153
  State of the Union speech 327
Carter, Rosalynn 129
Casey, Bill 30
Castro
  abuses 399
  troops 140
Castro, Fidel 139, 338, 345
catastrophe 35, 69, 402
  unanticipated 353
Catholic Relief Services 129, 274, 278
CATO Institute
  study 406
  threat comparisons 406
CBS Reports 34
CCIR (Citizens Commission on Indochinese Refugees) 32, 35, 97
  public awareness 30
  report 35
CDC (Centers for Disease Control) 169, 208, 331, 341
CDU
  Christian Democratic Union 385
cease-fire 427
  call 309
  plan in Libya 380
Ceausescu, Nicolai 251
Celeste, Dick 274
Celler, Emanuel 62
central
  strategic ingredients 418
Central America 319, 336, 337, 350, 373

civil wars 83, 336
  flight 159
  internally displaced 336
  military regimes 339
  undocumented aliens 336
Chad 383
challenges
  surging globally 425
changing the culture 355
charities
  private 352
Charry-Samper, Hector 337
Chavchavadze, Judy 105, 285, 306, 307
chemical
  attack 391
  attacks 427
  attacks 2015 380
  treatment 391
  weapons 390, 393
Cherne, Leo 30, 32, 35, 36, 45, 97
Chernyaev, Anatoly 262
Chicola, Phil 144, 228
Chidiac, Raya 389
children
  of the dust 215
  the South China Sea 35
Childress, Richard 204
China 78
  resettlement 240
Chinese
  ethnic 22, 116
  immigration 54
Christian
  Pentecostals 262
  values 375
  war crimes
    against 375
Christman, Pat 19
Christman, Paul 19
Christmas story 250
Christopher, Warren 38, 39, 40, 42, 43, 44, 91, 138, 164, 272

Chung Tan Cang 15
Church, Frank 10
CIA (Central Intelligence Agency) 11, 28, 70, 290
citizens
  Cambodian 23
civil
  conflicts tribal 275
  service employee 178
  service professional 179
  society 399
  society representatives 337
  war 342, 350, 380
  war Guatemala 343
civilians
  into crosshairs 419
civilization 76, 380, 393, 409, 413, 427
  at a crossroads 426
  challenges 410
  civilizational crisis 427
  demands 425
  new test 425
civilized
  defenders 427
  nations 391
  people 427
  society 389
  world xix, 76, 271
Clapp, Priscilla 268, 269
Clark, Bill 165
Clark, Dick 33, 38, 40, 45, 70, 72, 75, 78, 83, 96, 111, 119, 137
Clark, Joan 175
Clark, Ray 3, 4
Clark, William 159, 163
Cline, Garner (Jim) 119, 166
Clinton
  administration 140
Clinton, William (Bill) J. 142, 324
closest advisors 165
coalition 419
  international 329

partners 419
coalition of the willing 241, 413
Coast Guard 382, 383
    Italian 376
Coco River 344
coffers
    private 98
    public 98
Cohen, Hank 173
Cold War 7, 20, 60, 61, 256, 263, 264, 266, 271, 336, 423
Coleman, Joe 186
Collett, Elizabeth 382
Colombian 337
Colomoncagua 342
colonies 54
combatants 331
commitment
    renewed 82
Committees
    Judiciary reorganizing 160
communist 214, 247, 252, 253
    government 22, 210
    regimes 19, 159
    single-party 250
    systems 19
community
    international 69, 381, 425
compact
    members as negotiators 416
    migration 399
    partners 417
    two international 399
compassion 115
compromise 44
Conable, Barber 331
concern
    paramount in future 341
conclusion
    humane 414
conference call 318
configuration
    new organizational 29

Congress 9, 35, 38, 50, 71, 86, 90, 95, 96, 97, 98, 107
    admissions hearings 163
    advance consultation 202
    Amerasian legislation 215
    and Iranian compliance 379
    and low-level witnesses 166
    and refugee consultations 149
    and RP 134
    a principal concern 111
    Communist Party 263
    consultation hearing 221
    consultations 159
    consultations report to 303
    continuing resolution 159
    Cuba policy 143
    funding 52, 111
    funding pressure 226
    funds from 44
    gave RP authority 313
    hearings 274
    interest in Khmer 202
    refugee legislation 137
    RP-Soviet Jews 257
    shocked 179
    Simpson 177
    supplemental 71
    testifying 1980 139
    threatening 111
congressional
    admissions consults 164
    advocates 231
    appropriations 88
    committees 89, 91, 119, 314
    committee staffers 119
    consultation hearings 162
    consultations 164
    delay 101
    disapproval 166
    enactment 222
    funding 93, 98
    funding approval 86
    hearing 69

hearings 92
hesitancy 46
imperatives 97
imposed budget reductions 225
initiative 253
Kampuchea relief 129
leaders 75
letter 304
multiple committees 171
oversight 310
reform 89
refugee law 120
relations 85, 94
response 223
schedule 165
staff 101, 243
staffers 171
system 45
testimony 196, 221
threats 164
transfer threats 84, 109
witnesses 164
Connors, Calvin 175
conscience 114, 146, 424
consensus
   approval 238
   durable solutions 413
   international 73
   not reached 319
   on proposals 236
   original 333
   US mission 300
Con Son Island 15
Consular Affairs
   State bureau 105
consultations 167, 231
   hearing 91
   victory 172
containment policy 323
continuing resolution 45
   1988 224
Contras
   and Miskito Indians 344

rebels 336
contributions 73, 77, 106, 227, 414
   dedicated individuals 206
   equitable 417
   multilateral 295
   partner 107
contributors
   financial 226
Controls 99
controversy
   multilateral v. bilateral 408
convoys 420
Coolfont
   breakthroughs 106
   Conference 106, 107, 108, 186
   RPparlance 104
cooperation
   depended on American 118
   diminished 411
   expanded 416
   global 413
   global limited 96
   intergovernmental 227
   international 418
   protect refugees 242
   refugee systems paradigm 236
   successful intergov 241
cooperative
   action 409
   action missing 412
   agreement 103, 104, 105
   resettlement 104
coordinator
   Clark 83
   Douglas 175, 261, 320
   Gene Douglas 181
   interagency for refugees 38
   Palmieri 111
   refugee 216
   refugee affairs 90, 121
   US refugee 231, 280, 283
Corcos, Albert 19
Cordovez, Diego 328

Corr, Ed 343
courage 427
Court of Justice 386
covenant
    for conflict victims 61
CPA (Comprehensive Plan of Action) 238, 239, 241, 416
crackdown
    trade 252
Crawley, Heaven 378
creative thinking
    missing 412
Crimea 421
crimes 392
    against humanity 390
criminal 425
crises
    anticipate 358
    Cambodia 373
    future strategy 413
    humanitarian 96
    humanitarian ahead 369
    Rwanda 373
    strategic planning 369
crisis
    places 132
    resolution Germany 408
    victims 410, 416
criticism
    congressional 202
critics 92, 205, 379, 405
    resettlement 103
    US–Central America
        policies 339
Crocker, Chet 289, 290, 304
Crosette, Barbara 214
CSCE (Commission on Security and Cooperation in Europe) 257
Cuba 328
    anti-communists 61
    boat flotillas 140
    Castro 346
    criminal deportations 148

criminal element 142
crises 139
Cuban entrants 359
entrants
    unvetted 142
exiles policy 141
Georgetown meetings 144
interception-return 140
irregular immigration 141
Mariel Crisis 140
Mariel exodus 346
Marielitos 214
Migration Agreement 1984 346
missile crisis 20
negotiations 345
permanent residency 140
Port of Mariel 133, 345
Radio Marti 346
refugees 27
return 143
screening 143
South Florida and
        Washington 140
special case 340
US Immigration Agreement 346
US military bases 141
Cuban
    criminals 159
Culpepper, Patty 18
cultural
    differences 388
    norms 227
    shifts 243
cultural orientation 113
Cuny, Fred 279, 357
Cushing, Hank 13, 124, 170
Czechoslovakia 249
    Communist Party 249
    Sudeten 58
damage
    repair 203
Damascus 382
Dam, Ken 175, 184

danger
  imminent 202
dangers 195
  refugees 75
Daniels, Jerry 18, 25, 211
Daoud, Mohammad 326
Davis, Allen Clayton 303, 304
Davison, Henry 61
Dawson, Marney 107
Day, Dick 119, 178, 179, 218
Day, Nora 124
DEA agent 197
deadlock
  political 422
Dean, John Gunther 23, 184
death 304
  count 129
  march 59
  marches 24
  rate 24
  rates 279, 294
  refugees pushed back 76
  squads 339
  Stalin 255
  statistics 377
  Syria deaths 373
  toll 374
decision-making
  allied 415
  victims central 423
decision memorandum 72, 74, 221
  Vance-to-Carter 74
decisions
  strategic 415
Declaration
  Cartagena on Refugees 337
  of Independence 54
  of Universal Human Rights 1948 62
DeConcini, Dennis 341, 348
de Cuellar, Perez 297, 298
defenders 427
defense
  missile system 263
  of persecuted 427
  spending 20
Deffenbaugh, Ralie 53, 106
defunding
  UNRWA 320
de Haan, Dale 116
  UN offices and US mission Geneva 75
déjà vu all over again 164
delegation 337
  American 299
  pledging 320
deliver aid by crane 389
DeLouie, David 343
demilitarized zone 421
de Mistura, Staffan 380
Democratic
  German Republic 250
  Kampuchea 23
Denton, Jeremiah 215
Denton–McKinney 216, 217
departures
  orderly 116
deportation 337
deprived
  essential funds 420
Derian, Patricia (Pat) 40
Der Tagesspiegel 385
Derwinski, Edward (Ed) 180, 251, 286
  Romania negotiations 252
Des Moines Register 130
détente 259
  prerequisite 262
deterrence
  humane 123
  policy 190
Deterrence 198
DeVecchi, Bob 103
Dewey, Arthur E. (Gene) 165, 170, 174, 197, 198, 200, 207, 208,

  228, 278, 295, 299, 320, 322,
   332, 342, 357, 361
 airliner arranged 288
 and evacuation 314
 and Gersony 303
 and OEOA 297
 and Sudan 287
 Beirut 318
 cables concerns 284
 contact point 316
 deputy assistant secretary 283
 dispatched Harris 319
 Khartoum 291
 Lebanon 309
 Palestine region 322
 planning 292
 reform actions 355
diaspora 306, 307, 408
dictators 425
Dillon, Robert (Bob) 317
diplomacy 324
 humanitarian 399
 multilateral 296
diplomatic 22, 248, 380
 community
  meeting 304
 necessities 252
 vital elements 101
director
 first RP 137
 permanent needed 402
directorate 40
disagreements
 philosophical 231
disaster 130
 human 24
discrediting news 170
discrimination 267
DISERO (Disembarkation Resettlement Offers) 114, 195
displaced 424
 camps 303
 displaced persons 340
 in asylum 402
 eleven million 374
 in Syria 374
 internally 372
 internally displaced 340
displaced persons 59, 63, 130, 158, 249
displacement
 internal 370
 lacking solutions 412
dissenters
 Cuba 139
 Poland 252
 Soviet regime 247
 State Department 5, 32
 Vietnam 214
dissidents 139, 255, 260
distress at sea 114
distribution 106
DMC (Disaster Management Center) 357
Dobrynin, Anatoly 262
Doctor's Plot 255
Doctors without Borders 387
DoD (Department of Defense) 2, 4, 11, 27, 33, 90, 312
Doheny, Kevin 278
DOJ (Department of Justice) 33, 89, 106, 142, 216
Dole, Bob 217
domestic
 processing 46
 resettlement 175
 resettlement 71, 85, 91, 101, 102, 103, 104, 108, 136, 186
 resettlement system 100
Dominican Republic 56
Donnelly, Ann 405
donor
 conferences 208
 countries 122
 funds received 358
 governments 126, 225, 417

487

governments major 228
inattention 305
resettlement countries 122
supplies pilfered 342
support 331
US only 110
Douglas, Eugene (Gene) 175, 184, 185, 225, 226, 228, 261, 280, 320
draconian forces 113
dragons 321
dropout rates 266
drought-plagued 280
Dubcek, Alexander 249
Dubs, Adolph (Spike) 325, 326
Dukakis, Kitty 205, 206
Dukakis, Michael 205
Dunant, Henri 60
durable solutions 66, 68, 69, 78, 85, 87, 120, 183, 201, 323, 333, 344, 368, 371, 403, 412, 414, 415, 417, 424
  approaches 411
  comprehensive 236
  conventional 411
  efforts 200
  Indochina 234
  nonresettlement 187
  permanent 339
  planning 187
  practitioners 416
  priorities 338
  protection 195
  search comprehensive 187
  three pursued 60
  UNHCR mandate 207
Durenberger, David 211
dysfunctions 390, 417
  multi-year 415
  systemic 425
Eagleburger, Larry 10, 312
EAP (East Asia and the Pacific) 46, 70, 95

lights back on 47
East Asia
  and the Pacific 180
Eastern Bloc 247
  allies 252
Eastern Europe 248, 259, 352
  crises 83
  refugees 64
economic privation 337
educational centers
  Philippines and elsewhere 112
Eglin Air Force Base 142
Egypt 371
Eiland, Mike 125, 175
Eilberg, Joshua 119
Eisenhower, Dwight D. 7, 59
elections 253
electorate 152
eligibility
  presumptive 121
Eller, Don 42, 145
Ellis Island
  21st century 376
Ellison, Don 221
El Salvador 338
  displaced persons 341
  IDP 343
  joint initiative 341
  no clear mandate 340
  objections 343
  team assessment 340
emergency
  and exodus phase 185
  blue handbook 357
  phase 148
  response deficiencies 299
  response model 356
  response systems 299
  technical training
    techniques 357
  training for response 356
emergency operations
  US Forest Service 279

Emerson, Ralph Waldo 265
emigration 60, 247
    bans 254
    Jewish 258
    Soviet 258
    Soviet Jews 263
    waivers 258
EMU (Emergency Management Unit) 319, 358
    early warning alerts 358
endangered
    people 427
    populations epic levels 411
Endres, Skip 119, 167
English, Richard 184, 186, 200, 204, 216, 221, 228
entrants
    conditional 121
entrepreneurs
    as security threats 22
entry
    second ban 405
    third ban 405
environmental damage 331
EPP (Expanded Parole Program) 18, 19
Erdogan, Recep Tayyip 419, 421
Eritreans
    fighting 278
escapee
    program 61
escapes
    Vietnam 22
ESL (English as a Second Language) 112, 158
    threats overcome 113
Ethiopia
    famine 299
    Gondar region 293
    invasion of 132
    Jews 289, 294
    Jews starving 289
    Jews to Sudan 282

Ogaden 276
    scale of suffering 299
ethnic
    Chinese 193
    cleansing 375, 399
EU (European Union) 378, 386
    Kampuchea 126
EUR (Europe) 312
Europe 368, 382, 425
    and Middle East 378
    burden-sharing 248
    humanitarian groups 383
    massive disruptions 248
    overwhelmed 369
    refugee programs 253
    US refugee operations 248
European
    Council warned asylum seekers 378
    policy 374
    policy makers 376
    satellites 247
    Union 376
evacuation 5, 15, 290
    Ethiopian Jews 290
    expenses 17
    Falasha 290
    fleet 14
    flight 11
    Indochina 27
    Khartoum 284
    Lebanon 316
    planning 11
    PLO 314
    Saigon 6, 352
    South China Sea 13
evacuees 13, 14, 63
EVD (Extended Voluntary Departure) 338
Everson, Mark 349
Évian
    Conference 55
    Conference 1938 76

failure 77
    objectives 56
evidence 389, 392, 406, 411
executive
    order 404
    orders 405
executive branch 108
    agencies 90
    officials 92
    refugees 91
existential
    import 389
    threats 94
        ongoing 409
exit permits 116, 214
exodus 70
    Soviet Union 269
exonerated 94
experiment
    social engineering 23
expert
    management 89
external players 29
failure
    humanitarian 387
faith-based groups 211
Falasha 284, 361
    airlift 283
    Beta Israel 282
family
    Muslim 375
    reunification 184, 270, 385
    reunion 192, 231, 387
famine
    Cambodia 24
    Ethiopia 295
    historic 305
    Kampuchea 128
    multilateral response 297
    of the century 301
    plagued N. Ethiopia 278
    questions about 129
    relief 301

spread out 279
Sudan 294
worst of century 301
FAO (Food and Agriculture
    Organization) 81
Farah, Abi 302
farming
    subsistence 24
FBO (Foreign Buildings
    Overseas) 274
fear
    well-founded 257
Federal Reserve 44
feeding programs 304
Feighan, Michael 62
Feldman, Roger 42
FEMA (Federal Emergency
    Management Agency) 141
Fick, Steve 19
financial
    expenditures 340
first asylum 44, 74, 187, 233
    arrivals 71
    as anchor 241
    at risk 28
    camps 69, 77, 85
    countries 71, 193
    governments 45, 115
    help 189
    Holbrooke 73
    languishing 76
    Middle East 369
    next steps 417
    populations 28, 232
    populations (1979 to 1986) 188
    principle 238
    principles 235
    right 274
    safe 236
    Southeast Asia 69, 97, 158
    struggle for 188
    Thailand 190
    threatened 201

490

Fish, Hamilton (Ham) 168, 171, 261
Flatin, Bruce 187, 221, 325
flood gates 371
Florida
    politicians 346
FMLN (Farabundo Marti National Liberation Front) 342
Foggy Bottom 44
Food for Peace 92, 125
force
    deadly 370
    multinational 316
forced out 338
forced return 230. *See* refoulement
    opposed 230
forcible repatriation. *See forced return*
Ford
    administration 149
Ford Foundation
    emergency response training 356
Ford, Gerald R. 5, 9, 10, 11, 17
Ford, Robert S. 381
foreign
    affairs management 44
    aid bill 45
    fighters and rebels 327
    Foreign Operations 92
    landscape 96
    policy 81, 170
    policy avoid disaster 316
Foreign
    Service Officer 43
foreign aid
    constraints 20
Foreign Service
    assignments 49
    credibility 174
    environment 174
    Institute 26, 75
    Institute Senior Seminar 363
    job descriptions 82

Officer 39, 137, 174, 216
Officer careers 354
Officers 49
    rotation 146
    shining moment 244
Fornoff, Harry 280
framework 99
Free Democratic Party 385
freedom 260
    emigration 262
    fighters 25
    of choice 257
    religious 262
Freeman, Chas 39, 40, 41, 353
    on boar 39
Freeman Report 40, 41, 43, 50, 84, 85, 88, 94, 136
    reform agenda 88
    reforms 87
freighter
    Cap Anamur 115
    commercial 22
French ambassador
    UN 381
French soldiers 129
frigate
    Balny 115
FSO (Foreign Service Office/Officer) 5, 41, 82, 175, 354
    second look 179
Fulbright, J. William 8, 9
Fund
    Presiding Bishop's, of the Episcopal Church 107
funding 50
    congressional 47
    Congress reluctant 71
    crisis 98
    needed 96
    per capita rates 105
    refugees 110
    set aside 74
    supplemental 45

UNRWA 320
Funseth, Robert (Bob) 174, 175, 192,
    219, 228, 238, 361, 362
G20
    decisions 416
Gaddafi, Muammar 280, 397
    death 383
Ga'ez
    language 282
Galang Island 110
Gamayel, Bashir 317
Garbis, George 83
Gaza 322
    and West Bank 308
Gdansk 253
Gedaref 280, 291
Geibel, Ed 111
General Assembly vote 398
generosity
    US 339
Geneva 145, 248, 299, 386
    arms reduction 262
    Conference 106, 116
    Conference question 74
    Convention and subsidiary 385
    delegation members 75
    negotiating 263
Geneva Conference 75, 79, 82, 97,
    100, 101, 108, 109, 114, 122,
    129, 132, 133, 134, 183, 187,
    235, 241
    commitment hopes 158
    commitments 183
    initiatives 98
    International Conference on
        Indochinese Refugees 74
Geneva Convention
    1949 61
genocide 317, 375, 399
    ethnic populations 416
Gerard, Raf 226, 228
Germany 58, 369, 371, 383, 384
    asylum population 387

asylum seekers 387
case study 408
migration policy 385
preferred solution 408
Gerson, Michael 379
Gersony, Bob 303, 305, 340, 342,
    343, 344
    Honduras 345
    Luwero Triangle 304
    Southeast Asia 197
    stealth 303
Gettier, Joe 13
Ghouta
    2018 420
Giuliani, Rudy 166
glasnost 264
Glenn, John 206
Glienicke Bridge 263
global
    action allies 408
    activism 424
    admissions ceilings 404
    agreement 62
    American outlook 243
    America's emergence 65
    crises 85
    economy top 20 417
    effort 95
    engagement 60
    exodus 372
    humanitarian leadership
        400, 401
    humanitarian matters 179
    humanitarian spirit 393
    humanitarian system 412
    leadership 423
    needs 99
    neighbors 425
    network 95
    onslaught 132
    overview 250
    planning 132
    powers 421

programs 98
refugee programs 84, 189
refugee system 95
relief assistance 352
resettlement 186
solution 424
volume of crisis victims 425
global humanitarian consensus 400
global humanitarian leadership 401
global humanitarian response 403
global humanitarian system 409
Goldman, Jerry 89
good will 427
Goodwillie, Susan 205
Gorbachev, Mikhail 262, 264, 271, 334, 423
reform message 263
government 231
asylum-donor-resettlement 74
circles 180
intimidating 339
partner 95
puppet 327
state and local 95
governors 243
Governor's Advisory Committee on Refugee Resettlement
Massachusetts 205
Grace, Dennis 32
Gramm, Phil 265
Grant, Jim 296, 297
and OEOA 297
grants 90
federal 102
per capita 102
great divide 322
Greece 375, 382, 388
destination country 376
economically stressed 388
Supreme Court 386
Green Berets
resettlement advocates 210
Green, Marshall 162

Green Party 385
Gregg, Don 289
Griswold, Jack 102
Gromyko, Andrei 262
Guatemala 338
Esquipulas 350
Human Rights Commission 343
guidance 44, 119
Khmer 204
guidance to New York 321
guide
step-by-step 357
Gulf
of Siam 114
of Tonkin 8
Guterres, António 372
Gwertzman, Bernard 289
HA
Human Rights 304
Habibi, Samir 107
Habib, Phil 29, 311, 314
HA (Humanitarian Affairs) 21, 27, 28, 32, 33, 119
Antideficiency Act 27
Haig, Alexander 159, 161, 162, 165, 311
Hai Hong 22
Haiti 328
and UNHCR 347
and US Coast Guard 348
crises 139
exodus 347
Haitian economic migrants 340
Haitian entrants 359
Haitian immigrants 140
Haitian Refugee Center 347
interdiction 347, 348
Krome refugee camp 347
Mariel crisis 347
outflows 139
policy 347
repatriation 348
returnees 347, 348

493

UNHCR lawsuit 347
US bilateral accord 347
US Justice Department 347
US policy 346
Haley, Nimrata (Nikki) 391
Hall, Sam 168
Hamitic
   people 282
Hanoi 22, 25, 116
   de Haan 116
Haq, Fazle 330
Haratunian, William 167
Hare, Paul 5
Harris, Carl 186, 197
Harris, Tex 278, 279, 357
   Lebanon 319
Hartling, Poul 75, 114, 201, 299, 329
Hart, Phil 62
Hatfield, Mark 169, 348
haven
   temporary 19
Hawkes, Phillip 167
hearings
   high-stakes 164
Hecklinger, Carol 142, 165, 170, 186
helicopters
   Huey 14
hell
   unfathomable 23
Helsinki
   Final Act 259
Heng Samrin 123
Herblock cartoon 165
heroism 115
HEW (Health, Education, and Welfare) 10, 11, 27, 33, 90, 100, 101, 106, 108, 120, 121, 158, 166
HHS (Health and Human Services) 90, 216
   report 407
HIAS (Hebrew Immigrant Aid Society) 257

high
   seas 114
Hiller, Lewis 196
history
   Hmong and refugee 26
Hite, Peggy 43
Hmong 211, 233
   and Lowland Lao 242
   army 25
   Detroit 211
   hill-tribe 25
   hill-tribe people 211
Hoganson, Jerry 251, 330
Holbrooke, Richard (Dick) 31, 46, 69, 70, 73, 75, 96, 129
holding
   arrangement 417
   centers 200
Holmes, Chris 138, 139, 143, 145, 345
Holocaust 392
Holtzman, Elizabeth 36, 100
homeland 426
Honduras
   camps 334
   Government 342
   Miskito Indians 344
   Miskitos in 344
   security role fulfilled 343
   survivors to 341
Hong Kong
   camps 239
   closed camps 190
   Jubilee Camp 229
   lights out 47
Horan, Hume 283, 291
Horn of Africa 139, 328
   as massive catastrophe 295
   assistance 278
   civil wars1984 295
   countries 276
   famine 296
   Gedaref 279

RP 279
UN disaster 295
Wad Kowlie camp 279
Wad Sherife camp 279
hostage crisis 20
hostile
   environment 393
   to refugee policy 339
Hotel InterContinental
   basement 287
Houdek, Bob 305
House
   Appropriations 27
   Appropriations Committee 27
   Appropriations subcommittee 92, 141
   Foreign Affairs 92
   Foreign Affairs and Asian and Pacific Affairs 197
   Foreign Affairs Committee 252, 338
   Immigration subcommittee 100
   International Relations Committee 90, 180, 347
   Judiciary chairman 119
   Judiciary Committee 18, 36, 100, 101, 167, 168, 176, 221, 260
   Judiciary staffers 168
   Judiciary subcommittee 119, 348
   Judiciary subcommittee on immigration 62
   Rayburn Office Building 167
   subcommittee on Immigration, Refugees and International Law 166
House and Senate
   appropriations 86
   committees 90, 274
   Judiciary committees 91
House of Representatives 258
   letter 171

Huddle, Pancho 197
Hughes, Sam 2
human
   disaster 393, 399
   displacements to Europe 377
   resource management 354
   rights 39, 139, 247, 257, 259, 262, 264, 266, 278, 336, 399
   rights groups 378
      criticized Europe 376
   tragedies 318
humane
   asylum 417
   deterrence 188, 190, 199, 201
   deterrence and Ray Panel 233
   foreign policy 353
   outcomes 422
   problem-solver 414
   results 416
   solutions 417, 418
humanitarian 253, 374, 427
   action 130, 393
   activism 367
   Afghan refugees 333
   allies 355
   apparatus 36
   assistance 402
   challenge 44
   challenges 65
   corridors 381
   crisis 422
   disaster 420
   engagement 63
   flawed responses 369
   foundation 65
   interest 222
   international community 341
   law 318
   leadership 401
   maneuvers 292
   multilateral responses 358
   networks 102
   outcry 424

495

parole 32
policy Vietnam 237
political leaders 359
practices 351
programs 235
purposes 342
regime revitalized 416
regime Syria 410
response 12
solutions 57
successes 417
support 359
system 368, 426
system battered 425
system collapse 371
system future 409
system gap 340
system tested 367
timidity 393
Humanitarian Affairs (HA). *See* HA; *See* HA
humanity 426
　world solution 427
humankind 424
Human Rights
　Universal Declaration of 1948 270
Human Rights Watch 383
Hummel, Art 26
Humphrey, Hubert 92
Hungarian
　citizens 249
Hungary
　refugees trapped in 377
Hun Sen 123
　appeal 126
Hunter, Doug 61, 102, 192, 238
Hussein, Saddam 425
IATF (Inter-Agency Task Force) 17, 18, 21, 32, 160
　Bangkok 18
ICARA II

Second International Conference on Assistance to Refugees in Africa 303
ICARA (International Conference for Assistance to Refugees in Africa) 301
ICEM (Intergovernmental Committee for European Migration) 19, 63, 74, 111, 116, 169, 248
　Loan Fund 106
　transport costs 105
ICG (Informal Consultations Group) 227, 228, 234, 241, 412
　Kuala Lumpur meeting 238
　Tokyo meeting 236
ICMC (International Catholic Migration Commission) 112
ICM (Intergovernmental Committee for Migration) 253, 275, 284, 293, 314, 344, 359, 363
　port ships 314
ICRC (International Committee of the Red Cross) 60, 126, 196, 275, 303, 313, 315, 341, 359
　access 222
ICR (Intergovernmental Committee on Refugees) 57, 59, 60
identity theft 349
IDF (Israeli Defense Force) 309, 311, 317
Idlib 419, 420, 421
IDP (Internally Displaced Persons) 336, 340, 341
　Salvadorans 350
IFRC (International Federation of Red Cross and Red Crescent) 61
Ignatius, David 379
illegal immigrants 338
ILO (International Labor Organization) 59
immigrants

496

illegal 349
immigration 55
    ambivalence 64
    channels 348
    Cuba-Haiti debate 348
    dysfunctions 348
    enforcement 349
    legal channels 387
    legal status 349
    loopholes 405
    magnet 349
    patterns 54
    policy 57
    pressures 384
    reform 348
    reform parameters 348
    system 349
    systems 236
    work authorization 349
impacts
    developmental 303
imperative 409
improprieties 96
improvements
    competencies 355
    Coolfont 107
    first-asylum camps 189
    immigration law 61
    operational 293
    systemwide 187
improvisations
    amalgam 353
Inder, Rodney 118, 228
Indiantown Gap 345
individuals
    committed 95
Indochina 66
    appropriations 91
    beneath surface 1977 29
    crisis 30
    durable solutions 73, 94, 234, 239
    emergency measures 351

    exit plan 20
    Geneva Conference 427
    initiatives 45
    program 152
    program phases 241
    program years 240
    refugee conditions 21
    refugee crisis
        response 413
    Refugee Panel 231
    refugee populations 416
    refugee program 241
    refugee programs 87, 226
    refugees 31, 424
    refugees second wave 29
    response model 369
    solution architecture 236
    strategy 235
    triangle 25
    Triangle 199
    turmoil 26
    vast upheaval 424
    victims 241
    war victims 120
Indochinese
    citizens 19
    durable solutions 241
    emergency phase 148
    ethnic groups 200
    first surge 26
    parolees 121
    refugees 152
    refugee surge 21
    resettlement 36
    resettlement options 70
    US monthly intake 73
Indonesia 26
    military 70
    port denied 22
    refugee groups 70
    refugees reaching 76
industrialized democracies 387

INF (Intermediate-Range Nuclear
    Forces) 271
informant network 197
information technology 354
infrastructure
    impacts-asylum countries 302
    projects proposed 302
Ingersoll, Robert 5
initiatives
    global solutions 152
    nonresettlement 187
Inouye, Daniel 93
Inouye staff director
    Bill Jordan 93
INS (Immigration and
    Naturalization Service) 11,
    19, 90, 120, 158, 185, 203, 204,
    206, 231, 248, 268, 349
inspection 88
inspectors 85
institutional
    changes 186
institutions
    building process 187
    humanitarian 64
insurgencies 336
insurgents 342
    anti-Soviet 334
integrating
    long-stayers 301
integration
    local schemes 233
intelligence reports 214
interagency
    coordinator office 52
    efforts 27
    official 29
    partners 221
    refugee matters 181
    relations 17
    skirmishes 130
Interfacing 95
intergovernmental
    humanitarian organizations 60
internal
    assessment of refugee
        function 39
    coordination 17
    passport 255
    structures 33
internally-displaced people 273
international
    affairs 8
    anti-piracy 115
    help 29
    institutions 361
    institutions humanitarian-
        focused 65
    principles-practices 416
    response 127
international community
    resources and support 352
International Conference on
        Indochinese Refugees
    Geneva Conference 74
International Harvester
    Seattle 332
International Rescue Committee 32
Inter-Religious Mission for Peace
    Cambodia 205
Intertect
    crisis consulting 357
intervention 78
    INS and RP 205
investigations 51, 96
    congressional 44
    IG (Inspector General) 80
    investigative reports 80
    investigators 48
IO (International Organizations
    bureau) 42, 95, 296
    executive director 145
IOM (International Organization for
    Migration) 63, 111, 266, 269,
    275, 363, 410
    Bill Swing 375

consequences 270
director general 386
Moscow 270
report 382
Iowa
doctors-nurses 130
Iran 333, 380
and peace agreement 382
deal 379
nuclear deal 368
nuclear deal with 379
proxies 373
Shah Pahlavi overthrow 159
Iraq 333, 370, 371, 389
IRC (International Rescue
Committee) 30, 97, 103, 105
IRO (International Refugee
Organization) 59
Iron Curtain 61
irregular status 337
ISIS (Islamic State of Iraq and Syria)
370, 375, 380, 390
de facto capital 389
Islamabad 332
Islamic State coordinator 393
Israel 83, 257, 260, 266, 387, 397
Government 270
McBride Commission 317
self-serving actors 292
Soviet emigration 269
Israeli
and Palestinian peace
process 324
Mossad 287
relationship 306
Israeli Embassy
Addis Ababa, Ethiopia 293
ISSG (International Syria Support
Group) 379
Italian Senate
defense committee 384
Italy 382, 383, 388
and Libya deal 383

destination country 376
Jackson, Henry 258
Jackson, Robert 207, 295
Jackson–Vanik 251, 258
amendment 258
legislation 256
Jacobs, Paul 14
Japan 58, 359
pledge reaffirmed 77
Jaruzelski, Wojciech 252
Javits, Jacob 10
Jean-Juste, Gerard 347
Jerusalem 397
Jerusalem Post 289
Wolf Blitzer 288
Jewish
cultural life 264
emigration 258
Federations Council 270
NGO officials 281
Jewish Agency 289
Jews
accepted. *See* Dominican
Republic; *See* Dominican
Republic; *See* Dominican
Republic
and Palestinians 306
attempting to land 1944 58
Austria and Germany 56
Ethiopian 282
Latvian 255
Riga 256
Rome processing 257
Soviet 61
Soviet Union 258
Jihad 327
Jochum, Bruno 387
Johnson
administration 31, 64
Johnson, Lyndon B. 7, 62
Johnstone, Craig 5, 11, 18
Jordan 371, 389
battles 308

499

Crown Prince Hassan 323
Jordan, Bill 92, 93
Jubilee Camp
   family 230
Judiciary 91, 94
   Committee
      consultations 162
   committees 91, 166
   Committees 186
   consultation hearings 187
   consultations testimony 200
Juncker, Jean-Claude 375
jurisdiction 70
Jury, Alan 238
JVA (Joint Voluntary Agency) 19, 32, 105, 186, 248
Kabul 325
   government 326
Kahan Commission report 318
Kahan, Yitzhak 318
Kampuchea 79, 126, 128
   atrocities in 124
   border 126
   border crisis 124
   (Cambodia) 328
   Cambodia 122
   colleagues 128
   elections 209
   forces 200
   genocide survivors 134
   holocaust 122
   Iowa SHARES 130
   Kampucheans 200
   refugees 206
   refugees in Vietnam 75
   return 233
   rice-growing 131
   tragedy 125
   urgent food appeal 126
   US funding 126
Kamput
   Cables 204
   refugee processing 202

Karachi
   port 330
Karadzic, Radovan 318
Karmal, Babrak 326, 334
Kass, Jeff 196
Kasten, Robert (Bob) 310, 316, 320, 341, 344, 348
Kataeb Party
   leader 317
Kavaliunas, Mary 98, 99, 102, 103, 160
KEG (Kampuchea Emergency Group) 125
Kelley, Jim 274, 278, 280
Kemp, Kitty 48, 82, 84
Kennedy
   administration 139
Kennedy, Edward (Ted) 94, 116, 119, 121, 169, 171
Kennedy, John F. 8
Kennedy, Richard (Dick) 148, 160, 161, 173
Kennedy, Robert 64
Kennedy, Rory 14
Kerry, John 404
Keyes, Alan 301
Khan Sheikhoun 390
   chemical attacks 391
Khao-I-Dang 130, 199, 206
   camp 200
   refugee camp 127
Khartoum
   attack 280
   cables 286
   cable traffic 282
   evacuation 284
Khmer
   advocate 205
   ancient Empire 123
   at holding centers 206
   border 131, 240
   cases 204
   community 206

controversial processing 203
denial rates for 204
durable solutions 131
fighters 130
holding centers 201
in Thailand 123
Khao-I-Dang 202
Mak Mun camp 130
national attention 206
orphans 205
people 123
processing 205, 206, 229
refugee processing 205
regional settlement 200
repatriation 200
rereview 233
resettlement 175, 201, 204, 205
resettlement in United
    States 206
resistance 207
returned home 209
rice farmers 131
rough border camp 129
safety 209
survival 130
surviving barely 127
temporary relocation 208
Thailand 131, 200
trapped at border 207
voluntary repatriation 200
Khmer Rouge 23, 24, 78, 122, 127,
    129, 203, 342, 406
    camp Ban Sangae 127
    camp Mak Mun 127
    camp Nong Chan 127
    camp Nong Pru 127
    camp Nong Samet 127
    camp Tap Prik 127
    siphoned food 129
    tribunal against 210
Khrushchev, Nikita 255
    political trials 255
Killing Fields

actor 205
Kirk, Alan Goodrich 14
Kirkland, Lane 120
Kirkpatrick, Jeanne 178, 278,
    302, 320
Kissinger, Henry 3, 5, 9, 11, 18, 258
Klein, Wells 103
Kocher, Judy 18
Kocher, Rich 18
Ko Kra Island 115
Kompong Som 128
Koranic teachings 335
Kos
    island of 370
Krauthammer, Charles 349
KRG (Kampuchea Relief Group)
    125, 131
Kristallnacht 58
Krug, Bill 124
Krumm, Don 279, 344, 357
    at Wad Kowlie 279
Kunugi, Tatsuro 209
Kurdi, Alan (Aylan) 370
Laffer, Dennis R. 58
Laitin, Joe 1
land-based enforcement 199
land bridge 128
landmark legislation 121
landmines 24, 25
language
    training 19, 26, 75, 111, 113,
        158, 253
    training and orientation 220
Laos 19, 26, 29, 79, 211
    camps Ban Vinai and Ban Na
        Pho 190
    Long Tieng 26
    lowland Lao 26
    lowland refugees 212
    massive exodus 359
    Pathet Lao 25
    People's Democratic Republic
        25, 26

501

refugees 69, 199
Latorre, Nicola 384
Latvia 255
Lautenberg
    Amendment 268
Lautenberg, Frank 268
La Virtud 341
Law of Return 282
Lawrence, Jim 81, 106, 128, 273
laws and regulations
    flouted 376
Lazin, Fred 260, 267
leaderless
    international drift 389
leaders 98, 401, 423
    emulated 353
    HA 119
    long term 138
    political 153, 372
    political system 84
    super-power 422
    (turnover) 136
leadership 71
    after Arab Spring 390
    America complacent 373
    American 95
    American in Indochina 401
    breakout 423
    engaged 423
    humanitarian 78
    IO 301
    major powers 422
    military 58
    multilateral 415
    presidential transition 159
    refugee decade 413
    risk-averseness 410
    role abandoned 412
    RP temporary 74
    scramble 138
    traditional global 20
    uncertainties 146
    US-USSR changes 257

League of Nations 58, 59, 60
Lean, Graham 197
least of these 427
Lebanese resistance 311
Lebanon 308, 317, 333, 371, 389
    evacuation and Kasten
        hearing 316
    refugee population 389
    refugee problems 310
Le Duc Tho 9
left behind 19
legacy
    as guide 368
    shame 76
legislation
    aliens 67
    legislative base 118
    refugee 118
    voluntary work 97
Leningrad 256
Lenin, Vladimir 254
Lennox, George Gordon 356
Lesbos
    asylum seekers and
        migrants 376
leverage 201
    American 189
liaison
    congressional on budget and
        management 139
    State Department 139
Libya 333, 370, 382, 383, 390
    de facto blockade 382
Lierly, Tex 197
life
    family 24
    religious 24
LIRS (Lutheran Immigration and
    Resettlement Services) 102,
    106, 210
Lloyd, John 124
loan
    repayment 106

repayments 106
local integration 60
Lodge, Henry Cabot 31
loggerheads 420
logistical experience 128
logistics base
    Nong Chan 128
Long, Andrea 221, 291
long-stayers
    resettlement 233
Long Tieng 25
Lon Nol
    government 23, 202
    soldiers 24
Los Angeles (L.A.) Times 283, 290
Lowman, Shep 13, 26, 30, 69, 75, 109,
    110, 119, 124, 139, 141, 144,
    146, 160, 165, 170, 186, 187
loyalty 247
Loy, Frank 92, 93, 138, 139, 140, 143,
    144, 148
Luwero
    concentration camps 303
    Triangle 303
Luwero Triangle 304
Lyman, Princeton
    East Africa 283
Lynch, Paula 332
    to Pakistan 332
Maddry, Ted 279
magnet effect 115, 183, 190, 201
Malaysia 26, 29, 70, 73
    refugees reaching 76
Malloy, Mike 228
management
    financial 99
    fiscal 1
    senior 99
    skills 354
managing down 187, 188
Mandlebaum, Michael 425
Mangrum, Grady 107
Manila 110

Marcos, Ferdinand 15, 110
Marcos, Imelda 110
Mariel
    effect 222
    Marielito problems 150
    Port of 139, 140
    syndrome 222
Marine 14
martial law 252
Martin, David 119
Martin, Graham 5, 11
Marxist coup d'état 326
mass
    deportations 376
    grave 129
Maxwell, Sally 18
Mayer, Stephan 384
Maynes, Bill 145
Mayo, Bob 4
mayors 243
Mazzoli, Romano 119, 166, 167, 202
    letter 171
McBride Commission 317
McCarthy, John 103
McClory, Robert 171
McDonalds 103
McKelvey, Margaret 125, 274
McKinney, Stewart 215
McManaway, Clay 11, 17, 163
McNamara, Terry 13
McPherson, Peter 278
    Beirut 318
    Lebanon 309
mechanisms 106
    implementation 415
    international 359
    operational 106
medical
    care 74, 304
    personnel 331
    programs 308
Mediterranean
    Central 383

Sea 376
Meeker, Warren 30, 36
Meese, Edward 266
Meir, Golda 56, 255, 258
Meissner, Doris 166, 167, 204, 206
Mekong River 13
Mengistu, Haili Mariam 276
    regime 277, 278
Merkel
    mandatory quotas 377
Merkel, Angela 371, 377, 378
Mesa Grande 341
Mexico 337
    asylum country 350
MFN (Most Favored Nation) 251, 258
Miami
    care for minors 142
MIAs 27
Michener, James 31
Middle East 61, 83, 306, 307, 316, 323, 370, 378, 380, 398, 417, 423, 425
    failures 410
    host population 417
    Judy Chavchavadze 307
    policy of evenhanded 306
    primary solutions 416
    refugee crisis 416
    refugees 307, 404
    under siege 371
    UNRWA 334
Middle East Institute 382
migrants 60, 63, 382, 383, 415, 426
    Africa 369
    anti-migrant League 384
    Asia 369
    boat routes 382
    economic 338
    irregular 376
    potential 384
    sanctuary cities 338
    scapegoated 390

migration
    affairs 64
    and refugee solutions 63
    great American 54
    legal 238
    meetings-Prague 250
    orderly 183
    regular avenues 348
    responsibilities 64
    section 102
Migration Policy Institute Europe 382, 386
migrations
    forced 58
Miles, Carolyn 305
milestones 324
military
    and diplomatic colleagues 214
    Assistance Program 16
    desert escort 280
    dictators 336
    dictatorships 159
    hospital 601 392
    offensive 127
    operations 342
    Sealift Command 16
    strikes 393
    structure 247
    withdrawal 389
Military
    Sealift Command 77
Miller, Steve 29
Miller, Tom 29, 33, 75
Milliken, Bill 35
mindsets
    re-orient 415
Miskitia
    Krumm visit 344
Miskito
    fled to Honduras 344
    Indians of Nicaragua 344
Mitchell, Libby 206
Miziara 389

mobilized
    cooperative global action 418
Mocoron
    camp 344
Mogadishu 277
monarchy 23
Mondale, Walter 56, 75, 78, 114, 427
Mongo, John 200, 209
monitoring 98, 104, 105, 129, 186
Montagnard people 210
Moore, Jonathan 238, 361, 362
moral
    duty 425
    failings 380
    ground 426
    imperatives 389
    obligations 424
    outrage 425
Morgan, Ann 111, 219, 220, 224
Morgan, Doc 141
Morris, Diana 356
Morris, Nicholas 357
Morse, Brad 295, 297, 298
Moscow 268, 382
    Olympics 327
    Spaso House 266
Mosquitia 344
Moss, Frank 98, 103, 104, 160, 161
Mosul 390
Mother Teresa 278
Mount, Dayton (Day) 43, 46, 49
Moussali, Michel 114
MPC (Migrant Processing Center) 269
Mujahideen 326, 327
    aid to 334
    fighters 327
    morale 327
Muller, Robert 345
multilateral 236
    actions 408
    agencies 295, 351
    budgets 413
    context 355
    crisis response 300
    deficiencies 355
    initiative 234
    leadership 57
    mandate 355
    model 208
    organizations 414
    organizations autopilot 359
    partners 36, 413
    performance 294
    reform 207, 355
    relief effort 330
    solutions initiative 413
    system 225, 239, 300, 353, 354, 355, 392, 407, 413, 414, 416, 417
    talks 237
multilateralism
    new commitment 60
multilateral system 408
multilateral teams 403
multilateral vs. bilateral 408
multinational
    UN force 312
multiple partners
    sharing burdens 407
Murphy, Caryle 304
Murphy, Richard 316
Museum
    Holocaust Memorial 375
Museveni, Yoweri 303, 304
Muslim
    countries 332
    immigrants 404
Myanmar 399
Nansen
    Award 196
    International Office for Refugees 59
national
    interest 43

interests 355
NSC 290
security advisor 3, 373
security affairs 267
terrorism report 2015 373
unity government 380
National
    Congress on Soviet Jewry 265
    Governors Association 35, 129
    Security Advisor 325
national behavior 400
National Council on Soviet
    Jewry 263
nationalism
    ethnic 58
    rising 390
nationals
    Filipino 112
National Security Decision Directive
    NSDD-93 204
nations
    first-asylum 29
NATO (North American Treaty
    Organization) 247
naturalization 54
Navy 14, 77, 78
    planes 77
NBER (National Bureau of Economic
    Research)
    report 406
NC
    Greensboro 210
    Raleigh 210
negotiation
    among countries 189
    intense diplomatic 312
    negotiating process 422
    United States-Cuba
        negotiator 144
    with Congress 41
negotiation(s) 200
    direct 189
Neilson, Stu 48

Netherlands 356
networks 102, 103
    churches 107
Newsom, David 29, 70
New York
    meeting 103
    (UN headquarters) 296
New Zealand 387
NGO
    activists 281
    advocates 29
    American 346
    and multilateral teams 358
    and RP 134
    and World Bank liaison 331
    as experts 104
    camp staff 342
    community 104
    Cuban resettlement 142
    diversity 248
    European 253
    expanded operations 64
    expert testimonies 120
    faith-based 408
    favor of RP 107
    feelings 104
    history-refugees-Europe 64
    Hmong advocates 211
    Juba hospital 280
    Kitty Kemp-advocate 205
    monitor operations 105
    overseas 105
    refugee community 179
    resettlement 90
    State Department contracts 102
    support for Purcell 177
Ngo Dinh Diem 8
NGO (nongovernmental
    organization) 20, 64, 248
Nguyen Co Thach 214
Nguyen Hop Doan 13
NHA (National Housing
    Authority) 110

Nicaragua
  return 344
Nicosia 314
Niger 383
Nigeria
  Biafra War 275
Nimeiri
  Sudan president 289
Nixon
  administration 82, 177, 258, 261
  administration first year 1
  aides 4
  impeachment hearings 167
  plan 3, 4
  resigned 9
Nixon, Richard M. 1, 5, 8, 9
Nobel Peace Prize 252
noncombatants 334
Nong Chan
  camp 130
norm 99
North Korea
  advisors 303
North Vietnamese 22
Norway
  Trygve Lie 207
NRA (National Resistance Army) 303, 304
NSC (National Security Council) 4, 5, 75, 90, 159, 163, 204, 290
NSDD-93 (National Security Decision Directive)
  Khmer 204
nuclear
  deal 379
  fiasco 390
  missiles 264
  negotiations 379
  powers 271
  threats 423
  weapons reduction 271
Oakley, Bob 31, 47

OAR (Office for Asian Refugees) 46, 186
Obama
  administration surge operation 404
Obama administration 379
  sidelines 374
Obama, Barack H. 379, 381
Obote
  forces 303
  killings stopped 304
  regime 280, 303
occupation 58
O'Connor, John 198
O'Donohue, Dan 200, 209
ODP (Orderly Departure Program) 116, 117, 191, 193, 217, 222, 224, 236
  discussions 219
  problems 192
  reactivation 237
  restructuring 221
  stabilization vehicle 194
OEOA (Office of Emergency Operations in Africa) 297, 298, 300, 356
OFDA (Office of Foreign Disaster Assistance) 125, 340
Office of Foreign Disaster Assistance 274
officers
  consular or diplomatic 248
  experienced refugee 175
Ogaden
  region 132
Oliver, Rosanne 176
Olympics
  Moscow 259
Omar Bahket 357
OMB 71, 82, 98
OMB (Office of Management and Budget) 8, 90, 139, 162, 177, 180, 274

507

Onu, Peter 302
OPCW (Organization for the Prohibition of Chemical Weapons) 390
Operation
    Baby Lift 10
    Frequent Wind 14, 16
    Homecoming 9
    leaks 288
    Moses 287, 288, 289, 290, 293
    New Life 17, 141
    Sheba 290, 292
    Solomon 293
opposition
    Turkish 421
Oral History Project 317
order
    presidential 290
orderly departure
    negotiations 116
    program 74, 75. *See* ODP
    safety and protection 115
orderly emigration 56
organizational capability 187
organizations
    intergovernmental 95
    multilateral 95
    partner 19
orientation
    cultural 158, 253
origin
    countries and regions 416
origin countries 417
OR (Orderly Return) 239
ORR (Office for Refugee Resettlement) 121
Ortega, Daniel 336
Oslo Peace Conference 324
Ottawa meeting 238
overseas relief 174
oversight 102
Ovnand, Chester 7
P5+1 governments 379

Pakistan
    camps 331, 334
    exchange system 330
    Government 328, 332
    logistics 330
    refugee sites 333
    Taliban 335
    trucks to 332
Palestine 307
Palestinian
    and Israeli peace process 324
    and Jews 306
    Army forces 314
    civilians 317
    human rights 323
    mother 322
    poverty 322
    quality of life 322
    Red Crescent Society 317
    refugees 306, 398
    self-sufficient 323
    shadow government 307
Palmieri-Loy 138, 139
Palmieri, Victor 111, 138, 139, 141, 142, 143, 145, 148, 159
panel
    reviewed 232
paradigm
    humanitarian 413
    solutions 414
Paris 383
Parker, Addie 81
parole 61, 121
    humanitarian 32
    numbers 36
parole authority 185
    emergency admissions 121
    intention 121
partners
    allied 418
    partnerships 41
    resettlement partnership 107
    solution 416

partnership 118
Pashtun
    culture 334
    refuge 329
passengers jumping 15
Pathet Lao 25
patrols 77
peace
    and restoration 422
    initiatives 316
Peel, Terry 92
PER 46
Peres, Shimon 289
perestroika 263, 264
performance reviews 105
permission
    unilateral 121
persecuted
    politically 337
persecution 55, 203, 257, 313, 337, 375, 386
    Autocephalous 268
    behind the Iron Curtain 157
    burden of proof 268
    Christians 268
    evidence 185
    fear 18
    fear of 267
    Jews 268
    membersUkrainian Catholic 268
    systematic 19
personal relationships 400
personnel
    actions 45
PER (State Department central personnel) 49, 82, 173, 272, 273, 274
Peshawar Seven 327
Pew Research Center 385
Phalangists 318
    attacked refugees 317

Phanot Nikhon Transit Center 116, 215
Phnom Penh 23, 127, 200
PICMME (Provisional Intergovernmental Committee for the Movement of Migrants in Europe) 63
piracy 115
    attacks 114, 242
    data 196
    informant testimonies 199
    intervention 198
    on agenda 134
    penalties 198
    pirate attacks 114, 192, 199
    pirates 113, 115, 195
    pirates convicted 197
    smuggler networks 376
    solution 196
    victims 198
    witness intimidation 198
placements quality 186
Plain of Jars 25
plan
    international comprehensive 417
Platt, Nick 75
pledges 77
    ICARA 302
    pledging conference 320
PLO (Palestine Liberation Organization) 307, 308
    combatants 176
    destinations 314
    evacuation 312, 314
    forces 311, 317
    training 310
Poland 252
    invasion of 58
    sanctions on 253
police
    local 345
    military 345
policies

policy
 Central America-Caribbean
  refugee 338
policy
 and refugees 32
 announcement 201
 decision-making 353
 decisions 373
 deterrence 199
 EVD 338
 first-asylum 230
 foreign 20, 36, 91, 118, 360
 foreign policy implications 165
 guidance 181, 402
 humane 339
 humane deterrence 199
 issues 228
 lack of coherent in
  migration 376
 makers 70, 340
 officials 118
 open door 127
 opposites 339
 prescriptions 405
 punitive 197
 strategic goals 339
 trajectories 421
 transit status 28
 wet-foot, dry-foot 140
political
 activists 247
 and military configuration 415
 asylum 337, 387
  Europe 413
 asylum system Europe 406
 blunders 407
 briar patch 166
 courage 393
 entrenched refugee
  problems 323
 expediency 411
 no authority or mandate 137
 prisoners 192, 221
 prisoners release 213

 settlement 328
 will 393, 423
Pol Pot 23, 204
Pond, Peter 205
Pope, Louise 81
port
 Malaysia 22
 of Mariel 338
 Vung Tau 14, 23
portfolio
 Purcell 261
 refugee 40
post-World War II
 US structures 63
poverty
 high rates 417
Powell, Colin 266
Powers, Charles 283, 290, 291, 292
POWs 27
PPRC 99
 review system 187
Prague Spring
 revolt 249
Prasong, Soonsiri 189, 190, 198,
 201, 211
Pravda 255
Preah Vihear Temple 70
precedents
 historical 368
predators 142
president
 executive office of 33
 prerogatives 202
President Carter 71, 73, 74, 120, 137,
 138, 164, 259, 326, 327, 359
 open arms speech 142
President Clinton 363
President Ford 12
President Gorbachev 263
Presidential Determination 89–15
 267, 268
President Johnson 1, 8, 62
President Maduro abuses 399

President Reagan 157, 159, 161, 175, 177, 182, 193, 195, 204, 252, 260, 261, 262, 263, 264, 265, 266, 271, 278, 282, 304, 316, 322, 359, 363, 423
   post-summit address 265
President Truman 67
President Trump 420
press 292
   briefing 4
   calls 4
   clippings 143
   conference 8, 35
   corps 2
   coverage 114
   international 56
   members 167
   secretary 1
presumptive eligibility 185
priorities
   time-sensitive 81
prisoners
   Jewish prisoner 263
   of war 215
   political 193, 219
private
   contributions 401
   diplomacy 262
   sector reductions 407
private sector 107, 243
PRK (People's Republic of Kampuchea) 122
PRM (Population, Refugees, and Migration bureau) 398, 402
process 99
professional classes 22
program
   officers 99
Program
   Reception and Placement 101
propagandist slant 255
propose safe zones
   Clinton 381

Panetta 381
Petraeus 381
protagonists 71
protection 28, 60, 61, 63, 67, 68, 75, 109, 114, 115, 131, 182, 195, 199, 200, 209, 213, 218, 231, 233, 288, 299, 300, 303, 331, 334, 337, 340, 355, 358, 414
   first asylum 28
   for weak, vulnerable, defenseless 426
protectionism 58
protocol
   government 99
   refugee 63
   Refugee Protocol 68, 118
   refugees 67
PRPC (Philippine Refugee Processing Center) 111, 113, 220
public
   service 152
Public Law 96–212 120
pull factor 199, 201
Purcell, James 167, 292
   congressional testimony 171
   director (bureau) 283
   director general IOM 266
   temporary-assignment memo 143
purges
   1930s 255
Putin, Vladimir 421, 427
PVO (private voluntary organizations) 17
qualifications 62
Queen Sirikit 205
quick exodus to Israel 269
Quinn, Kenneth 5, 13, 23, 34, 78, 130, 175
quota system 62
Rabin, Yitzhak 324
Radio Free Europe

511

under Nixon 82
Radio Liberty
    under Nixon 82
rail tunnel
    link 377
rapid response
    UN inability 208
Raqqa 390
    2018 420
RASRO (Rescue at Sea Resettlement Offers) 114, 195
Rayburn Office Building 221
Ray Indochina Refugee Panel 231, 236, 241
    and regional settlement 233
    historic report 232
    Report 233
Ray, Robert 34, 36, 75, 78, 129, 130, 231, 234
Read, Ben 38, 39, 40, 41, 42, 44, 47, 74, 80, 81, 82, 84, 87, 89, 125, 138, 139, 145, 273, 353
    team 174
Reader's Digest 113
Reagan
    administration 113, 148, 151, 206, 213, 277, 289, 323, 339, 345, 347, 359, 363
    administration appointees 162
    administration (perceived as) 166
    administration support 339
    administration witnesses 164
    and Gorbachev 257, 423
    early years 191
    on Cold War 158
    refugee issues 160
    Soviet agenda 262
    Soviet Jews 359
    White House team 179
Reagan, Ronald W. 117, 134, 148, 157, 199, 317
Rear Admiral 14

rebel
    areas 420
    forces 421
reception
    and placement 91
reconstruction
    funding 420
Red Cross
    American 61
    Haitian 347
    movement 60
    National Societies 275
reeducation
    SRV centers 213
reform 80, 100
    attempts 355
    commenced 29
    Freeman Report reforms 84
    Hoganson-type reforms 251
    multilateral 225
    refugee reforms 75
    urgent reforms 38
reforms 89
    Hogenson's 251
refoulement 347. *See* forced return; *See* forced return; *See* forced return
refugee
    admissions 121, 185
    advisory group 162
    advocates 19, 45
    annual appropriation 27
    apparatus 146
    appropriated funds 46
    approval and departure 269
    arrivals spiked 26
    assistance programs 91
    backwater status office 21
    bona fides 225, 267
    budget approved by State 274
    bureau 47, 92
    camps 19
    camps in Sudan 289

Chad refugees 279
concerns off State's radar 27
conferences and American
  participation 44
decade 335, 340, 351, 360, 368,
  407, 415
decade and action 392
decade and crisis training 356
decade and humanitarian
  response 352
decade experience summary 359
decade participants 417
decade record 408
definition 337, 340
dynamic strategy 34
emergency fund 128, 276,
  290, 316
Ethiopia refugees 279
explosion 118
Falasha camps 284
Falasha developments 286
field operations 47
first surge 21
flows in Asia 27
former HA program 45
functions 40
funding requests 45
global landscape 135
global populations 150
global relief 159
Indochinese influx 119
international assistance
  funding 403
international assistance to 101
international obligations 339
issues 94, 107, 118, 165, 177, 273,
  306, 348
issues Washington 64
Jewish in Ethiopia 281
Jewish refugees and moral
  right 267
Jewish refugees Sudan 288
job 43

leadership 367
legacy 150
major processing partner 19
medical screening 19
Middle East refugees 367
modern programs 52
new bureau 80
new State Department team 34
new team 31
officials 174
organization reform 31
parlance 28
parole 267
population 28
  Egypt 417
  populations 26, 109, 189
  overseas 352
preferences 417
president's emergency refugee
  fund 313
problems scope 359
problems worldwide 29
processing 19, 185
  centers 77
  guidelines 204
  moratorium 250
  operations 248
  recommendations 233
programs 34, 38, 43, 44, 52, 86,
  90, 91, 93, 118
  and personnel 50
  director 40
  in trouble 38
  Latin America 340
  partners 33
  pioneer 41
  reorganization 40, 64
  transfer plans 81
proper funding 48
refugee decade 254, 260
refugee decade programs 408
relief 277
  overseas 38, 119

513

WW II 53
reporting from Khartoum 284
resettlement 35, 201, 216,
    229, 232, 248, 268, 345,
    367, 403
resettlement priority
    categories 201
Salvadoran population 341
second surge 32
selection efforts 105
selection-processing 269
self-sufficiency 158
six processing priorities 105
solutions 27, 182
Somali commissioner for
    refugees 277
Soviet processing 267
staffers 95
stalwarts 36
State Department dilemma 33
State Department new
    bureau 45
status 216, 238, 257, 337, 339
status and labels 242
status definition 66
statutory responsibilities for 29
surge postwar 30
Syrian refugees 404
Syria refugees 367
team 35, 70, 71, 80, 96, 185
transportation 19
tsunami 26
Uganda refugees 279
Um Rakuba refugees 288
Refugee
    Programs budget 1981 92
    Programs hearings 97
refugee arrivals 188
    discouraged 188
refugee budgets
    declining 219
Refugee Convention 1951 63, 66, 68,
    70, 118, 120, 347, 403

asylum principle 386
Central America-Caribbean 340
formal refugee definition 67
governments 416
(*refugee* definition) 336
signatories 67
US not ratifying 66
refugee programs 177, 209, 225,
    344, 367
action-oriented 121
catapulted 351
interagency 232
team 124
worldwide 120
Refugee Programs 120
field team 95
hearings 41
testimony 97
third-country resettlement 110
training programs 111
refugees
and HA 27
and taxes 406
armed 334
assure start 101
at sea 77
boat 28
budget lobbying 96
Cambodia 201
collected for profit 22
defined 63
deserving 425
encamped in boat 28
endangered in camps 342
exodus 372
external processing regime 414
foreign policy implications 89
from camps 77
Greece 386
Hmong 18, 25
in danger at sea 115
Indochina 17, 119
Indochinese 31

514

in first asylum 23
  influx 332
  Iraq 417
  Jewish 56
  Jordan 417
  land 28
  Laos 18, 201
  Laotian 26
  Lebanon 417
  legal 336
  less likely to kill 406
  major resettlement 337
  new tide 24
  Palestinian 159
  persecuted 416
  processing on-board 22
  pushed back 69
  resettlement 17
  right of return 323
  screening 232
  solutions 83
  Somalia-Ethiopia 359
  Southeast Asia 34
  special humanitarian
    concern 120
  surge operation 404
  team 78
  transit and rescue 75
  Turkey 417
  Vietnam 201
  Vietnamese 22, 34
  villages 329
Refugee Studies Center 372
refugee work 18, 175, 179, 196, 274
  as a discipline 353
  disciplinary imperative 353
Refugee work
  out of backwaters 354
refuseniks 260, 262, 266
regimes 59
  processing-protection 185
regional
  asylum 333

  settlement 68, 183
Regis, Pete 119, 167
regulated movement 194
relationships
  collaborative 119
relief 126
  emergency 357
  organizations 129, 130
  services 129
  World Relief
    and Miskitos in
      Honduras 344
relief and development 301
religious
  minorities 61, 247, 256
Renzi, Matteo 384
reorganization 41, 51, 136
repatriation 60, 130, 187, 339
  forced 122
  voluntary 68
repatriation program 200
repeat offenders 197
reports
  inspection 89
  investigative 136
Republic
  South Vietnam 22
reputation 51
  crisis management 138
  RP programs 137
requirements (grants) 103
rescue 414
  action 59
  American mechanism 37
  by freighter crew 196
  helicopter 12
  Military
    Sealift Command 75
  Navy 75
  no mechanisms for 29
  war victims 58
resettlement 32, 41, 60, 69, 185, 189,
    199, 240, 333, 339, 340, 371

515

2016 403
abroad 22
access 190
agreed numbers 202
burden 416
capacities 26
costs 406
countries 28
domestic 85, 101, 107, 150, 170
domestic office 186
domestic overhaul 120
doubling 74
Eastern European 64
funding 46
lowest annual 407
moratorium amendment 169
options decline 403
performance 186
permanent 17, 28, 190, 253
personal stake in 106
prepared to stop 97
priorities 105
private 101
program 186, 402
programs remaining 352
projections 176
reorienting strategy 231
resettled safely 415
solution 416
Southeast Asia refugees 74
Soviet 261
stabilization 184
surge 106
third country 200, 411
third-country 28, 36, 68, 183, 416
third-country 414
US 104
US regime 405
resolution
humane 414
resources 97
response capabilities 355

restrictions
resettlement 201
restructuring
communist 22
return
voluntary and safe 230
review
models 99
Policy and Program Review 99
UNHCR 177
revitalized organization 273
Revolution
1917 254
rice
crop 24
production 130
rights
civil rights advocates 339
civil rights leader 120
Civil Rights movement 62
refugee civil rights 59
rivalries 422
RMA (Refugee and Migration Assistance) 64
Rodino, Peter 18, 119, 171
Rohingya 399
Romania
anomaly 250
moratorium decision 251
resettlement dilemma 250
Romanov tsars 254
Rome 81
Romero, Berta 19
Roosevelt
administration ambivalence 58
Roosevelt, Eleanor 62, 66
Roosevelt, Franklin D. 55, 58
Rose City 196
Rose, Gerald 11
Rosenblatt, Lionel 5, 11, 18, 26, 32, 69, 75, 91, 125, 129, 165, 172, 173, 211
Roth, Andrew 262

RP 99, 398
  acting director 162
  advocacy 331
  Africa 273
  Africa Office 49
  air bridge involvement 128
  a linchpin 362
  Amerasians decision 216
  American foreign policy
    influence 134
  and Falasha rescue 283
  and IDP gap 340
  and international cost-
    sharing 355
  and Kampuchea refugees 124
  and KRG 125
  and Miskitos 344
  and World Bank 331
  annual appropriation 310
  assessment Sudan 280
  border advice 341
  budget 243
  budget expansion 86
  cable traffic embargo 293
  congressional relations 231
  continuity Indochina 174
  credibility 170
  Cuba 338
  deputies) 200
  Dewey arrival 275
  director 81
  director de facto 146
  director Frank Loy 92
  director selection 41
  director support 178
  durable solutions 244
  dynamo 95
  early months 111
  emergency management
    training 294
  Emergency Management Unit
    295, 311

EMU (Emergency Management
    Unit) 341
Europe and Near East
    director 251
existential threats 109
first global budget 96
foreign and civil service 355
formative emphasis 353
funding 91
geopolitical environment 83
Horn of Africa 294
Horn of Africa assessment 356
immigration channels 243
information cut-off 285
information flow 293
in-house reform 355
July 30, 1979 82
key staff 105
launch priorities 88
lawyer 313
leadership 84
leading donor for refugees-
    Africa 275
lead role 106
led reforms 356
legal authorities 316
multilateral reform
    initiatives 225
obstacles 343
officers and staff 272
operating style 180
planning-management 355
PLO evacuation authority 315
program and asylum
    division 119
proposed reforms 251
protection and relief 275
reassigned to 80
recovery challenges 158
reforms 83
reporting system 294
reputation 84
required competencies 354

517

resettlement problems 243
resettlement team 221
resilient staff 137
SA-2 160, 171, 174
second director 138
seventh-floor headquarters 126
skeletal 98
sole witness 165
stabilization 83
staff 128, 324
start-up 45, 80
strategic goals 355
Sudan operation 292
Task Force Afghan 328
Task Force Afghanistan 133
Task Force Cuba 142
Task Force Cuba-Haiti 133, 141, 345
Task Force Kampuchea 133
Task Force Somalia 133, 276
team 103, 131, 132, 195, 214, 334, 363
teams 89
transformation significance 354
unique position 308
volunteer appeal 125
R&P (Reception & Placement) 107
RP (Refugee Programs bureau) 48, 80, 101, 133, 143, 146, 152, 231, 248, 250, 261, 264, 265, 270, 275, 305, 306, 310, 311, 312, 313, 315, 320, 328, 339, 354, 362
   budget 352
   developed profile 352
   influenced 356
   Kampuchea Relief Group 274
   stabilize asylum 350
RP team 87
RTG (Royal Thai Government) 200
Rubicon 52
Rumbula
   massacre 256

Runkles, Norman 81, 98
Rusch, Terry 186
Rusk, Dean 31
Russell, Chris 75, 84
Russell, Richard 92
Russia 380, 423
   and peace agreement 382
   condemns strikes 391
Russian
   Jews 254
Rustin, Bayard 30, 36, 120
RVN (Republic of Vietnam) 12
Rydbeck, Olof 310, 311, 320
   UNRWA 321
SA–2 162
Sabra 319
   attacks 319
   camp massacres 324
   massacre 318
safe
   asylum 330, 333, 344
   first asylum 203
   haven 56
   repatriation 233, 333
   return 232
   voluntary repatriation 183
   voluntary return 184
safety
   refugee 115
Saigon 23
   airlifts 18
   evacuation 148, 352
   evacuations 19, 37
   evacuees 21
   fall 12
   fall of 53
   Fall of 27
   fell 22
   last day 13
   River 13
   River 14
   withdrawal 19
Sa Kaeo

518

refugee camp 127
SALT II 259
Salvadorans
  civil war 339
salvage
  RP 100
Samrin, Heng 122
Sandinistas 336, 344
  voted out 350
Sargisson, Phil 356, 357
Sasser, Bruce 228
satellite 277
Saudi Arabia 316, 333, 420
Save the Children 304, 305
Save the Children UK 303
Saydnaya 392
SCA (Security and Consular
    Affairs) 64
scenario
  best-case 415
Schifter, Richard 266
Schill, Jim 124
Schlesinger, James 15
Schwartz, Abba 64
Schwartz, Carmi 270
Schweiker, Richard 161
Schweitzer, Ted 115
Scott, Dick 19
screening 233, 238
secretary of state 27, 33, 40, 159
  testimony 165, 223
  the assistant 31
Secretary Shultz 177, 178, 179, 180,
    192, 193, 201, 209, 216, 217,
    218, 221, 222, 223, 227, 232,
    262, 263, 296, 300, 310, 311,
    314, 321, 322, 359, 362, 363
  and candidate Purcell 363
  briefing 251
  senior staff meetings 250
  testified 359
  Vietnam speech 244
security 191

breakdowns 348
checks 404
concerns 188
concerns for cities 406
conditions 420
conditions Vietnam and
    Laos 243
homeland debates 367
screening 404
US camp concerns 142
Security
  Homeland 398
Security Council
  emergency 391
  failures 381
  veto 381
Security Council vote 398
Seder 294
self-selected
  asylum 371
  countries 369
  destination 411
self-sufficiency
  agricultural 131
Senate
  Appropriations 92, 93, 310
  Appropriations Committee
    93, 341
  Appropriations
    subcommittee 315
  Clark confirmation 33
  consultation letter 171
  Foreign Operations 348
  Foreign Relations 92
  Foreign Relations Committee 8,
    9, 90, 301
  Judiciary Committee 176,
    260, 359
  Judiciary subcommittee 348
  Palmieri confirmed 138
  RP hearings 315
September 11, 2001 367, 404,
    407, 418

September surprise 202
settlement
   regional 187, 188, 274, 339
seventh
   floor office 174
   floor reception 218
Seventh Fleet Task Force 76 14, 15
seventh floor 38, 173
   leadership 80
   staffers 75
   worried 44
seven-year war 422
Sharansky, Anatoly 263
Sharansky, Avital 263
Sharansky, Natan 254
shared
   mission 352
   values 427
Sharon, Ariel 309, 311, 314, 318
Shatila 318, 319
   attacks 319
   camp massacres 324
   massacre 318
Shayrat
   air base 390
Sheehan, Terry 226, 228
Shevardnadze, Eduard 262
Shia
   groups 327
   Iraqi Shia 373
shippers
   commercial 114
shipping
   commercial shippers 114
   industry 77
shoot-on-sight 70
Shultz
   and Chernyaev 262
   and Dobrynin 262
   and OEOA initiative 297
   appointed Purcell 261
   approval 321
   confirmation 311
   direction to delegation 321
Shultz, George P. 177, 201, 244, 261, 271, 321, 359
Siblin
   Center 311
   Vocational Training Center 310
Sieverts, Frank 162
Sihanouk, Norodum 209
Sihanoukville port 128
Simington, Ian 118, 228
Simpson, Alan 119, 171, 177, 202, 216, 218
Singapore 114
Sir Jackson Technique 208
Six-Day War 307
Slovakia
   hardened policy 375
Smith, Julie 373
Smith, Marvin 81, 98
Smith, William French 161, 302
smugglers 378
Smyser, Dick 139, 144, 160, 162, 163, 227, 228
Snepp, Frank 13
society
   civilized 426
   restructured 22
Solarz, Stephen 197, 205, 253
Solidarity 252
   international 226
   leaders 252
   leadership 252
solution 69
   durable political 209
   integrated and comprehensive 414
solutions
   anchor 414
   approach for Syria 418
   bilateral 407
   compact 236, 413, 414
   compact informal 241
   contribute 416

durable solutions 274
historical assessment 244
humane 387, 412
humanitarian 359, 375, 415
longer-term 355
low comprehensive priority 368
multilateral approach 359
nonresettlement 190
only viable solution 416
political asylum 412
primary 416
refugees 68
replicated 239
resettlement as option 68
solution framework 241
solution phase 417
solutions compact 415, 416, 417, 422
solutions compact members 416, 417
solutions compact results 415
tailor-made 410
targeted 339
workable 410
world
solution 427
solutions phase 187
Somalia 276
RP emergency program 277
wars 139
South Africa
deaths 304
South Asia 368
foreign influences 335
madrassas 335
South China Sea 7, 13, 77, 114, 196
Southeast Asia 2, 18, 19, 21, 29, 38, 39, 69, 71, 74, 76, 78, 79, 93, 98, 109, 118, 133, 199, 325, 328, 352, 373, 417
camp populations 110
camps 74, 334
crisis population 241

most vulnerable people 195
operations 239
program questions 113
refugee problems 43
refugee resettlement 107
refugee surge 96
Southern Cross 22
South Lebanon 307
South Vietnam 9
endangered groups 242
evacuation 13
officers 6
Souvanna Phouma 25
Soviet
admissions to US 257
Aeroflot 269
American trade 258
bloc 78
bombing 334
dissidents 263
empire 259
exit visa 257
exit visas 266
forces 249
government 256
Government 269
identity 255
invasion 252
Jewish emigration 256
Jewry 255, 256
crises 83
Jews 254, 255, 257, 260, 265, 267, 268, 270
Jews and options 267
Jews and Soviet
liberalization 266
Jews and US admissions 261
Jews embattled 270
Jews emigrate 270
Jews' lawful emigration 270
minorities 270
pogroms 254
power 255

521

refugees 264
refugee (status) applicants 268
reprisals 334
Soviet-American relations 269
Soviets and Eastern Europe 247
Soviet Union 7, 20, 60, 248, 254, 255, 266
Soviet Union and Afghanistan invasion 139
Soviet Union arrests 263
Soviet Union emigration 158
Soviet Union in Afghanistan 20
Soviet Union in Angola 20
Soviet Union in Ethiopia 20
Soviet Union in South Yemen 20
Soviet Union refugees 249
Soviet Union sanctions 265
tempers 259
troops 334
willful destruction 334
Spain 383
SPATE (Soviet Pan American Travel Effort) 269
Spiers, Ron 175
sponsor
    identification 19
    local sponsors 71
    resettlement 210
SRV
    unilateral cessation 193
SRV (Socialist Republic of Vietnam) 70, 75, 78, 115, 116, 191, 193, 213, 214, 237, 238
stability
    operational 64
stabilization 31, 80, 256
    plan 333
    regime 183
staff 45, 48, 84
    agonized 295
    career opportunities 138
    cut 64
    training 358

Stalin, Joseph 255
Star Trek Enterprise 136
startup
    RP 137
starvation 301
starved
    and beat to death 303
Star Wars 263, 264
State
    new refugee bureau 66
    refugees mission-central 40
    refugee team 26
State Department 11, 33, 35, 44, 95, 102, 107, 128, 177, 231, 244, 248, 251, 301, 304
    Administration bureau 43
    advocates for refugees 69
    Africa burea 287
    American diplomacy 52
    and Middle East 323
    backbone 99
    backwater 64
    backwaters 354
    budget 91
    burgeoning responsibilities 52
    capability 134
    central budget 95
    concern diminished 64
    culture change 353
    disengagement 64
    executive branch refugee locus 89
    field officials 26
    foreign policy problem 49
    Foreign Service 178
    funding 403
    George Warren 57
    heroics 97
    historian 326
    Historian 63
    humanitarian performance 38
    humanitarian priority 82
    Indochina 26

inspector general 27
interagency refugee
    coordinator 38
IO (International Organizations
    bureau) 145, 298
Kitty Kemp 48
leadership 398
leadership unresponsive 26
Medal of Valor 13
new refugee team 31
Office of Congressional
    Relations 165
officers 18
parallel investigation 27
powerful officials 39
refugee assistance 403
refugee operations 18
refugee policy role 108
refugee portfolio 27
refugee programs 352
Refugee Programs bureau 259
refugee stewardship 86
refugee team 402
resettlement reports 21
R & P grants 100
RP in State Magazine 354
salvage 44
seventh floor 29
Southeast Asia advocates 29
specific engagements 402
stewardship 186
team 323
witnesses 166
statement
    American 300
status
    legal 349
    permanent resident alien 121
statutory base 46
Stennis, John 9
Sternberg, Carel 103
Stockman, David 162
Stoessel, Walter J. 167, 222, 260

Vietnam negotiation(s) 214
strategic
    analysis 63
    approach 235
    change 352
    decision 306
    issues 329
    partner agreement 368
    question 348
    reason 259
strategies
    cost-efficient strategy 407
    decrease deaths 278
    guiding 418
    humanitarian 415
    incorrect strategy 410
    Indochina strategy 413
    prosecution 199
    solutions strategy 414
    strategy deficiencies 409
    strategy renewal 410
    workable 411
strategy
    critical phases 182
Strong, Maurice 297, 298
Stubbs, Bill 175
Studds, Gary 347
Subic Bay 15
subsistence services 188
substance
    over form 158
success
    institutional efforts 353
Sudan
    civil war 279
    contacts 287
    emergency conference 299
    escapes and intriguers 292
    escapes leaks 292
    escapes roles publicized 292
    highest mortality/morbidity 279
    measles epidemic 294
    Omdurman children dying 297

523

South Sudan 280
supply problems 294
Um Rakuba camp 282
vice president imprisoned 288
Sudan Embassy 287
Sullivan, William (Bill) 15
Summit
    Asian Economic 71, 73
    Geneva 262
    Iceland 264
    Moscow 265
    Rome on Libya 380
    Washington 265
    World Humanitarian 399
superman syndrome 146
supplemental
    urgent 45
Supreme Court
    entry ban 405
Surena, Andre 313
surge capacity 107
survivors 197
    death camp 59
    imprisoned, killed 22
    relief difference 402
    survival challenges 359
    survival problems 425
    survivor testimonies 197
Swaebe, Geoffrey 314
Swing, William (Bill) L. 375
    migrants 376
syndicate
    Hong Kong 22
Syria 333, 380, 389, 390, 392, 399,
    402, 406, 409, 423, 427
    Abramowitz warning 373
    ad hoc responses for 368
    admissions issue 404
    Aleppo destruction 381
    and Middle East crisis 401
    Arab Spring 371, 390
    barriers to renewal 394
    chemical 390

citizen harm 381
citizens displaced 381
civil war 368, 416
crematorium 392
crisis 370, 402
crisis and solutions compact 415
crisis seventh year 414
crsis outcome 393
Deraa 370
displaced citizens 371
early warnings 373
envoy for 380
failures 410
fifth-year destruction 371
Ghouta 390
historic civilization 378
human crises 373
humanitarian apparatus 393
humanitarian disaster 389
humanitarian need 402
Iran proxy force 379
Jordan border 389
mistaken strategies 369
needs in 403
non-strategic crisis response 369
opposition 380
peace process 380
reconstruction 416
red line 393
refugee admissions from 407
rehabilitation 422
return 422
Saydnaya Military Prison 391
survivors 381
Syrian Network for Human
    Rights 392
Syrian War 415
systematically starve 381
US paralysis 390
war accelerated 404
weak humanitarian
    response 392
Syrian

opposition parties 374
peace agreement 382
refugees 377
system
   global humanitarian 118, 134
   international refugee 93
   political 137
   welfare 121
systematic resettlement 186
systems 81, 99
   modern 41
Taft, Julia 10, 11, 17, 160, 161
   nomination 163
Taliban 259, 406
   Pakistan 335
Tan Son Nhut
   identify and process 11
Tarah, Abdi Mohamed 277
Taraki, Noor Mohammad 326
targeted resettlement 201
Task Force
   Cuba-Haiti 133
   Somalia 132
Tayeb, Omar 283
Taylor, Maxwell 31
Taylor, Myron C. 56
TB
   communicable 169
TCP (Third Country Processing) 250, 252
team
   new 134
   over-worked 144
teamwork
   professional 149
   results 139
Tegucigalpa 342, 343
Tehran Eight 327
terrorist
   attacks 367
   deny entry 425
   expansion 368
   ISIS 380
   shootings 404
test
   civilization 426
   crisis recognition 355
testimony
   cooperation 107
Thai
   border 126, 130, 131
   camps 201
   fishermen 197
   foreign minister 127
   Friends Relief Foundation 205
   Government 115, 123, 190, 197, 199
   humane deterrence 127
   Khmer populations 123
   Navy 197, 198
   officials 196
   one exception 123
   opened camps 127
   police 198
   prosecutors 197
   UNHCR mandates 207
Thailand 25, 26, 36, 73, 128
   Abramowitz calling 124
   flow 124
   Gulf 115, 197
   Hmong 211
   IRC 105
   Khmer 127, 200
   piracy 196
   refugee camps 35
   refugees reaching 76
   Rosenblatt 32
   Songkhla 115
Thatcher, Margaret 73
Thessaloniki 388
third-country resettlement 68, 248, 360, 415
Thomas, Evan 7, 8
Thomas, John 39, 43
Thompson, Mac 18, 32, 204
Thompson, Paul 357

Thorne, Nick 141, 142
threat
    to United States 143
threats 88
    expulsion 19
    impending 409
Thurmond, Strom 171
Tigrayans
    fighting 278
Tinker, Jerry 94, 119
Tobias, Gaudencio V. 110
Tokyo 71
tool
    integrating foreign and domestic 101
top officials 312
TPP (Trans-Pacific Partnership) 417
trade 257
    imbroglio 258
tragedies
    begged commitment 82
Tragic Triangle 27
training
    center 111
    center incursion 311
    emergency 357
    English language 75
    ESL skills 112
    insurgent 344
    Morgan and Geibel 112
    pre-entry 220
    program accomplishments 111
    survival skills 112
training program
    implementing partners 112
Tran Quang Co 237
Transatlantic Council on Migration report
    2017 412
transit
    impacts 417
transport
    dilapidated system 128
    loan system 105
    system 332
Treasury Building 1
treaty
    multilateral 66
trends
    immigration 55
Triangle
    Indochina 199
Trojan horse 367
troops
    US 389
    withdrawal of 391
Truman
    administration 66, 67
Truman, Harry S. 61
Trump, Donald J. 390, 391, 420, 427
tuberculosis
    medical clearance checks 168
Tucker, John 18
Turay, Greg 196
Turkey 371, 419
    and 1951 Refugee Convention 378
    Coast Guard 383
    to Europe 378
    tragic results 370
Tusk, Donald 378
two insurgent ideologies 334
tyrants
    impunity 426
    murder 426
    torture 426
Udorn Air Base 25
Uganda 303
    crackdown headline 304
    human rights abuses 304
    soldiers 303
Ugandan Army 304
UIA (United Israel Appeal) 287
Ukraine 421
Ukrainians 59
UN

Afghanistan resolutions 329
Commission of Inquiry on
    Syria 391
General Assembly 62, 66, 317,
    323, 398
headquarters in New York
    City 296
in Geneva 162
Regional, Refugee, and
    Resilience Plan 416
Resolution 2231 379
responses 208
secretariat 208
secretary general 73, 126, 317
Security Council 309, 328
Security Council members 374
terms 66
Third Committee 66, 67
Tribunal on Cambodia 209
UNBRO (UN Border Relief
    Organization) 207, 295, 297,
    300, 334, 355, 356
border Khmer 209
protection force 208
undesirables 338
UNDP (UN Development Program)
    275, 295, 297, 302
Ethiopia 297
UNHCR
field staff 284
Geneva 284
global training 294
near paralysis 294
protection mandate 207
staff 294
Sudan 282
UNHCR (UN High Commission for
    Refugees) 62, 69, 73, 74, 75,
    77, 109, 110, 114, 115, 116, 123,
    126, 130, 131, 177, 192, 196,
    200, 201, 209, 226, 228, 234,
    237, 238, 239, 241, 243, 244,
    248, 275, 276, 277, 279, 287,
    299, 305, 319, 329, 331, 341,
    343, 344, 345, 356, 357, 359,
    361, 403, 412
Central America 339
elections 299
executive committee
    chairman 386
officials 197
returns 209
Smyser appointment 163
UNICEF
Jim Grant 296
UNICEF (UN International
    Children's Emergency Fund)
    126, 208, 275, 294
Unitd States
and Indochina refugee
    admissions 158
United Nations 59, 60, 126, 415, 426
headquarters 361
United States 253, 338, 368, 380, 423
2016 resettling 403
and asylum regime 387
and Syria 391
Congress 33, 118
Constitution 54
coordinator for refugee
    affairs 33
countrymen in savage
    captivity 157
donation announcement 420
existential question 393
honest broker 275
immigration 54
intervened with vaccine 294
Jewish resettlement 269
leadership 34, 83
opted out of the conflict 380
planning 25
prime mover 60
prisons 159
processing 205
Public Health Service 169

527

refugee applicants 406
Refugee Policy 1970s 152
refugee program 46
resettlement cuts 403
responses to complex crises 131
Sealift Command 77
self-serving actors 292
Syria relief 402
timidity 389
travel to 19
warned 419
Universal Declaration of Human
    Rights 62, 270, 395
University
    Brandeis 263
    Brown 31
    Concordia 211
    Coventry 378
    Furman 206, 363
    Georgetown 348
    Kent State 8
    of Wisconsin 357
    Ohio 280
    Oxford 372
    Tulane 11
UNRRA (UN Relief and
    Rehabilitation
    Administration) 59, 60
UNRWA (UN Relief and Works
    Agency) 62, 159, 306, 314, 319,
    321, 323, 398
UNTAC 209
US
    accomplishments 360
    acculturation 242
    and Uganda 304
    and UN New York City 320
    Attorney General 266
    budget cuts 403
    camps budget 109
    channels 298
    Coast Guard 347
    commitment 356
    concern 225
    connections 405
    critics 350
    delegation 299
    delegation head 319
    durable solutions 242
    Embassy in El Salvador 342
    Embassy in Honduras 342
    engagement 400
    Ethiopia 278
    excluded peace negotiations
        Syria 382
    exposing role 305
    Indochina success 243
    intelligence reports 213
    justice system 346
    law forbids 310
    medical teams 294
    Pacific Command 228
    permanent residents 242
    Poles' resettlement 252
    presidents 418
    programs 351
    reawakening 242
    refugee coordinator 137, 165
    refugee policy 349
    resettlement solution phases 240
    sanctions on Russia 391
    Soviet refugee policy 268
    team 208
    trade bill 258
    vetting procedures 406
    wheat 330
USAID 27, 40, 81, 86, 92, 96, 310,
    340, 341, 398
USAID (US Agency for International
    Development) 27, 31, 33, 90,
    91, 101, 125, 273, 296
USEP (US Escapee Program) 61
USIA (US Information Agency) 8
USRP (US Refugee Program) 61
USS *Kirk* 14, 15

USSR (Union of Soviet Socialist
   Republics) 133, 247, 252, 254,
   255, 256, 257, 259, 260, 263,
   264, 325
USS *St. Louis* 58
Uzbek immigrant
   attack 405
vaccine
   measles 294
Vance, Cyrus 29, 39, 70, 72, 78,
   123, 273
vanden Heuvel, William 70, 75
Van Egmond, Alan 321
   evacuation action 314
   to UN 321
Vang Pao 25
Vanik, Charles 258
Veatch, Ellis 3
vessels
   commercial 114
vetting 404, 405, 406
   careful refugee 406
   NGOs 105
   refugee applicants 405
victim
   unwillingness 197
victims 61, 115, 371, 392
   central 418, 423
   conflict 372
   crisis 407
   displaced 339
   politically exiled 368
   protection central 415
Vieira de Mello, Sergio 209, 238
Vietcong 5, 8, 10, 12, 22, 25
   victory 18
Vietnam 20, 26
   discrimination in 220
   emigration and political
      prisoners 224
   evacuees 17
   massive exodus 359
   military against Khmer 207

orderly departure 191
refugee(s) 18
refugees 199
survivors 16
Vietnam War 1, 3, 11, 14, 20, 25,
   92, 177, 351
Vietnamese 28, 129
   asylum seekers 239
   community in US 214
   deterrence 199
   escapees 113
   family visit 229
   forces 200
   Government 192
   Land group 212
   North 23
   ODP 233
   orphans 10
   refugees crisis 242
   Sikhiu camp 190
Vine, Dick 172, 174, 177, 199, 200,
   202, 204, 251
violence
   Central America and
      Caribbean 340
   violent offenders 345
visa 214, 232, 257
   Amerasian applications 215
   lottery 405
   processing stopped 267
voluntary agencies 60
voluntary repatriation 68, 274
vulnerability
   takeover 101
Vung Tau port 15
Wad Sherife 294
Wahed, Rama 388, 389
Waldheim, Kurt 73
Walesa, Lech 252, 253
Walters, Ingrid 102, 103
Walters, Vernon 281
war crimes 381
   against Christians 375

529

against Kaka'I 375
against Sabaean-Mandaean 375
against Shabak 375
against Turkmen 375
against Yazidis 375
Ward, June 145
warfare
    guerilla 25
War Powers Resolution 20
Warren, George 57, 58, 60, 66
Warren, George, Jr 119
wars
    fifteen erupted-reignited 372
Warsaw 253
    Ghetto and Jewish boy 35
    Pact 247, 249
    Pact countries invaded 249
Washington viii, 21, 23, 38, 78, 102, 109, 116, 342
    chaos 140
    official 29
Washington Monument 44
Washington Post 291, 304, 379
Washington-Tel Aviv 283
Watergate 9, 20, 145
Waterston, Sam 205
water trucks 279
Watson, Jack 143
weapon
    possession culturally integral 334
Weaver, Jerry 280, 283, 285, 287, 290, 291, 292
Webster, Lelia 19
weekend campaign 314
West Bank and Gaza 308
Western Europe 248, 253
Western Hemisphere 336, 339
West Germany 247
West Virginia
    Coolfont 104
WFP (World Food Program) 60, 125, 275, 295, 305

Wharton, Chris 19
Whitehead, John 218, 231, 253
White House 33, 35, 74, 90, 103
    advisors 404
    alerted 142
    chat 262
    face-to-face 10
    OMB 180
    press
        room 2
    press conference 1
    Ron Ziegler 164
    RP nomination 178
    transition team 160
    visit 143
Whitehouse, Charles 26
Whitmire, Donald 14
Wiesner, Louis A. 31, 36
Winter, Roger 197
Wisner, Frank 5, 11, 31, 32, 34, 69, 75
withdrawal
    military, diplomatic 19
witness 93
Wolfowitz, Paul 180, 200, 206, 209
work
    gangs 24
    habits 151
world
    advocacy 424
    combatants 427
    community success 408
    conscience 424
    focus 46, 85
    protagonists 427
    World Bank 331
    World Learning 112
    World Relief 107, 344
World War II 36, 60, 248, 372, 375, 401
Wright, Lacy 13, 204
Yarborough, Trin 224
Yazidis
    war crimes against 375

year zero 23
Yevrei 255
Yom Kippur War
 refugees created 308
Yosef, Ovadia 282
Zepa
 and Srebrenica massacres 318
zero sum thinking 413
Ziegler, Ron 2, 3
Zieman family 266
zone
 demilitarized 421